Shareholder Protection Reconsidered

This book examines the role and potential of derivative actions in shareholder protection in public limited companies. Derivative actions have been a focal point of legislators' agendas on shareholder protection, in the past few decades, throughout Europe and beyond. Nevertheless, there remain jurisdictions, such as Greece, which are still devoid of this remedy. Against this backdrop, this book examines whether and how the derivative action may improve shareholder protection, constituting thus a mechanism that justifies legislative attention. It does so in three parts. First, it analyses the desirable role derivative actions assume in protecting shareholder property, monitoring corporate management and mitigating agency costs, alongside their economic implications, introducing the reader to the contemporary international debate on the topic. Having set the desiderata, the second part proceeds with the comparative analysis of Greek, German and UK law – jurisdictions that have recently reformed their provisions on shareholder protection – examining not only the law on derivative actions and their Greek counterpart remedy but also mechanisms of shareholder protection that do, or could, assume functions similar to those of the derivative action. By critically assessing the merits and failures of the respective UK, German and Greek shareholder protection laws, the book then proceeds to offer (in Part III) a model framework of shareholders' derivative litigation for jurisdictions considering reform. Written in an accessible format, it will be an invaluable resource for anyone interested in this important aspect of company law and corporate governance.

Georgios Zouridakis, PhD (Essex), is a qualified attorney at law and member of the Athens Bar Association, Greece, Lecturer at the University of Essex School of Law, UK and research fellow at the Athens Institute for Education and Research, Greece.

Routledge Research in Corporate Law

Available titles in this series include:

Regulation and Inequality at Work
Isolation and Inequality Beyond the Regulation of Labour
Vanisha Sukdeo

Regulation and the Credit Rating Agencies
Restraining Ancillary Services
Daniel Cash

Law and Responsible Supply Chain Management
Contract and Tort Interplay and Overlap
Edited by Vibe Ulfbeck, Alexandra Andhov and Kateřina Mitkidis

Shareholder Primacy and Global Business
Re-clothing the EU Corporate Law
Lela Mélon

Corporate Law, Codes of Conduct and Workers' Rights
Vanisha Sukdeo

Insolvency Law and Multinational Groups
Theories, Solutions and Recommendations for Business Failure
Daoning Zhang

Employee Rights in Corporate Insolvency
A UK and US Perspective
Hamiisi Junior Nsubuga

Shareholder Protection Reconsidered
Derivative Action in the UK, Germany and Greece
Georgios Zouridakis

Shareholder Protection Reconsidered

Derivative Action in the UK, Germany and Greece

Georgios Zouridakis

Routledge
Taylor & Francis Group
LONDON AND NEW YORK

First published 2020
by Routledge
2 Park Square, Milton Park, Abingdon, Oxon OX14 4RN

and by Routledge
52 Vanderbilt Avenue, New York, NY 10017

Routledge is an imprint of the Taylor & Francis Group, an informa business

British Library Cataloguing-in-Publication Data
A catalogue record for this book is available from the British Library

Library of Congress Cataloging-in-Publication Data
A catalog record has been requested for this book

ISBN: 978-0-367-23582-6 (hbk)
ISBN: 978-0-429-29334-4 (ebk)

Typeset in Galliard
by Swales & Willis, Exeter, Devon, UK

Dedicated to my son, Stylianos-Marc

Contents

Acknowledgements ix
Abbreviations x

PART I
Derivative actions in abstracto: the theoretical framework of this study **1**

1 Introduction 3

2 The importance of an effective shareholder remedy for wrongs against the company 21

PART II
Derivative actions de lege lata: a comparative and functional analysis **67**

3 Comparison of functionally equivalent rules on shareholders' enforcement of corporate claims 69

4 The Greek framework for shareholder protection in a comparative context and the (in)existence of alternatives to derivative actions 124

PART III
Derivative actions de lege ferenda: suggestions based on comparative considerations **163**

5 Proposals for a functioning and truly protective derivative action 165

6 Conclusion 213

Bibliography 219
Table of cases 234
Annex 239
Index 255

Acknowledgements

This book is a revised, extended and updated version of my doctoral thesis, written during my time as a member of the School of Law, University of Essex, UK and submitted in February 2016. Derivative actions and shareholder protection may be interesting, but at the same time they are possibly the most complex issues in the area of corporate law and corporate governance. Adding to the challenge of this task was researching in three different languages and the ever-changing legal landscape. The exquisite Albert Sloman Library and funding from the Essex School of Law and the University of Essex Scholarship significantly facilitated my doctoral research.

Several people helped and supported me throughout this journey and this is the place to mention a few. I am deeply grateful to Dr Marios Koutsias, who has been an exemplary supervisor, for his guidance and support. I would also like to thank my PhD examiners, Professor Janet Dine and Dr Youseph Farah; the president, Dr Thomas Papanikos, and fellow members of the Athens Institute for Education and Research; the fellow faculty members of the Essex School of Law; and Dr Paul Hughes and Dr Thomas Papadopoulos for their interest in my research. My sincere gratitude also goes to my wife, Stephanie and my parents, Stylianos and Chrysanthi, for their love and day-to-day support.

Abbreviations

i) Select terms and statutes

ABA	American Bar Association
AE	*anónymos etaireía* (Greek, public limited company)
AG	*Aktiengesellschaft* (German, stock corporation); *Amtsgericht* (German, district court)
AktG	*Aktiengesetz* (German, Stock Corporation Act)
BGB	*Burgerliches Gesetzbuch* (German, Civil Code)
BGH	*Bundesgerichtshof* (German, Federal Supreme Court)
BJR	Business Judgment Rule
BSP	Blackwell Scientific Publications
BT-Drucks	*Bundestags-Drucksache* (German, parliamentary documentation)
BverfG	*Bundesverfassungsgericht* (German, Federal Constitutional Court)
BR-Drs	*Drucksachen des Deutschen Bundesrates* (German, Federal Council documentation)
CA 2006	Companies Act 2006
CEPEJ	European Commission for the Efficiency of Justice
CPR	Civil Procedure Rules
CUP	Cambridge University Press
ECHR	European Convention on Human Rights
EE	Edward Elgar
EPE	*etaireía periorisménis efthýnis* (Greek, private limited company)
FamFG	*Gesetz über das Verfahren in Familiensachen und in den Angelegenheiten der freiwilligen Gerichtsbarkeit* (German, Act on Proceedings in Family Matters and Matters of Non-Contentious Jurisdiction)
FEK	*Fýllo Efimerídas Kyverníseos* (Greek, Government Gazette Issue)
FG	*Finanzgericht* (German, Finance Court)
FSMA 2000	Financial Services and Markets Act 2000
FRC	Financial Reporting Council
GCC	Greek Civil Code
GrCivPrC	Greek Civil Procedure Code
HGB	*Handelsgesetzbuch*

IPO	initial public offer
KonTraG	*Gesetz zur Kontrolle-und Transparenz im Unternehmensbereich* (German, Act on Control and Transparency in Business Matters)
LG	*Landgericht* (German, regional court)
MBCA	Model Business Corporations Act
NED	non-executive director
OLG	*Oberlandesgericht* (German, Higher Regional Court)
OUP	Oxford University Press
Plc	Public Limited Company
SA	*Société Anonyme*
SRD	Shareholder Rights Directive
TFEU	Treaty on the Functioning of the European Union
UCP	University of Chicago Press
UMAG	*Gesetz zur Unternehmensintegrität und Modernisierung des Anfechtungsrechts* (German, Act on Corporate Integrity and Modernisation of Rescission Law)
ZPO	*Zivilprozessordnung* (German, Civil Procedure Code)

ii) Law journals and reports in English

ALER	American Law and Economics Review
All ER	All England Law Reports
Am J Comp L	American Journal of Comparative Law
App Cas	Appeal Cases
BCC	British Company Law Cases
BCLC	Butterworths Company Law Cases
Brook J Int'l L	Brooklyn Journal of International Law
Bus Law	Business Lawyer
CLR	California Law Review
Co Law	Company Lawyer
Co LN	Company Law Newsletter
Colum L Rev	Columbia Law Review
Cornell L Rev	Cornell Law Review
Deakin LR	Deakin Law Review
Del J Corp L	Delaware Journal of Corporate Law
DR	European Commission of Human Rights Decisions & Reports
DULJ	Dublin University Law Journal
EBLR	European Business Law Review
EBOR	European Business Organisation Law Review
ECL	European Company Law
EHRR	European Human Rights Reports
ER	English Reports

ECFR	European Company and Financial Law Review
EWHC	England and Wales High Court
Ex D	Exchequer Division
Geo LJ	Georgetown Law Journal
Geo Wash L Rev	George Washington Law Review
Harv Bus L Rev	Harvard Business Law Review
Hong Kong LJ	Hong Kong Law Journal
ICCLR	International Company and Commercial Law Review
ICLQ	International and Comparative Law Quarterly
JBL	Journal of Business Law
JCLS	Journal of Corporate Law Studies
JL Econ & Org	Journal of Law, Economics, and Organization
KB	King's Bench
LCP	Law and Contemporary Problems
LQR	Law Quarterly Review
LR	Law Reports
Md L Rev	Maryland Law Review
Mercer L Rev	Mercer Law Review
Miss CL Rev	Mississippi College Law Review
MJECL	Maastricht Journal of European and Comparative Law
Notre Dame L Rev	Notre Dame Law Review
Nw UL Rev	Northwestern University Law Review
OJ	Official Journal of the European Communities
OJLS	Oxford Journal of Legal Studies
PLC	Practical Law for Companies
Syd LR	Sydney Law Review
Tex L Rev	Texas Law Review
U Chi L R	University of Chicago Law Review
UCL JL & J	UCL Journal of Law and Jurisprudence
U Ill L Rev	University of Illinois Law Review
UNSWLJ	University of New South Wales Law Journal
Va L Rev	Virginia Law Review
Vand L Rev	Vanderbilt Law Review
WLR	Weekly Law Reports
Wm & Mary L Rev	William and Mary Law Review
Yale LJ	Yale Law Journal

iii) Greek law journals and reports

ChrID	Chroniká Idiotikoú Dikaíou (Private Law Chronicles)
ChriDik	Chrimatopistotikó Díkaio (Financial Law)
DEE	Díkaio Epicheiríseon kai Etairión (Business and Company Law)
DForN	Deltíon Forologikís Nomothesías (Tax Legislation Bulletin)
EEmpD	Epitheórisi Emporikoú Dikaíou (Commercial Law Review)

EEN	Efimerís ton Ellínon Nomikón (Greek Lawyers' Bulletin)
EllDni	Ellinikí Dikaiosýni (Hellenic Justice)
EpiskED	Episkópisi Emporikoú Dikaíou (Commercial Law Review)
NoV	Nomikó Víma (Legal Tribune)
PeirN	Peiraïkí Nomología (Peiraeus Jurisprudence)

iv) German law journals and reports

AcP	Archiv für die civilistische Praxis (Archive for Civil Practice)
AG	Die Aktiengesellschaft (The Stock Coproration)
BGHZ	Entscheidungen des Bundesgerichtshofs in Zivilsachen (Decisions of the Federal Supreme Court in Civil Matters)
BverfGE	Entscheidungen des Bundesverfassungsgerichts (Decisions of the Federal Constitutional Court)
CCZ	Corporate Compliance Zeitschrift
DB	Der Betrieb (The Enterprise)
DstRE	Deutsches Steuerrecht (German Taxation Law)
NJW	Neue Juristische Wochenschrift (New Juristic Weekly Bulletin)
NZG	Neue Zeitschrift für Gesellschaftsrecht (New Journal of Company Law)
RabelsZ	Rabels Zeitschrift für ausländisches und internationales Privatrecht (The Rabel Journal of Comparative and International Private Law)
ZGR	Zeitschrift für Unternehmens- und Gesellschaftsrecht (Journal of Business and Company Law)
ZHR	Zeitschrift Für das gesamte Handels- und Wirtschaftsrecht (Journal of the Entire Trade and Commercial Law)
ZIP	Zeitschrift für Wirtschaftsrecht (Commercial Law Journal)

Part I

Derivative actions in abstracto

The theoretical framework of this study

1 Introduction

1.1 The subject and the objectives of this book

It would be an understatement to say that shareholder protection is (and has always been) an integral, yet highly complicated, part of modern company law. Jurisdictions go to great lengths to set intricate systems of checks and balances on the administration of corporate affairs and to devise armouries of rights exercisable in and against the company, elaborate in their construction and application, only to protect the varying interests of shareholders. As suggested by its title, this book focuses on a mechanism of shareholder protection known as the derivative action. It aims to investigate whether Greek shareholder law should be reformed and whether and how this mechanism should be introduced into it. The research purports to evaluate, from the perspective of shareholder protection, the applicable Greek legal framework, identify its shortcomings and inquire how the derivative action may address them, with the view of re-establishing the effectiveness and competitiveness of the national law. To achieve these ends, this book conducts (in Part II) a comparative analysis with two jurisdictions which provide for derivative actions, namely Germany and the UK.[1]

Derivative actions can be broadly defined as follows: *in cases where a wrong is suffered by the company, a (group of minority) shareholder(s)* (otherwise barred from litigating directly in their own name and on their own behalf, by virtue of the no reflective loss principle and the principle that only the company may litigate its claims through its competent organs – the 'proper plaintiff rule') *may be allowed to seek remedy on behalf of the company.*[2] In practice, a derivative action

1 Capital letters will be used herein when referring to this book's Parts and Sections, in order to avoid the risk of confusion with other sections or parts of statutes, etc.

2 This is the definition of what is referred herein as 'genuine' derivative actions. See also the discussion on the features of derivative actions in Harald Baum and Dan W Puchniak, 'The Derivative Action: An Economic, Historical and Practice-Oriented Approach' in Dan W Puchniak, Harald Baum and Michael Ewing-Chow (eds), *The Derivative Action in Asia: A Comparative and Functional Approach* (CUP 2012) 7. See Georgios Zouridakis, 'Introducing Derivative Actions in the Greek Law on Public Limited Companies: Issues of Legal Standing and Lessons from the German and UK Experience' (2015) 26 *ICCLR* 271, 272 regarding pp. 3–5 in this Section.

is useful, if not essential, in cases where those in control of the company (thus able to act – and litigate – on behalf of the company or to instruct those with such capacity) are the ones who wronged the company. The wrong will not be remedied, due to this conflict of interests, to the detriment of all involved in the company – and thus its shareholders – but for the wrongdoers, unless another person derives the right to sue them from the company, acting on behalf and for the benefit of the latter.

Unlike personal shareholders' claims, derivative actions serve the purposes of reinforcing the accountability of those in control of the company and protecting shareholders cumulatively. They do so by removing the impasse which the 'proper plaintiff rule' may create, when necessary.[3] The direct beneficiary of a successful derivative claim is the company only, whilst shareholders benefit indirectly or, more precisely, reflectively. However, the shareholders' right to litigate on behalf of the company evidently constitutes a decisive interference in the ordinary administration of corporate affairs. The law has therefore to facilitate the pursuit of meritorious derivative claims whilst, at the same time, weed out and deter litigation that would disturb the efficient running of the company and run contrary to the company's and shareholders' interests. The difficulty in this task resides in that filters against frivolous and vexatious litigation inherently run the risk of disenfranchising shareholders and preventing meritorious claims from being brought, whilst any incentives to shareholders to enforce the corporate claims may be exploited by malicious litigants.

Derivative actions have been considered by many academics as one of the most potent means of (minority) shareholder protection, assuming thus a cardinal role in corporate governance.[4] Notwithstanding being a landmark feature of common law,[5] they have progressively expanded to civil law jurisdictions.[6] The outspread of provisions on derivative actions throughout Europe during the last decade is evidence of voluntary regulatory convergence,

3 Known, under common law, as the rule in *Foss v Harbottle* (1843) 67 ER 189; (1843) 2 Hare 461.

4 Indicatively: Robert C Clark, *Corporate Law* (Little, Brown 1986) 639; Arad Reisberg, *Derivative Actions and Corporate Governance: Theory and Operation* (OUP 2007) 9; see also *Cohen v. Beneficial Industrial Corp* 337 US 541 (1949), 548, hailing the derivative action as 'the chief regulator of corporate management'.

5 See GR Sullivan, 'Restating the Scope of the Derivative Action' (1985) 44 CLJ 236: 'Derivative actions have been allowed at least since *Atwool v. Merryweather* (1867) LR 5 Eq 464n'.

6 For categorisations of jurisdictions into 'legal families', see the seminal work of René David and John EC Brierley, *Major Legal Systems in the World Today: An Introduction to the Comparative Study of Law* (Simon & Schuster 1978). An explanation for the spread of statutory provisions on derivative actions across jurisdictions from the late nineties onwards may be the normative influence of the 'law and finance' literature (see Subsection 2.4.3.2). Evidence supporting this explanation can be found in Italy: see Paolo Giudici, 'Representative Litigation in Italian Capital Markets: Italian Derivative Suits and (if ever) Securities Class Actions' (2009) 6 ECFR 246.

on a matter which institutional harmonisation – through the proposal for a fifth company law directive (whose article 16 provided a minimalistic form of a derivative action) – has so far been unsuccessful in the EU.[7] The recent history of one of the core continental jurisdictions of this study, Germany, supports this observation.[8] Almost a decade ago, the *Gesetz zur Unternehmensintegrität und Modernisierung des Anfechtungsrechts* ('Act on Corporate Integrity and Modernisation of Rescission Law'; hereinafter UMAG)[9] introduced the new section 148[10] to *Aktiengesetz* (German Stock Corporation Act of 1965) in an attempt to strengthen the protection afforded to *minority* shareholders.[11] The emphasised word alerts the reader of comparative corporate law to the difference from the UK statutory provisions and English common law. Contrary to the continental European approach of conferring the right to sue on behalf of the company only to ex lege minorities, usually determined on the basis of participation in share capital, any shareholder can individually bring a derivative action under English law. This characteristic of derivative actions remained unchanged despite the advent of the new statutory provisions under the Companies Act 2006.[12] What also remained largely unaffected, despite various reforms of its national company law statute, is the Greek approach of not providing for a 'genuine' derivative action.[13]

7 OJ C 7 11.1.1991.

8 Notable civil law jurisdictions having introduced derivative actions to their corporate law statutes during the past three decades include Belgium (since 1991 by virtue of Lois coordonnées sur les sociétés commerciales [Belgian Company Code] art 66bis, of 26 July 1991, Moniteur Belge [MB] [Official Gazette of Belgium]), Italy (since 1998, by virtue of Decreto Legislativo 24 febbraio 1998, n. 58 (It.); Testo Unico in Materia di Intermediazione Finanziaria [TUIF] [Rules and Regulations Concerning Stock Market Trading] art 129, D. Lgs. n. 58); and (People's Republic of) China (since 2005, by virtue of Standing Comm. Nat'l People's Cong, 27 October 2005). For a historical overview of this incident of voluntary convergence, see Martin Gelter, 'Why do Shareholder Derivative Suits Remain Rare in Continental Europe?' (2011–12) 37 Brook J Int'l L 843; Baum and Puchniak (n 2) 2.

9 BGBl I, 2802. On the replacement of the older provisions, see, indicatively, Nikolaos Paschos and Kay-Uwe Neumann, 'Die Neuregelungen des UMAG im Bereich der Durchsetzung von Haftungsansprüchen der Aktiengesellschaft gegen Organmitglieder' (2005) 33 DB 1779; Holger Fleischer, 'Das Gesetz zur Unternehmensintegrität und Modernisierung des Anfechtungsrechts' [2005] NJW 3525; see also the decisions in OLG Hamburg, Beschluss vom 19.1.2007 – 11 Wx 33/06, AG 2007 331; Finanzgericht Hamburg Urt. v. 11.09.2009, Az. – 3 K 124/08, DStRE 2010 594, making reference to the UMAG reforms on shareholder-led litigation.

10 Titled: 'Complaint Admission Proceedings (Derivative Actions)'.

11 UMAG also amended s 147, which constituted the only possibility for shareholder-initiated representative litigation, analogous and functionally equivalent to derivative actions. However, a form of derivative action was provided in the Law on Corporate Groups (*Konzernrecht*). See AktG ss 310, 317, 318, 323.

12 Now 'derivative claims' (as the term applies under CA 2006 Pt 11).

13 (Codified) Law 2190/1920 on (Public) Companies Limited by Shares (Sociétés Anonymes; SAs).

Alas, the Greek law on shareholder litigation on behalf of the company remains somewhat obsolete.[14] Despite the fact that members of private limited companies may sue derivatively before Greek courts,[15] legislators have continuously refrained from introducing a similar mechanism to the law of public limited companies.[16] The provision conceptually and functionally closest to a derivative action under the respective law is the 'company's action' whereby a 5% minority may demand that the board brings the action and, in case the board does not comply with this request, the majority of that minority may petition the court to appoint special representatives to bring the claim.[17] The company's action was introduced to

14 Concurring: Evanghelos Perakis 'The Greek and International Discussion on Acceptance and Restriction of the Derivative Action brought by a Shareholder of a Public Limited Company' in Hideo Nakamura, Hans Fasching, Hans F Gaul and Apostolos Georgiades (eds), *Festschrift für Kostas E Beys dem Rechtsdenker in Attischer Dialektik* (5th edn, Eunomia 2003), 3700. The existing (functionally equivalent to derivative actions) remedy has not changed much since its introduction in the 1960s. On the evolution of legal rules, see John Armour, Priya Lele, Simon Deakin and Mathias M Siems, 'How Do Legal Rules Evolve? Evidence from a Cross-Country Comparison of Shareholder, Creditor and Worker Protection' (2009) 57 Am J Comp L. 579.

15 This does not mean that the respective provisions in the law on private limited companies, whether in the form of EPE (limited liability company) or IKE (private capital company), are free from ambiguity, nor that they constitute optimal means of protecting members' interests. Case law is virtually non-existent and, regarding EPE, it is unclear whether the statute provides for a derivative action or another form of actio pro socio.

16 See further explanations for the phenomenon in Subsection 2.4.3.3.

17 Law 4548/2018 arts 103–106, replacing Law 2190/1920 art 22b(1), (3). The minority right is pronounced as follows (in my translation):

Article 104, Enforcement of the company's claims, following minority petition:

1. Shareholders representing one twentieth of the paid-up share capital have the right to submit/file, in writ, to the board of directors a request whose subject is the filing of the company's claims according to article 103. The corporate constitution may decrease the above percentage. Applicants must prove that they became shareholders six months prior to the submission of the request.

2. The request of the paragraph above includes the information possessed by the applicant shareholders regarding the facts substantiating, according to their judgement, the liability of the members of the board of directors and the damage suffered by the company. In their request, the shareholders have to set a reasonable deadline, within which the board of directors ought to assess the content of the request and decide whether the company will bring an action for the claims described in that request. The above deadline cannot be shorter than one month since the request was submitted to the board of directors.

3. The board of directors decides upon the shareholders' request, after considering the comments and explanations of those members of the board of directors named in the shareholders' request. The members of the board of directors named in the shareholders' request do not have the right to vote in the board meeting deciding upon the shareholders' request. If the inability to vote concerns so many members that the rest do not fulfil quorum requirements, the board of directors is considered as not taking a decision, in deviation of the provisions in paragraph 3 of article 97; and the provisions of article 105 apply. The decision of the board of directors on the shareholders' request, as well as the possible inability of the board of directors to decide, are communicated to the applicants with diligence by the latter and at the expense of the company.

Greek law in 1962, by means of legal transplant from German law and, contrary to its mother jurisdiction, still constitutes the exclusive way for shareholders to enforce corporate claims in Greece.[18] The efficacy of the company's action has been questioned widely and the need for the introduction of derivative actions into the Greek law on public limited companies has been pronounced by a variety of prominent Greek academics over time.[19] However, attempts in that direction have so far been unsuccessful.[20]

Against this backdrop, this research embarks on the objective of investigating whether the reform of Greek law and the introduction of the derivative action are desirable and whether and how they may improve shareholder protection in

4. In case the request in paragraph 1 is submitted by the majority of the shareholders, the board of directors has the duty to proceed to filing the corporate action without ado.

Article 105, Appointment of special representative to file the claim:

1. If: a) the board of directors dismisses the minority's request in whole or in part, or b) the deadline in the second sentence of paragraph 2 of article 104 passes without action being taken, or c) four months pass since the board of directors' decision to file an action, without the action having been filed, as decided by the board of directors, or d) board of directors cannot decide upon the request of the minority, or e) in the case of article 104, paragraph 4, the company does not file the action, the majority of the shareholders that submitted the request as per the previous article have the right, within two months since the decision of the board of directors was communicated as per the third sentence of paragraph 3 of article 104 or since the deadlines above of cases (a) and (c) passed without action being taken, to submit a petition before the single-member court of first instance regarding the appointment of a special representative to file the action against the members of the board of directors, according to the content of the minority's request of article 104.

2. ... The court accepts the shareholders' petition and appoints special representative, provided there is no overriding interest of the company, justifying that proceedings against the members of the board of directors are not conducted.

18 By virtue of LD 4237/1962. The Greek proviso was modelled after AktG 1937. The German framework already reformed in 1965.

19 See, indicatively, Georgios Triantafillakis, 'From the Protection of the Minority to the Protection of the Shareholder' in Minutes of the 18th Panhellenian Conference on Commercial Law (Collaborative Work), *Trends and Prospects of the Law of the Public Limited Company* (Nomiki Bibliothiki 2009) 117–119; Christina Livada, 'Filing of Company Claims against the Members of the Board of Directors' in Perakis Evanghelos (ed), *Sociétés Anonyme's Law* (3rd edn, Sakkoulas 2013) 1017–1018. Reference (not extensive) is made there to international literature on derivative actions, including *Gower & Davies' Principles of Modern Company Law*, ed Paul Davies and Sarah Worthington (9th edn, Sweet & Maxwell 2012); Reisberg, *Derivative Actions* (n 4); Susanne Kalss, 'Shareholder Suits: Common Problems, Different Solutions and First Steps towards a Possible Harmonisation by Means of a European Model Code' (2009) 6 ECFR 324; as well as the European Model Company Law Act project.

20 Significant efforts were made by Professor Perakis: notably, his proposal to introduce derivative actions into the law of listed companies through the 2002 law on corporate governance (a similar approach of including provisions on derivative actions in a CG code is followed in the USA: the ALI's Principles of Corporate Governance. See Stephen M Bainbridge, 'Independent Directors and the ALI Corporate Governance Project' (1992–1993) 61 Geo Wash L Rev 1034) was eventually dismissed.

public limited companies. From the outset, this is a rather complex and challenging task.

To begin with, it necessitates the identification of the perceived role derivative actions assume in shareholder protection, their function and their importance, in order to construe an analytical framework. The book has therefore to explain which interests of shareholders this remedy is destined to protect, as well as the kinds of behaviour it is meant to protect from. Furthermore, it will examine why it is necessary to confer on shareholders the right to litigate on behalf of the company in order to protect such interests and the circumstances where this right may be invoked. Moreover, in order to better explain the importance of derivative action, this book has to identify and explain the broader objectives of shareholder law this remedy helps pursue.

Equally significantly, this book's primary objective calls for the evaluation of the broader Greek legal framework on shareholder protection, as compared to the derivative action. The desirability of reform depends on whether Greek law fails to protect shareholders effectively in the ways the derivative action is meant to. The analysis thus needs consider not only the existing functionally equivalent remedy (the company's action) but also other mechanisms of shareholder protection that do or may assume functions similar to those of the derivative action.[21] This assessment of Greek shareholder law de lege lata also determines the impact any improvement on shareholder remedies may have on the overall levels of protection.

To achieve these objectives, this book adopts a comparative methodology.[22] Legal comparisons have great value as a cognitive exercise in evaluating national law and comparative law is a trusted companion in the quest for ways to conduct profound and critical analysis.[23] Consideration of 'foreign' rules broadens the horizons of the researcher, illuminating characteristics of his familiar law otherwise clouded by established doctrine and jurisdictional bias. Importantly for this book, comparative law enables the researcher to 'stress weaknesses … because he has not lived with them to the point where they have become second nature and thus acceptable'.[24] Therefore, the comparative analysis herein purports to remove any such doctrinal blindfolds and illustrate whether and how other jurisdictions address issues of shareholder protection better than Greek law does, with a rather refreshing element of objectivity. Accordingly, instead of using a hypothetical 'ideal' derivative action as the benchmark for evaluation, a rather utopic benchmark to set a priori anyhow, this book compares Greek law with the existing German and UK frameworks on

21 For an explanation of the term 'functional equivalent', see Subsection 1.3.1.

22 Schlessinger et al. (n 30) 1. Comparative law (*Rechtsvergleich*) has been considered a form of legal methodology, a 'species of law' and a discipline or a science in its own right. See Peter De Cruz, *Comparative Law in a Changing World* (3rd edn, Cavendish-Routledge 2007) 231–232.

23 De Cruz (n 22) 22.

24 Basil Markesinis, *Foreign Law and Comparative Methodology* (Hart 1997) 17.

shareholders' derivative litigation.[25] The comparative analysis also serves the purpose of assessing the competitiveness of shareholder protection in an international context: a particularly worthy task given the effects of globalisation on the market for equity investment.

The methodology herein employed is primarily functional.[26] Functionalism identifies a 'tertium comparationis', a point of reference to which the studied subjects are compared[27] in (hypothetical) factual circumstances in need of a legal solution. Functionality thus involves contemplating how the law addresses factual problems.[28] Accordingly, rules that may differ in their wording may be functional equivalents, in that they provide a similar solution to a given problem. Functionalism can be said to have its ancestry in social sciences: it followed the precept that social systems should be compared on the basis of how they 'satisfied certain needs'.[29] Hence, the analysis selected and compared rules on the basis of the functions they perform in the contexts of shareholder protection and corporate governance. For instance, it examines how the selected jurisdictions protect shareholders from reflective loss and how they address certain agency problems, by considering – in tandem with the functional method – an array of functional equivalents. Within the course of analysis, such relatively broad questions are followed by more specific ones, such as 'how can a shareholder enforce a breach of directors' duties', 'on what grounds may a shareholder pursue the company's claims' and 'what criteria does a claimant have to satisfy in order to enjoy legal standing?'

Building upon the findings accruing from the evaluation of the Greek law and the identification of its shortcomings, this research advances its proposals for reform, in order to complete its primary objective. After all, stripped to its essentials, this book is a call for the legislator to reconsider the law on the enforcement of corporate claims by shareholders. The de lege ferenda proposals for a derivative action aim to improve shareholder protection under Greek law and reassert its position in the international context, aspiring to set an example for other jurisdictions to follow.

Comparative law played a cardinal role in pursuing these goals. On a level of diagnosis, it helped assert that some of the approaches undertaken by Greek law are unsatisfactory from certain points of view and should be reformed. But at the same time, it provided tangible examples of the 'better law'. That is, it illustrated *how*

25 'Derivative litigation' herein refers to shareholders' litigation on behalf and for the benefit of the company, not litigation related to 'derivatives' as financial instruments.

26 The 'functional method' of comparative law, introduced by Zweigert and Kötz, can be considered as the most accepted method of legal comparisons. See M Graziadei, 'The Functionalist Heritage' in P Legrand and R Munday (eds), *Comparative Legal Studies: Traditions and Transitions* (CUP 2003) 101.

27 M Bogdan, *Comparative Law* (Kluwer 1994) 60.

28 This definition also reflects Kaden's description of 'dogmatic comparison' (*dogmatische Rechtsvergleichung*). See HC Gutteridge, *Comparative Law: An Introduction to the Comparative Method of Legal Study and Research* (CUP 1946) 7.

29 Mathias M Siems, *Comparative Law* (CUP 2014) 25.

foreign rules protect shareholders better than their Greek counterparts; it also highlighted the ways other jurisdictions attempt to address questions of shareholder protection not considered by the existing Greek legal framework.[30] The utilisation of such insight accruing from a comparative analysis, in the formulation of reform proposals (the normative function of comparative law), constituted a further reason for selecting the methodology followed herein. Comparative law brings to the surface a number of alternative solutions to given factual problems, whose effect is tested in practice, enabling the researcher to identify the ones suitable for his objectives. Accordingly, in devising proposals for a new framework for shareholders' derivative litigation, an arduous task where fine equilibria must be met, this book relied on the British and German experience with the remedy.

However, utilisation of the insight offered by comparative law does not assume the form of 'transplantation' of foreign rules, (a much-debated topic in any case), at least if we are to conceive legal transplants as the verbatim transposition of a legal rule from one legal order to another without any modifications and with the expectation that the transferred rule shall have identical an application in the donee jurisdiction. Experience shows that such expectation will be frustrated.[31]

The task of the methodology employed in this book instead, is to seek avenues for cross-fertilisation of legal thought on the topic of shareholder protection. This is an objective clearly discernible from that of legal convergence and harmonisation of laws. Essentially, this study constitutes 'Applied Comparative Law'.[32] The comparative considerations have a purpose, a telos, which is the identification of problems in shareholder protection and measures the legislature may take to solve them, within the context of the national company law. From the outset, it is recognised that the jurisdictions selected operate in an environment of regulatory competition and it is also on this foundation where the normative part of the book is built. As will become obvious, the proposed framework for shareholder litigation is neither a verbatim transposition of the 'better law', nor the result of regulatory 'cherry-picking'. What it is instead, is the synthesis of the elements that – by virtue of the preceding comparative analysis in Part II – are found to be in tandem with the objectives of effective shareholder protection and to be compatible with the core principles of the company law set by this book's jurisdictional focus.

1.2 The jurisdictional focus

As mentioned above, derivative actions, despite being the two-centuries-old creation of English common law, have in the past decades found their way into civil law jurisdictions. In fact, for various reasons and in varying ways, they have

30 Rudolf B Schlessinger, Hans W Baade, Mirjan R Damaska and Peter E Herzog, *Comparative Law, Cases-Text-Materials* (5th edn, Foundation Press 1988) 6.

31 Frederique Dahan and Janet Dine, 'Transplantation for Transition: Discussion on a Concept around Russian Reform of the Law on Reorganisation' (2003) 23 Legal Stud 284, 308–309, arrive at a similar conclusion.

32 Gutteridge (n 28) 9.

spread by now to every inhabited continent.[33] The following paragraphs illustrate this global phenomenon and the divergence involved therein and explain the reasons behind the selection of the jurisdictions studied by this book and how the latter relate to their counterparts internationally.

1.2.1 The international debate on derivative actions: An overview

It is common knowledge that most of the popularity – academic, legislative or other – enjoyed by the derivative action is attributed to the significant role it has been playing for many decades in US corporate governance, particularly in the states of New York, California and Delaware. Interestingly, the law developing independently of English common law, the remedy was much more frequently invoked there as compared to its use across the Atlantic, even after the espousal of the rule in *Foss v Harbottle*[34] by American courts.[35] In the absence of state intervention, private enforcement of directors' duties by means of the derivative action soon became an integral component of the corporate governance toolbox and met with judicial and academic acclaim. However, controversy was not avoided. Already since the early decades of the past century, abuse was reported[36] and measures were taken to restrict it.[37] The abuse centred mainly on so-called 'strike suits': that is, derivative suits brought by shareholders with a minimal stake both in the company and in the proceedings, with little – if any – chance of success, which often ended in meaningless settlements. It was submitted that, at some point, mainly attorneys benefitted from such practice.[38] However, the measures taken did not prevent the resurgence of derivative suits, including strike ones, in the 1960s.[39] Once again, measures were necessitated to tackle abuse and, this time, the response was (first) provided by the courts. The pivotal decision by the Federal District Court of

33 As is illustrated below, derivative actions are provided by most European countries, besides having a strong presence in North America (US, Canada). Many countries in Oceania (Australia, New Zealand), Africa (e.g. Nigeria), South America (e.g. Chile, Colombia) and Asia (e.g. China, Japan, Singapore) also provide for some form of derivative action.

34 (1843) 67 ER 189.

35 AJ Boyle, 'The Minority Shareholder in the Nineteenth Century' (1965) 28 MLR 317.

36 Franklin S Wood, 'Survey and Report Regarding Stockholders' Derivative Suits' (1944) (the Wood report).

37 The State of New York amended the relevant provisions of its Business Corporations Law to require that shareholders provide security for expenses in filing a derivative suit. The appropriateness of this measure is debatable, since it disenfranchises financially weak claimants. On the arguments against financial disincentives, see analysis below, Section 3.2.

38 John C Coffee Jr, 'Understanding the Plaintiff's Attorney: The Implications of Economic Theory for Private Enforcement of Law through Class and Derivative Actions' (1986) 86 Colum L Rev 669.

39 According to John C Coffee Jr and Donald E. Schwartz, 'The Survival of the Derivative Suit: An Evaluation and a Proposal for Legislative Reform' (1981) 81 Colum L Rev 261, shareholders soon found ways to circumvent this requirement by pursuit of a federal cause of action, as claims arising under the Securities Exchange Act of 1934 were not subject to state security-for-expenses statutes.

New York in *Gall v Exxon Corp* brought to the forefront the role of the Special Litigation Committees.[40] Accordingly, the possibility arose that a committee, instituted with the special purpose to review whether pursuit of the action is in the company's best interests, may opine against a claim, resulting in its rejection. However, it has been reported that, more often than not, SLCs show solidarity with their fellow directors (standing as defendants in the case before them), dismissing claims against them as unmeritorious.[41] In any case, the derivative action nowadays retains much of its importance within the US corporate governance framework, despite the rise to prominence of class actions in the past decades, often getting the media limelight with cases such as *In re Walt Disney Derivative Litigation*.[42]

The brief description of the law and practice on derivative actions across the Atlantic reveals that the remedy assumes a cardinal role in shareholder protection and corporate governance there. This 'success' of the derivative action in the US accounts for the numerous – usually piecemeal – legal transplants of the respective provisions around the world, including civil law jurisdictions. As will be explained in the second and third Parts of this book, echoes of American law are discernible in both the German and the Greek law on public limited companies.[43] The previous paragraphs also showed that, for decades, in the epicentre of the American discussion on derivative actions lies the issue of strike suits and the ways to restrict them.

Contrary to the aforementioned jurisdictions, in the majority of countries, proceedings on derivative actions constitute a rather rare phenomenon: possibly the only jurisdiction with numbers of derivative suits per year comparable to those of Delaware and New York is, somewhat intriguingly, Japan.[44] Comparatists attribute the scarcity of litigation to, among other things, the lack of economic incentives for claimants, the various restrictions and requirements set for claimants to sue. The analysis in Chapter 3 shows that, to different extents, this is the case regarding the herein studied jurisdictions. To illustrate, all three impose the loser-pays rule. Absent the possibility for indemnification, such a rule will most certainly discourage the aspiring corporate champions from instigating proceedings which, if successful, *may* leave little return for them but, if unsuccessful, *will* make them liable to pay the winning party's (often substantial) litigation costs.[45] Furthermore, the scope of misfeasance covered by the remedy is restricted in Germany.[46] It is also the case regarding English common

40 W Chen, *A Comparative Study of Funding Shareholder Litigation* (Springer 2017) 43.

41 Coffee and Schwartz (n 39) 262–263.

42 907 A 2d 693 (2005)

43 The latest legal transplant being that of independent committees (that could in practice become SLCs) to Greek law: Law 4548/2018 art 102(4).

44 Dan W Puchniak and Masafumi Nakahigashi, 'Japan's Love for Derivative Actions: Irrational Behavior and Non-Economic Motives as Rational Explanations for Shareholder Litigation' (2012) 45 Vand J Transnat'l L 1.

45 See Section 3.2.

46 See Section 3.3.2.

law and the 'fraud on the minority' doctrine, still applicable in England to disputes falling outside the scope of the UK CA 2006.[47] Importantly, the availability of the remedy is further restricted by screening devices, whose form, purpose and function differ from one studied jurisdiction to another.[48]

Contrary thus to the US, in the biggest part of the world, the academic and legislative discussion revolves around identifying the reasons for the remedy's disuse and incentivising private enforcement of directors' duties or, at least, removing the obstacles therefrom. However, there still remains a part of the world, Greece included, where derivative actions are not available (at least regarding public limited companies). There, the topic of discussion is whether derivative actions are at all necessary. European countries fall into both the latter categories. The ensuing paragraphs look closer into the matter.

1.2.2 Derivative actions in Europe: Work in progress

Some European jurisdictions have long provided for derivative actions, yet the remedy has rarely featured in their courtrooms.[49] This observation applies to both common law and civil law countries. A prime example from the latter group is France, where the action sociale ut singuli has been available since 1867, without ever becoming a popular means of shareholder activism though.[50] Nevertheless, recent legislative action has, on occasions, led to a change. The advent of the CA 2006 in the UK, for example, has resulted in an increase of cases brought to court by derivative claimants in the UK.[51] Definitely, however, nowhere in Europe is the frequency of derivative suits comparable to that of the US, as mentioned above.

In addition to the countries that recently reformed their derivative actions, there are many that introduced the remedy to their laws only in the past few decades,[52] the latest addition to this ever-growing group being Luxemburg.[53] In certain cases, derivative actions replaced or complemented existing functionally

47 As do multiple derivative actions.

48 See Subsections 3.3.1, 3.3.3, 3.3.4, 3.3.5.

49 Gelter (n 8).

50 The German HGB of 1884, s 223, on the other hand, promoted the company's action over alternatives, the rationale being that individual right could paralyze the company. As D Latella, 'Shareholder Derivative Suits: A Comparative Analysis and the Implications of the European Shareholders' Rights Directive' (2009) 6 ECFR 307, 318 aptly observes, 'German lawmakers had therefore introduced a mere Iniziativrecht (initiative right)'.

51 See Annex 1 for a list of reported cases under CA 2006 ss 260–264; see also D Milman, 'Shareholder Litigation in the UK: The Implications of Recent Authorities and Other Developments' (2013), 342 Co LN 1, 2.

52 In addition to Belgium, Italy and Germany (see n 8), the Czech Republic (1992), Latvia (1993), Lithuania (2004) and Slovenia (1997) are among the EU countries who introduced the remedy to their company laws within the past thirty years, whereas Russia followed suit in 1996.

53 Since August 2016. This reform improved its rankings in the World Bank's relevant 'ease of shareholder suits' index (<www.doingbusiness.org/en/reforms/overview/economy/luxembourg> (accessed 2 March 2019)).

equivalent rules. The obvious (and often express)[54] reason for this legislative activity is the strengthening of shareholder protection and enforcement mechanisms for corporate management liability. Explaining the timing of its occurrence is harder, however. For one, regulatory competition has played a role,[55] which may have been amplified by the 'law and finance'[56] literature that emerged in the early nineties and found its way to the World Bank's highly influential 'doing business' indices, published annually.[57] It is important to note, though, that this legislative activity has not always met with the desirable results. For instance, Italian law has been tinkering with ownership thresholds for legal standing for some time, in a search of how to spur shareholder activism, despite the fact that the remedy was introduced to it in 1998.[58] Definitely, the introduction of the derivative action did not open wide the floodgates of litigation anywhere in Europe: it is well reported that quite the contrary is true.[59]

There remain, of course, few countries in Europe where derivative actions do not form part of shareholders' arsenal, at least concerning public limited companies. Within the EU there are only few such states, Austria, Estonia, Greece and the Netherlands included. However, within this group, functionally alternative remedies are provided. Some of them even closely resemble the derivative action in its purpose, structure and scope,[60] such as the company's action, available in Austria and Greece.[61]

Regarding the mechanics of derivative actions and functionally equivalent remedies in each country, the restrictions mentioned in the previous paragraphs constitute core components of regulatory design. To begin with, most European countries avail the remedy only to qualified shareholder minorities:[62] this is the case not only for Germany, but also for the Greek functional equivalent company's action.[63] Within this group, many jurisdictions complement this requirement with further conditions, such as minimum holding periods and continuous

54 Company Law Reform White Paper (Cm6456), DTI, London, March 2005, 3; UMAG (n 9).
55 Company Law Reform White Paper (Cm6456), DTI, London, March 2005, 9.
56 Rafael LaPorta, Florencio Lopez de Silanes, Andrei Schleifer and Robert W Vishny, 'Law and Finance' (1998) 106 Journal of Political Economy 1113.
57 As stated in its website <http://doingbusiness.org/methodology> (accessed 2 March 2019).
58 Giudici (n 6) 250.
59 Indicatively, Gelter (n 8); Latella (n 50).
60 Some authors contend that the shareholders right to request a special audit or investigation is also a functional equivalent to the derivative action, especially if the investigating body has the power to impose sanctions or penalties (as happens in the Netherlands). I beg to differ. Even though this minority right has much potential in uncovering corporate misfeasance, it is not an enforcement mechanism and has no compensatory function; it is to be noted that in most countries it purportedly assumes a complementary role to provisos on shareholder-led litigation on behalf of the company.
61 Austrian *Aktiengesetz* s 134; Greek Law 4548/2018 arts 103–106.
62 Based on a share ownership percentage or aggregate capital participation thresholds. Within the EU, 19 countries place such restrictions on derivative actions.
63 Interestingly, this also applies to the UK CA2006 derivative action applicable to unauthorised donations or expenditure, s 370.

ownership of shares. Similarly common are restrictions on the scope of misfeasance covered. Admission proceedings on the other hand rarely constitute a screening mechanism, whereas Germany is one of the few providing for an American-style demand requirement.[64] Besides, quite a few countries attempt to remove financial disincentives by means of indemnification of the derivative litigant by the company.[65] Furthermore, access to litigation related information is afforded to shareholder-claimants by various means: a common fact-finding mechanism among continental law jurisdictions being the shareholder-requested extraordinary audit.[66]

The previous paragraphs show that, as regards providing the remedy in abstracto, a good level of voluntary convergence has occurred among European countries. However, when one looks closer at the details of the respective provisions, a more diverse picture emerges. This lack of uniformity shows that there is no such thing as a 'European derivative action': the results of the latest studies, commissioned by the EU on related topics, support this observation. In fact, each country construes its derivative action as an – often unique – mixture of the aforementioned restrictions, indemnification strategies and information rights.

In light of the above it becomes clear that, within the EU (to say the least), the discussion on how to improve shareholders' enforcement of directors' duties (or, even more generally, the company's claims) has revived over the past decades, the derivative action assuming a central role thereat. Despite that and the recent waves of legislation at national level amending or instituting the remedy the latter has little practical significance in most countries, whereas it is completely absent in some. It is therefore topical to investigate whether and why the derivative action is a necessary component of shareholder protection and corporate governance, which aspects of regulatory design are accountable for shareholders reluctance or failure to enact the remedy and, ultimately, how a functioning and truly protective derivative action should be construed.

The jurisdictions studied herein constitute examples of the different stages of the remedy's progress throughout Europe. Furthermore, their legal frameworks cover a great part of the wide spectrum of rules on costs allocation, fact-finding mechanisms, restrictions and conditions to enact derivative actions (and functionally equivalent remedies) applicable within this broader area. Their comparative study can thus be said to not only provide conclusions, de lege lata and de lege ferenda, regarding this book's defined jurisdictional scope, but also provide

64 'Demand' can be defined as the requirement for shareholders to make a formal request to the board(s) to initiate proceedings, before filing a derivative action. However, countries that provide for the functionally equivalent remedy of the 'company's action', such as Greece and Austria, originating and still applicable in Germany (AktG s 147), also require that shareholders demand the board to take action before filing a petition at court for the appointment of special representatives to pursue the claim.

65 The Czech Republic, Cyprus, Germany, Greece, Ireland, Latvia and the UK.

66 Available in a host of countries, such as Austria, Bulgaria, Croatia, Finland, Germany, Greece, Italy, Latvia, Poland, Romania, Slovenia and Sweden.

a better understanding of derivative actions in Europe. The following paragraphs focus on the reasons behind the selection of the laws to be compared, their comparability and the context within which they operate.

1.2.3 The comparison of Germany, Greece and the UK

The development and evolution of the laws in question not only are duly considered in the analysis herein but also determined the selection of countries and national rules to be compared. Given that the Greek law on public limited companies does not provide for derivative actions and that the existing functional equivalent is disused and presumed to be problematic, it would make little sense to compare it with a jurisdiction where derivative actions have long comprised an everyday phenomenon. In the latter case, the law expectedly would be currently focused more in constraining abuse of the remedy, than asserting its role in shareholder protection and corporate governance. On the contrary, it stands to reason to examine the law of jurisdictions which find themselves in an evolutionary stage closer to the Greek one; that is, where recent legislative efforts aim to make shareholder litigation on behalf of the company a workable and appealing option. Germany and the UK are therefore suitable candidates for this research, whereas Delaware is not.

The analysis concerns comparable legal rules and practices, in the effort to produce a meaningful comparative study. Comparability, the compelling yet frustratingly vague methodological commandment that 'like must be compared with like',[67] is contingent on the focus of the comparison and, more profoundly, intertwined with its purpose.[68] A functional study, as this book is, follows an approach purposive in character. Therefore, contrary to contextualist approaches, it focuses more on the objectives of the laws under comparison, paying less attention to (yet not disregarding) the general cultural context in its search for comparables. In any case, it is nowadays common ground that the selected jurisdictions belong to comparable legal families. Yet, even the notion of 'legal families' often divides jurisdictions more than they deserve. Considered in a global context, the laws in general and company law in particular of the UK, Germany and Greece share a good deal of proximity, further reasserted by recent research on the categorisation of jurisdictions.[69]

67 Gutteridge (n 28) 73.

68 Antonios Emmanuel Platsas, 'The Functional and the Dysfunctional in the Comparative Method of Law: Some Critical Remarks' (December 2008) 12(3) Electronic Journal of Comparative Law, <www.ejcl.org/123/art123-3.pdf> (accessed 12 September 2014).

69 Professor Siems conducted research based on statistics methodology, the results of which group the aforementioned countries in the same cluster. See M Siems, 'A Network-Based Taxonomy of the World's Legal Systems' (2014) Durham Law School Working Paper March 2014, <http://papers.ssrn.com/sol3/papers.cfm?abstract_id=2387584> (accessed 12 September 2014).

Some general observations are useful at this point. First, apart from the commonly applicable European Union legislation, the sources of law vary among the legal orders comprising this research's domain. In the UK, common law assumes an important role as a source of law and often influences the content and application of statutory provisions.[70] The role of precedent (stare decisis) and the congruent fact that 'the life of the law has not been logic: it has been experience', constitute defining characteristics of this jurisdiction.[71] As opposed to the heirs of Westminster, the heirs of Rome do not regard precedent to have the status of hard law.[72] In the cases of Germany and Greece, precedent mostly serves the role of providing interpretation of the applicable (statutory) law. The above basic differences must be kept in mind when reference is made hereinafter to the 'law'.

Secondly, the domain of this book is shareholder rights protection in public limited companies, which can be defined as corporate bodies exhibiting corporate personality, freely tradable shares, centralised management and membership based on capital contributions with limited liability.[73] Therefore, reference will be made to other corporate types and formations only when necessary. The first point of divergence among the examined jurisdictions lies in that the law of public limited companies is encompassed in statutes constructed ad hoc for this purpose in Germany and Greece, whereas in the UK a gigantic statute covers limited liability companies more generally and reference to public limited companies therein constitutes the exception rather than the rule. Further divergence exists from the perspective of numbers of public limited companies registered in each country. In Greece, public limited companies are the backbone of the economy and for long have constituted the most widespread corporate formation. A look at the Greek registry for commercial companies suggests that this situation has not changed significantly, despite the emergence and recent popularity of the private capital company (IKE).[74] In this respect, the Greek corporate landscape differs prima facie from the German and UK ones. In the UK, the overwhelming majority of companies are registered as private limited companies and in Germany the equivalent *Gesellschaft mit beschränkter Haftung* (GmbH) has traditionally been the most popular.[75] However, a closer look at the factual

70 This book focuses mostly on the law of England and Wales.

71 Oliver W Holmes Jr, *The Common Law* (1881), <www.gutenberg.org/files/2449/2449-h/2449-h.htm> 1 (accessed 15 May 2015).

72 Maurice Sheldon Amos, Frederick Parker Walton, and Alexander Elder Anton, *Amos and Walton's Introduction to French Law* (Clarendon Press 1963), 4.S.

73 Reinier Kraakman, John Armour, Paul Davies, Luca Enriques, Henry Hansmann, Gerard Hertig, Klaus Hopt, Hideki Kanda and Edward Rock, *The Anatomy of Corporate Law: A Comparative and Functional Approach* (2nd edn, OUP 2009) 5.

74 By 2016, there were 3,581 registered SAs, 6,184 private limited companies (EPE) and 10,349 IKEs. IKE is an initiative similar to the German *Unternehmersgesellschaft* (UG) and the French *Société par actions simplifiée* (SAS). cf Heribert Hirte and Christoph Teichmann, *The European Private Company – Societas Privata Europaea (SPE)* (Walter de Gruyter 2012), 337.

75 See Janet Dine and Marios Koutsias, *The Nature of Corporate Governance* (EE 2013) 275.

reality reveals that most Greek companies registered as public limited ones, exhibit a strong 'personal' element, drawing thus them closer to the British 'Ltd'.[76] Accordingly, case law in the latter two countries on private companies is of comparative interest for this book, to the extent that it concerns rules applicable to public companies as well.

Given that this is a book written in English, it encountered the challenge of using the same term (in English) for three jurisdictions, even though each one of them speaks a different language.[77] In the majority of the legal terms examined herein, further explanation was redundant, as both the original and the translated term stand for identical concepts (e.g. 'limited liability'), familiar to lawyers across the world. Often though, further explanation of the terminology is offered, as the translation of the original word may refer to a narrower or wider notion.[78]

Another challenge was, in admittedly rare instances, to devise an English term for a concept not found in UK law, or vice versa; an example being the term 'company's actions' (*etairikí agogí*). 'Company's actions' are considered to be functional equivalents of derivative actions (which in turn should translate into Greek as *parágogi agogí*).[79] Yet, as explained in Section 3.1.2, reference to them as derivative actions would be inaccurate and would lead to confusion.

Overall, 'there are certain terms in every system of law which cannot be translated into another language simpliciter but must be explained at some length',[80] and this book duly considered the importance of the use of language and terminology in its effort to accurately communicate its arguments.

1.3 Outline of the issues considered

Throughout this study, three major questions are posited and addressed. The first relates to the ratio legis and the functions of the derivative action, inquiring whether it is important to protect shareholders by allowing them to sue on behalf of the company. Chapter 2 provides an affirmative response, advancing its arguments from three perspectives. The first perspective is that of shareholders' property and proprietary interests. It is explained that the derivative action provides a refuge for shareholders suffering reflective losses in their property, by allowing remedy thereof, a remedy designed to benefit shareholders as a group

76 To that effect Peiraeus Court of Appeal 277/2005 DEE 2005, 685.

77 All translations herein are by the author, save for the instances where it is expressly stated that this is not the case.

78 M Van Hoecke in M Van Hoecke (ed), *Epistemology and Methodology of Comparative Law* (Hart 2004) 175; Konrad Zweigert and Hein Kötz, *An Introduction to Comparative Law*, tr Tony Weir (3rd edn, OUP 1998) 44ff; De Cruz (n 22) 222.

79 To that matter, see Cypriot law, which provides for a derivative action [exceptions to the rule in *Foss v Harbottle* (1843) 67 ER 189] under this heading (*Theodoros Pirillis and Another v. Eleftherios Kouis*), Civil Appeal No. 11387 (2004) 1A SCJ 136.

80 Gutteridge (n 28) 125.

and to not frustrate the application and the objectives of fundamental principles of company law. The next viewpoint is that of corporate governance. Focus is therein attributed to the role of derivative actions in the alignment of shareholders' interests with those of other constituencies within the firm. It is illustrated how, by means of compensation and deterrence of misfeasance at a board level, derivative actions shelter shareholder interests from both the directors' and fellow shareholders' opportunism. It is further argued that, by effecting the accountability of corporate management, derivative actions assign a stewardship role to the shareholder-litigant, to the benefit of all interests involved in the company. Lastly, the importance of this form of shareholder protection is assessed from an economic perspective. The first level of assessment looks into the function of the derivative action as a means to minimise agency costs and internalise externalities, building upon the discussion in the 'corporate governance perspective', as well as it examines the implications derivative litigation has on corporate wealth. The second level of assessment moves away from the concrete concept of the firm towards the more abstract theme of the market and the economy as a whole. It is argued that provisions on derivative actions, as a form of shareholder protection, may determine investors' (prospective shareholders/corporators) confidence in corporate business and the equity market, and therefore form part of initiatives and policies in favour of stock market development and economic growth.

Having identified the importance and the implications of provisions on derivative actions and given the jurisdictional focus of this book, a second question suggests itself: in which ways and how successfully does the Greek legal framework attempt to protect shareholders, in the ways the derivative action is meant to? Addressing this question is the task of the second Part of this book. Accordingly, Chapter 3, availing itself of the cognitive function of comparative law, compares the laws of two jurisdictions providing for derivative actions, with the Greek functional equivalent remedy of the corporate action. In essence, this Chapter aims to provide a diagnosis on the respective Greek provisions, identifying their problems and comparative disadvantages, from the viewpoint of shareholder protection. Studies on derivative actions often focus on the respective substantive legal rules, usually found in corporate law statutes, as well as rules on allocation of litigation costs and the availability of contingency fees arrangements. But there is more to derivative litigation than that. A comparative study on this topic needs to consider issues that are usually found elsewhere than in the provisions on derivative actions or functionally equivalent remedies, in order to illustrate whether this avenue of litigation is a viable option for shareholders to protect their and their company's interests. Such issues include the allocation of litigation expenses, waiver and settlement of corporate claims, ratifiability of breaches of directors' duties, as well as access to corporate information. This is precisely the approach of Chapter 3, in an effort to provide an accurate and objective analysis.

Nevertheless, rules and practices within a legal system may perform the same or similar functions as a rule in another legal system. Therefore, Chapter 4 investigates whether Greek law provides for effective substitute or alternative (to the derivative action) mechanisms of shareholder protection, outside the narrow scope of Law 4548/2018 articles 103–106, in order to conclude the task of the second Part of this book. This question is answered in the negative, following a comparative analysis on oppression remedies, direct shareholder claims, actions challenging the validity of corporate resolutions, as well as the ability of shareholders to contractually arrange the conduct of corporate affairs. This Chapter also offers an updated view on the levels of shareholder protection offered by Greek law, in a comparative and international context. It is illustrated that, despite some laudable efforts to make the Greek legal framework more protective, it still suffers from comparative disadvantages. The analysis also leads to the conclusion that an improvement of shareholder remedies against mismanagement could result in an 'upgrade' of shareholder protection under Greek law.

The final question to be posed concerns how the Greek law on shareholder-initiated litigation on behalf of the company should be, de lege ferenda. This is the normative part of this book. Chapter 5 avails itself of the diagnosis in Part II, in order to formulate and substantiate its suggestions, envisaging a derivative action that truly lives up to its important role in shareholder law. The proposed framework for a 'derivative action' aims to capture the merits of the respective German and UK laws and learn from their mistakes. The structure of and the issues considered in Chapter 5 accord to those of Chapter 3.

Even though the suggestions de lege ferenda purportedly avoid calling for a radical review of Greek company law as a whole, the proposed framework markedly distances itself from the existing standards of shareholder litigation. It consists of an individual shareholder right to sue on behalf and for the benefit of the company, free from arbitrary constraints on legal standing. The scope of the cause of action is inclusive, aiming to accommodate the enforcement of directors' duties and the protection of shareholders' interests. The proposed framework removes barriers from shareholder litigation, enabling shareholders to take over pending litigation and allowing suits to be brought against the management of connected companies. It prevents wrongdoers from keeping their misfeasance concealed, by providing claimants with access to litigation-related information. Furthermore, it relieves claimants from excessive pecuniary risks, by making the company, as the direct beneficiary of the proceedings, the bearer of litigation costs by default. Most importantly though, the proposed derivative action puts the company's interests to the fore and respects the organisational structure of the company. The court, as a neutral arbiter, is called in admission proceedings to weigh the views of claimants and of the company's board, in order to decide whether the suit at hand is important enough for the company to proceed. The book concludes in Chapter 6, summarising the findings and the arguments of this research and delineating its implications.

2 The importance of an effective shareholder remedy for wrongs against the company

2.1 Introduction

As illustrated in Chapter 1, derivative actions are gaining ground internationally, being considered as a potent means to facilitate enforcement of directors' duties and shareholder protection. However, is this perception justified and, if so, why? What are the functions of the derivative action in shareholder protection, and what is its importance in the broader framework of company law and corporate governance? These challenging questions emerge at the very outset of this research. In essence, they inquire into the rationale for the shareholders' right to enforce the company's claims and its role in protecting certain interests. This Chapter employs three, interrelated, perspectives to explain why an effective framework on shareholder protection against wrongs done to the company is important.

The first perspective is discussed in Section 2.2 and concerns the protection of shareholders' proprietary interests. This explains how considerations of property serve as the rationale for granting shareholders rights in the company in general and how the right to sue on behalf of the company in particular assumes an integral role in protecting shareholders' property. The second perspective is that of corporate governance, as explored in Section 2.3. This focuses on the role of derivative actions in addressing conflicts of interests within the company. It places the issue of protection of shareholder wealth within the theoretical framework of 'agency problems', explaining how derivative actions protect shareholders, from which and whose behaviour they protect them and the relationship between such protection and the interests (and, indeed, wealth) of other corporate stakeholders. The last perspective relates to economic efficiency. This is a particularly topical theme, due to the ongoing struggles the Greek economy and stock market is experiencing. Section 2.4 investigates the economic implications of the agency problems which derivative actions seek to address. To that end, it considers the role of derivative actions in addressing 'agency costs' and internalising externalities, and the effects, direct and indirect, derivative litigation has on corporate and shareholders' wealth. It then examines whether derivative actions, as a means of shareholder protection, have further (macro-)economic effects. In doing so, it assesses differing views on the role of shareholder law in promoting stock market development. Section 2.5 summarises and concludes.

2.2 The proprietary perspective

2.2.1 Introduction

In Greek academia, advocacy in favour of the introduction of derivative actions to the legal system is largely based on the premises of protection of shareholders' property.[1] Derivative actions are viewed as an ingenious device for remedying shareholders' reflective loss: references to jurisdictions which provide for such a remedy often betray envy for the 'better solution'.[2] This Section will explain the important role that shareholder litigation on behalf of the company assumes in the protection of shareholders' proprietary interests.

2.2.2 Shareholder protection, shareholder rights and private property

In order to avoid a petitio principii in formulating a position based on the premise of shareholders' proprietary interests, we should consider whether shareholders do actually possess property rights by their status as members of the company per se and, if so, which property spheres they extend to. It is internationally accepted, including the jurisdictions studied within this book, that shares are 'an item of intangible personal property', representing a variety of rights.[3] However, it is not an easy task to provide a conclusive definition of the incidents and the precise subject of this kind of property. The multiplicity of rights accruing from share ownership complicate any such endeavour.[4]

1 Indicatively: Lucas Kokkinis, 'I apokatástasi tis émmesis zimías ton metóchon ferengyos AE' (1997) 3 DEE 256.

2 This impression is left by the perusal of Nikolaos K Rokas, 'Corporate Organisation and Shareholders' Individual Action', (2007) NH' EEmpD 1, 18, who, following a (very) brief overview of the European and American derivative actions posits that 'in Greek practice, ***particularly in comparison with other countries***, the ineffective protection of the minority is particularly noticeable' (emphasis added).

3 Regarding the UK, see CA 2006 s 541: shares are 'personal property … and are not in the nature of real estate' (in Scotland: moveable property); Sarah Worthington, 'Shares and Shareholders: Property, Power and Entitlement: Part 1' (2001) 22 Comp Law 258. Regarding Greece, the prevailing opinion is that Greek Constitution art 17 protects merely the shareholders' rights in rem, yet the share as property is protected by the ECHR: see Supreme Court Plenary Session 14/1999 DEE 1999 1017; Supreme Court 795/2000, NoV 2001 1307; A. Alexandropoulou, '«Squeeze-out» kai nomiká zitímata pou anakýptoun apó tin efarmogí tou' [2008] DEE 404. Regarding Germany, see *Grundgesetz*, art 14 (Constitution of the Federal Republic of Germany); to that end the decisions of the German Federal Constitutional Court: BVerfG 20.09.1999, ZIP 1999 1798, NJW 2000 349 (*Walter/Daimler-Benz*); BVerfG 23.08.2000 NJW 2001 279, ZIP 2000 1670 (*Moto Meter*). Regarding the European Convention on Human Rights (Annexed Protocol 1 art 1), to which they are all parties, despite the use of the term 'possessions', it is clear that article 1 is about the right of property, particularly so by looking at the *travaux préparatoires*: see *Marckx v Belgium* (-1979–80) 2 EHRR 330, 355.

4 As held in *Company S. and T. v. Sweden*, no. 11189/84, Commission decision of 11 December 1986, DR 50, 138: 'a company share is a complex thing. It certifies that the holder

Much of the literature on shareholder law endorses the axiom that the company is owned by its shareholders. In the work of Kraakman et al., which has become a standard reference internationally for the study of comparative company law and corporate governance, the notion of 'ownership of the firm' is defined in the terms of 'the right to control the firm' and receive its 'net earnings'.[5] Accordingly, shareholders are perceived as 'owning' the corporation and to have ceded all but the fundamental decision-making to a centralised management for efficiency reasons.[6] This view can be reinforced by the consideration that the distinctive characteristic and necessary prerequisite for the creation and proliferation of the company, its equity capital, is provided by shareholders and remains bound by the company.

In legal terms, however, shareholder 'ownership' of the corporation and its assets is, at best, 'indirect'.[7] Any contrary assertion is hard to reconcile with the fundamental principle of company law: that the company is a person distinct from its members and is therefore the proprietor of its own assets and the subject of its own liabilities (the separate juristic personality principle: in German, *Trennungsprinzip*; in Greek, *archí tis aftotéleias tou n.p.*).[8] Therefore, unlike the members of unincorporated business formations, the shareholders' sphere of property is, abuse notwithstanding, clearly distinguished from that of the company's.[9] The oft-cited example in Greek literature, that the sole shareholder of the company commits a criminal misdemeanour when damaging an asset of

possesses a share in the company together with the corresponding rights. This is not only an indirect claim on company assets but other rights, especially voting rights and the right to influence the company, may follow the share.'

5 Reinier Kraakman, John Armour, Paul Davies, Luca Enriques, Henry Hansmann, Gerard Hertig, Klaus Hopt, Hideki Kanda and Edward Rock, *The Anatomy of Corporate Law: A Comparative and Functional Approach* (2nd edn, OUP 2009) 14.

6 ibid. 6, 14.

7 See Supreme Court Plenary Session 14/1999 DEE 1999 1017; Supreme Court 795/2000, NoV 2001 1307.

8 As is under German law 'bound for the purpose of business' (*Zweckbindung des Gesellschaftsvermögens*); see also Greek Supreme Court, 1285/1980 EEmpD LB' 394, 397. As described by Evanghelos Kourakis, if the sole shareholder of a Greek corporation physically damages the latter's infrastructure, he/she will be held liable for the relevant misdemeanour of the Greek Criminal Code: see 'Division of Share Capital in Shares' in Evanghelos Perakis (ed), *Sociétés Anonyme's Law* (3rd edn, Nomiki Bibliothiki 2013) 552.

9 Under exceptional circumstances, the corporate personality may be overridden and shareholders can be held personally liable. 'Piercing the corporate veil', as this phenomenon is known in English law, dates back to the exceptions to the rule in *Salomon v Salomon & Co Ltd* [1896] AC 22 and is common to the subsequent case law in Greece (indicatively: Greek Supreme Court Plenary Session 2/2013 DEE 2013 321) and Germany (indicatively: BVerfG, BVerfGE 13, 331; BGH, BGHZ 20, 4, NJW 1956, 785). For a comparative perspective, see Georgios Zouridakis, 'Tortious Liability of Parent Companies: Some Thoughts in Light of the Recent English Case Law and a Comparative Law Overview' [2015] DEE 990. The recognition by the law of the fact that shareholders are capable of (ab)using the corporate form as a façade, concealing the true owners of the corporate assets and/or the true debtors, shows that there is an element of truth in the notion of 'indirect ownership' of the firm.

the company, so illustrates.[10] The decision of the Athens Court of Appeal, according to which not even the sole shareholder of a company can sue for a loss suffered by the company, draws the same conclusion.[11] It follows that neither the corporation nor its assets form the item of shareholders' property in law and therefore shareholders are not afforded the ordinary legal remedies for property infringement regarding corporate assets.

Shareholders may not own the company from a legal perspective, but they undeniably own their shares. The share is protected as an item of property not only in the jurisdictions examined by this book but also under the ECHR.[12] It represents the membership of its holder in the company and confers a bundle of rights (or powers),[13] exercisable against others.[14] It is this aggregation of rights – which may vary not only from jurisdiction to jurisdiction and company to company but also among the shares of the same company – that defines the shareholding's status and value as property, as well as the protection thereof. An important implication of this view is that the level of protection afforded by law to shares, due to their status as property, will accord to these different 'species' of rights and their importance in the shareholding. Thus, it is acceptable for a minority to be squeezed out of the company and be compensated for the financial value of their shares, even though their participation rights are in such a way nullified.[15]

The fact that shares are an item of property helps explain the extent to which the share is protected against expropriation and why a minimum array of rights is necessary for the logical (and legal) construction of the share as such an item.

10 Kourakis (n 8) 553. Similar example is provided by common law: *R. v. Phillipou* [1989] Crim LR 559; see Janet Dine, 'Fiduciary Duties as Default Rules: European Influences and the Need for Caution in the Use of Economic Analysis' (1999) 20 Co Law 190, 191.

11 Athens Court of Appeal 924/1998 Dikaiosyni 1999 407.

12 See n 3.

13 See Evanghelos Perakis, *Contractual Restrictions of the Shareholder's Voting Right* (1976) 100, viewing the share as enshrining a single right to membership, from which various powers stem; see also BGH, BGHZ 90, 92, 95.

14 Brenda Hannigan seems to arrive at a similar conclusion in 'Altering the Articles to Allow for Compulsory Transfer: Dragging Minority Shareholders to a Reluctant Exit' [2007] JBL 471, 489, 491. For the theory according to which property consists of bundles of rights, exercisable against others, see AM Honoré, 'Ownership' in AG Guest (ed), *Oxford Essays in Jurisprudence* (OUP 1961) 113. WN Hohfeld proposes a slightly different construction of the bundle of rights theory, in 'Fundamental Legal Conceptions as Applied in Judicial Reasoning' (1916) 26 Yale LJ 710. This theory is particularly useful regarding intangible property, as the approaches on what constitute rights in rem cannot reflect the practical and conceptual complexity of many forms of intangible property and particularly financial instruments. See discussion in Zachary Douglas, Joost Pauwelyn and Jorge E Viñuales, *The Foundations of International Investment Law: Bringing Theory Into Practice* (OUP 2014) 370ff.

15 This issue has been considered by German case law. See BVerfG, BverfGE 14 263, 276ff (*Feldmühle*); BVerfG, BverfGE 100, 289, 301ff (*DAT/Altana*); BVerfG 23.08.2000, NJW 2001 279, ZIP 2000 1670 (*Moto Meter*). For the Greek (concurring) perspective, see I Papadimopoulos, 'Ta dikaiómata tou squeeze-out kai tou sell-out ypó to fos tis Odigías 2004/25/EK schetiká me tis dimósies prosforés exagorás' [2005] DEE 396.

However, in order to comprehend the full scope, rationale and purpose of shareholder participatory and monitoring rights, we have to consider the close interrelationship between the two, otherwise distinct, spheres of property: that of the company and that of shareholders.

Investment in shares is temporally indefinite[16] and its returns are uncertain and contingent upon the profitable running of the company.[17] Accordingly, a share may contribute to its holder's wealth if, for example, it is sold for a price greater than it was purchased for, or if dividends are paid to it. But these primary forms of financial return depend on the performance of the company: if the company suffers losses, then the shareholders' investment suffers too, either yielding no dividends or diminishing in value. It is this *dependency* of the enjoyment of *share* property on the status of *corporate* property, which makes investment in shares unique and explains the scope, rationale and importance of shareholders' rights. Absent of any right to partake in or monitor the administration of corporate affairs, investing in shares would be an irrational option due to its residual character and the uncertainty involved, at least compared to other forms of investment.[18] Creditors, for example, have claims of a value stipulated independently from the fluctuations in corporate value, claims that become due at a contractually specified point in time, insolvency notwithstanding. If investing in shares loses rationality, then the very purpose and nature of the corporation as a capital company (i.e. an institution created to accumulate capital contributions) is frustrated. On the other hand, shareholders can be expected to have the incentive to see the company do well, due to this proprietary dependency. From a certain perspective, these considerations provide the shareholders' rights, both proprietary and administrative in character, with a doctrinal justification.[19]

Therefore, a share constitutes a complex item of property, whose value and enjoyment depend on the property of another (juristic) person, distinct from the shareholder. This dependency explains the rationale behind and the importance of shareholders' rights. On a different reading, the previous paragraphs suggest that the protection of shareholders' proprietary interests can only be effective if it addresses the detrimental effects that expropriation of or damage to the corporate property may have on their shares. Due to the interdependence between the two spheres of property – the share and the company – the law's objective of protecting the share as an item of property may be frustrated, if the company is left prey to the malicious intents of those seeking to achieve private benefits at its expense. Rights to participate in the administration of corporate affairs may assist in this respect, principally in a preventive manner, by ensuring

16 This indefinite character of investment in shares comes in contrast with finite human life.

17 From this perspective only, shareholders possess merely a 'chose in action', as pronounced in *Colonial Bank v Whinney* [1886] App Cas 426 (FitzGerald LJ).

18 See Ross B Grantham, 'The Doctrinal Basis of the Rights of Company Shareholders' (1998) 57 CLJUK 554, 583; for an institutionalist perspective, see Oliver Williamson, 'Corporate Governance' (1983–84) 93 Yale LJ 1197, 1210, 1227.

19 Grantham (n 18).

that the persons at the helm of the company are trusted by the shareholders to preserve and grow corporate wealth and by reserving part of the corporate decision-making directly to the latter. The preventive potential of shareholders' (participatory) rights is of great significance in non-listed companies, where the effects of dissatisfactory governance cannot be avoided by nimbly switching companies. However, when damage to corporate property has occurred, litigation emerges as the primary option to protect either or both spheres of property. Nevertheless, the company itself may not litigate, particularly in cases where its centralised management is liable for the proprietary damage. Accordingly, the derivative action, being the right to litigate on behalf of the company, emerges as a prima facie potent and important element of shareholder protection. In order to better comprehend its importance, we shall now focus on the inability of shareholders to sue on their own behalf for damage suffered by the company.

2.2.3 Setting the boundaries of shareholders' property protection: The 'no reflective loss principle'

The principle that shareholders cannot litigate on the grounds of their 'reflective loss' (in Greek, *anaklastikí zimía*; in German, *Reflexschäden*) is commonly accepted across jurisdictions.[20] What the shareholders may view as damage suffered by their investment is not recoverable by direct action, unless the damage of the shareholder's property resulted directly from wrongdoing. Accordingly, if someone, including the company's directors (by breach of the directors' statutory duties or otherwise), damages the company, the entity vested with the right to sue is normally the company not the shareholders. The adverse effect the wrongdoing may have on stock property is considered reflective of the loss suffered by the company: it may amount to a drop in the (market) value of the shares (particularly if listed), lower than expected dividends – the importance of which cannot be overstated in non-listed companies – or restricted access to the proceeds of liquidation.[21]

The inability of shareholders to achieve redress for their reflective loss seemingly runs contrary to what was previously discussed as the rationale for shareholder

20 For a comparative study, see Bas J De Jong, 'Shareholders' Claims for Reflective Loss: A Comparative Legal Analysis' (2013) 14 EBOR 97. Regarding Germany, see Theodor Baums, 'Ersatz von Reflexschäden in der Kapitalgesellschaft' [1987] ZGR 554; regarding England, see Stephen Griffin, 'Shareholder Remedies and the No Reflective Loss Principle: Problems Surrounding the Identification of a Membership Interest' (2010) 6 JBL 461; regarding Greece, see Konstantinos G Pampoukis, 'Liability of Corporate Directors for Shareholders' Reflective Loss' (1995) A' EpiskED 333.

21 See also Christina Livada, 'Filing of Company Claims against the Members of the Board of Directors' in Perakis (n 8) 1018–1019; *Gower & Davies' Principles of Modern Company Law*, ed Paul Davies and Sarah Worthington (9th edn, Sweet & Maxwell 2012) 664; Uwe Hüffer, *Aktiengesetz* (C.H. Beck 2012) 637.

rights and protection, namely the share as an item of property. However, the 'no reflective loss principle' sits comfortably with the orthodox perception of shareholders' property and its relation with that of the company. The underlying rationale behind the rule is based on the fundamental principle, in company law, of separate legal personality.[22] In corporations, where members are not equated with the company itself, the former cannot receive compensation owed to the latter. Within the Greek legal context, this becomes apparent from the reoccurring wording in court decisions:

> In such cases of a damaging act or omission against the legal person … the claim for compensation belongs only to the legal person suffering direct loss … which is exclusively entitled to bring the action … . The individual shareholders of the company, if they have suffered losses, which may consist of a decline in the market value of their shares, the diminution of their real value or the distribution of lesser dividend … do not have a parallel claim for compensation for this loss.[23]

A similar, if not identical, view is undertaken by English law. As stated by Lord Millett in *Johnson v Gore, Wood & Co*:

> A company is a legal entity separate and distinct from its shareholders. It has its own assets and liabilities and its own creditors. … If the company has a cause of action, this is a legal chose in action which represents part of its assets. Accordingly, where a company suffers loss as a result of an actionable wrong done to it, the cause of action is vested in the company and the company alone can sue.[24]

Setting aside the doctrinal basis for the no reflective loss principle outlined above, it has to be noted that any proposal to allow direct shareholder claims for reflective loss would have a multiplicity of adverse effects and lead to controversies, in theory and in practice.

22 It follows that in cases where this principle does not or should not apply, according to the judging court, then direct recovery may be possible for the shareholders, who in this case voluntarily attempt to 'pierce the veil' in order to establish their position as the wronged persons and therefore acquire legal standing to sue. See *Agrotexim and Others v. Greece* (A/330) (1996) 21 EHRR 250 [65].

23 Athens Single-Member Court of First Instance 9669/2014 DEE 2014 1055, 1056. This wording appears also, indicatively, in Greek Supreme Court 1888/2005 DEE 2006 392; Athens Court of Appeal 5864/2011 DEE 2012 468; Athens Court of Appeal 252/2007 EpiskEmpD 2007 558; Thessaloniki Court of Appeal 2500/1994, Armenopoulos 1995 1424; Athens Court of Appeal 3469/1991 EEmpD 1993 424. The wording originates from Greek Supreme Court, 1285/1980EEmpD LB' 394, 397. Notably, Law 4548/2018 expressly provides for the shareholder right to claim direct loss (art 107).

24 [2000] UKHL 65 [2002] 2 AC at [61]. Lord Millett repeated his position in *Waddington Ltd v Chan Chun Hoo Thomas* [2009] 2 BCLC 82.

First, recovery directly by the shareholders would deprive the company of its own respective right. Such deprivation would prejudice not only the rest of the members but also corporate creditors: voluntary or not.[25] The no reflective loss principle can thus be said to serve the maintenance of corporate capital.[26] Even though it can be argued that the remaining shareholders could join the action, since they suffered damage arising from the same wrong, this is not always easy or profitable, and, in any case, this argument does not consider the adverse effects direct recovery by shareholders may have on the interests of creditors of any sort.

Direct recovery of corporate losses by shareholders could also result in double recovery and double jeopardy (*Doppelschaden*): the wrongdoer might have to compensate twice for the same wrong and shareholders would benefit not only directly by their recovery but also indirectly by the company recovering its losses.[27] Furthermore, such a possibility would frustrate the organisational distribution of powers within the company. In Greek and German literature, shareholders' individual direct action for reflective loss is primarily precluded on the premises of the strict delimitation of powers within the company and the character of shareholders' membership: investment in shares follows the fortune of the company, the latter being placed in the hands of directors.[28] If shareholders were allowed to sue directly for their reflective loss, on the same factual grounds as the company, then the board would be deprived of their power to run the company effectively.[29] In this respect, the continental views and the common law approach coincide.[30] In British literature and case law, the argument is that the power to manage and distribute the company's assets is normally vested to the board,[31] and – where permitted by law or contract – to shareholders acting collectively; any receipt of compensation in advance of the company would amount to a de facto distribution that bypasses the core corporate characteristic of centralised management.[32] *Johnson* is illustrative of how direct recovery of reflective loss would frustrate this organisational structure:

25 See concurring rationale in BGH 20.03.1995, BGHZ 129, 136, 166 (*Girmes*).

26 This concurs with the German decisions: BGH 10.11.1986, ZIP 1987 29 WM 1987 13, 16; BGH 11.07.1988, ZIP 1988 1112, 1115.

27 The oft-cited English decision supporting this argument is *Johnson* v. *Gore Wood & Co* [2000] UKHL 65; [2002] 2 AC 1; [2001] 2 WLR 72; [2001] 1 All ER 481. For the German and Greek concurring legal perspectives, see Hüffer (n 21) 511; Pampoukis (n 20) 338.

28 See Eleftherios Levantis, *Commercial Law: Companies with Limited Liability* (Sakkoulas 1998) 560; Hüffer (n 21) 637.

29 To that effect the German decisions: BGH, BGHZ 94, 55, 58ff; BGH, BGHZ 105, 121, 130ff.

30 The English decision in *Prudential Assurance Co Ltd v Newman Industries Ltd (No2)* [1982] Ch 204, 224 (Brightman LJ) illustrates this point succinctly: 'when a shareholder acquires a share he accepts that the value of his investment follows the fortunes of the company'.

31 See B Hannigan, 'Drawing Boundaries Between Derivative Claims and Unfairly Prejudicial Petitions' [2009] JBL 606, 613.

32 *Gower & Davies* (n 21) 664.

> If he (Mr Johnson) were allowed to do so then, if the company's action were brought by its directors, they would be placed in a position where their interest conflicted with their duty; while if it were brought by the liquidator, it would make it difficult for him to settle the action and would effectively take the conduct of the litigation out of his hands.[33]

A final point is that bypassing the no reflective loss principle could potentially frustrate the company's interests as a whole. This returns to the argument against depriving the company of its claim, but extends well beyond that given the damage litigation may cause to the business. For example, litigation may incur bad publicity for the company in cases where the board sits in court as a defendant: this is a cost to be borne by the company and not offset by the litigant shareholder's direct recovery. It is a strong argument that some (corporate) claims are better left not litigated and it is precisely for this reason that shareholders may not always sue even *on behalf of the company*. We will revisit this issue in Chapter 3.

2.2.4 Synthesis: Shareholders' property, reflective loss and the importance of being able to litigate on behalf of the company

The no reflective loss principle leaves shareholders dependent on the company to litigate its cause of action and thus achieve recovery for their losses. However, in cases where the company does not pursue its claims, the shareholders' loss remains. In view of the earlier discussion about the rationale for shareholder rights residing, at least in part, in the protection of shareholders' proprietary interests, it becomes evident that this rationale is largely frustrated if the shareholders' arsenal of rights cannot address such situations. The no reflective loss principle can lead to injustice, a fortiori, if adherence to the rule creates an impasse in cases where the competent corporate organs are indifferent, negligent or even in conflict of interests regarding the prospect of litigation.[34]

Let us now focus on the last point. As explained above, one of the doctrinal bases for the no reflective loss principle is the organisational structure of the company. However, from a proprietary perspective, this structure may fail its cause if the authorised bodies do not promote the proprietary interests of the company. In most jurisdictions the authority to pursue these interests and litigate on behalf of the company normally rests with the board(s) of directors. This is the case under the Greek law on public limited companies, whereby the board is granted a general (delegable) power of representation by statute,[35] and its power and duty to litigate on behalf of the company is expressly stipulated in

33 [2000] UKHL 65 [2002] 2 AC [66].

34 This is the prevalent opinion in Greek academia. See Rokas, 'Corporate Organisation' (n 2) 16. For the German, concurring, perspective, see Baums (n 20) 561.

35 Law 4548/2018 arts 77, 86.

law.[36] However, the board may opt against bringing a claim, particularly in instances where the damage suffered by the company resulted from their wrongdoing. In view of the possibility that an omnipotent board would deplete corporate and shareholders' property and remain unpunished, the authority to litigate corporate claims is shared with other corporate organs. Accordingly, in all three jurisdictions considered by this book, the shareholders' assembly – the GM – enjoys competence to decide whether corporate claims are litigated; particularly when they consider claims against the board.[37] Germany goes a step further, adding an extra organ competent to litigate such claims, namely the supervisory board.[38] In a similar vein, independent directors are gaining popularity across jurisdictions:[39] from a legislative point of view, this trend can be evidenced in the requirement to have independent directors in listed companies under the Greek Law on corporate governance.[40]

Nevertheless, this strategy does not always yield satisfactory results for the company and its shareholders. The board may be unwilling to litigate claims against its members. A dual board structure on the other hand does not in itself provide a solution: particularly if the supervisory board itself appointed the delinquent management board, as the German experience shows.[41] Independent directors do not have a good record in pursuing corporate claims,[42] nor is the GM's authority always sufficient in protecting shareholders' property. In cases where ownership of the shares is widely dispersed – and therefore voting power is demarcated – shareholders suffer from a collective action problem.[43] Even in cases where this problem is overcome, due to the concentration of voting power in the hands of a few, injustice may still occur, as it is these few who appointed the board, their acquiescence in the wrongdoing is a genuine possibility.

Accordingly, if the board composition and the majority rule do not work towards protecting the company's proprietary interests, the right of shareholders to achieve redress for their reflective loss, as is the derivative action, assumes an important role

36 ibid. art 103.

37 Regarding Greece, Law 4548/2018 art 104; regarding Germany, AktG s 147; regarding England, The Companies (Model Articles) Regulations 2008 (SI 2008/3229), Model Articles For Public Companies, arts 3, 4; *Alexander Ward & Co Ltd v Samyang Navigation Co Ltd* [1975] 1 WLR 673 (but see also *John Shaw & Sons (Salford) Ltd v Shaw* [1935] 2 KB 113).

38 Indicatively: Rokas, 'Corporate Organisation' (n 2) 14; Hans C Hirt, *The Enforcement of Directors' Duties in Britain and Germany: A Comparative Study with Particular Reference to Large Companies* (Peter Lang 2004) 262ff. On the influence and the implications of this model at EU level, see Janet Dine, 'Implications for the United Kingdom of the EC Fifth Directive' (1989) 38 ICLQ 547, 548–550.

39 Indicatively: Arad Reisberg, *Derivative Actions and Corporate Governance: Theory and Operation* (OUP 2007).

40 Law 3016/2002 art 3.

41 See, among many others, Klaus J Hopt, 'Die Verantwortlichkeit von Vorstand und Aufsichtsrat: Grundsatz und Praxisprobleme – unter besonderer Berücksichtigung der Banken' [2013] ZIP 1793, 1794.

42 See Subsection 1.2.1.

43 Reisberg (n 39) 26; Kraakman et al. (n 5) 62; Mancur Olson, *The Logic of Collective Action: Public Goods and the Theory of Groups* (Harvard University Press 1965).

in the protection of their property. The absence of this right, in such cases, denies shareholders access to justice to protect their proprietary interests, creating a void hardly reconcilable with the ratio of shareholders' rights and protection resting on the dependency of their interests to those of the company. This restriction of access to justice raises in turn further legal concerns, as the latter – apart from constituting a human right[44] – is protected constitutionally at a national level.[45]

These considerations are particularly relevant for Greece, as evidenced by the multiplicity of court decisions dismissing shareholders' claims on the grounds of the no reflective loss principle. This 'trend' has gained momentum since the early eighties and continues, with slight detractions, to this date.[46] By fate or coincidence, it also happens that Greece sat as defendant in the leading case on the subject before the ECHR, *Agrotexim*.[47] The explanation for this undesirable phenomenon resides mainly in the unavailability of an existing remedy against maladministration, functionally equivalent to the derivative action, to shareholders owning a small portion of the company's share capital. As will be explained in Chapters 3 and 5, legal standing in such cases is, for questionable reasons, severely restricted and the whole procedure is cumbersome and unappealing to shareholders.[48] Further explaining the magnitude of the problem of reflective loss is the incapacity of other shareholder rights under Greek law to

44 ECHR art 6 (right to a fair trial). Also of relevance is ECHR art 13 (right for an effective remedy).

45 Greek Constitution art 20. Concerns about the shareholders' access to justice under Greek law have been voiced by Athanasios Liakopoulos, *Zitímata emporikoú dikaíou IV* (Sakkoulas 1997) 179, 188, 189; Georgios Mentis, 'Liability of Corporate Administrative Organs for Investor's Loss' in Minutes of the 11th Panhellenian Conference of Greek Corporate Lawyers (Collaborative Work), *The Societe Anonyme and the Stock Market. The Protection of the Investor* (Sakkoulas 2003) 105. Notwithstanding the validity of these arguments under Greek constitutional law (which has yet to be attested before the Greek courts), the contention of some Greek academics that the absence of a shareholders' right to bring an action in respect of damages suffered by the company constitutes a violation of ECHR art 6 was dismissed in *Agrotexim and Others v. Greece* (A/330) (1996) 21 EHRR 250 [73], despite the dissenting opinions of Judge Walsh and four commissioners which, by and large, resonate with the views of the aforementioned Greek academics. However, the ECHR did not consider in this case – for procedural reasons (ibid [75]) – whether such violation or a violation of ECHR art13 exist when neither the company 'nor its shareholders ha[ve] any remedy whatsoever' against the wrongdoers (ibid [74]). Anyhow, such considerations would probably make no particular difference in the particular case, as the court found that the liquidators performed their tasks diligently (ibid [70]).

46 Athens Single-Member Court of First Instance 9669/2014 DEE 2014 1055, 1057; Athens Court of Appeal 877/2014 DEE 2014 505, 506; Athens Court of Appeal 5864/2011 DEE 2012 468; Piraeus Single-Member Court of First Instance 3884/2011 EEmpD 2012 684; Thessaloniki Court of Appeal 2399/2005 EpiskEmpD 2006 486; Greek Supreme Court 1888/2005 DEE 2006 392; Athens Court of Appeal 924/1998 Dikaiosyni 1999 407; Greek Supreme Court 1405/1998 DEE 1998 972; Thessaloniki Court of Appeal 2500/1994, Armenopoulos 1995 1424; Greek Supreme Court, 1285/1980EEmpD LB' 394, 397.

47 *Agrotexim and Others v. Greece* (n 45) 250.

48 Part of the analysis featured in Chapters 3 and 5 has been published by Sweet & Maxwell in Georgios Zouridakis, 'Introducing Derivative Actions in the Greek Law on Public Limited

provide remedy and act as alternatives to the derivative action, as explained in Chapter 4.

Adding to the importance of the right to sue on behalf of the company, in protecting shareholders' property, is the fact that it uniquely provides this function, leaving the no reflective loss principle intact. The direct beneficiary of any award is the company, not the shareholder-litigants. Double jeopardy is avoided and both the maintenance of corporate capital and the separate legal personality are respected. Apart from adherence to doctrinal orthodoxy, this characteristic of derivative litigation has important practical implications. First, the complications regarding the computation of the shareholders' loss are avoided. Assessment of the damage on shareholder property caused by a wrong to the company is challenging, particularly regarding the calculation of the losses suffered by members individually.[49] Derivative actions strike this problem at its heart, as by remedying the company as a whole – and thus shareholders reflectively – the need to compute is eclipsed. Furthermore, a derivative claim provides compensation not only to the claimant, but also to all fellow shareholders. As such, derivative actions are a means of collective redress, similar to class actions.[50] In the contrary case of a direct claim for reflective loss, any award directly to the shareholder-claimants would entail the danger of prejudicing both the proprietary interests of the company's other members and those of other stakeholders, for the reasons previously explained.

2.2.5 Conclusions

The primary conclusion is that the shareholders' right to achieve redress for wrongs done to the company assumes an integral role in the protection of their property. Due to the dependence of the latter on a different sphere of property – that of the company's – and the impasse resulting from the no reflective loss principle regarding judicial redress for their losses, the shareholders' right to sue on behalf of the company emerges as a necessary element in an effective framework of protection. Moreover, a derivative suit has the merit of not frustrating the no reflective loss principle: a rule based on solid doctrinal grounds and

Companies: Issues of Legal Standing and Lessons from the German and UK Experience' (2015) 26 ICCLR 271 and is reproduced by agreement with the Publishers.

49 This computation has puzzled some Greek academics. See for example Pampoukis (n 20), who views the shareholders' reflective loss as one of an uncertain value, due to the residual character of the shareholders' investment; Lucas Kokkinis, 'I zimía ton metóchon kai i apokatástasí tis. Sképseis me aformí tis AP Ol 14/1999 kai AP 795/2000' (2002) 6 DEE 574. Kokkinis supports the idea that the shareholders' reflective loss is nothing else than the difference between the proprietary value of the share prior to and following the event of the wrongdoing.

50 Paolo Giudici, 'Representative Litigation in Italian Capital Markets: Italian Derivative Suits and (if ever) Securities Class Actions' (2009) 6 ECFR 246, 249; Theodor Baums and Kenneth E Scott, 'Taking Shareholder Protection Seriously? Corporate Governance in the United States and Germany' (2005) 53 Am J Comp L 31, 50.

worthy of respect. Derivative suits also protect shareholders collectively, avoiding the pitfall of protecting the interests of some equity holders to the detriment of others. Lastly, it was illustrated that the need for derivative litigation emerges in cases where the corporate organs entrusted with the administration of the company's property do not act. The next Section focuses on this last point, from a different standpoint: that of (enforcement of) responsible corporate governance practices.

2.3 The corporate governance perspective

2.3.1 Introduction

In corporate governance literature, an oft-invoked justification for derivative actions is their role in addressing 'agency problems'.[51] The notion of agency problems has assumed a prominent position in the study of shareholder law and corporate governance since its emergence in economics literature in the mid-1970s.[52] As an explanatory mechanism, they provide valuable insight for legal research, as they highlight the intra-corporate conflicts of interest and provide a framework of analysis.[53] The task of this Section is to explain what they are, how derivative actions and functionally equivalent rules relate to them and why the latter shareholder remedies have the potential of assuming an important role in corporate governance: one that goes beyond shareholder protection and becomes, essentially, a public good.

2.3.2 The management-shareholders agency problem: Derivative actions as a means of shareholder protection

The modern corporation has the distinctive characteristic of centralised and delegated management. Shareholders, being members of the company, entrust the administration of the corporate property to the board, thereby ceding control of the company to the directors and officers. Centralised management provides experienced, specialised, swift and efficient decision-making at corporate

51 'Agency' in economics does not necessarily coincide with the homonymous legal term. According to Michael C. Jensen and William H Meckling, 'Theory of the Firm: Managerial Behavior, Agency Costs and Ownership Structure' (1976) 3 Journal of Financial Economics 305, 308: 'We define an agency relationship as a contract under which one or more persons (the principal(s)) engage another person (the agent) to perform some service on their behalf which involves delegating some decision-making authority to the agent.'

52 Indicatively: Eugene F Fama, 'Agency Problems and the Theory of the Firm' (1980) 88 Journal of Political Economy 288.

53 As an explanatory mechanism, 'agency problems' retain their suitability for legal analysis even under the perception of the company as a real entity (the 'legal fiction' assumption of Jensen and Meckling (n 51) 310, 311), because they focus on the intra-corporate relations underlying the legal and organisational structure of the company: concurring, Lia Athanasiou, *Shareholders' Activism and Corporate Monitoring* (Nomiki Bibliothiki 2010).

level, which would be impossible if the multitude of members had to convene for every corporate decision. It also enables shareholders to pursue other ventures and/or invest in a multiplicity of companies, by relieving them from the time and other costs involved in corporate decision-making.[54] Shareholders therefore hand the fortunes of their investment to a management they perceive as efficient, basing their decision on reputation, the past and prospective profitability of the company and, in the case of listed companies, market performance. Of course, when these considerations do not apply, as in single-member entrepreneur-owned companies, shareholders are expected to take the helm of the firm themselves.

All this is hardly new for a corporate law study, but these considerations are essential for understanding the substratum of the first agency problem examined herein, namely the one related to the conflicts of interest between the management and the shareholders. Akin to an agency relationship, shareholders being the (indirect) owners of the firm – the 'principals' – entrust the promotion of their interests to the corporate decision-makers – the 'agents'.[55] The 'management–shareholders agency problem' refers to the divergence of pursued interests between those principals and agents.

Reference to the relevance of the 'agency theory' to the thesis of Adolf Berle and Gardiner Means on the 'separation of ownership and control' in the 'modern corporation' has become a cliché in the study of corporate law, but a few words are necessary.[56] Much of the analysis in *The Modern Corporation and Private Property* focuses on the observation that, in companies showcasing diffuse share ownership, those who have their stakes in the company do not run it, whilst the converse is equally true:[57] to put it otherwise, directors and officers administer, in the words of Adam Smith, 'other people's money'.[58] Why this observation is valid and relevant from a legal perspective is obvious, in light of the preceding discussion and explanation in Section 2.2 regarding the shareholding's dependency on corporate property. What aggravates the disparity between ownership and control in diffuse share capital structures are the practical difficulties for any control to be exerted on the management, due to the collective action problems shareholders face. Hence, directors and officers in the 'Berle and Means Corporation' enjoy sizeable power and privilege: they control the company and shareholders' wealth, while being de facto situated beyond

54 Mike Wright, Donald S Siegel, Kevin Keasey and Igor Filatotchev, *The Oxford Handbook of Corporate Governance* (OUP 2013) 99.

55 Jensen and Meckling (n 51) 308.

56 Adolf Berle and Gardiner Means, *The Modern Corporation and Private Property* (first published 1932, Macmillan 1962).

57 Franck Easterbrook and Daniel Fischel, *The Economic Structure of Corporate Law* (Harvard University Press 1996), 91 argue that the less the corporate management's wealth is tied to the company, the less they are expected to run the latter efficiently.

58 Adam Smith, *An Inquiry into the Nature and Causes of the Wealth of Nations*, ed RH Campbell, AS Skinner and WB Todd (first published 1776, Clarendon Press 1976) 741.

and above the latter constituency's reach. They are presented with opportunities to enrich themselves, to the detriment of the company and the shareholders and, in the absence of any monitoring, lack the incentive to provide quality services.

In an effort to address this agency problem, the law imposes rules and standards of behaviour upon corporate decision-makers.[59] Rules refer to the outright prohibition of certain activities or the prescription of actions to be taken in given circumstances.[60] Standards on the other hand are more open-ended and usually come in the form of director's duties, as they are pronounced in company law statutes;[61] further – usually more precise – standards of conduct may be found in corporate governance codes, whether as a matter of mandatory law or soft-law.[62] Focusing on directors' duties, the effort to address the management–shareholder agency problem is all too obvious in jurisdictions where the company's interests are conceived as those of shareholders as a whole, present and future. This is because the basic directors' (fiduciary) duty, the duty of loyalty in the positive sense, is pronounced as the duty to promote the interests/success of the company, placing the corporate interests above their own individual ones. In doing so, directors are expected to exhibit certain levels of diligence (duty of care). But even in jurisdictions where shareholders do not enjoy such exclusivity, their interests form part of the corporate ones.[63] Accordingly, despite the fact that directors' duties are typically owed to 'the company', the ultimate (and often exclusive) beneficiaries of the duties are the shareholders.

However, within both rules and standards strategies an essential component is enforcement.[64] The management cannot be expected to abide by these standards simply because of its goodwill. Every human being, including the people ultimately deciding and acting on behalf of the company, carries their own perfections and imperfections. It is to be expected that some directors and officers, at some point in time, will take advantage of their power positions in order to

59 This is the 'standards strategy' in corporate governance (Kraakman et al. (n 5) 39, 40). For the application of this strategy on shareholder litigation see Hirt (n 38) 63ff.

60 Kraakman et al. (n 5) 39.

61 e.g. directors' duties as applicable under Greek law, Law 4548/2018 art 102; under German, law AktG, ss 93, 116; under UK law, CA 2006 ss 170–177.

62 e.g. the UK Corporate Governance Code and the German Corporate Governance *Kodex* (available at: <www.dcgk.de//files/dcgk/usercontent/en/download/code/2015-05-05_Corporate_Governance_Code_EN.pdf> (accessed 12 August 2015)), both soft law in nature and following a comply-or-explain approach; cf Greek Law 3016/2002 on corporate governance, which is mandatory in nature.

63 The perception that the company's interests refer to the company as an abstract, autonomous entity has been pronounced most prominently by Otto von Gierke, *Das Deutsche Genossenschaftsrecht* (first published 1868, Wissenschaftliche Buchgemeinschaft 1954); Walther Rathenau, *Vom Aktienwesen – Eine Geschäftliche Betrachtung* (Fischer 1917). This view is not generally followed in academia and deservedly so, as beneath the company lies a socio-economic phenomenon.

64 Kraakman et al. (n 5) 40.

promote their individual interests, to the detriment of others involved in the corporate business.[65]

Enforcement of directors' liability can and does come from various sources. The public enforcer has an interest in ensuring that the controllers of the company do not act against the law, particularly in view of the impact corporate decision-making has on the economy and society. However, the public enforcer has neither the infrastructure nor the political fiat in liberal Western economies to closely observe the conduct of corporate affairs and intervene in every case where the management-shareholders agency problem gets out of hand. Even in jurisdictions with the reputation of strong public enforcement of corporate governance, authorities are mainly concerned with the securities market and therefore their monitoring is limited to the companies listed therein.[66] In any case, close state supervision of the broader spectrum of corporate activity would be impractical in economies with tens of thousands of registered corporations, such as the economies forming the study area of this book. This would necessitate vast amounts of public funds and large numbers of personnel in order to have any effect.[67]

Another source of enforcement may be a body of monitors within the board structure of the company. Looking at the company laws of different jurisdictions, we observe that executives answer to the board of directors; independent (non-executive directors) members are put in place and, in some cases, supervisory boards are assigned with the task of monitoring the management.[68] The main problem with this strategy is that those monitors have, at best, as much a stake in the company's performance as the management. Their exposure to opportunities for taking advantage of the company may be minimal compared to that of the management (as they have the task of monitoring rather than managing), but at the same time they have no material incentives to prevent the latter from exploiting their power position.[69] On the contrary, they have good reasons to not displease the persons at the helm of the company, as they would if they embroiled them in litigation. The monitors' career prospects depend – or may at some point in time depend – on those who may stand as defendants. The market for the

65 These are known in economic terms as 'agency costs'. I do not refer here exclusively to a breach of the duty of loyalty; in discharging their duties in a negligent manner and in breach of the duty of care/diligence, the corporate management also promotes its own interest, as they place less effort in their work while maintaining their position (shirking).

66 This is the case with Australia and its national Securities and Investment Commission (ASIC). See also Alexandra Mikroulea *Scope of Corporate Managers' Duties and Liability* (Nomiki Bibliothiki 2013) 290.

67 See also John C Coffee Jr, 'Rescuing the Private Attorney General: Why the Model of the Lawyer as Bounty Hunter is Not Working' (1983) 42 Md L Rev 215.

68 E.g. UK CGC B.1.2 (2014), requiring half of the board to be comprised of non-executive directors (NEDs) in FTSE 350 companies.

69 Wolf-Georg Ringe, 'Independent Directors: After the Crisis' (2013) 14 EBOR 401, 417–418.

services of corporate management and directorship is a narrow one: those who may assume office as monitors may later run a company and vice versa. This may be true not only for independent directors, but also (even more so) for members of supervisory boards, where applicable.[70]

The derivative action, being an enforcement mechanism, suggests itself as an important part of a strategy to address the agency problem between management and shareholders. It does so in two ways. First, it is a means of compensating directly the company and, indirectly, the shareholders. As was explained in Subsection 2.2.4, the derivative action has the benefit of remedying shareholders' reflective loss en masse, along with safeguarding other corporate constituencies' interests, as any reward goes to the company rather than the claimant. The effect of this function of the remedy obviously takes place ex post facto, as does any form of compensation.

The second function of the derivative action in corporate governance is more complicated and, as elaborated in the next Section, is similarly – if not more – important than the compensatory function. The threat of enforcement, so far that it is a credible threat, deters misfeasance on the part of those running the company. This tenet, quite familiar to the criminal lawyer,[71] has an application to civil matters within the corporate context that is well discussed in academia[72] and evident in the ratio legis of modern legislation.[73] Accordingly, the persons in charge of the corporation have reasons to abstain from wrongful behaviour, in view of the possibility that they will be punished. 'Punishment' within the context of corporate governance should not be understood under the narrow prism of compensating the damage caused to the company but instead should be perceived as including further effects, such as the reputational damage incurred by the defendants in such litigation.[74] Those in control of the company have thus a disincentive to behave opportunistically in view of the possibility of being 'punished' (prevention) and, in cases where an action has successfully been brought against them, to avoid behaving in such a way again (recidivism). Deterrence can also be said to be reinforced by the accumulation of relevant precedent. Actions brought by shareholders not only signal that misfeasance does not go unpunished but also help clarify the boundaries of acceptable

70 Klaus J Hopt in Klaus J Hopt, Hideki Kanda, Mark J Roe, Eddy Wymeersch and Stefan Prigge, *Comparative Corporate Governance: The State of the Art and Emerging Research* (Clarendon Press 1998) 227–259.

71 Indicatively, Dan M Kahan, 'Social Influence, Social Meaning, and Deterrence' (1997) 83 Va L Rev 349.

72 e.g. JD Cox, 'Compensation, Deterrence, and the Market as Boundaries for Derivative Suit Procedures' (1984) 52 Geo Wash L Rev 745; John C Coffee Jr, 'New Myths and Old Realities: The American Law Institute Faces the Derivative Action' (1992–1993) 48 Bus Law. 1407, 1428ff.

73 Coffee 'New Myths' (n 72) 1428, referring to the ALI's Principles of Corporate Governance s 7.10(b).

74 ibid. 1437.

behaviour in the administration of corporate affairs.[75] The deterrent effect of shareholder litigation enforcing directors' duties can thus be seen as taking place ex ante, despite the fact that litigation is a corporate governance mechanism operating ex post.[76]

A counter-argument to the deterrent function of derivative actions may be the existence of directors' and officers' (D&O) liability insurance schemes. Indeed, having the company pay for insurance raises the possibility of moral hazard on the part of the management, as it effectively shelters their private wealth from the financial consequences of their wrongdoings. On balance though, D&O insurance enhances the prospects and magnitude of compensation.[77] Furthermore, it would be a misstatement to say that all sorts of misconduct are covered by insurance, in practice or by law. Fraud, dishonesty and wilful illegality are usually exempted, not only because of insurance practices but also because the law so prohibits on the grounds of public policy.[78] In fact, insurance can be viewed as a complement to the safe harbour for business decision-making set by the Business Judgment Rule, protecting negligent decisions taken in good faith, which fall outside the ambit of the latter exemption from liability. Moreover, misconduct may well translate into an increase in insurance premiums, an unwelcome event for the company, which may weigh heavily against directors. Lastly, any argument that D&O insurance nullifies deterrence completely disregards the reputational damage litigation may have on the management and its deterrent effect. For these reasons, D&O insurance can be held to have marginal adverse effect on the role of derivative actions in shareholder protection and corporate governance.

2.3.3 The minority shareholders–majority shareholders agency problem: Derivative actions as a means of minority protection

The considerations outlined above are relevant to the Greek corporate governance landscape. To begin with, accountability of corporate directors is a long standing problem for Greece, one that can be accounted for by the lack of an effective shareholder remedy against directors' misfeasance and the absence of a 'genuine' derivative action.[79] An influential Greek academic whose contribution to the study of Greek company law and whose impact is impossible to overstate, summarises the problem in a few lines:

75 Reisberg (n 39) 53.

76 ibid. 51.

77 Deirdre Ahern, 'Directors' Duties: Broadening the Focus beyond Content to Examine the Accountability Spectrum' (2011) 33 DULJ 116.

78 This is the case under Greek law. See analysis (with comparative considerations on German law) in Mantha Varela, 'I kálypsi tis améleias sti genikí asfálisi tis astikís efthýnis' [2008] DEE 412.

79 See Zouridakis (n 48) 271.

> Two are the essential elements for the sustainable operation of public limited companies: substantial oversight and activation of the provisions for civil liability of members of the BoD. … In Greek practice of corporate law, precisely these two crucial points are the most disused. In particular, rare are the judicial decisions dealing with the issue of directors' liability, even rarer to the point of non-existence are the ones ordering directors to compensate.[80]

Despite being published more than two decades ago, this observation retains its relevance. The volume of reported decisions on the enforcement of directors' duties has remained low ever since.[81] In view of the problematic construction of the statutory provision on the enforcement of directors' duties, as explained in Chapter 3, this is an expected phenomenon.

Absence of civil liability litigation does not mean that misfeasance does not occur. This concern bears relevance in the German context too, as can be deduced by Chancellor Merkel's declaration in 2008, in which she asserted that statutory rules on directors' liability are practically unused.[82] Germany has been struck by various corporate scandals over the years, such as the recent Volkswagen gas-emissions debacle.[83] Allegations and complaints for directors' misfeasance in the Greek context may not be of such a magnitude to attract frequent international media attention, due to the small size of the national economy, yet they exist and they are numerous.[84] Notable examples of proceedings attracting extensive domestic media attention include the claims related to the Greek bubble-stock saga in 1999[85] and a recent series of litigation against the boards

80 N Rokas, 'Comments on Athens Multi-Member Court of First Instance 4831/1992' [1993] EEmpD 596.

81 A review of the most comprehensive legal database reveals that, since 2005, less than 20 decisions have been reported. See also Annex I.

82 Declaration by Chancellor Dr Angela Merkel, Deutscher Bundestag: Drucksachen und Protokolle [BT] 16/181, 7 October 2008; see also Gerhard Wagner, 'Officers' and Directors' Liability Under German Law: A Potemkin Village' (2015) 16(1) Theoretical Inquiries in Law 69, 71: cf. Klaus J Hopt, 'Die Verantwortlichkeit von Vorstand und Aufsichtsrat: Grundsatz und Praxisprobleme – unter besonderer Berücksichtigung der Banken' [2013] ZIP 1793, 1794.

83 'Why Volkswagen's Share Price has Fallen so Far' [21 September 2015] The Economist, <www.economist.com/news/business-and-finance/21665452-18-billion-fine-not-carmakers-only-worry-why-volkswagens-share-price-has-fallen-so> (accessed 25 September 2015).

84 A notable exception is that of the 'Koskotas' scandal in the 1990s (where $210 million disappeared from the Bank of Crete), which made the cover of Time magazine (13 March 1989).

85 'The 'bubble' period of the ASE coincided with repeated instances of fraudulent practices and corporate scandals', claim Apostolos Dasilas and Stergios Leventis in 'Corporate Governance, Dividend Status, Ownership Structure, and the Performance of Greek Seasoned Equity Offerings' (2013) 20 International Journal of the Economics of Business 387, 390. Forty-two defendants were recently acquitted in criminal proceedings before the Athens Three-Member Criminal Court of Appeal, on allegations of market manipulation. See Kollia Eleftheria, 'Areios Págos gia metochés- foúskes: Oi dikastés den

of several Greek banks, such as the Hellenic Postbank[86] and Proton Bank.[87] The Proton Bank case, where the corporate directors were systematically involved in the tunnelling of corporate assets to 'connected enterprises',[88] leading to the default of the company, is an exquisite example of the inadequacy which the applicable framework exhibits on the enforcement of directors' duties in allowing shareholders to achieve redress for their losses. This issue is further discussed in Chapter 4.

Enforcement of directors' duties is an existing problem for Greek law, yet its roots are not identified in the separation of ownership and control in the given national context. The management–shareholders agency problem, as defined above, has only limited relevance for Greek companies. The reason for this is that very few companies are diffusely owned and, in the international context, Greece exhibits high levels of share ownership concentration. LaPorta et al. provided the first available comprehensive empirical evidence of the ownership structure of Greek firms, studying the largest 20 listed corporations in the Athens Stock Exchange in 1999. Their results showed that almost two-thirds of them were owned by block-holders (mainly families), 30% were state-owned, whilst the remaining 5% were diffusely owned.[89] Comparatively, the study showed that Greece stood in the extreme of ownership concentration, exhibiting higher levels than most continental European countries, including Germany and Italy, whilst the UK and other Anglo-Saxon jurisdictions stood at the opposite extreme with high-level share ownership diffusion.[90] Later country-specific studies by Greek scholars show that ownership concentration has remained high during the past decade.[91]

Of course, we should not overlook the fact that the few companies with diffuse ownership have large capitalisation and are important participants in the Greek market and economy as a whole.[92] Another factor that should not be

ángixan tin ypóthesi «Chastoúki» to skeptikó tis aítisis anaíresis apó to anótato dikastírio' [15 March 2014] To Vima, < www.tovima.gr/society/article/?aid=577096> (accessed 1 October 2015).

86 See Ioanna Mandrou, 'Se díki 35 átoma gia ta dáneia ekatommyríon evró tou T.T.' [30 September 2015] Kathimerini, <www.kathimerini.gr/832828/article/epikairothta/ellada/se-dikh-35-atoma-gia-ta-daneia-ekatommyriwn-eyrw-toy-tt> (accessed 1 October 2015).

87 See Athens Single-Member Court of First Instance 12468/2012, EEmpD 2012 275; Athens Single-Member Court of First Instance 9669/2014, DEE 2014 1055.

88 Athens Single-Member Court of First Instance 9669/2014, DEE 2014 1055, 1057.

89 Rafael LaPorta, Florencio Lopez-De-Silanes and Andrei Shleifer, 'Corporate Ownership Around the World' (1999) 54 Journal of Finance 471, 493, statistics at a 10% shareholding cut-off.

90 ibid The UK exhibited 90% of studied firms being widely held, the percentage for Germany being 35% of firms studied.

91 Panayotis Kapopoulos and Sophia Lazaretou, 'Corporate Ownership Structure and Firm Performance: Evidence from Greek Firms' (2007) 15 Corporate Governance: An International Review 144, 147; Loukas J Spanos, 'Corporate Governance in Greece: Developments and Policy Implications' (2005) 5 Corporate Governance: The International Journal of Business in Society, 15, 22.

ignored is the projected privatisation of most of the state-owned Greek companies, which may have the effect of shifting the ownership paradigm, by introducing a multiplicity of institutional investors. In all recent memoranda of understanding on structural economic reforms Greece has signed with its lenders, extensive privatisations have been agreed and some have already taken effect.

Yet, in order to properly comprehend the lack of enforcement of directors' duties in the Greek corporate governance context and the importance of an effective minority shareholder remedy, we should switch focus to the other agency problem, namely that which exists between majority shareholders and minority shareholders (the 'majority–minority agency problem'). In concentrated ownership, shareholders owning significant blocks of the share capital are perceived to be able to both monitor and influence the management.[93] Control of the company thus remains with shareholders, or more precisely *some* shareholders. Their ability to influence management has the potential not only of minimising the management–shareholders agency problem but also of disenfranchising minorities, by virtue of decisions taken – at least typically – at board level.

As illustrated previously, directors' duties are owed to the company and thus to members as a whole. Adherence to directors' duties therefore serves the purpose of minority protection, as the term 'members as a whole' excludes the discriminatory placement of some intra-corporate interests above others.[94] It also follows that a breach of duty may arise despite directors serving the interests of some shareholders, even if the latter hold the majority of the shares. In concentrated ownership structures, directors may act to the detriment of the company and hence against the interests of minority shareholders, only to serve the (conflicting) interests of the majority. They have good incentives to do so. Majority shareholders appoint and remove directors, have a decisive say on their pay and seek to be closely involved in the administration of corporate affairs, as a large part of their private wealth is bound with the fortunes of the company.[95] It is also not so rare for the majority shareholder to reserve a key position on the board for himself/herself, where ownership concentration is high.[96]

92 The most diffused listed corporations are those active in health services, financial services and construction. See Kapopoulos and Lazaretou (n 91) 155.

93 See Andrei Shleifer and Robert W Vishny, 'A Survey of Corporate Governance' (1997) 52 Journal of Finance 737.

94 As Evanghelos Perakis observes in *Rights of Minority Shareholders* (Bruylant 2004) 33, the principle of equal treatment flows naturally from the directors' duty of loyalty.

95 So suggests behavioural economic theory. See Martin Gelter and Geneviéve Helleringer, 'Lift not the Veil! To Whom are Directors' Duties Really Owed?' [2015] U Ill L Rev. 1069, 1117.

96 Empirical studies in the Greek context affirm this assertion. Kapopoulos and Lazaretou (n 91) found significant correlation between block-ownership and shareholder-held positions in corporate boards.

However, majority shareholders do not always think and operate under the criterion of benefitting the company as a whole. Their power position presents them with the opportunity to extract private benefits at the expense of all others involved in the company. Having subdued the corporate board to their will, they can expect the board to actively effectuate or, at least, forebear their opportunistic behaviour. Conversely, opportunism on the part of the management as a whole, to the detriment of minorities, is easily facilitated when the only constituency left to be persuaded not to hold them liable is a familiar – and often amicable – majority. In such cases, those primarily affected by such behaviour – and consequently having the incentive for seeking prevention and remedy thereof – are minority shareholders. It so follows that the efficacy of the derivative action much depends on its availability to minority shareholders, as this would entail practical difficulties for delinquent directors to 'greenmail' a multiplicity of shareholders not to sue.[97]

These considerations lead by necessity to the conclusion that the enforcement of directors' duties is of significant relevance to the majority–minority agency problem. This is why derivative actions are construed as an individual or minority shareholders' right, even in jurisdictions with concentrated ownership. This rationale can also be traced in the fact that in such jurisdictions, the scope of defendants in a derivative action often extends to persons exerting influence on decision-making at board level.[98] It follows that derivative actions aim to address either the management–shareholder agency problem or the majority–minority issue or both scenarios, depending on the given corporate ownership context. The remedy focuses on control of the company effectuated at board level and the effects that the conflict of interest between those in control and the company may have on shareholders as a whole, irrespective of whether these effects originate in the pursuit of private benefits by the board, majority shareholders or both. Accordingly, the compensatory and deterrent value of derivative actions retains relevance in concentrated ownership structures. The wording employed above, using terms such as 'those in control of the company' instead of 'the directors', was not a stylistic touch; rather, it was a deliberate choice to show that these functions of derivative actions fit within the contexts of both agency problems.

2.3.4 The corporate controllers–stakeholders agency problem: Derivative actions as a public good

There is currently a reignited discussion on whether the third agency problem in corporate governance, concerning the management and non-shareholder constituencies, should be 'internalised' in the standards of behaviour designated for management.[99] In legal jargon, the issue is whether the interests of

97 See also Subsection 5.3.1.

98 e.g. German AktG ss 147(1), 148(1).

99 The discussion's origins in the US can be traced in Merrick E Dodd Jr, 'For Whom are Corporate Managers Trustees' (1932) 45 Harv L Rev 1145.

the company, the subject of the directors' duty of loyalty, should be perceived to coincide with those of its shareholders or whether the interests of other constituencies should be included. Even though 'corporate interests' constitute a core, yet often vague in its content, concept of corporate governance, there is certainly no uniformity of definition, neither among academic views, nor within the definitions given by different jurisdictions.[100]

Accordingly, in some countries the company's interests are equated with those of its shareholders,[101] whilst in others the interests of the company are co-defined by those of various stakeholders.[102] For sure, most jurisdictions nowadays distance themselves from the strict and complete disregard of non-shareholder interests, while at the same time reserving a special place for (long-term) shareholder value in defining corporate interests. National laws can be said to be converging on this matter, yet differences in detail and emphasis pertain.[103]

The UK CA 2006 section 172(1) now pronounces that the board has to consider a range of stakeholders in promoting the 'success of the company for the benefit of its members as a whole', in the long term.[104] Whilst the precise content of this provision has not yet been satisfactorily clarified by the judiciary, it resonates with a move towards an 'enlightened shareholder value' approach,[105] prescribing consideration of other stakeholders' interests in the course of running the company, up to the extent that such consideration accords to the pursuit of corporate profit, value maximisation and therefore shareholders' – present and future – benefit.[106] However, the fact that only shareholders fall under the definition of 'members' within the company law statute has led academics to conclude that shareholders remain the point of focus for corporate management under the statutory duties.[107]

Similarly, the prevailing – if not undisputed – view in academia and case law regarding Greek company law perceives the company's interests to be its long-term profitability and sustainability, for the benefit of the members.[108] The

100 The topic has been extensively discussed by Janet Dine and Marios Koutsias, *The Nature of Corporate Governance* (EE 2013); Michael Galanis and Alan Dignam *The Globalization of Corporate Governance* (Ashgate 2013).

101 Shareholder primacy/supremacy is perceived as a characteristic of the US and, particularly, the law of Delaware.

102 The most commonly referred example is that of Germany: see Dine and Koutsias (n 100) 272–275. Similar observations apply to French law and Chinese law.

103 Mathias M Siems, *Convergence in Shareholder Law* (CUP 2008) 178–182, aptly observes that convergence takes place on two levels: both in law and in practice.

104 See also UK Corporate Governance Code, A.1 (2014).

105 Both title and content of the ESV are reminiscent of Professor Jensen's 'enlightened value maximization' and 'enlightened stakeholder theory'. See Michael C Jensen, 'Value Maximization, Stakeholder Theory, and the Corporate Objective Function' (April 2002) 12 Business Ethics Quarterly 235.

106 *Gower & Davies* (n 21) 542.

107 ibid; Dine and Koutsias (n 100) 183.

108 Georgios Triantafillakis, *To Symféron tis Epicheírisis os Kanónas Symperiforás ton Orgánon tis AE* (Sakkoulas 1998) 122; Harris E Apostolopoulos, *The Business Judgment Rule and the Challenge of the Firm's Insolvency* (Nomiki Bibliothiki 2014) 16; Eleni Karamanakou,

emphasis on the long-term perspective can also be identified in the European Commission's objectives[109] and the OECD's guiding principles[110] and is said to consider the benefit of all stakeholders in the company, as only in a prosperous business can the persons dealing with and involved in it prosper themselves.[111] As in the UK, Greek company law does not seem to allow corporate decisions to disregard shareholders. Rather, it recalibrates the content of the *protected* shareholders' interests within the ambit of general directors' duties, so as to fit a sustainable running of the corporate business, whose purpose remains closely interrelated to the benefit of shareholders (namely corporate profit and the augmentation of corporate value). Of course, these considerations do not apply for companies established for non-profit or non-commercial purposes, up to the extent permissible by national company law and the numerus clausus of corporate forms and types.

On the other hand, Germany, despite being regarded traditionally as *the* example of corporate pluralism, is observed to be moving towards a more shareholder-orientated paradigm.[112] The voices in academia favouring a more shareholder-friendly approach are growing stronger and recent reforms reflect this viewpoint.[113] This does not deny that other stakeholders' interests, and particularly those of employees, are considered under German company law. Rather, it demonstrates that shareholders are enjoying increasing priority within the context of German corporate governance, from academic, statutory and factual points of view.

Therefore, the enforcement of directors' duties, as long as it aims to align their behaviour with 'corporate interests', protects – or, at least, aims to protect – the interests of all constituencies included in the definition of the latter term. Accordingly, derivative actions can be said to attain a broader social value than merely protecting shareholders. It seems that this conclusion involves a contradiction:

Shareholders' Fiduciary Duties (Nomiki Bibliothiki 2013) 76; see also Peiraeus Single-Member Court of First Instance 5826/2006 DEE 2007 452.

109 See European Commission, 'Action Plan: European Company Law and Corporate Governance: A Modern Legal Framework for More Engaged Shareholders and Sustainable Companies', Brussels, 12 December 2012, COM (2012) 740/2; Commission Recommendation 2014/208/EU of 9 April 2014 on the quality of corporate governance reporting ('comply or explain') [2014] OJ L 109/43.

110 G20/OECD Principles of Corporate Governance <www.oecd.org/daf/ca/Corporate-Governance-Principles-ENG.pdf> (accessed 21 November 2015).

111 See also Jensen (n 105) 236.

112 Siems *Convergence* (n 103) 178–180. Galanis and Dignam (n 100), in their general advocacy for an inclusive approach lament that, in the aftermath of the global financial and economic crisis, Germany is 'in the crossroads' instead of leading the way towards what they perceive to be the appropriate response to the problem.

113 Academic views and legislative trajectories should not be considered as independent from each other. Academia has an influence on legal drafting, evident from the impact that leading German professors' reports had on UMAG, as well as from the assignment of the drafting of Law 3604/2007 and Law 4548/2018 to groups of Greek scholars.

a corporate constituency, whose (short-term) interests might conflict with the rest, is perceived to champion the interests of all constituencies. A closer look on the nature of derivative actions resolves this conundrum.

It is true and reasonable that the underlying motive behind derivative litigation can generally be expected to be compensation of the claimant's reflective loss, as explained in Section 2.2. However, the final arbiter in shareholder-initiated *derivative litigation* is the court, and derivative actions are brought on behalf of the company, not the shareholder-claimant. Accordingly, in cases where the complained of behaviour relates to alleged breaches of directors' duties, only the court will judge whether such breaches occurred and should be remedied. Given that the duties sought to be enforced are owed to the company and that the content of these duties is defined in and by the law, courts can and should be reasonably expected to reach a decision not on the basis of the claimant's underlying interests and motives but instead on the basis of the interests protected by virtue of directors' duties.[114] Therefore, if the behaviour complained of ran against a particular interest of (some) shareholders, such as the short-term maximisation of their investment's value, but did not run against the company's interests as they are defined by law, then courts ought to reject the derivative claim. In this case, derivative actions have the effect of protecting the right-holder's welfare to the extent that other corporate constituencies are not adversely affected. Conversely, directors' behaviour against the company's interests, even where the statute defines them as coinciding with those of shareholders, may often affect all persons involved in the company. This might be the case where such behaviour directly affects corporate assets, or where directors' negligence is such that their decisions put the corporate business in danger. The compensation achieved on behalf of the company and the effected disciplining of the wrongdoers, if litigation is successful, achieve a benefit enjoyed as much by shareholders, as by employees, suppliers, creditors and so on.

It follows that the ultimate recipients of judicial redress within the ambit of the enforcement of the directors' duties may well extend beyond the claimants and shareholders in general. Therefore the 'bundling of atomistic individual interests and the observance of diffuse or corporate interests on the part of the shareholders' is attempted by the law.[115] This consideration is reflected in the Germanic doctrinal basis for the derivative claimant as a *Gesetzliche Prozessstandschafter*: that is, the procedural steward, on behalf of the company, by virtue of law. Derivative actions can thus be viewed as enabling – or even ascribing – a stewardship role on shareholders. The successful exercise of the right to enforce directors' duties – by bringing an action on behalf of the company –

114 Compare the interests protected by other shareholder rights and remedies, such as the right to dividend and the unfair prejudice remedy, which are closely connected with the protection of individual shareholders.

115 Anne van Aaken, 'Shareholder Suits as a Technique of Internalization and Control of Management: A Functional and Comparative Analysis' (2004) 68 RabelsZ 288, 289.

thus becomes a public good, enjoyable not only by shareholders cumulatively but also by all the constituencies involved in the definition of the company's interests.[116]

2.4 The economic implications of derivative actions

2.4.1 Introduction

Section 2.3 focused on how derivative actions and functionally equivalent rules relate to issues of corporate governance, as foregrounded within general academia by economists. This Section takes a step further and seeks to discover the economic implications of this kind of shareholder-initiated litigation. It first examines the economic effects of derivative litigation on a corporate level. To that end, it shows how the function of derivative litigation as a minimiser of agency problems translates in economic terms and whether it yields tangible economic results. The discussion moves to the macro-economic implications an advanced (and competitive) framework for shareholder protection may have. The focus of the analysis is the potential of legal provisions on shareholder protection to operate as a drive for market and economic development. This Section will evaluate the different positions regarding the matter (hereinafter referred to as 'the causality issue'), in order to reach its own conclusions. The objective is to examine whether reasons of economic efficiency call for an effective and internationally competitive national legal framework on shareholder remedies.

2.4.2 Agency costs, related economic perspectives on intra-corporate conflicts of interest and the role of derivative litigation

In economics, agency problems entail costs for the parties.[117] Following the discussion in Section 2.3, it is no surprise that much of the advocacy for derivative actions rests squarely on the arguments surrounding the existence of 'agency costs' and the role of law in minimising them. As succinctly put by Posner:

> The derivative suit is a monument to the problem of agency costs; it would make no sense to allow a shareholder to bypass the corporate management in bringing a suit against an officer if one could be confident that management always acted in the shareholders' interests[118]

116 ibid 317–18.

117 Cardinal elements of the 'agency costs' analytical schema can be traced in Williamson's 'transaction costs economics' analysis, which identified the costs involved in contracting with the company as an institution, suggesting that, due to the uncertainty involved in shareholders' contracting with the company, private ordering may not suffice to safeguard shareholders' interests and shareholder monitoring over the board is justified. See Williamson (n 18) 1204–1205, 1228.

118 Richard Posner, *Economic Analysis of Law* (3rd edn, Little, Brown 1986) 389.

Jensen and Meckling identified three kinds of 'agency costs' within the firm, alongside the costs of incorporation: monitoring costs, incurred by the shareholders to constrain the management/controller's opportunism; bonding costs, incurred by the management/controller to assure shareholders that their interests will not be frustrated; and residual loss, namely the decrease in welfare experienced by the shareholders due to the divergence of interests with the management/controller, in an action or omission of the latter.[119]

The role of derivative actions in addressing the last type of costs can be adduced by the analysis in Section 2.2. Reflective loss arising from directors' misfeasance falls under the definition of residual loss, as it constitutes the decrease in shareholder welfare due to a conflict of interests between shareholders as 'principals' and directors and/or insiders as 'agents' (in economic terms).[120] Derivative actions constitute the means of recovering reflective/residual loss collectively for all shareholders.

Legal provisions on the enforcement of directors' duties also aim to minimise the other two categories of agency costs. They provide constraints on managerial behaviour (set by directors' duties) with a 'bite'. Therefore, they reduce the expenditure on the part of shareholders to seek guarantees from the corporate controllers that they will not misappropriate perquisites from the company[121] and, conversely, limit expenditure on the part of controllers to ensure shareholders that their behaviour will not be opportunistic. In both cases, directors' duties provide parties with an agreeable framework of controller's behaviour; derivative actions, as a threat of enforcement, attempt to guarantee that this framework will be respected. They relieve both shareholders and controllers from the time, effort and money involved in reaching contractual arrangements to protect their investment in the company.

These studies examine intra-corporate affairs in general and, as such, only provide a starting point in understanding the economic implications of shareholders' derivative suits. Van Aaken's analysis however, is better focused on the issue. In her view, the damage directors' misfeasance may cause on the private wealth and utility of shareholders and other constituencies is viewed as an externality.[122] She concludes that derivative actions help internalise those externalities and, apart from 'individual utility of internalisation', they provide a public good, as the utility of the enforcement of the company's claims is shared with all corporate constituencies.[123]

119 Jensen and Meckling (n 51) 308.

120 ibid.

121 See Davide Lombardo and Marco Pagano, 'Law and Equity Markets: A Simple Model' in Joseph A McCahery, Piet Moerland, Theo Raaijmakers and Luc Renneboog (eds), *Corporate Governance Regimes: Convergence and Diversity* (OUP 2002) 343.

122 'Externalities are those consequences of decisions or actions which affect other persons than the decision-maker, without the former being compensated (if it is a negative externality) or without these persons having to compensate the decision-maker (if it is a positive externality)' (Van Aaken (n 115) 298).

123 ibid 317.

On a similar note, recent studies show that the strength of shareholder remedies against expropriation significantly diminishes the cost of capital for firms, affirming the intuitive conclusion that the higher the risk of insider expropriation the greater the returns prospective shareholders would demand from the firm in order to decide to invest.[124] It follows that the existence of legal safeguards, such as the derivative action, is financially beneficial for firms, as it encourages equity investment at a lower cost.

Of particular interest for the Greek corporate landscape is the study of Davis, who found that derivative actions have significant compensatory value for non-listed closely held corporations.[125] However, a different picture is painted by earlier American empirical studies, suggesting that derivative suits have little compensatory value and may not result in a significant increase of share value.[126] These studies should be read with caution by comparatists and, a fortiori, non-American policy-makers. Originating from the US, their results are bound to the characteristics of American derivative suits. Accordingly, whilst the methodology followed therein may be of good and direct use to non-American scholars, any wholehearted espousal of their conclusions outside the US would be arbitrary, unless a jurisdiction bears many similarities with the US in that respect. The unique characteristics of derivative litigation in the US, such as the absence of the loser pays principle, the widespread practice of contingent fees and the crude amount of settlements should be born in mind when trying to draw conclusions for one's own jurisdiction.

In any case, these studies have been much disputed by academics and to date have not been espoused either by the American legislature or by the influential American Bar Association (ABA) and American Law Institute (ALI).[127] The strongest line of argument against them rests in the fact that the deterrent effect of the derivative suit is either overlooked or not properly considered.[128] In their

124 A recent study focuses particularly on derivative actions in the US and the impact of the 'universal demand rule' (Joel F Houston, Chen Lin and Wensi Xie, 'Shareholder Protection and the Cost of Capital' (16 September 2015), <http://ssrn.com/abstract=2661292> (accessed 1 October 2015)). Similar studies on the broader topic of shareholder rights are Kevin CW Chen, Zhihong Chen and KC John Wei, 'Agency Costs of Free Cash Flow and the Effect of Shareholder Rights on the Implied Cost of Equity Capital' (2011) 46 Journal of Financial and Quantitative Analysis 171; Joan Elston and Laura Rondi, 'Shareholder Protection and the Cost of Capital: Evidence from German and Italian Firms' (2007) 18 (2) Statistica Applicata 153.

125 Kenneth B Davis, 'The Forgotten Derivative Suit' (2008) 61 Vand L Rev. 378.

126 For an overview of related empirical studies, see Bryant G Garth, Ilene H Nagel and Sheldon J Plager, 'Empirical Research and the Shareholder Derivative Suit: Toward a Better-Informed Debate' (1985) 48 LCP 137; see also Reisberg (n 39) 56ff.

127 The ALI placed considerable focus in the design of the derivative action under its Principles of Corporate Governance, as did the ABA in the context of Model Business Corporations Act (MBCA) (§ 7.40).

128 See John C Coffee Jr, 'The Unfaithful Champion: The Plaintiff as Monitor in Shareholder Litigation' (Summer 1985) 48 LCP 5, 10; Reisberg (n 39) 57.

defence, deterrence – unlike compensation – is not readily quantifiable.[129] Whereas compensation can be readily measured by focusing on the outcomes of litigation, deterrence is situated in the mentality of its recipients.[130] However, it would be wrong to underestimate the potential which deterrence of managerial misconduct has for the promotion of good corporate governance. Deterrence has its own economic implications. To clarify, a decision finding against a defendant in derivative litigation may not only deter him/her from future misfeasance, but also signal to the management of all other companies within the jurisdiction that misconduct is not tolerated.[131] One outcome then may be that agency costs are minimised within the jurisdiction as a whole and corporate directors and managers think twice before making decisions that are potentially value-decreasing.

2.4.3 Hard law as a facilitator of equity investment, market development and economic growth

2.4.3.1 Introduction

The suggestion that shareholder protection, individual or minority, incentivises investment in shares, appears to constitute conventional wisdom amongst legislators internationally. Even a cursory look at the preambles to recent company and securities law reforms reveals that the rationale for shareholder protection is often based on such, purely economic, considerations.[132] Despite its popularity, the idea that protection attracts investment has not been unanimously embraced by academics. In fact, a fruitful academic debate, initiated originally by economics scholars, has occupied much of the contemporary literature on company law and corporate governance, focusing on this causal relationship between law and financial development. In particular, this unidirectional causality thesis has been questioned on a variety of grounds and rival theses suggest alternative explanations of the law-market relationship. Given that, as explained, derivative actions are a means of protecting minority

129 Coffee, 'New Myths' (n 72) 1437.

130 Reisberg (n 39) 60.

131 Empirical studies also demonstrate that derivative actions are correlated with changes towards better CG standards (Stephen P. Ferris, Tomas Jandik, Robert M. Lawless and Anil Makhija, 'Derivative Lawsuits as a Corporate Governance Mechanism: Empirical Evidence on Board Changes Surrounding Filings' (2007) 42 Journal of Financial and Quantitative Analysis 143).

132 See, for example, the reasoning in the Company Law Reform White Paper (Cm6456), DTI, London, March 2005 s 3. Regarding international organisations, prominent examples are the OECD and the World Bank. The latter bases its 'Doing Business' index methodology on Simeon Djankov, Rafael LaPorta, Florencio Lopez-de-Silanes and Andrei Shleifer, 'The Law and Economics of Self-Dealing' (2008) 88 Journal of Financial Economics 430, as stated in its website <http://doingbusiness.org/methodology> (accessed 21 November 2015).

shareholders, it is interesting to scrutinise the relevant discussion and attest the normative claim in favour of strong shareholder protection from the (macro-) economic perspective of market efficiency.

2.4.3.2 The 'law matters' position

Two decades ago, a group of academics (known by the acronym LLSV) led by Professor Rafael LaPorta produced a comparative study that could rightfully be considered a 'breakthrough' in the fields of company law and corporate governance: namely, the 'law and finance' study.[133]

LLSV's original 'Legal Determinants of External Finance' and 'Law and Finance' studies, alongside the related works that followed from the members of the group,[134] argue that 'legal protection of outside investors limits the extent of expropriation of such investors by corporate insiders, and thereby promotes financial development'.[135] Much of their argumentation in support of this main theory, as well as their methodology, was original. As conceded by Professor Roe, the fact that the group was composed of financial economists 'should embarrass many … corporate law professors who have not even attempted' what the group completed.[136] LLSV paved the way for 'law and finance' studies,[137] influenced a number of reforms[138] and provided a strong indication that an interdisciplinary approach has much to offer to comparative law studies, especially regarding comparative methodology.

LLSV hypothesised that the better the protection afforded to investors, the more developed the respective debt and equity markets are, and, therefore, economic disparities can be attributed to the differences among legal frameworks.[139] In order to empirically attest this hypothesis,[140] the group engaged in an innovative comparative law method. Akin to econometrics, this 'numerical comparative method', 'comparative statistical analysis'[141] or (as subsequently named by another duet of

133 Rafael LaPorta, Florencio Lopez de Silanes, Andrei Schleifer and Robert W Vishny, 'Law and Finance' (1998) 106 Journal of Political Economy 1113.

134 Rafael LaPorta, Florencio Lopez-de-Silanes and Andrei Shleifer, 'The Economic Consequences of Legal Origins' (2008) 46 Journal of Economic Literature 285; Rafael LaPorta, Florencio Lopez de Silanes, Andrei Schleifer and Robert W Vishny, 'Legal Determinants of External Finance' (1997) 52 Journal of Finance 1131–1150.

135 LaPorta et al., 'Law and Finance' (n 133) 1121.

136 Mark J Roe 'Corporate Law's Limits' (2002) 31 J Legal Stud 233, 252.

137 Even at a higher education level. A visit to the SOAS University of London website (<www.soas.ac.uk/courseunits/C338.html> (accessed 21 October 2018)), for example, shows that there is a course on the topic which, among other things, teaches how to interpret the regression results of LLSV.

138 An example is the introduction of derivative actions to Italian law. See Giudici (n 50).

139 LaPorta et al., 'Law and Finance' (n 133) 1114.

140 This was not so original an assumption eo ipso, as betrayed by their reference to Robert Clark, *Corporate Law* (Little, Brown 1986).

141 LaPorta et al., 'Law and Finance' (n 133) 1115.

scholars) 'leximetrics',[142] essentially attempted to quantify the legal protection afforded to 'external investors' (including shareholders), in order to associate its results with the data collected on the accessibility to external finance and thereby establish a link between law and investment. The hypothesis was supported by the results of their statistics and the conclusion they reached is important for the objectives of this book. Their study suggests that a causal relation between law and investment exists, in which it is investment that follows: otherwise put, 'legal rules do matter. It is not just the stance of the law or the political sentiment of the day that shapes financial markets'.[143]

The second hypothesis LLSV made is that with low shareholder protection comes concentrated ownership.[144] The underlying reasoning for this assumption is twofold. First, should protection for shareholders be inadequate, blockholders have to raise high percentages of shares so as to monitor managers. As the group points out, in such a case concentrated ownership becomes a substitute for protection by law.[145] Apparently, this argument is based on the works of agency theorists and the analysis on agency costs. Second, they argued that minority investors' demand for low prices regarding their perspective investment discourages firms to issue new stock and consequently ownership remains concentrated.[146] The empirical study conducted by LLSV confirmed their primary assumption that efficient protection is an incentive for investors in equity and leads to dispersed ownership; the more enhanced protection shareholders enjoy, the more dispersed the ownership of the corporation.[147]

Moreover, by considering the law-structure linkage in conjunction with later findings and related works, the group concluded that countries showcasing diffuse ownership structures, also exhibit thriving financial markets.[148] This finding logically aligns with the other conclusion the group reached, that the strength of equity markets depends on investor protection. Interestingly, the group went further to claim that high-level (minority) investor protection leads to general economic growth at a national level, in tandem with Levine and Zervos' finding that 'stock market liquidity and banking development are both positively and robustly correlated with contemporaneous and future rates of economic growth'.[149]

142 See Mathias M Siems, 'Shareholder Protection around the World (Leximetric II)' (2008) 33 Del J Corp L 111; Priya P Lele and Mathias M Siems, 'Shareholder Protection: A Leximetric Approach' (2007) 7 JCLS 17.

143 Rafael LaPorta, Florencio Lopez de Silanes, Andrei Shleifer and Robert W. Vishny, 'Investor Protection and Corporate Governance' (2000) 58 Journal of Financial Economics 3.

144 LaPorta et al., 'Law and Finance' (n 133) 1145.

145 This argument is reminiscent of Jensen and Meckling (n 51).

146 LaPorta et al., 'Law and Finance' (n 133), 1145.

147 ibid. 1148.

148 ibid. 1150.

149 LaPorta et al., 'Law and Finance' (n 133) 1152; Ross Levine and Sara Zervos, 'Stock Markets, Banks, and Economic Growth' (December 1996) World Bank Policy Research Working Paper No. 1690; A1.213 Working Paper No. 297 29.

In drawing their conclusions in the 'law matters' study, LaPorta et al. formulated the 'legal origins' thesis.[150] In summary, it argues that legal traditions are determinative of the protection afforded to investors and therefore of corporate structures and firm growth. LLSV concluded that common law countries are the most protective, French origin countries are the least protective, and German and Scandinavian origin countries are situated in the middle but closer to the French standards than the common law ones.[151]

There is overlap in the above theses. As part of the 'law matters' theorem, the essential goal of the 'legal origins' thesis is to ascertain the optimal legal framework for protecting investors. As a logical construction, it does not dismiss the existence of a competitive market of legal culture; rather, it aims to track the best available solutions to similar problems and eventually offers suggestions to national legislators, although the group (almost) never explicitly advocated for reform.

LLSV's findings were impressively original, yet they did not avoid controversy or criticism. Criticism focused mainly on the fact that their methodology was incomplete and inaccurate.[152] More specifically, critics persuasively argued that the variables used by LLSV did not address all aspects of shareholder protection.[153] For example, LLSV's research did not include the right to request a special audit, the right of the General Meeting to have a say on executive pay and the right to remove directors, particularly those appointed by individual shareholders by virtue of corporate by-laws. Their approach failed to consider all solutions provided by jurisdictions to the factual problems posited, as the design of the 'law and finance' indices appears to reflect an element of bias towards American legal and corporate culture and practice. This is demonstrated by the 'focus on protection of shareholders from directors and the comparative disregard of the expropriation of minority shareholders by majority blockholders'.[154] In comparing the solutions given to the management–shareholders agency problem within the 49 jurisdictions examined, their study did not duly consider the minority–majority shareholder conflict, which – in contrast to the situation in the US and the UK – is of paramount importance for countries where concentrated ownership prevails, as in Greece and Germany. Indeed, subsequent works

150 LaPorta et al., 'Legal Origins' (n 133). For the classification regarding comparative law scholarship, see Raffaele Caterina, 'Comparative Law and Economics' in M. Jan Smits (ed), *Elgar Encyclopedia of Comparative Law* (EE 2012) 191.

151 LaPorta et al., 'Law and Finance' (n 133) 1151.

152 To list a couple, Udo C Braendle, 'Shareholder Protection in the USA and Germany: "Law and Finance" Revisited' (2006) 7 (3) German Law Journal 257; Mathias M Siems, 'What does not Work in Comparing Securities Laws: A Critique on La Porta et al's Methodology' (2005) 16 ICCLR 300.

153 For detailed re-examinations of the indices used in the 'law and finance' thesis, see Lele and Siems (n 142); Holger Spamann, 'Law and Finance Revisited' (2009) 23 Review of Financial Studies 467.

154 Lele and Siems (n 142) 5, 6.

by LaPorta et al. have admitted some initial shortcomings and enriched the criteria used to measure protection, albeit reaching conclusions similar to their original studies.[155]

Focusing on the construction of indices often diverts attention from the most significant problem of the 'law and finance' study, namely that 'a qualitative assessment of the rights seems to be missing'.[156] Of particular interest for the purposes of this book is the fact that LLSV did not take into account the preconditions bound to the enactment of the rights attested, such as the right to bring a derivative suit.[157] As will become apparent in Chapter 3, legal rules may look similar when read superficially and in isolation, whereas they showcase significant divergence when studied in detail and within the legal context in which they operate. Furthermore, the group did not elaborate on whether some rights are more important than others from the shareholders' perspective: in the jargon of statistics, variables were not weighed. The end result is thus somewhat confusing; for instance, it is debatable whether 'oppression remedies' should rank equally with 'proxy voting', especially within the context of concentrated ownership structures.[158] The 'fallacies' of the LLSV methodology may be explained by the fact that there was no previous work of the kind to rely upon. Their approach to quantifying law became a notable contribution to legal and economic academic research;[159] however, being the first of its kind in the field of comparative company law, it navigated uncharted waters. Despite the numerous attempts of notable scholars to refine it, no quantitative index on shareholder protection can claim yet to be perfect.

When it comes to derivative actions, the LLSV approach did not get everything wrong. Notably, later work by members of the LLSV group focused on case-study functional comparisons, whose subject is directly related to derivative litigation and the legal rules connected to it.[160] The study posits a hypothetical situation of minority expropriation facilitated at board level and involving

155 See Djankov et al. (n 132), where the group revised the so called 'anti-director' index.

156 Perakis, *Minority Shareholders* (n 94) 102.

157 ibid.

158 'Proxy voting' represents a right which aims at facilitating participation in the *collective* organ of the General Meeting, whose authority does not cover the totality of corporate decision-making, whilst 'oppression remedies', defined by the group as encompassing both derivative actions (e.g. UK CA 2006 ss 260–269; German AktG ss148–149) and oppression remedies (such as what is now CA 2006 ss 994–996 on unfair prejudice claims), covers a broader scope of corporate decisions. It could thus be argued that the latter variable should be weighed more than the former.

159 Among many other proponents, see Lele and Siems (n 142); Cristoph Van der Elst, 'Law and Economics of Shareholder Rights and Ownership Structures: How Trivial are Shareholder Rights for Shareholders?' Tilburg Law and Economics Center (TILEC) Law and Economics Discussion Paper No. 2010–009; Tilburg Law School Legal Studies Research Paper No. 008/2010 (15 February 2010).

160 Djankov et al. (n 132).

a controlling shareholder, examining the legal avenues which different jurisdictions avail minority shareholders in order to protect their investment. This comparative study differs from the original LLSV papers, not only as a matter of focus, but also as a matter of detail. Despite the deviations from the original paradigm, significant correlations between shareholder protection and stock market development were still observed. This refined methodology attracted international attention and is currently endorsed by the World Bank in its 'Doing Business' reports, published annually.[161]

Later 'leximetric' studies also found significant statistical correlations between the levels of shareholder protection afforded by provisions on derivative actions and stock market capitalisation, despite finding no significant correlations between other shareholder rights and the latter.[162] The consistency between these studies regarding the findings on derivative actions – studies which are in other respects contradictory in their results – is explicable. The key difference between derivative actions and other variables used in 'leximetric' and similar indices, is their applicability as a means of shareholder protection to different ownership-structural contexts. As previously explained, derivative actions are designed to combat both shareholder-orientated agency problems and minimise the related agency costs. Therefore, a focus on derivative actions evades the perils involved in the use of a catch-all, multi-shareholder-rights coding, as the latter may provide a confusing picture on how the law addresses different agency problems in different jurisdictions with different ownership structures. In fact, one of the very few normative suggestions the LLSV group voiced explicitly and confidently for European countries with concentrated share ownership was that:

> legal reforms may need to be considerably more radical in nature, and give shareholders explicit rights to either prevent expropriation or seek remedy when it occurs, such as the opportunity to sue directors (perhaps through derivative or class action suits) for oppressive conduct[163]

However, Professor Siems, despite finding a correlation between the availability of derivative actions and market capitalisation, refrains from asserting that a causal relationship exists between the two, a fortiori so between general shareholder protection and market development.[164] He is not alone. Other academics have also pronounced their doubts. A different view on 'the causality issue', concerning law and economic (corporate) structures and market performance,

161 Two of the six indices ('extent of director liability' and 'ease of shareholder suits') directly concern derivative litigation. See n 140.

162 M Siems, 'Private Enforcement of Directors' Duties: Derivative Actions as a Global Phenomenon' in Stefan Wrbka, Steven Van Uytsel and Mathias Siems (eds), *Collective Actions: Enhancing Access to Justice and Reconciling Multilayer Interests?* (CUP 2012) 115.

163 'Corporate Ownership Around the World' (n 89) 512.

164 Siems, 'Private Enforcement' (n 162) 115.

suggests that the latter precede rather than follow the former. Consequently, two different theories have been formulated on the emergence of strong and diffuse equity markets, namely 'law follows' and 'path dependencies'.

2.4.3.3 The response to 'law matters': Refutations and clarifications

The 'law follows' thesis has been best articulated by Professor John Coffee Jr.[165] His position is that strong and diffuse private equity markets can arise even in the absence of a robust protective regulation and that historical evidence suggests different conditions for the occurrence of such a trend towards investment in equity.[166] More specifically, Coffee argues that what gave rise to the corporate governance model of the 'separation of ownership and control' in Anglo-Saxon countries was private initiative and not political sentiment[167] or high levels of regulatory investor protection;

> private institutions – most notably, stock exchange rules and bonding mechanisms by which investment bankers pledged their reputational capital – probably played a greater role than mandatory legal rules in the early rise of dispersed ownership.[168]

Accordingly, legislative action follows actual developments, as 'the legislature cannot anticipate problems that it has never seen … law appears to be responding to changes in the market, not consciously leading it'.[169] Essentially, it is argued that regulatory action is only taken in hindsight. Concerning the legislations that offered original solutions to given factual problems, such an explanation of the causality issue is utterly logical (even from the viewpoint of legal realism). Human law-making is the product of a rather complex cognitive process and therefore cannot be parthenogenetic. Supporting this position in the corporate law context is the fact that new regulation on corporate governance is usually a response to a pathogen or, in John Coffee's words, 'scandal driven'.[170] Indeed, most of the recent significant reforms on corporate governance followed notorious scandals; notably, the Sarbannes–Oxley Act[171] was a response to

165 John C Coffee Jr, 'The Rise of Dispersed Ownership' (2001) 111 Yale LJ 1.

166 ibid. The author further supports his argument with case studies in England, the US and the Netherlands.

167 i.e. it did not matter whether a socialist or conservative party or leader was in power (Coffee, 'The Rise of Dispersed Ownership' (n 165) 71ff). Evidence for this observation can be found in the Greek stock exchange ratings, which were at their highest while the Panhellenic Socialist Movement was in power.

168 ibid 87, 88.

169 ibid 65, 81.

170 ibid 23.

171 Pub. L. No. 107–204, 116 Stat. 745 (2002).

Enron and WorldCom and the Dodd–Frank Act was a response to the 2008 economic crisis.[172]

From a certain point of view, this observation does not disprove the 'law matters' thesis and can even be understood as fortifying it. It concedes that a shift in regulation can adjust inefficient corporate practices.[173] Coffee's historical perspective does not posit that law has no relevance to the size of equity markets, rather it claims that strong markets initially grew in the absence of a strong investor protection framework. A lato sensu definition of this framework, as encompassing general legal protection outside the narrow confines of securities regulation, makes in my opinion the validity of his claim more nuanced. In any case, law is not denied its role in fostering the development and sustainability of equity markets, even in Coffee's view. As he concedes:

> Even though equity markets can arise in the absence of strong minority protections, it hardly follows that they can develop to their full potential in such an environment.[174]

In essence, the 'law follows' approach qualifies the claim that strong legal protection of minority investors is conditio sine qua non for market development, adding private initiative – or, defined negatively, absence of state interventionism – to the debate, as a factor in the emergence of a reliable market. Examined closely, the empirical results and conclusions reached by LLSV and Professor Coffee provide valuable insight into two distinct issues. While LLSV elucidate on why common law countries display disperse corporate ownership structures (providing a 'snapshot' of how the corporate world was in the late 1990s, rather than a time-series study), Coffee discovered the preconditions that led to the emergence of this corporate model. As long as these conditions are met, regulation has to follow as a proxy for trust on the part of investors that they will not be expropriated, or, as Coffee summarises, 'ultimately, this Article has advanced two claims that are novel only to the academic world: law matters, and trust is efficient'.[175]

Another perspective on the evolution of capital markets and the prospects of convergence towards an efficient model of share ownership structures and investor protection regulation, suggests that history matters, as it shapes the trajectories (paths) upon which persistent disparities depend.[176] Accordingly, continuing

172 Coffee, 'The Rise of Dispersed Ownership' (n 165) 30.

173 On the position that mandatory rules may restore confidence to markets, see Troy A. Paredes, 'A Systems Approach to Corporate Governance Reform: Why Importing U.S. Corporate Law Isn't the Answer', (2003–2004) 45 Wm & Mary L Rev 1055, 1143ff.

174 Coffee, 'The Rise of Dispersed Ownership' (n 165) 64.

175 John C Coffee Jr., 'The Future as History: The Prospects for Global Convergence in Corporate Governance and its Implications' (1998–1999) 93 Nw UL Rev 641, 707.

176 The leading article concerning 'path dependencies' in law is Lucian Bebchuk and Mark Roe, 'A Theory of Path Dependence in Corporate Ownership and Governance' (1999) Harvard

regulatory and functional divergence is attributed to the archetypal corporate structures and rules that vary among jurisdictions and set unswerving trajectories. What path dependencies suggest, under the obvious influence of the homonymous economic theory, is that these 'paths' are not necessarily determined by efficiency considerations.[177] As long as corporate rules and practices arise, whether efficient or not, they stand a chance of becoming persistent according to this strand of literature.[178] Evidently, this theory is in stark contrast with the view that a universally optimal model of corporate governance will eventually prevail, leading to global legal and structural convergence due to its predominance over alternative economically inefficient models.[179]

'Path dependencies' provide valuable insight regarding the forces resisting change towards different ownership structures and patterns of investor protection. Bebchuk and Roe posit that 'a country's initial pattern of corporate ownership structures influences the power that various interest groups will have in the political process that produces corporate rules'.[180] Accordingly, in a jurisdiction such as Greece, dominant block-holders are expected to lobby against any pro-minority legislation. This might have been the case during the 2007 reform of Greek company law, when suggestions to introduce a form of 'genuine' derivative action were eventually dismissed: in the words of a prominent Greek scholar: 'the legislator's ado … conceals adherence to big, strong shareholder interests'.[181] The same conclusion may be reached regarding the latest reform.

Indeed, actors benefitting from an established corporate structure and legal framework can be expected to resist any change to the status quo. But they will do so only as long as they benefit. Equally, interest groups themselves may demand change, when the system that their practices rely upon collapses. It could be the case that in such situations, different interest groups will become more active. Bebchuk and Roe do not pay due attention to those considerations. For instance, in their analysis on the path-dependent trajectory of block-ownership, they disregard the influence of minority shareholders and its potency: 'surprisingly they do not describe another sort of pressure on the existing system, namely the role of the minority shareholders. If the latter are not happy

Law School John M. Olin Center for Law, Economics and Business Discussion Paper Series, Paper 266.

177 See Brian W Arthur, 'Competing Technologies, Increasing Returns, and Lock-In by Historical Events' (1989) 99 Economic Journal 116.

178 Bebchuk and Roe (n 176) 3: 'The focus of the analysis … is not on the possibility that corporate structures and corporate rules might be inefficient – but rather on the possibility that those structures and rules might be path dependent.'

179 For a concurrent view, see Reinhard H Schmid and Gerald Spindler, 'Path Dependence, Corporate Governance and Complementarity' (2002) 5 International Finance 311, 313.

180 (n 176) 131.

181 Rokas, 'Corporate Organisation' (n 2) 18: 'the committee responsible for the reform of L.2190/1920 hesitated to introduce a … ground-breaking, for Greek standards, provision'.

with their yield, they can sell the shares.'[182] Block-holders and managers may indeed have an interest in maintaining their power position in the firm alongside political leverage to pursue this interest at a regulatory level. However, if minority investors flee to more attractive destinations, within or outside the jurisdictional borders, the firm's value diminishes to the loss of the incumbent shareholders, the company and the market as a whole. Accordingly, by exiting the firm, minority shareholders can exert considerable pressure to both blockholders and efficiency-minded policy-makers.

Yet again, the persistence of a given regulatory framework may be explained by reasons other than efficiency or the influence of interest groups. McCahery et al. give a convincing explanation for this phenomenon, availing themselves of the teachings of psychology. They focus on the persons drafting and passing statutes, an 'elite' group of 'legislators, judges, practitioners, regulatory agencies, professional groups and legal scholars'.[183] They posit the reason behind their inaction lies in behavioural psychology, as 'people exhibit a "status quo bias," in that, all else equal, they prefer to leave things as they are'.[184] This might in part explain not only the slow and frustratingly incremental development of Greek company law in the past decades but also the continuing presence of obsolete terminology (such as the 'prudent pater familias' standard for directors' diligence, until 2007) and the use of classical Greek in a company law statute otherwise worded in modern Greek until very recently (Law 2190/1920 was replaced on 1 January 2019).

2.4.3.4 Synthesis: The role of law

The examination of the above views helps crystallise the relationship between regulation, economic performance and structures. The attested theories differentiate on how strong a link there is among these three notions, as well as on whether regulation is the cause or the effect of corporate structures. However, synthesis remains possible. This Section concludes accordingly, that shareholder protection has a pivotal, yet not exclusive, role in attracting investment in equity. It acts as a positive catalyst, in the sense that it accelerates a reaction amongst different reagents.[185]

182 Udo C Braendle and Juergen Noll, 'On the Convergence of National Corporate Governance Systems' (2006) 17 Journal of Interdisciplinary Economics 57, 72.

183 Joseph A McCahery, Erik PM Vermeulen, Masato Hisatake and Jun Saito, 'Traditional and Innovative Approaches to Legal Reform: The 'New Company Law'' (2007) 8 EBOR 7, 15.

184 Jennifer Arlen, 'The Legal Implications of Psychology: Human Behavior, Behavioral Economics, and the Law: Comment: The Future of Behavioral Economic Analysis of Law' (1998) 51 Vand L Rev 1765, 1772.

185 Cheffins quotes 'the fact that the law did not act as a catalyst for change in the US and the UK does not preclude the possibility that this could occur elsewhere' in 'Law as Bedrock, The Foundations of an Economy Dominated by Widely Held Public Companies' (2003) 23 OJLS 1, 2.

The approaches examined on the causality issue help to identify the reagents in this chemistry-related allegory: these can be grouped in three categories. Macro-economically, it is the economic strength of a country and a pro-shareholder, non-interventionist public policy that encourages investment in equity. Meso-economically, it is interest groups that influence such a policy.[186] Micro-economically, it is the corporate structures and the existing 'agency' relations that could attract (or repulse) investors within the firm. None of the above factors can independently determine the prosperity of the market. Consider the following, abstract example. A functioning market could be the outcome of a successful public policy, which adhered to the demands of interest groups formulated in accordance to the existing corporate environment. Now consider excluding each of the factors. Without the voice of pressure groups, there would be little incentive for policy-makers to work towards creating a suitable business environment. Without a coherent investment policy, business could be subject to extensive state intervention that dissuades entrepreneurship (e.g. red tape, disproportionately high taxation, or an outdated corporate framework). Lastly, even if both the macro-economic and meso-economic paragons cooperate towards attracting investment, incumbent shareholders and directors may themselves decelerate the equity market, if they consider the maintenance of ownership control as beneficial. This example, albeit general and brief, highlights an otherwise conventional truth that is not readily discernible in the works of the 'law and finance' theorists: successful financial markets are the outcome of numerous variables working in harmony. There is no silver bullet solution to a problematic market.

Law is the coordinator of interaction between the aforementioned factors, determining their outcome. Concerning policies, the law expresses political will, being its main 'tool'. Legislative initiative thus often reflects existing or (ideally) anticipated social needs that should be treated by policy-making. Accordingly, when it comes to a policy that favours investment in equity, instead of high debt financing leverage, appropriate implementation necessitates a competitive shareholder protection array of provisions. This is evidenced in the reports preceding the Companies Act 2006, as well as the Law 2190/1920 reform in 2007 and Law 4548/2018. Regarding the CA 2006, the white paper published by the Department of Trade and Industry preceding the final bill is clear as to the objectives of the latter:

> Our framework must reflect the challenges of modern capital markets in which business and investment decisions are increasingly determined by global conditions ... investors can choose where to put their money.[187]

The wording in the preamble of Law 3604/2007 reforming the Greek company law statute is similar:

186 See also Siems, *Convergence* (n 103) 236.
187 Company Law Reform White Paper (Cm6456), DTI, London, March 2005 9.

> The dynamics of the evolution in the fields of corporations, market economics and competition imposed the adjustment of the existing framework to the new facts regarding the markets' function and international competition[188]

The preamble of Law 4548/2018 is even more explicit:

> Many countries nowadays, European or not, realizing the importance of the global competition of laws, care to modernize their laws on public limited companies, so that they advertise their national market and render it more welcoming for foreign investment.[189]

It becomes evident that the aforementioned acts took into consideration the fact that investors worry about the value of their investment, be it short-term or long-term. If investors fear that their prospective shareholding is imperilled by potential expropriation by the insiders, the anticipated high risk of the respective stock will be a deterrent to any decision to purchase and other options provided by more competitive legislations will be preferred. The protection to shareholders afforded by company law thereby becomes crucial to building trust in an equity market. By principle, trust is crucial for investment.[190] The Greek legislator is not unaware of its importance, as seen in the preamble of Law 3604/2007, amending the law on public limited companies.[191] To summarise the position undertaken in this Section, regulatory action should be considered as an inaugural part of a pro-shareholder policy, not just an accompaniment.

This policy may well be influenced by the pressure enacted by contemporary shareholder groups. Such pressure groups are usually formed during crises, whether scandal-driven or not. Legislative action is then a response to concerns regarding liquidity and management by the firms' members: such concerns are usually expressed in the financial press.[192] Yet, incumbent shareholders are not the only to benefit by a pro-shareholder legislation; prospective shareholders benefit too and they can exert influence, voluntarily or inadvertently, towards

188 Explanatory statement (preamble) to Law 3604/2007, <www.hellenicparliament.gr/UserFiles/2f026f42-950c-4efc-b950-340c4fb76a24/a-eurodikaio-eis.pdf>, 1 (accessed 20 November 2015).

189 Explanatory statement (preamble) to Law 4548/2018, 2.

190 This notion is supported by Mariassunta Giannetti and Andrei Simonov's empirical study, 'Which Investors Fear Expropriation? Evidence from Investors' Portfolio Choices' (2006) 61 Journal of Finance 1507.

191 In my translation: 'as is proven, empowering the shareholder's position constitutes an investment incentive and contributes to creating a climate of trust in the market. Law 2190/1920 has never been friendly to shareholders and the minority', 1.

192 'Already much of the pressure to act on directors' remuneration has been generated by the media maintaining a focus on the issue, which forces politicians and regulators to respond' (Brenda Hannigan, 'Board Failures in the Financial Crisis: Tinkering with Codes and the Need for Wider Corporate Governance Reforms: Part 2' (2012) 33 Comp Law 35, 36).

such a policy. However, external shareholders ('outsiders') complicate the issue. In a globalised economy, their options are anything but national: their decisions largely depend on the comparisons made by themselves or by credible institutions regarding investment prospects. Jurisdictions are aware and should be mindful of this reality: they are reportedly engaged in regulatory competition. This is a 'race to the top' rather than a 'race to the bottom', as legislators struggle to offer the most efficient and competitive shareholder rights protection.[193] Thereby, outsiders can push for regulatory incentives even by choosing not to invest in a jurisdiction.

It is to be expected that individuals focus at the firm level when considering a prospective investment. If their interests could be easily compromised by insiders, then buying the firm's shares is not good business. As a matter of fact, insiders are often willing to take the risk of making the firm unpopular to investors, for the simple reason that extracting short-term private benefits has always been an alluring option.[194] Consequently, it is up to mandatory legal provisions to adopt the substantial role of formulating an investor-friendly environment. Accordingly, shareholders would feel safer if they can be remedied for unfair prejudice or fraudulent management.[195] Moreover, they would be interested in appointing auditors, dismissing them or even contesting their reports in order to monitor their investment.[196] Additionally, investors (even those least interested in actively participating in corporate decisions) would be in dire straits if the GM could adopt a resolution that would compromise their interests (even without prior notice), either by altering the ownership structure of the company or by waiving corporate rights to compensation.[197] Shareholders are also concerned with their right to dividend: its allocation, its percentage of the annual profit and any bonuses that the law might offer. Notwithstanding this enumeration of shareholder rights being indicative, the point is clear; enforceable mandatory rights are important for investment decisions.

As regards the shareholders' rights explored within this book, there is no comprehensive qualitative study available, to the best of my knowledge, on whether provisions on derivative actions strengthen investor confidence in a market. However, as mentioned above, 'leximetric', 'law and finance' and other empirical studies seem to point to an affirmative conclusion. Examination of the yearly fluctuations on share value in different jurisdictions paints a similar picture, as shown in Table 2.1.

193 Kraakman et al. (n 5) 26; Andrew Johnston and Phil Syrpis, 'Regulatory Competition in European Company Law after Cartesio' (2009) 34 EL Rev 378.

194 See Rui Albuquerue and Neng Wang, 'Agency Conflicts, Investment, and Asset Pricing' (2008) 63 Journal of Finance 1.

195 e.g. UK CA 2006 Pts 11, 30; French Code de Commerce arts L.225–252; German AktG ss 147–149.

196 e.g. AktG s 142, 258, 260; Code de Commerce arts L.225–218 f.

197 See AktG ss 93, 116, 117, 302, 309; Law 4548/2018 art 102(7).

Table 2.1 Fluctuations in share value following legislation on derivative actions

Year	Fluctuation in stock market turnover ratio compared to previous year * where statutory derivative actions came into force	Mean fluctuation of stock market turnover ratio in 18 richest economies **	Median fluctuation in stock market turnover ratio in 18 richest economies
2005	0.235783 Germany***	0.034078	0.062213
1998	0.534044 Italy	0.003046	0.028888
2007****	1.094210 United Kingdom	0.207825	0.131012

Notes

* Ratio of the value of total shares traded to average real market capitalisation; see World Bank's World Development Indicators, available at <www.worldbank.org/data/> (accessed 21 November 2015). Fluctuation calculated as the difference between values in a given year (t1) and the year before (t2), divided by the value of the previous year (t2), Δ (Vt1-Vt2)/Vt2.

** According to annual GDP (constant 2005 US$) data, retrieved from the World Bank website, <http://data.worldbank.org/indicator/NY.GDP.MKTP.KD?order=wbapi_data_value_2004+wbapi_data_value+wbapi_data_value-last&sort=asc&page=2> (accessed 21 November 2015). The countries considered are Australia, Brazil, Canada, China, France, Germany, India, Italy, Japan, Korea Republic, Mexico, the Netherlands, Russia, Spain, Switzerland, Turkey, the UK and the USA

*** UMAG came into force late in the year (November 2005). However, the examined variable continued to exhibit an increase for the following year (2006), in the rate of 0.189601.

**** Companies Act 2006 (Commencement No. 3, Consequential Amendments, Transitional Provisions and Savings) Order 2007 (SI 2007/2194) art.2(1)(e).

The jurisdictions in the table above experienced a rise in their stock-market turnover ratio, in all instances where statutory derivative actions were introduced. Also, this rise dwarfed the performance of their foreign counterparts at the time. It is notable that other countries coming close to such increases in the given timespan either introduced a similar kind of shareholder protection or reformed their existing statutory provisions on derivative actions. In 2005, for instance, Italy lowered the quorum thresholds for legal standing in derivative suits and South Korea introduced class actions, exhibiting a rise in their stock market turnover ratio, with rates of 0.277322 and 0.214683 respectively. Whether the newly introduced statutory provisions on derivative actions account exclusively for the above observations cannot be said with absolute certainty. For example, in most instances, the reform of national company or securities laws touched upon a broader array of issues. The CA 2006 changed much of UK company law as we previously knew it: UMAG considered matters such as shareholders' rescission suits and the Italian Legislative Decree 58 (of year 1998) introduced ideas other than just the derivative action that were novel to Italian law, such as mandatory bid rules. In any case, the fact that the table reflects a repeated phenomenon cannot be ignored.

Nevertheless, some may argue that a vibrant equity market is not necessary for corporations to grow. This might be true for jurisdictions where debt financing can support the liquidity of firms to an extent that the need to turn to the market as a source of finance is rendered minimal. This is not necessarily the case for many European countries today and is definitely not so regarding Greece. Predictably, the aftermath of the crisis as regards debt finance was a globally significant increase in the reluctance of banks to lend. Europe, in particular, experienced such an effect as early as 2009: 'according to the European Central Bank, loan rejection rates in the eurozone increased from 12% to 18% between the first and second half of 2009'.[198] The main reason for such a response by the financial institutions is obvious: banks suffered a critical hit in their financing options and subsequently sought to reduce the volume of outgoing capital by tightening debt and credit terms.[199] Switching focus to Greece, the picture gets even darker for companies, particularly for small and medium enterprises (SMEs): Greek banks were the most reluctant financiers in Europe during the first semester of 2013.[200]

Greek SMEs finance themselves internally, by making use of the equity available from the founding family.[201] Nowadays, few of them are able to continue this practice.[202] As the study by Daskalakis et al. reports, the SMEs preferred method of financing is debt, since it does not affect corporate control.[203] Keeping in mind, however, the fact that Greek SMEs consider 'access to finance' to be their primary problem, according to the ECB statistics, alternative ways of financing should be investigated.[204] This is particularly significant for the so-called 'young' firms (recently incorporated companies), as they do not have capital reserves sufficient to support their operative needs.

From a corporate finance perspective, bank financing – which is closely connected with concentrated ownership – can be viewed as a less efficient alternative. A major reason for such inefficiency, according to Lanoo and Khachaturyan, is that 'the banking market may be dominated by a few players, who may not be

198 J Potter and J Thompson, 'Government Responses to the Impact of the Global Crisis on Finance for Young and Small Enterprises' (2011) 20 Strat Change 145, 147.

199 ibid. 146.

200 European Central Bank, 'Survey on the Access to Finance of Small and Medium-Sized Enterprises in the Euro Area' (ECB 2013) <www.ecb.europa.eu/pub/pdf/other/accesstofinancesmallmediumsizedenterprises201304en.pdf?bb16b7e4d7d49e53249f2be976653b18> (accessed 20 November 2014), 12.

201 'Own funds are a priori the main financing equity source'. See Nikolaos Daskalakis, Robin Jarvis and Emmanouil Schizas, 'Financing Practices and Preferences for Micro and Small Firms' (2013) 20 Journal of Small Business and Enterprise Development 80, 89.

202 European Central Bank (n 200) 4.

203 Daskalakis et al. (n 201) 94.

204 ECB statistics available at <www.ecb.int/stats/money/surveys/sme/html/index.en.html> (accessed 5 October 2015).

interested in financing certain higher-risk segments of the market'.[205] Indeed, financing ventures that involve a respectable amount of risk is a task for wealthy financial intermediaries; not exactly the case for the majority of Greek banks. Not so long ago, Greek banks were bailed-out once again and capital controls were instituted for the first time in Greek history.[206] Equity finance can provide a solution and a shareholder- friendly environment might just work to that end.

2.4.4 Summary and conclusions

The time is ripe for efforts to be made to reinstitute investor confidence in the Greek equity market. A revision of the Greek framework for shareholder protection against mismanagement, by means of the introduction of a genuine derivative action, could help in that respect, as long as it increased the levels of shareholder protection. This would minimise agency costs, resulting in economic and financial benefits at both a firm and a market level. Of course, such an increase cannot be expected to render the Greek stock market efficient on its own. However, as part of a general pro-investment strategy and perhaps a broader reform of corporate and securities law, an introduction of derivative actions to Greek law may help facilitate this.

2.5 Conclusion

The inquiry into the functions and the role of the derivative action in shareholder law and corporate governance showed that it serves the purpose of remedying the infringement of certain interests; directly those of the company's shareholders whilst, indirectly, those of corporate stakeholders, shareholders – present and future – within a given jurisdiction and the market as a whole.

The nature of these interests, from a shareholders' perspective, is predominantly proprietary at firm level. Derivative actions constitute a means of recovering reflective loss, protecting the proprietary interests of all members of the company, as compensation goes to the company and not the shareholder-claimant exclusively. Protection is provided against the opportunistic behaviour of corporate management, notwithstanding whether the latter originates in the promulgation of directors' or controlling shareholders' interests. Similar protection of welfare is afforded to all stakeholders in the company, to the extent that it is affected by a diminution in corporate property.

Derivative actions assume an important role in the alignment of conflicting interests within the company and help effectuate one of the basic objectives of corporate law, namely the regulation of intra-corporate affairs. By facilitating the enforcement of directors' duties, derivative actions provide the latter with

205 Karel Lanoo and Arman Khachaturyan, 'Reform of Corporate Governance in the EU' (2004) 5 EBOR 37, 40.

206 See 'Recapitalising Greek Banks: The Damage' [7 November 2015] The Economist 79.

meaningful content. They thus ensure that corporate decision-making at board level accords to the tenets of law and does not frustrate the interests which company law aims to protect.

From a financial perspective, derivative actions reduce agency costs. They not only provide a means of redeeming residual loss but also reduce the cost of capital for firms, as they reinstate investor confidence in corporate management. This has further, economic implications, as confidence is the most important factor in the development and sustainability of equity markets.

This Chapter effectively justifies the advocacy in favour of derivative actions. Many of the arguments herein are particularly topical for Greece, due to the native concentrated corporate ownership structures and the contemporary (un) available financing options. At the same time, this Chapter outlined the desiderata of provisions on shareholder remedies against maladministration in general, by explaining the objectives, functions and operation of an effective remedy. Accordingly, the ensuing Chapters will evaluate the applicable Greek 'company's action', the functionally equivalent provision to derivative actions, against these desiderata.

Finally, this Chapter has demonstrated that law matters in investment decisions. In the age of globalised investment decisions, the implication of this conclusion is that the effectiveness of a national framework on shareholder protection is weighed against its foreign counterparts by prospective investors. From this perspective, the comparative examination of Greek law stops being a matter of methodological preference and becomes imperative.

Part II

Derivative actions de lege lata

A comparative and functional analysis

3 Comparison of functionally equivalent rules on shareholders' enforcement of corporate claims

3.1 Introduction

3.1.1 Preliminary remarks

As stated in Chapter 1, there had been numerous calls, sometimes fervent, sometimes reluctant, for a review of shareholder remedies under Greek law. Many of them focus on the absence of a derivative action.[1] The reason was that the available functional equivalent mechanism, the 'company's action' or 'corporate action', had been repeatedly characterised as dysfunctional.[2] The provisions on the 'new'

1 See Section 1.1.

2 The egregious (due to the obscurity of its wording) text of Law 2190/1920 art 22b can be translated as follows: '1. Corporate claims against the members of the board of directors arising from the management of corporate affairs shall be mandatorily pursued, if the General Meeting so decides, by resolution reached according to paragraphs 1 and 2 of article 29 and paragraph 1 article 31, or if shareholders representing one tenth (1/10) of the registered (paid up) share capital so demand from the board of directors or the liquidators. This percentage may be reduced by the corporate constitution. The minority's petition is considered only if it is ascertained that the petitioners became shareholders three (3) months at least prior to the petition. The conditions set in the first sentence are not required in case damages are due to the members of the board of directors' fault (dolus).

2. The action shall be brought within six months from the day the General Meeting was convened or the petition was submitted.

3. The General Meeting may appoint special representatives regarding the conduct of proceedings. If pursuit of the claim is demanded by the minority or in case that the deadline set in the above paragraph lapses without any action being brought, the Chair of the Court of First Instance in the district where the seat of the company is situated may, upon application of the minority submitted within one month from the expiration of the deadline set in the above paragraph, under the procedure set in article 634 Civ. Procedure, appoint special representatives of the company for the conduct of judicial proceedings. The court expenses for appointment of special representatives and pursuit of the company's claims are borne by the latter'. See Georgios Zouridakis, 'Introducing Derivative Actions in the Greek Law on Public Limited Companies: Issues of Legal Standing and Lessons from the German and UK Experience' (2015) 26 ICCLR 271. Slightly different translation can be found in Lambadarios Law Firm (tr and ed), *Law 2190/1920 on Companies Limited by Shares (Sociétés Anonymes); Law 3190/1955 on Limited Liability Companies: Greek & English text* (Nomiki Bibliothiki 2011) 185–186.

company's action came to effect on 1 January 2019. Once again, no derivative action is provided by the Greek law on public limited companies. The question thus persists: are such calls warranted?

It is illustrated hereinafter that shareholder-initiated litigation on behalf of a company is a highly complex issue, as the law has to strike a fine balance between the availability of the remedy and its abuse. Its availability might guarantee the enforcement of the company's claim and work towards the protection of every interest involved, in the ways explained in Chapter 2, but, at the same time, a readily available remedy may increase the possibility of undesirable litigation, providing the frivolous with access to court and presenting the extortionist with the means to coerce. A truly protective remedy thus has to make the best of both worlds. The law-maker and the judge are therefore caught in the struggle between those two opposing forces, which, as is shown below, carve the content of the law and its application. Accordingly, this Chapter shows that, depending on the jurisdiction, different responses are expected to the question: under which circumstances and how can a shareholder enforce a company's claim? This divergence accrues from balancing the aforementioned competing goals and transcends rules on costs allocation, legal standing, the cause of action, procedure and admissibility of the claim, as well as rules on access to litigation-related information.

This Chapter uses the above considerations to compare the company's action with the German and UK derivative actions. The comparative study directly serves two objectives. Firstly, it purports to explain the relevant law and bring to the surface any problems in its construction and function. Secondly, it aims to show how protective the Greek framework is compared to the German and UK ones. The ensuing analysis identifies a variety of problems regarding this facet of Greek shareholder law and illustrates that other jurisdictions protect shareholders better, in many respects. Contingent upon these conclusions is the further objective, to identify the points where Greek law is – still – in need of change and the ways in which the comparative considerations may be of help to that direction.

3.1.2 Conceptual considerations and their relevance to regulatory design

Chapter 2 explained that derivative actions have the potential to assume an important role within a legal system and an economy. Furthermore, as illustrated in Chapter 1, many jurisdictions provide for derivative actions, even more provide for rules functionally equivalent to derivative actions. Yet, those rules are designed and perform very differently compared to each other. The reason for this divergence resides in the complexity involved in this kind of shareholder litigation. This Subsection explains that, in order for a shareholders' remedy to become protective for shareholders and assume the role envisaged in Chapter 2, its regulatory design has to consider and respect this complexity.

Derivative actions (and functionally equivalent remedies) are construed as a minority shareholders' remedy in view of the impasse created by the no reflective loss principle and the possibility that the collective intra-corporate organs fail to achieve redress on behalf of the company. From this perspective, the effectiveness of the remedy depends on its availability to minorities and individual shareholders. As is illustrated in the ensuing Sections, this is determined primarily by rules on legal standing. The more shareholders enjoy access to justice, the better the availability of the remedy and the greater the possibility for recovery of their reflective loss. Availability of the remedy is further determined by the admissibility of claims based on the nature of the complaint. The scope of corporate misfeasance shareholders are allowed to seek judicial redress for is directly connected with recovery of their reflective loss. To explain, this kind of litigation may achieve recovery of shareholders' losses only within the boundaries of the scope of misfeasance it is designed to remedy, notwithstanding the fact that other forms of misfeasance may equally harm shareholders' interests. Similar considerations apply to the number of potential defendants to the suit, as a variety of actors within and outside the company are potential wrongdoers: directors, shadow directors and contracting parties, to name but a few. Lastly, the use of the remedy relates to the availability of corporate information to shareholders. Litigation cannot be expected to be brought, at least not with any possibility of success, if shareholders are unaware of the reasons and the persons responsible for their reflective loss, or if they cannot support their claims with sufficient evidence.

Recovery of reflective loss via compensation on behalf of the company and – indirectly – shareholders as a whole, falls under the topics of corporate governance, agency problems and agency costs. In Section 2.4 we saw that the dilution of recovery among all shareholders may act as a disincentive for claims and thus incapacitate much of the derivative action's potential in addressing agency costs. In such a case, the aggregate welfare of shareholders is endangered due to the irrationality involved in the pursuit of the individual welfare of the derivative claimant, when he/she has to bear alone the costs and the risk of litigation but also share recovery with everyone else in the company. It is illustrated below that incentivising shareholders and addressing free-rider concerns are key elements of regulatory design, situated mainly within the ambit of the allocation of litigation costs, in recognition of the derivative and representative nature of the remedy.

Staying with agency problems and costs, derivative actions and functionally equivalent remedies address them not only by providing a means of compensation but also a means of deterrence. For this deterrent function to take effect, enforcement of corporate claims should be a *credible* and *considerable* threat. Accordingly, the effectiveness of the remedy from that perspective depends on the possibility for a claim to be brought, even more so for a claim to be brought successfully. This possibility runs back to the issues of shareholders' accessibility to and incentives for derivative litigation, given that enforcement is initiated by them. Furthermore, deterrence also depends upon the severity of punishment, as, if the extraction of private benefits outweighs compensation, wrongdoers are less likely to be inhibited.[3]

3 Arad Reisberg, *Derivative Actions and Corporate Governance: Theory and Operation* (OUP 2007) 64.

It so follows that a derivative action – or a functionally equivalent remedy – is as much protective for shareholders' interests as it is available to them. But this is only half the story. Litigating on behalf of the company may run to its detriment and therefore be against the interests of shareholders as a whole, sometimes including even the shareholder-claimant. This is because litigation engages much of the company's resources. In fact, in order to assess the efficacy of derivative actions following this rationale, recovery should be offset by the costs involved in the litigation and thereafter.[4] Taking into consideration the time, human capital and expenses engaged in the court proceedings, it is doubtful that the compensatory order, if achieved, will always make up to them. Cases like *Prudential* illustrate that the litigation costs may reach dazzling heights,[5] whilst cases like *Smith v Croft* show that the protraction of proceedings may render proceedings a 'shambles', especially where the claim does not eventually meet with success.[6] Also likely to be affected by such litigation is the market value of the shares, regarding traded companies. The stock market is an information-sensitive sector and, even though any signal of incoming compensation may raise demand of the company's stock,[7] publicity of court proceedings against the management of the company might result in loss of confidence by the investors, at least in the short run.[8] A derivative claim may also be detrimental to the interests of the company, if it results to the resignation of directors who, due to their unique personal and professional qualities, are irreplaceable for the company. This concern was apparent in the affidavit of Mr Baldock, director of a minority shareholder (Wren Trust) opposing the derivative proceedings brought by other minority shareholders in *Smith v Croft (No 3)*:

> I am of the view that Mr. Soames represents the principal asset of the company. ... There is therefore no reason why if Mr. Soames became so disenchanted with the present litigation he could not either set up business on his own account in this country or seek alternative employment in the same industry in the US.[9]

Consequently, when shareholders attempt to initiate litigation on behalf of the company, an 'agency problem' is created between the shareholder-litigant and

4 Indicatively: Susanne Kalss, 'Shareholder Suits: Common Problems, Different Solutions and First Steps towards a Possible Harmonisation by Means of a European Model Code' (2009) 6 ECFR 324, 332.

5 *Prudential Assurance Co Ltd v Newman Industries Ltd (No 2)* [1982] Ch 204: the temporal length and the size of the litigation costs involved in this case added to the notoriety of the common law derivative action.

6 (1987) 3 BCC 218, 258 (Knox J).

7 Kalss (n 4) 332.

8 Mark L Cross, Wallace N Davidson and John H Thornton, 'The Impact of Directors and Officers' Liability Suits on Firm Value' (1989) 56 Journal of Risk and Insurance 128–136.

9 (1987) 3 BCC 218, 257. The irony in this statement is that derivative suits in the US were far more numerous than those of the UK.

the company as a whole, due to the representative nature of the remedy. The minority shareholder becomes the 'agent' in such cases, upon whose hands depend the interests not only of fellow shareholders, but also of all persons contracting with (or otherwise involved in) the company. This agency problem's severity is determined by the degree to which the law allows a shareholder having interests competing to those of the company's to bring proceedings with the sole objective of extracting private benefits. If no safeguards are in place, agency costs may skyrocket and firms be left helpless to be plundered by predatory shareholders, rendering the corporate environment a miserable view and unattractive to investors.

The aforementioned considerations on safeguards against undesirable litigation permeate much of the legal thought. Apart from the rather rich literature on the matter, the wording of the consultation and preparatory reports prior to the statutes introducing such a form of litigation, alongside the relevant case law, reveal that the fear of excessive litigation is seriously contemplated:[10] from the earliest stages of rule-making to judicial interpretation and application.[11] The importance of such considerations for the purposes of this book is paramount since, reportedly, the threats of frivolous and predatory litigation have vehemently influenced the Greek law-maker not to take any incisive step regarding the matter during the 2007 reform of Greek corporate law, impugning the contrary voices from the academia.[12] Rather disappointingly, the latest reform followed suit and, by and large, maintained the previously applicable set of restrictions on the remedy. It can even been argued that Law 4548/2018 places stricter conditions for a claim to be brought than its predecessor.[13] As will be seen, many of the differences among jurisdictions derive from the approaches taken so as to prevent abuse of the remedy. In order to constrain frivolous and vexatious litigation, they impose restrictions on legal standing, on

10 Exquisite analysis in Anne van Aaken, 'Shareholder Suits as a Technique of Internalization and Control of Management: A Functional and Comparative Analysis'(2004) 68 RabelsZ 288 with numerous references to American and German scholarship.

11 See Andrew Keay and Joan Loughrey, 'An Assessment of the Present State of Derivative Proceedings' in Joan Loughrey (ed), *Directors' Duties and Shareholder Litigation in the Wake of the Financial Crisis* (EE 2013) 187ff; Janet M Dine and Brian R Cheffins, 'Shareholder Remedies: Lessons from Canada' (1992) 13 Co Law 89.

12 Among others, Panagiotis K Panagiotou, 'Actio Pro Socio and the Principle of Fiduciary Duty as a Means to Limit the Latter in Company Law' (2013) B' EEmpD 291, 301; Christina Livada, 'Filing of Company Claims against the Members of the Board of Directors' in Perakis Evanghelos (ed), *Sociétés Anonyme's Law* (3rd edn, Sakkoulas 2013) 1018–1019; Georgios Triantafillakis, 'From the Protection of the Minority to the Protection of the Shareholder', in Minutes of the 18th Panhellenian Conference on Commercial Law (Collaborative Work), *Trends and Prospects of the Law of the Public Limited Company* (Nomiki Bibliothiki 2009) 116–117.

13 Achilleas Christodoulou, 'Remarks on Articles 103–105 of Law 4548/2018 Regarding the Filing of the Company's Action' (2018) 11 DEE 1267, expresses the view that the newly inserted discretion of the court (to dismiss the minority's petition, if the latter preponderantly runs against the company's interests) materially curtails minority protection. Further restricted is the scope of misfeasance covered by the remedy.

the cause of action, as well as they subject the decision to sue to court's review, under various criteria. The availability of the remedy to shareholders is thus curtailed, in view of the detrimental effects litigation may have on the company and shareholders as a whole.

It therefore follows that an *effective* and *truly protective shareholders' remedy* against wrongs to the company is the one that strikes the right balance between its availability and the restrictions to its abuse. This is so because only in such a way can this type of litigation fulfil its full potential in assuming the role envisaged in Chapter 2. Otherwise, the law runs the risk of not remedying shareholders' reflective loss, but instead allowing for further loss to occur; it runs the risk of not mitigating agency problems and their costs, but creating additional ones instead; and, finally, it runs the risk of devastating investors' confidence in a market, instead of promoting it.

3.1.2.1 Nature, typology and terminological considerations

The very nature of derivative actions interlocks with civil procedure rules and principles.[14] They effectively constitute a means to circumvent the ordinary rules on the legal standing of juridical persons: in common law parlance, a derivative claim[15] is an exception to the 'proper plaintiff rule', as established in *Foss v Harbottle*.[16] Further procedural matters are also dealt within the ambit of the law on derivative actions, such as litigation costs and the extent to which a decision becomes res judicata.[17] On the other hand, derivative actions, being a form of corporate redress against managerial misconduct, constitute part of the substantive company law. Interestingly, even their procedural aspects are usually dealt with in company law statutes.[18] These observations are important, for the implication that a comparative study on such rules needs to consider the applicable procedural law.

Consistent with the procedural nature of derivative actions is the fact that shareholders are required to go through an admission stage for their claim to proceed. Given the expenses involved in and the potential length of proceedings, until the court reaches decision on the merits, the examined jurisdictions attempt to filter out frivolous and vexatious suits early on, in order to protect parties from such

14 This is evident in the differentiations in terminology made in CA 2006 with respect to Scottish law. Further evidence of this 'dual' nature of derivative claims is the fact that CPR Pt 19 and Practice Direction 19 C supplement the provisions under CA 2006 Pt 11.

15 According to the wording of the statutory provisions, CA 2006 ss 260ff.

16 (1843) 67 ER 189.

17 Evanghelos Perakis, 'The Greek and International Discussion on Acceptance and Restriction of the Derivative Action brought by a Shareholder of a Public Limited Company' in Hideo Nakamura, Hans Fasching, Hans F Gaul and Apostolos Georgiades (eds), *Festschrift für Kostas E Beys dem Rechtsdenker in Attischer Dialektik* (5th edn, Eunomia 2003), 3679; reaching further analytical detail on the matter is Panagiotis I Kolotouros, *Actio Pro Socio: The Procedural Dimension of the Corporate Action* (Sakkoulas 2006).

18 See, for instance, AktG s 148(2), where court jurisdiction is determined, along with other procedural matters (e.g. suspension of limitation period), matters which could well be addressed within the ZPO.

undesirable effects, by entrusting this task to courts and setting certain criteria upon which permission to pursue/continue a claim may be granted. Evidently, procedure plays its rule in the pursuit of regulatory objectives.

In Germany, admission proceedings take place in a single hearing and attest the standing to sue of the claimant(s) based on the criteria set in *Aktiengesetz* section 148(1).[19] Similarly, the petition for appointment of a special representative under Greek law[20] can be seen as an admission procedure for the claim to be asserted.[21] In the UK, a two-stage procedure is provided for permission to continue the derivative claim. In fact, a late entry to the statute was the procedural screening mechanism of adjudicating, in a separate stage (ex parte), whether the claimant has a 'prima facie case'.[22] The requirement for permission to continue a claim as a derivative one to be granted has also many procedural connotations, given the representative nature of the derivative claim. Recently, the court in *Wilton UK Ltd v Shuttleworth and Others (No 2)*[23] held that the claimant taking steps (service of claim to defendants, etc.) without permission was acting without authority. However, in certain circumstances, such as the ones before it, the court may retrospectively grant permission, even when the ex parte stage has not taken place, and validate with retrospective effect steps taken in the proceedings without permission.[24] However, the law seems to be unclear as to whether establishing a prima facie case is an exercise clearly discernible from the examination as to whether the claimant has standing based on the criteria set in CA 2006 section 263: a task also for the second stage (inter partes).[25] The criteria, in their majority reflecting the rules formulated under

19 AktG s 148 (2).

20 Law 2190/1920 art 22b(3); now Law 4548/2018 art 105.

21 Hans C Hirt, 'The Enforcement of Directors' Duties Pursuant to the Aktiengesetz: Present Law and Reform in Germany: Part 1' [2005] ICCLR 179, 187, described the then equivalent procedure under German Law as 'preliminary'.

22 Paul L Davies and Sarah Worthington, *Gower and Davies' Principles of Modern Company Law* (9th edn, Sweet & Maxwell 2012) 659. If the application is successful at first stage, the court may give directions as to the evidence to be provided by the company (s 261(3)), in what resembles an intermediate stage in the application for permission. See Janet Dine and Marios Koutsias *Company Law* (8th edn, Palgrave MacMillan 2014) 206.

23 [2018] EWHC 911 (Ch).

24 At [158] f. It is interesting to note here that the judge went on to explain in some detail why his decision was consistent with the 'filtering' policy underlying the statutory derivative claim provisos and that only for good reason may the procedural requirements (including the 'prima facie case' stage) be by-passed.

25 One would expect that establishing a prima facie case would necessitate only satisfaction of the formal requirements in filing a claim, such as membership status of the claimant, legal and factual basis of the action specified and relevant to the procedure, etc. (requirements specified in CA 2006 s 266, for derivative actions in Scotland). However, courts have occasionally taken a different view, adding to these elements the criteria and requirements in CA 2006 s 263.See, regarding Scotland, *Wishart v Castlecroft Ltd & Ors* [2009] CSIH 65 [31] (Lord Nimmo Smith, Lord Reed, Sir David Edward, QC); regarding England, *Stimpson v Southern Landlords Association* [2009] EWHC 2072 (Ch)

common law, fall under two categories. Under the first one (section 263 subsection 2), should the set requirements not be met by the claimant, the court must refuse permission.[26] Under the second category (section 263 subsections 3, 4), a non-exclusive list is set of factors which the court must consider in exercising its discretion to give permission.[27] In judicial practice, considerations under section 263(3) and (4) have intruded most of the judgments in the early cases under the new statute.[28] Interestingly, the parties may in some instances opt to merge the two-stage admission procedure in a single hearing, as this would save time and money. The courts seem not only to permit but also to applaud such initiatives, as can be adduced by the words of Floyd J in *Mission Capital*:

> Sections 261 and 262 of the Act describe a two-stage process for the granting of permission to continue such an action which is given effect to by CPR 19.9(a). In the first stage, the court considers on paper whether there is a *prima facie* case for permission to be given. If so, a permission hearing is held on notice to the company; in this case the parties have *sensibly* agreed to combine the two parts of the process.[29]

It is therefore likely that the ex parte and inter partes stages will in practice often be held in a single hearing, and, in any case, telescoping of the criteria set in section 263 may be facilitated in adjudicating a prima facie case.[30]

Some clarifications regarding the terminology used in the ensuing analysis are necessary at this point. The adjective 'genuine' used for derivative claims under CA 2006 Part 11 and the derivative action under common law is selected due to the long tradition of the remedy in the UK, temporally preceding the

[2010] BCC 387 [46] (Pelling QC). Further discussion in Chapter 5 and Keay and Loughrey (n 11) 192–193.

26 'Leave' in Northern Ireland; and Scotland (CA 2006 s 266). As noted in Geoffrey Morse (ed), *Palmer's Company Law* (Sweet & Maxwell 2015) para 8.3717, regarding the Scottish provisions: 'The delay in having to seek permission to commence proceedings (which does not arise in English law) is a serious defect in the Scottish provisions, since it might result in the substantive claim prescribing before the necessary action to recover loss can be commenced'.

27 In *Mission Capital Plc v Sinclair* [2008] BCC 866 (Ch) 874 the application of CA 2006 s 263 was described as follows 'Section 263 explains the basis on which the court is to consider the giving of permission. The relevant part here is section 263(2)(a) … . This section is mandatory in character. If the relevant facts are established the court must refuse leave. Section 263(3) sets out the discretionary consideration' (Floyd J). Regarding Scotland, we read in Morse (n 26) para 8.3721 'Section 268 mirrors the provisions applicable in England and Wales and Northern Ireland (s 263) and decisions on those provisions will carry considerable weight in Scotland.'

28 See on the discussion Keay and Loughrey (n 11) 190ff.

29 *Mission Capital Plc v Sinclair* [2008] BCC 866 (Ch) 874 (Floyd J, emphasis added).

30 See also David Gibbs, 'Has the Statutory Derivative Claim Fulfilled its Objectives? A Prima Facie Case and the Mandatory Bar: Part 1' (2011) 32(2) Comp Law 41.

(somehow inaccurate) translation as such of foreign provisions that bear comparative similarities; thus exhibiting an element of originality.[31]

The use of the term 'derivative action' when referring to Greek Law 4548/2018 articles 104–106 (and its German equivalent old version of *Aktiengesetz* section 147[32]) would amount to coining an academic misnomer for what actually is the ad hoc replacement of the board with 'special representatives' of the company, by court decision, with the (exclusive) mandate to initiate litigation against the misfeasant board of directors.[33] Arguably, this procedure has more resemblance with the provisions of the Greek Civil Code on the placement of 'interim administration' for the company – by court decision[34] – in cases where the incumbent directors are found in conflict of interest than the common law's 'genuine' derivative action.[35] Thereby, claims are asserted *indirectly* by shareholders, whereas a core component of derivative actions is that shareholders maintain their own legal standing[36] in the main proceedings.[37] Therefore, for the purposes of consistency and clarity, the literary translation of the Greek provision will be preferred – corporate (or company's) action(s) – and (pre-UMAG) section 147 of *Aktiengesetz* and articles 104–106 of the Greek statute will otherwise be referred to as indirect and quasi-derivative actions. Conversely, reference

31 Note that, despite the existence of a provision for a minority shareholders' action in the same statute (s 370), only claims regulated in CA 2006 Pt 11 are explicitly described as derivative ones.

32 Its predecessor, Law 2190/1920 art 22b was modelled after the old (German) AktG s 147. See Themis K Skouras, 'Appointment and Replacement of Special Representatives in the Societe Anonyme' [1983] EEmpD 553; Ioannis Passias, *To Díkaion tis Anonýmou Etaireías* (1969) 685, 691. For a translation of the old German law, see Gerhard Wirth, Michael Arnold and Mark Greene *Corporate Law in Germany* (CH Beck, 2004).

33 Proceedings follow the non-contentious jurisdiction procedure of Greek Code of Civil Procedure (GrCivPrC) art 786. The same procedure was followed by Law 2190/1920 art 22b; see Paris Arvanitakis, 'Article 786' in Michael Margaritis and Anna Margariti (eds), *Commentary on the Code of Civil Procedure*, vol. 2 (Sakkoulas 2012) 1551.

34 Greek Civil Code (GCC), art 69.

35 Nevertheless, GCC art 69 is of narrower scope, from certain perspectives, compared to the company's action under Law 4548/2018 arts 104–105: for instance, it does not cover inaction of the board to pursue corporate claims or instances where the board operates under the directions of the majority of the share capital. See Nikolaos K Rokas, 'Corporate Organisation and Shareholders' Individual Action' (2007) NH' EEmpD 16; Leonidas N Georgakopoulos, *To Díkaio ton Etaireión* (4th edn, Sakkoulas 1991) 208–210; see also Patrai Court of Appeal 226/1997 DEE 1997, 591, 592 (with commentary by Lucas A Kokkinis), asserting that GCC art 69 application to conflicts of interest is strict and does not extend to cases of maladministration/mismanagement.

36 In German, *eigener Klagebefugnis*. See Karsten Schmidt and Marcus Lutter, *Aktiengesetz: Kommentar* (Otto Schmidt 2010) 2130. Part of the analysis on legal standing featured herein has been published in Zouridakis (n 2) 271–283 by Sweet and Maxwell and is reproduced by agreement with the publishers.

37 Harald Baum and Dan W. Puchniak, 'The Derivative Action: An Economic, Historical and Practice-Oriented Approach' in Dan W Puchniak, Harald Baum and Michael Ewing-Chow (eds), *The Derivative Action in Asia: A Comparative and Functional Approach* (CUP 2012) 7.

herein to the 'derivative action under UK law' points to CA 2006 Part 11, unless stated otherwise. In a similar fashion, reference to the 'German derivative action' normally connotes the sections 148 and 149 of the German Act.

3.2 The strategies adopted regarding costs allocation

Let us first examine the jurisdictions that provide for direct derivative actions. Both the UK and Germany adopted the strategy of imposing procedural hurdles on shareholders. In neither of them are the barriers of economic/financial nature: both rejected the idea of making derivative litigation expensive.[38] From the perspective of equal access to justice, such a decision is rather justified. Besides other obvious jurisprudential reasons not to use costs as a means of restricting the volume of litigation, there are efficiency considerations suggesting that such a strategy is not optimal. First, such measures do not guarantee that the volume of litigation will remain to reasonable standards for the right reasons. Even though they would be an important deterrent to rational actors, not all actors in the trade act rationally (in the economic sense of the term). In fact, the Japanese experience on derivative actions shows that quasi-rationally /irrationally motivated proceedings are anything but a rare phenomenon.[39] A costs strategy might thus impede litigants whose action will in effect be beneficial to the company, whilst it would leave undeterred wealthy claimants, who seek to disrupt – or even damage – the corporate business by involving the company in (possibly lengthy) litigation. Second and more importantly, derivative actions are destined to operate as checks and balances against bad corporate governance. In effect, they constitute a mechanism for shareholder activism, by disconnecting the harm caused personally to each shareholder from the cause of action and availing direct redress for the company exclusively. Therefore, due to their nature, derivative actions are a cost that the claimants should not prima facie bear, as the claim to be enforced is the company's and compensation goes (directly at least) to the company.

Accordingly, an enabling approach is suggested regarding litigation costs. The perspective that the minority is a disadvantaged, weaker party to the corporate dispute in (among others) economic terms, suggests that, in order for the protection to be effective, there should be some relief from the costs entailed, at least when the litigation is not vexatious. This consideration encompasses also the problems of 'free-riding' and 'rational apathy' inherent in derivative actions. Simply put, it is hard to explain rationally why litigants should undertake

38 See Carsten Paul, 'Derivative Actions under English and German Corporate Law: Shareholder Participation between the Tension Filled Areas of Corporate Governance and Malicious Shareholder Interference' (2010) 115 ECFR 81, 110ff.

39 Dan W Puchniak and Masafumi Nakahigashi, 'Japan's Love for Derivative Actions: Irrational Behavior and Non-Economic Motives as Rational Explanations for Shareholder Litigation' (2012) 45 Vand J Transnat'l L 1; cf MD West, 'Why Shareholders Sue: The Evidence from Japan' (2001) 30 JLS 351.

a costly and potentially lengthy procedure for the benefit of the company, a shared benefit that they can only *reflectively* enjoy through the economic output of the shares owned. It is submitted that, to do away with the claimants' concerns as to free-riding, an award/incentive strategy must be implemented.[40] That is, upon a successful claim the claimant should be directly entitled to part of the award or the award should go directly to the body of shareholders.[41] Such an approach is not followed in the countries herein examined or by the EMCA.[42] Nevertheless, the matter of costs has, as already stated, much occupied legal thought.[43] The general impression is that the solutions adopted eventually attempt not to enrich the claimants but at least not to leave them worse off.

The continental law provisions follow the strategy of costs indemnification by the company, thus curbing the 'loser pays' principle (the English rule). Given that the Greek provisions confer a right only to appoint special representatives, who will in turn assert the corporate claims against the management, it is only reasonable that Law 4548/2018 articles 104–106 do not put any further qualifications on such relief. Deservedly so, as bearing the litigation costs in what essentially is a preliminary procedure to the substantive claim (which is pursued by the special representatives) would be too high a burden for petitioners to carry. However, the rule displays some disparity regarding the provisions on special audit, where the court is afforded discretion to allocate (part or the total of) the expenses to the petitioner.[44]

The latter approach resembles that of the German derivative action. The sixth paragraph of *Aktiengesetz* section 148 distinguishes between costs in the admission proceedings and the ones to be determined in the final judgment. Regarding the former, shareholder-applicants bear the costs, unless the company's behaviour is to blame for them bringing an unmeritorious claim by not notifying them of opposing corporate interests, if the application is dismissed on such grounds.[45] However, if shareholders succeed in the admission proceedings but eventually lose the case of damages/compensation, they should bear the costs only when they were culpable or grossly negligent in bringing the claim.[46] Apparently, German derivative claimants have fewer chances in being reimbursed

40 Indicatively: Andreas Cahn, 'Vorstandsvergütung als Gegenstand rechtlicher Regelung' in Stefan Grundmann, Brigitte Haar, Hanno Merkt, Peter O Mülbert, Marina Wellenhofer, Harald Baum, Jan von Hein, Thomas von Hippel, Katharina Pistor, Markus Roth and Heike Schweitzer (eds), *Festschrift für Klaus J. Hopt zum 70. Geburtstag am 24. August 2010: Unternehmen, Markt und Verantwortung* (Walter de Gruyter 2010) 452.

41 Baum and Puchniak (n 37) 37.

42 Section 11.39(1) reads: 'Shareholders who commence such proceedings must pay the legal cost involved, but may have such cost reimbursed by the company to the extent that they do not exceed the amount recovered by the company as a result of the proceedings.'

43 For an illuminating discussion in the European context, see Kalss (n 4) 332ff.

44 Law 4548/2018 art 143(3).

45 AktG s 148 (6).

46 Uwe Hüffer, *Aktiengesetz* (CH Beck 2012) 872.

by the company for their litigation expenses than Greek petitioners in a company's action; this disparity with the holistic 'company-pays' Greek approach is only mitigated by an applicable cap on litigation expenses.[47] The EMCA is even less encouraging, as it only allows reimbursement of litigation costs in the event that the derivative claim is successful, 'to the extent that they do not exceed the amount recovered by the company as a result of the proceedings'. Apparently, reimbursement may be available only upon the success of the claim, subject to the recovery cap.

The English approach, as per the common law exceptions to the rule in *Foss*, provided indemnity, pursuant to a relevant order by court. What was subsequently called a '*Wallersteiner* order',[48] assuming the name of the decision where such indemnity was first granted, much resembles the German rule on the decision on costs in the final hearing. Unless the claim is not reasonable, the company should bear full costs regardless of the outcome of the proceedings: the test to be applied to attest the reasonableness was that of the 'independent director'.[49] Nowadays, the rule has statutory footing in the Civil Procedure Rules: Practice Direction 19 C 2(2), on the claim form, makes reference (yet not express) to the rule in *Wallersteriner*, providing also some guidance regarding when such an order can and should be sought.[50] Consequently, it appears to be possible to have the expenses covered in full following such practice, provided that the court so orders.

It can thus be held that a claimant (or petitioner) with some possibility of success will at least not be worse off in all the examined jurisdictions. Why do shareholders pursue derivative claims so scarcely then? The oft cited – and maybe deplored – argument of lack of incentives is substantiated, yet it does not provide a full explanation. For one thing, culture seems to have little to do with the phenomenon regarding the countries comprising this study's domain. Investors in German, British and Greek companies are not litigation averse: in fact, quite the contrary. There have been recent nation-wide studies on the frequency of shareholder litigation in both Germany[51] and the UK[52]

47 Under Greek law (Law 4194/2013 'Attorneys' Code' art 63), a statutory minimum cap also applies, based on a scaled ratio and depending on the value of the claim.

48 *Wallersteiner v Moir (No2)* [1975] QB 373, 391ff (Lord Denning).

49 Ibid. 404 (Buckley LJ).

50 See also Paul (n 38) 96–97.

51 Theodor Baums, Florian Drinhausen and Astrid Keinath, '*Anfechtungsklagen und Freigabeverfahren: Eine empirische Studie*' [2011] ZIP 2329, 2331. Notice that this study concerns actions challenging the validity of GM resolutions, an individual right under German law. Court decisions [BGH 29.1.2001, NJW 2001, 1428, AG 2001, 263 (*Aqua-Butzke*); also BGH, BGHZ 146, 179, NJW 2001 1425 (*MEZ*)] and recent legislation (UMAG) have placed restrictions to abuse. See also Mathias M Siems, *Convergence in Shareholder Law* (CUP 2008) 122.

52 Roman Tomasic and Folarin Akinbami, 'Shareholder Activism and Litigation against UK Banks' in Joan Loughery (ed), *Directors' Duties and Shareholder Litigation in the Wake of the Financial Crisis* (EE 2013) 143ff: Westlaw-based research evidencing rather scarce

(yet none in Greece) which show that, if anything, frustrated members do actually bring matters before court. Aside claims under article 22b and its recent successors, articles 103–106, excessive litigation has been for long a major concern in Greece and recent amendments to the Civil Procedure Code made big effort to lower the workload of the Courts of First Instance by reallocating jurisdiction on several matters to minor courts.[53] A third reason for the scarcity of shareholders' litigation on behalf of the company lies in the construction of the provisions themselves. As is demonstrated below, this is probably the most persuasive explanation. The applicable restrictions on a variety of matters (other than costs and award allocation) related to this form of litigation determine its possibilities of success and expectedly influence the quantum of claims brought before court; few would pursue a lost cause. In any case, economic incentives are not the exclusive factor to be considered regarding the availability of derivative actions.

3.3 Restrictions on litigation in particular

3.3.1 Legal standing[54]

3.3.1.1 Legal standing in general

The primary observation as to who enjoys legal standing under the different forms of derivative (or corporate) actions, is that such right is conferred either to individual members or to a minority of the contributors to share capital. Indeed, the span of the rights holders has much occupied the legislators' thought in recent reforms. Accordingly, the selection of a 1% qualified minority (*Minderheit*) threshold by the German legislature, purports to make derivative actions available to a bigger forum than that of the action in section 147 of *Aktiengesetz*, as it stood before the UMAG.[55] Remarkably, Greek legislators also considered this facet of the availability of corporate actions in the 2007 reform, but preferred to lower the then existing threshold to one tenth of registered capital, instead of introducing genuine derivative actions to the law

occurrence of derivative claims (eight in number then). However, there is evidence that since CA 2006 Pt 11 came into force litigation is becoming more frequent. Concurring: David Milman, 'Shareholder Litigation in the UK: The Implications of Recent Authorities and Other Developments' (2013) 342 Co LN 1, 1–2. It is submitted that actions under CA 2006 s 994, are more frequent.

53 Indicatively: amendments by Law 3994/2011; Law 4055/2012; Law 4139/2013.

54 See Zouridakis (n 2) 274–280.

55 See further Hüffer (n 46) 865: 'Forum of only 1% of the share capital participation or the amount of 100,000 euros is low, especially in smaller AGs; what actio pro socio on one hand and de lege ferenda makes unnecessary, on the other hand could strain the authorization procedure' T Bürgers and T Körber (ed), *Heidelberger Kommentar zum Aktiengesetz* (CF Müller 2008) 970; Schmidt and Lutter (n 36).

on public limited companies.[56] This reform also introduced a novelty: it enabled the corporate by-laws to limit the requisite threshold to petition for a corporate action to what could in practice amount to one share.[57] The practical impact this contractual freedom may have on shareholder protection is questionable, being a matter of the founders' and the majority's discretion.[58] Nevertheless, Law 4548/2018 maintained this approach, further lowering to one twentieth of registered capital the ownership threshold required for shareholders to demand the company take action.[59] If the company does not (or cannot) decide to sue, then the majority of the aforementioned minority may file a petition for judicial appointment of special representatives.[60] It is to be noted that the EMCA also places qualified minority requirements in its version of the derivative action, despite ostensibly conferring the right to sue to shareholders individually. This is because it sets the condition that a 10% minority oppose any resolution to grant exemption from liability or waive the right to take legal action; thus, rendering legal standing dependent on the behaviour of that minority, in a fashion similar to the Greek provisions. The significant difference between the two, however, is that the derivative claimant as per the EMCA needs not be a member of the dissenting group of shareholders, whereas the petitioners under Greek law need have been members of the bigger minority demanding the company (via its board) to sue. The distinction made by the EMCA, between the two minorities involved in the process of the derivative action, mitigates the restriction placed by the high ownership threshold required to oppose the resolution on discharge, as any shareholder – even those not being members of the company at the time of the General Meeting – may sue, if the latter requirement is met.

In the selected jurisdictions and regarding both derivative and company's actions, legal standing to sue or file the relevant petition is afforded to minority shareholders. Minority protection is indeed an objective of such rules, as explained above. At least concerning company's actions, as is the one of Law 4548/2018, minority protection is necessitated by the alleviation of the right to request the company to pursue a claim to the body of the General Meeting. In light therefore of the possibility that the GM, because of interlocking interests with those of the wrongdoers, fails to enact this right, it is fair for the minority to be empowered to take action.[61] A similar rationale seems to apply to the German and UK jurisdictions, yet in neither of them is the inaction of the shareholders' majority a mandatory precondition for a claimant to sue. The GM

56 Explanatory statement (preamble) to Law 3604/2007, <www.hellenicparliament.gr/UserFiles/2f026f42-950c-4efc-b950-340c4fb76a24/a-eurodikaio-eis.pdf> (accessed 15 August 2015).

57 Law 2190/1920 art 22b(1), (3).

58 Triantafillakis (n 12) 116. See also Section 5.3.1.2.1.

59 Art 104.

60 Art 105.

61 Athens Court of Appeal 3494/2007, DEE 2007 1191.

retains, of course, the power to demand the *Aufsichtsrat* to assert corporate claims under section 147 of the German statute, but inaction thereof is no precondition to bringing a claim under *Aktiengesetz* section 148.

A point where the examined jurisdictions differ materially though, is the definition of 'minorities' capable of initiating proceedings. The continental ones define as such the holders of a proportion of the company's share capital, whereas the UK statute does not limit the availability of the remedy in such a way and considers each shareholder to be a minority for the purposes of CA 2006 Part 11.[62] The said ownership thresholds employed by Greek and German law are supposed to constitute a *screening device* to frivolous litigation.[63] As the argument goes, a contribution of 1% or more reflects a stronger connection with the corporate interests than that of a single share and renders slimmer the possibility of predatory litigants buying shares with a view to damaging the corporate interests.[64]

Nevertheless, restrictions on legal standing based on share capital participation may necessitate a number of shareholders to cooperate, in order to reach the requisite thresholds. The plethora of claimants (petitioners in the case of Greece), in such situations, may give rise to a variety of problems. The first concerns the collective action itself. Shareholders need undergo the additional costs of forming alliances with the view to litigate: a task further hindered by the hardships of identifying counterparts willing to participate in this endeavour.[65] The German legislature instituted the 'shareholders' forum' to that end, in an effort to alleviate some of these costs.[66] Greek law only recently followed suit, by means of transplantation of the German provisos. However, as will be further discussed in the next Chapter, shareholder associations and forums entail their very own costs and are designed to primarily serve the exercise of shareholder rights related to the General Meeting.[67] It is further to be noted that, at the moment, the Greek provisions lack detail compared to the – rather unused in practice – German ones.[68]

62 CA 2006 s 260(5) confers locus standi to both members and non-members to 'whom shares in the company have been transferred or transmitted by operation of law'.

63 Baum and Puchniak (n 37) 88.

64 Paul (n 38) 104.

65 Law 4548/2018 art 141(11) provides for the right to be informed about the fellow shareholders and their contact details, if the articles of association so provide. However, the practical significance of this right remains to be seen, as its exercise might lead to the infringement of the law on the protection of personal data, particularly in view of the regulation (EU) 2016/679 on the protection of natural persons with regard to the processing of personal data and on the free movement of such data, and repealing Directive 95/46/EC [2016] OJL119/1.

66 See Nikolaos Paschos and Kay-Uwe Neumann, 'Die Neuregelungen des UMAG im Bereich der Durchsetzung von Haftungsansprüchen der Aktiengesellschaft gegen Organmitglieder' (2005) 33 *DB* 1779, 1780.

67 The wording of the Greek proviso seems to restrict the scope of the shareholder forums operation to the rights relevant to the General Meeting.

68 Ulrich Noack, 'Aktionärsforum im Bundesanzeiger: ein Flop' [18 March 2013] Handelsblatt Rechtsboard, <https://blog.handelsblatt.com/rechtsboard/2013/03/18/aktionarsforum-im-bundesanzeiger-ein-flop> (accessed 20 June 2019).

An additional burden for minority shareholders is the requirement that the ownership thresholds are maintained throughout the proceedings. If part of the applicants lose their membership status or do not wish anymore the claim be pursued and the remaining shareholders do not satisfy the requisite threshold, the claim (or petition) will be rejected.[69] Further perplexing the law on legal standing are cases where the claimants' aggregate participation in the company diminishes in the course of proceedings, for reasons beyond their control, such as a capital increase. This seems to be a concern mainly for petitions to appoint a special representative, as the latter's appointment is contingent upon the minority's mandate. Under the German derivative action such requirement does not seem to exist, yet the position of German law remains unclear.[70]

The German statute further attempts to combat abusive litigation by imposing another temporal restriction, regarding 'the point in time' the claimants became members. This provision targets 'professional' litigants buying shares with the mere intent of engaging the board members and the company in court proceedings, in order to serve interests that do not align with corporate ones. Mitigating this restriction is the setting of the benchmark according to actual or imputed knowledge (instead of occurrence) of the complained act or omission.[71] To a great extent this mirrors the civil law approach regarding calculation of limitations on claims.[72] Therefore, a constraint is imposed that, although not necessarily in contrast with the approach adopted by the CA 2006 section 260 subsection 4 (where it is expressly provided that it is 'immaterial' whether the claimant became a member after the cause of action arose), is not to be found among the mandatory restrictions under UK law. It is expected, however, that courts – in exercising their discretion – consider whether claimants purchased their shares in view of prospective litigation, within the ambit of *good faith*.[73] Such a concern was contemplated in *Smith v Croft (No. 2)* by the representative of the company (Aldous QC);

> It is said that even if the board is independent and 99 per cent of the shares were to be held by 'outsiders,' the remaining one per cent could bring a derivative action; if that were so it would have far reaching consequences,

69 Concurring: Ioannis Delikostopouos and Labros D Sinaniotis, 'Mi peraitéro stírixi ton eidikón ekprosópon anónymis etaireías sto 1/3 tou metochikoú kefalaíou tis' [2000] Diki 990.

70 T Bürgers and T Körber, *Heidelberger Kommentar Aktiengesetz* (3rd edn, CF Müller 2013) 1290. The prevailing opinion is that the quorum is necessary only when filing the application; cf the opposing view in Gerold Bezzenberger and Tilman Bezzenberger, 'Aktionärskonsortien zur Wahrnehmung von Minderheitsrechten' in Georg Bitter, Marcus Lutter, Hans-Joachim Priester, Wolfgang Schön and Peter Ulmer (eds), *Festschrift für Karsten Schmidt zum 70. Geburtstag* (Otto Schmidt 2009) 105, 112ff.

71 S 148 (1)(1).

72 See GCC art 937 (torts only), s 199(1)(2).

73 Keay and Loughrey (n 11) 211.

> since it would enable a trade rival to buy a single share in order to maintain a derivative action for wholly improper reasons.[74]

It can further be observed here that the above temporal restriction, is not to be found in the pre-UMAG section 147 of *Aktiengesetz*. This evidences the legislators' effort to keep frivolous claimants at bay, by imposing further screening mechanisms on a direct action which is perceived as more attractive than the regime of special representatives.

Greek law imposes a strict restriction in its functionally equivalent provision: petitioners have to adduce evidence of possessing membership status six months prior to filing the petition.[75] However, criticism of the Greek approach regarding the duration of membership status as too harsh compared to the German one is nuanced by contextual reading of the German provisions. Duration of membership, as a requirement for legal standing that is disconnected from the occurrence of the directorial wrong (thus similar to the Greek approach), found its way through *Aktiengesetz* section 142 to derivative proceedings. According to the latter, the applicant minority for a special audit has to prove membership for at least three months preceding the petition and maintain it throughout the audit procedure.[76] Given the importance that discovery of evidence has with the filing of derivative claims and the fact that the special audit under the aforementioned section is, effectively, the only worthy means of facilitating such discovery under German law, the scope of section 148(1)(1) is curtailed.[77] Therefore, save for the cases that there is no need to resort to such a procedure,[78] petitioners under section 148 have, in practice, to satisfy a strict requirement of longstanding membership in the company.

It is safe to adduce that UK law is more generous regarding legal standing. Not only the right to bring a claim under Part 11 is an individual one, but also contemporaneous ownership of shares might only be considered in court within the context of good faith.[79] As regards Germany and Greece, the 'minority approach' is followed. Nevertheless, given that the German provisions confer a form of direct derivative action, the justification of such an approach lingers on the controversial argument of 'substantial share of and commitment to the corporate interests'; thereby, the German solution is doctrinally questionable, leading to the outcome that an action aiming to

74 [1988] Ch. 114, 142.

75 Art 104(1). Notably, Law 4548/2018 doubled the threshold set by Law 2190/1920 art 22b (1).

76 OLG München Beschl. v. 11.5.2010 – 31 Wx 14/10, NZG 2010 7884, ZIP 2010 1032.

77 The duration of ownership requirement in s 142 applied similarly to s 147 (pre-UMAG).

78 e.g. in case of 'whistle-blowing'.

79 Explanatory notes on CA 2006 s260: '*subsection (4)* provides that a derivative claim may be brought by a member in respect of wrongs committed prior to his becoming a member. This reflects the fact that the rights being enforced are those of the company rather than those of the member and is the position at common law'.

safeguard the corporate interests and constituting a control mechanism for good corporate governance is rendered a 'millionaire's action'.[80] Indeed, in case of large (capitalisation) corporations, 1% of *registered* capital (its trade value can be far greater) can lead to some level of eclecticism: a minori ad maius, this applies to rules requiring larger percentages, such as the old version of *Aktiengesetz* section 147 and the default minority threshold set in Law 4548/2018 article 104. As Professor Baums persuasively illustrated in anticipation of the KonTraG,

> (i)n the case of Daimler Benz, for example, with an equity capital of about DM 2.3 bn this means that one would have to hold shares with a nominal value of DM 230 million or gather and convince other shareholders with equivalent shareholdings.[81]

Imposition of a threshold therefore entails an amphisemy. It may reflect a policy that favours block holders in listed corporations, on the one hand; on the other hand, it may suggest that the rule is intended for closely held non-listed corporations, where ownership of high percentages of share capital is more common. In any case, other filters may work in the same direction with less ambiguity as to their rationale. A closer and systematic look at the relevant case law across jurisdictions provides evidence in support of this assumption. The Greek experience, compared to the British one as it stands since CA 2006, exhibits comparable numbers of reported cases in the past seven years, in view of the difference in size between the two economies.[82] Importantly, there is evidence that, even though the 'floodgates' remained sealed in the UK, claimants whose shareholdings would fall short of the Greek (and even German) threshold were successful in their applications in the UK, whilst others who held much bigger percentages of the company's share capital were not.[83] Apparently, a qualitative approach can achieve the same results in restricting the numbers of litigation as a quantitative one.

However, one cannot help but notice that minorities in Greece have a role to play only in the preliminary proceedings. It is thus important to further elaborate on legal standing post-admission: as already explained, there lies the fundamental difference between direct derivative actions and corporate actions. Instead of the applicant shareholders, it is special representatives who have standing in the 'main'

80 G Bezzenberger and T Bezzenberger, 'Section 148', in K Hopt and H Wiedemann (eds), *Großkommentar AktG* (Walter de Gruyter 2008)para 81.

81 Theodor Baums, 'Personal Liabilities of Company Directors in German Law' (1996) 9 ICCLR 318, 322.

82 See Annex 1.

83 In *Stainer v Lee* [2010] EWHC 1539 (Ch) the successful applicant held about 0.08% of the company's share capital and was judged to be acting according to the company's interests in bringing a derivative claim. cf *Kleanthous v Paphitis* [2011] EWHC 2287 (Ch), where the unsuccessful applicant held 15.5 % of the company's shares.

proceedings (on the merits of the action), on behalf of the company and it is up to the court's discretion to select the special representatives of its preference.[84]

Benefitting from the comparative nature of this study, useful insights can be drawn from the German experience of the 'special representatives' regime in order to assess the merits and demerits of the Greek approach. Notably, the German 'enhanced' minority right to appoint special representatives by court decision had a very short lifespan; section 147(3) was introduced by the KonTraG only to be removed seven years later.[85] In fact, the approach was deemed problematic from the very beginning, for a variety of reasons, including the very institution of special representatives.[86] Even though the theoretical bases of the rule promulgated the incompatibility of mere member status with that of corporate representative, drawing on the strict separation of powers within the company, the underlying rationale was bluntly to dis-incentivise (unmeritorious) litigation.[87] Indeed, due to petitioners having no further control over the course of the proceedings, company's actions are not an appealing option; however, this applies equally to both shareholders wanting to bring an action that is to the company's benefit and predatory litigants. There seems to be little reason for a member (or group of members) to invest time and money in a procedure they have no longer control of from the point the court makes the respective appointment.[88] Furthermore, it can be argued that the alienation of the petitioner from the background and the consequences of the claim might result in a prudent and objective conduction of the proceedings; however, it might also result in relative lack of interest from the part of the representative. This comprised one of the arguments in favour of reform, as it is highly unlikely that the appointed representative exhibits similar zeal to a member that suffered a reflective loss in pursuing a claim.[89] The possibilities for moral hazard are obvious: the special representatives enjoy only an interim and ad hoc position in

84 The court is by no means bound by the petitioners' submissions as to who should be appointed special representative. See Alexandra Mikroulea, *Scope of Corporate Managers' Duties and Liability* (Nomiki Bibliothiki 2013) 254; AI Freris, 'Judicial Enforcement of Corporate Claims against the Members of the Board of Directors' in VG Antonopoulos and S Mouzoulas (eds), *Sociétés Anonymes*, vol. 2 (Sakkoulas 2013) 208. Similarly under the old s147 of the German *Aktiengesetz*. See AG Nürtingen AG 1995 287, ZIP 1994 785.

85 (Gesetz zur Kontrolle-und Transparenz im Unternehmensbereich) BGBl. I, 786.

86 cf the contributions of Adams, Baums, Hopt, Kübler, Lutter and Wenger in 'Die Aktienrechtsreform 1997' [1997] AG-Sonderheft 6/1997.

87 Hirt (n 21) 188.

88 Baums, 'Personal Liabilities' (n 81) 322; Hirt (n 21) 189–190; Peter Ulmer, 'Die Aktionärsklage als Instrument zur Kontrolle des Vorstands- und Aufsichtsratshandelns' (1999) 163 ZHR 290, 334–336; Jens Koch, 'Das Gesetz zur Unternehmensintegrität und Modernisierung des Anfechtungsrechts (UMAG)' (2006) ZGR 769, 771.

89 See, on the matter of special representatives, the works of the two academics who heavily influenced UMAG, Theodor Baums, 'Empfiehlt sich eine Neuregelung des aktienrechtlichen Anfechtungs- und Organhaftungsrechts, insbesondere der Klagemöglichkeiten von Aktionären?' in *Gutachten F zum 63. Deutschen Juristentag Leipzig 2000* (CH Beck 2000); Ulmer (n 88).

the administration of corporate affairs, have no stakes in the company and therefore have few incentives to discharge their duties diligently. In such a case, instead of mitigating existing agency costs, the procedure prescribed by articles 104–105 creates new ones.

3.3.1.2 Multiple derivative actions

An important dimension of legal standing is the possibility of 'multiple' derivative actions. In situations where a company is controlled by a parent corporation, the boards of the two corporate entities may have the same composition. Even when this is not expectedly the case, as for example in Germany where the interlocking composition of boards in parent-subsidiary structures is precluded by law,[90] the independence of the board members may be questionable: after all, particularly in cases of sole proprietorship, it is the owner company who appoints and dismisses the board. In such cases, where the parent company owns the subsidiary, the damage made to the subsidiary by its directors can only be remedied by the parent company assuming action and thus the process reaches an impasse. Therefore, unless there is an option for a shareholder in the parent company to instigate litigation on behalf of the subsidiary (*double derivative action*) the wrong cannot be remedied. This is especially the case where the subsidiary is fully owned by the parent, because of the absence of other potential 'champions' of the company's claim.

At first glance, the requirement that only a member of the company has standing to sue under the UK CA 2006 seems dismissive of multiple derivative actions or, at best, is silent as to the matter. British scholarship, in its early responses to the newly introduced statute, identified the issue and highlighted the adverse consequences that might arise from the abolishment of multiple derivative actions. Reisberg in particular contrasted the effect Part 11 might have on this matter in relation to the approaches followed by other members of the common law family, hinting at a potential comparative disadvantage.[91] His concerns over the availability of multiple derivative claims have now been addressed, by and large, by the decision in *Universal Project Management Services Ltd v Fort Gilkicker Ltd and Others*,[92] which refuted his prediction that English courts would respond negatively to such a possibility. Regarding the intent of statutory provisions, Briggs J asserted that

> there is … no persuasive reason why Parliament should have wished to provide a statutory scheme for doing justice where a company is in wrongdoer control, but none where its holding company is in the same wrongdoer control.[93]

90 AktG s 100; see further Hüffer (n 46) 537–536.

91 Arad Reisberg, 'Shadows of the Past and Back to the Future: Part 11 of the UK Companies Act 2006 (In)action' (2009) 6 ECFLR 219, 241ff.

92 [2013] EWHC 348 (Ch).

93 At 173. Note the reference (repeatedly in the judgment) to 'wrongdoer control'. Following Briggs J's rationale that, the statute being silent, multiple derivative actions can be brought under common law, common law rules extend generally to admissibility and particularly to standing to

Briggs J went further to conclude that the statute should be interpreted as allowing multiple derivative actions[94] and that the admission procedure in the Civil Procedure Rules clearly applies also to multiple derivative actions.[95] It is interesting to note that in reaching his decision the judge considered academic writings (including Reisberg's) alongside foreign case law.[96] This observation demonstrates the complementary role the literature still assumes in adjudicating matters where the statute offers little guidance. Notably, much of the scholarship referred to in this decision offers a comparative law overview on multiple derivative claims and expresses concerns as to the efficiency of the UK statutory provisions if interpreted as not permitting such claims.[97] Considering the judgment in *Gilkicker*, it may be inferred that the court opted to assert the English legal framework on shareholders' protection as an internationally competitive model.

In the light of these considerations, there seems to be a significant caveat in the continental jurisdictions.[98] No action can be initiated by the shareholder of a parent company against the management (and the persons connected to the wrong complained) of the subsidiary, on behalf of the latter. Doctrinally, multiple derivative actions can be perceived to frustrate the sacrosanct principle of separate legal personality.[99] However, the latter principle is common amongst all jurisdictions examined; particularly in the UK. The relevant rule in *Salomon v Salomon* is applied in utmost strictness but, as evidenced by Briggs J's rationale that derivative actions constitute a procedural exemption designed to prevent injustice, such doctrinal obstacles proved to be surmountable.

3.3.1.3 Assessment

Restrictions on locus standi formed an integral part of the continental legislators' strategy to combat abusive litigation. The arguments put forward by the German and the Greek legislators do not seem persuasive, as the approach therein followed carries the danger of barring meritorious actions.[100] Importantly, inquorate

sue. Thereby, reintroducing, inter alia, in their former might, the criteria of 'wrongdoer control' and 'fraud on the minority' in the context of multiple derivative actions. *Abouraya v Sigmund* [2014] EWHC 277 (Ch) followed this rationale. See also Milman (n 51).

94 At 175.

95 At 53.

96 Arad Reisberg and DD Prentice, 'Multiple Derivative Actions' (2009) 125 LQR 209; *Waddington Ltd v Chan Chun Hoo Thomas* [2009] 2 BCLC 82 (Hong Kong Court of Final Appeal).

97 e.g. Sh Goo, 'Multiple Derivative Actions and Common Law Derivative Action Revisited: A Tale of Two Jurisdictions' (2010) JCLS 255.

98 Similar concerns expressed by Pavlos Masouros, 'Is the EU Taking Shareholder Rights Seriously? An Essay on the Impotence of Shareholdership in Corporate Europe' (2010) 7 ECL 195, 203 (pre-dating *Gilkicker*).

99 Milman (n 52) 2.

100 Baum and Puchniak (n 37) 88.

minorities face a dead end regarding their reflective loss, becoming easy prey for opportunistic directors and block-holders.[101] Furthermore, multiple derivative actions under continental law regimes do not enjoy the availability they do under common law. Therefore, it can be asserted that in respect of who can bring a claim before court, the British approach is more protective to shareholders. The German and, to a greater extent, the Greek provisions prevent shareholders who are unable to reach the legal standing requirements from enforcing the company's claims, restricting their access to justice to recover their reflective loss while, at the same time, they limit the numbers of potential claimants and therefore increase the possibility that wrongs remain unpunished.

3.3.2 Restrictions regarding the scope of misfeasance remediable and the persons against which the action may be brought

Considering the persons whom a derivative claim may be brought against, the limitations on the scope of the UK statutory remedy are slight. CA 2006 Part 11 provides that defendants may be persons in breach of their directors' duties and/or third parties or even non-shareholders.[102] Similarly, yet somewhat more restrictively, in Germany, the derivative action may be brought against a variety of defendants,[103] ranging from the members of the boards to persons exerting their influence to the latter.[104] Articles 102–105 of Law 4548/2018 are thus rather restrictive regarding this matter, given that 'third parties' are nowhere mentioned, even though express reference is made[105] to the persons stipulated in article 87, limiting therefore the scope of the remedy to directors and persons to whom they have delegated powers.[106] Notably, the Greek provisions can be held to fall below the EMCA standards in this respect, as the latter allows for a derivative action to be brought against fellow shareholders too.[107]

The view that law in the UK is more protective in this regard is reinforced by the recently re-asserted availability of multiple derivative actions, extending thus the scope of defendants to persons wronging a connected company. The divergence in approach herein identified is of obvious practical significance as, in some jurisdictions, holding jointly and severally liable everyone involved in the complained

101 A problem aggravated when no other remedy is available. See Chapter 4.

102 S 260(3); see *Goodwin v Cook* [2018] 6 WLUK 425, where the claim was brought against shadow director; cf the approach as per the EMCA, where shareholders are expressly pronounced as potential defendants.

103 S 148(1) in conjunction with AktG s 147 (1).

104 AktG s 117, alongside the persons connected with the formation of the company and the corporate issuers, ss 46–48, 53.

105 Art 102(5).

106 However, the consensus in Greek academia is that the definition of 'director' within the ambit of Law 4548/2018 arts 77ff includes de facto directors.

107 Yet with an interesting twist: shareholders may only be liable for fault or gross negligence, contrary to what applies for directors.

misfeasance may not be as possible as it would be in others. Congruently, in the UK and Germany, claimants stand a better chance of holding a variety of persons extending beyond the incumbent administration accountable and thereby achieve for the company relief which materially reflects the damage caused. Greek law is lacking also from a deterrence perspective, as the threat of civil liability is not felt outside the confines of the board.[108]

An idiosyncrasy of German law has to be highlighted here. As already stated, a tradition of particular legislative focus to the regulation of (de lege and de facto) groups of companies (*Konzernrecht*) exists. Within the ambit of the law applicable to domination agreements,[109] a form of *direct derivative action* is procured, whereby the scope of defendants extends to the legal representatives and the directors of the controlling enterprise.[110] The action under section 309 relates to domination agreements, which ex lege are express and written, but its scope is broadened by virtue of sections 310, 317, 318 and 323 to other structures of inter-corporate control.[111] Two observations are of particular interest. First, the rule significantly predates the general statutory derivative action. The fact that a genuine derivative action was available to shareholders in inter-corporate disputes arising from mismanagement by the controlling enterprise's representatives, whilst for intra-corporate ones[112] the only way to remedy a wrong done to the company was through the appointment of special representatives, is rather astonishing on its own.[113] This approach evidences a disproportionate evolution of the law on groups of companies, compared to general anti-mismanagement rules.

Secondly, *Aktiengesetz* section 309 is seemingly more permissive for any shareholder of the controlled company to instigate litigation. Locus standi is afforded to individual shareholders and there is no 'screening' process or other equivalent demands to limit litigation. Therefore the conundrum arises that, whilst the *Konzernrecht* derivative action assumes a complementary role regarding wrongs that fall within the ambit of *Aktiengesetz* sections 147–149, the latter action undergoes much less judicial scrutiny regarding its admissibility. Furthermore, there appears to be some mismatch regarding costs, as there is no provision equivalent to that in section 148 (paragraph six) within the ambit of *Konzernrecht*-litigation. This is one

108 More problematic is the approach taken by Volos Single-Member Court of First Instance 141/2011 DEE 2011 686 which, on a rather narrow and mistaken interpretation of the law, considered inadmissible any petition to appoint special representatives in order to pursue a claim against former directors.

109 Under the German law on groups of companies, domination agreements put the subsidiary under the directions of the parent company.

110 AktG s 310.

111 Baums, 'Personal Liabilities' (n 81) 322.

112 i.e. claims accruing from the mis-management of a given company.

113 The provision is particularly intended for litigation brought by the subsidiary's shareholder-(s) against the controlling company's management; according to Martin Schwab *Das Prozeßrecht gesellschaftsinterner Streitigkeiten* (Mohr Siebeck 2005) 81, the very reason that the parent might hold almost in full the capital of the controlled company, explains why the remedy is afforded to individual shareholders.

of the reasons (along with its limited scope of intra-group affairs) put forward for its obsolescence, as up until 1999 it remained 'completely without any function in 30 years of its existence.'[114] Nothing much has changed since.[115]

In any case, this approach is remarkable for its uniqueness. There is nothing similar to be found in the other two countries herein considered. Functionally, accountability of the parent company's management, if its influence had a damaging effect to the subsidiary, can be enforced in the UK by means of the general statutory derivative action, up to the extent that their influence is connected with a breach of the subsidiary company's directors' duties. However, there appears to be no such leeway available under Greek law, as the wording of articles 102–105 specifically refer to the 'company's directors' and their delegates as the only possible defendants to such litigation.

This difference as to who may stand as defendant is not entirely connected to differences in the nature of the misfeasance giving rise to the action. In all three jurisdictions, it is principally directors' breach of law or duty that is considered in the provisions for derivative actions.[116] Consequently, even the scope of the persons to be held liable against the company is curtailed. Indeed, the Explanatory Notes to the UK CA 2006 section 260 pronounce that

> *Subsection (3)* also provides that the cause of action may be against the director or against a third party, or both. Derivative claims against third parties would be permitted only in very narrow circumstances, where the damage suffered by the company arose from an act involving a breach of duty etc. on the part of the director.

However, a closer look on the relevant provisions and their application in court reveals that the Greek and UK remedies cover a broad range of wrongs done to the company, whilst their German counterpart is reserved only for gross violations and misfeasance.

A company's action may be brought under Law 4548/2018 articles 103–105 in respect of claims 'accruing from 'any act or omission that constitutes breach of duty. Notably, the applicable law adopts a more restrictive approach compared to its predecessor. As per Law 2190/1920 article 22b, the scope of the remedy not only covered breaches of directors' duties as they are prescribed by the company law statute or corporate by-laws but also extended to other forms of misfeasance.[117] The UK CA 2006 follows a similar, if not more permissive, approach regarding the matter. But this has not always been the case.

114 Martin Gelter, 'Why do Shareholder Derivative Suits Remain Rare in Continental Europe?' (2011–2012) 37 Brook J Int'l L 843, 879 quoting in translation Ulmer (n 88) 300.

115 Indicatively: Hirt (n 21) 192.

116 For Germany, AktG s 148 para 1(3); for Greece, Law 4548/2018 arts 103–105.

117 It covered claims 'accruing from the management of corporate affairs'. This can also be viewed as a restriction to the cause of action, as it does not cover misfeasance not accruing from the management of corporate affairs. See, regarding a similar provision of Chinese law,

The 2006 'codification' of derivative actions in the UK resulted in a remarkable change as to the scope of misfeasance covered.[118] Until then, the 'fraud on the minority' rule, formulated under common law, operated as a restriction to shareholder litigation: arguably, it was the only true ground upon which derivative actions could proceed.[119] It is argued that, along with the expenses involved, this rule constituted the most significant reason why derivative actions scarcely occurred in the UK, contrary to the other prominent member of the common law legal family, the USA.[120] In fact, the replacement of the aforementioned grounds with breach of duty, breach of trust, default and negligence as causes for action led to concerns over a possible increase in litigation numbers.[121] As made obvious in this Chapter, the increase is not dramatic and certainly the UK is way afar from experiencing the American numbers of derivative suits being filed annually.

From the early cases applying the newly introduced statutory derivative claim, it became apparent that a change in approach was indeed effected. In *Wishart*, Lord Ordinary held that 'one of the objects of the 2006 Act was to introduce more flexible criteria than the former "fraud on the minority" exception to the rule in *Foss v Harbottle*'.[122] This dictum can be viewed as reference to the provisional recommendations found in the Law Commission's report(s).[123] That wrongdoer control and fraud on the minority do not

Li Xiaoning, *A Comparative Study of Shareholders' Derivative Actions* (Kluwer 2007). Indeed, Greek scholarship made reference to the facilitation of 'internal' (i.e. intra-corporate) liability of directors, when analysing Law 2190/1920 art 22b.

118 The reader should not be misled that CA 2006 Pt 11 had the purpose of simply codifying the common law rules. The intention was to introduce a new, statutory, derivative action; this can be adduced by the wording of the Law Commission, *Shareholder Remedies* (Law Commission No 246, 1997) para 1.21: 'we still consider that it would be desirable for a new derivative procedure to be introduced along the lines of the provisional recommendations.'

119 Possibly alongside ultra vires etc., as long as they were not grounds for a personal action. Derek French, Stephen Mayson and Christopher Ryan, *Mayson, French & Ryan on Company Law* (31st edn, OUP 2014) 563.

120 See Brian R Cheffins and Bernard S Black, *Outside Director Liability Across Countries* (2006) 84 Tex L Rev 1385, 1463, 1404–1405.

121 S 260(3) (for England, Northern Ireland and Wales); s 265 (3) (for Scotland). The move towards remedying negligence is significant, as under the 'fraud on the minority' regime the additional requirement that the negligent wrongdoer benefitted individually had to be fulfilled for a derivative action to proceed. See *Pavlides v Jensen* [1956] Ch 565; cf *Daniels v Daniels* [1978] Ch 406. According to Victor Joffe, David Drake, Giles Richardson, Daniel Lightman and Timothy Collingwood, *Minority Shareholders, Law, Practice and Procedure* (4th edn, OUP 2011) 38, the restrictions in Pt 11 regarding the remediable misfeasance do not apply when a derivative claim is brought following an order under CA 2006 s 994.

122 At 38.

123 *Shareholder Remedies* (Law Commission No 246, 1997) para 1.13. See also explanatory notes on CA 2006 s 260: 'a derivative claim may be brought in respect of an alleged breach

constitute mandatory preconditions for bringing a derivative claim, was further affirmed in *Bamford v Harvey*,[124] where explicit reference to *Wishart* was made (despite the latter Scottish decision not being binding).[125] To paraphrase the wording in *Gower & Davies* regarding the rule in *Foss v Harbottle*, 'fraud on the minority' seems to be 'consigned to the dustbin'.[126] The impact of the widening of the scope of misfeasance covered by the statutory remedy is all the more apparent from the fact that only one application has so far been refused on the grounds that the complained conduct fell outside that scope.[127] Fraud on the minority might conceptually retain relevance though, in the context of ratifiability, as such misconduct 'inherently' cannot be ratified under the approach determining ratifiability on the basis of the nature of the wrong.[128]

Turning to the other facet of the common law regime, on the appropriate cause of action in respect of which a derivative claim may be brought, wrongdoer control has also been 'downgraded' in judicial practice to a discretionary factor in formulating a judgment. Still, this development cannot be seen as welcome. There is a problem inherent in what amounts to 'wrongdoer control', regarding the possibility that a derivative claim meets with success: it is not easy to track down ownership and de facto control of the shares.[129] It is even more difficult to prove by evidence that the wrongdoers are in control in large companies, should the question be on whose behalf the shares are held. This situation arises particularly when disclosure requirements fail to identify actual ownership.[130] Disclosure of shareholdings is, remarkably, an area of law where the realms of company law and the law of finance meet.[131] Therefore, unless the latter is highly developed, particularly regarding disclosure of actual (end) share ownership, the concept of wrongdoer control may (to a large extent) insulate directors. Given that no express reference to the criterion is made in the statute, wrongdoer control survived through the context of ratifiability, ratification and the views of disinterested members. It remains to be seen whether wrongdoer

of any of the general duties of directors in Chapter 2 of Part 10, including the duty to exercise reasonable care, skill and diligence (section 174)'.

124 [2012] EWHC 2858 (Ch) [2013] BCC 311.

125 At [29].

126 (n 21) 654.

127 *Re Seven Holdings* [2011] EWHC 1893 (Ch).

128 See *Parry v Bartlett* [2011] EWHC 3146 (Ch [2012] BCC 700 [79]).

129 Keay and Loughrey (n 11) 218.

130 ibid. 217–220. The Kay report ('The Kay Review of UK Equity Markets and Long-Term Decision Making' (2012) available at: <http://lawcommission.justice.gov.uk/docs/kay-review-of-equity-markets-final-report.pdf> (accessed 30 August 2015)) attributed much significance to the matter.

131 For reflections on this international phenomenon, see Triantafillakis (n 12) 115; see also Nicolaos Vervessos, 'The Relationship between the Law on Societes Anonymes and the Law of Capital Markets' in Michael-Theodoros Marinos (ed), *The Public Limited Company among Company, Insolvency and the Law of Capital Markets* (Sakkoulas 2011) 328–356.

control will feature as a decisive factor in future cases, given that the list of discretionary factors in CA 2006 section 263 is not exclusive.

Another matter related to the cause of action is the availability of alternative remedies. This, again, is a factor to be considered by the deciding court in exercising its discretion in the UK.[132] The rationale is simply that, in case another remedy exists (in UK law this usually is the unfair prejudice remedy under CA 2006 Part 30), it might be more appropriate for shareholders to pursue the same cause of action in their own right, otherwise than by derivative action: the latter being an exceptional means of redress to reflective loss suffered by the shareholders and enforcement of directors' duties. This is evident in the very recent decision in *Bridge v Daley*:

> The focus of Mr Bridge's complaints … are not upon breaches of duty owed to the company, but are complaints that he has been disadvantaged as a shareholder by the way in which the company has been managed and operated by the present Board.[133]

Indeed, despite the apparent advantage, from the disgruntled shareholder's perspective, of the unfair prejudice remedy in that it compensates (if successful) petitioners directly, shareholders may opt to 'dress' their claim as a derivative one only to avail themselves of a *Wallersteiner* order.[134]

In fact, there was the impression that under common law the availability of another remedy constituted an absolute bar for a derivative claim to proceed;[135] mainly because of the 'sixth principle' set by Gibson LJ in *Barrett v Duckett*:

> The shareholder will be allowed to sue on behalf of the company if he is bringing the action bona fide for the benefit of the company for wrongs to the company for which no other remedy is available. Conversely if the action is brought for an ulterior purpose or if another adequate remedy is available, the court will not allow the derivative action to proceed.[136]

132 Ss 263(3)(f), 268(2)(f).

133 [2015] EWHC 2121 (Ch) [82] (Hodge QC).

134 See *Kleanthous v Paphitis* [2011] EWHC 2287 (Ch); [2012] BCC 676 [80] (Newey J): 'One is left with the suspicion that Mr Kleanthous has chosen to pursue derivative proceedings alone in the hope that that he will be able to obtain a costs indemnity'.

135 In *Hughes v Weiss* [2012] EWCH 2363 (Ch) [61], Keyser QC dismissed the idea that the 'alternative remedy' criterion constituted an absolute bar to derivative claims pre-2007, citing the decisions in *Mumbray v Lapper* [2005] EWHC 1152 (Ch) and *Konamaneni v Rolls Royce Industrial Power (India) Ltd* [2003] BCC 790; [2002] 1 WLR 1269.

136 [1995] BCC 362, 367.

This is certainly not the case nowadays. Under the statutory regime, such availability is a matter to be considered and quite often adds to weigh against permitting a derivative claim when the court exercises its discretion:[137] on its own, however, it does not render an application impermissible.[138]

It can be observed that in its early application, the new statutory derivative claim has been challenging for the judiciary. References made to the Law Commission's consultation papers and reports, alongside academic works, reveal a laborious effort to grasp the rationale behind legislation. On the other hand, parallels are sought in case law to bridge any gaps between the pre-existing rules and the provisions in force. In any case, the experience on the statutory regime signals a more permissive approach regarding the cause of action.

The approach as to the misfeasance covered by the provisions on derivative actions is quite different in Germany. According to section 148(1)(3), only 'dishonesty or gross violation of the law or of the articles of association' constitute grounds for derivative claims. Apparently, the German statute is more restrictive regarding the cardinal matter of the cause of action. Dishonesty has to reach 'criminal' levels of disloyal behaviour, whilst 'gross violations' are understood as absolutely unacceptable and extraordinary wrongs, in terms of both their nature and their effect on the company.[139] Case law so far has rejected a complaint about excessive (well above average) remuneration of officers as not meeting this requirement.[140]

It is a peculiar phenomenon that such a restriction survived the UMAG: much criticism had been levied by academics on the equivalent rule found in the old version of section 147(3) of *Aktiengesetz*, yet this screening mechanism was introduced to the direct derivative action.[141] This restriction creates a disparity between duties and their enforcement by shareholders. As will be further argued in Chapter 5, this approach is dysfunctional, unjust and partly responsible for the practical insignificance of the stillborn German derivative action. Accordingly, it is asserted that German law suffers a comparative disadvantage, as the cause of action has little to do with restricting the

137 See *Iesini v Westrip Holdings Ltd* [2009] EWHC 2526 (Ch) [2010] BCC 420 (at 126); *Mission Capital* (at 46).

138 Indicatively, Roth J in *Stainer* (n 83): 'I consider that given what is at the heart of the present case, a derivative action is entirely appropriate and therefore the theoretical availability to the applicant of proceedings by way of an unfair prejudice petition is not a reason to refuse permission' (at 52). See also *Kiani v Cooper* [2010] EWHC 577 (Ch); [2010] B.C. C. 463 [38]–[40] (Proudman J); *Cullen Investments Ltd v Brown* [2015] EWHC 473 (Ch); *Montgold Capital LLP v Ilska* [2018] EWHC 2982 (Ch).

139 Hüffer (n 46) 867.

140 See LG München I, Beschluss vom 29.3.2007 – 5 HK O 12931/06, AG 2007 458 and the relevant commentary (m. Anm. Spiekermann) 'LG München: Zur Frage der Angemessenheit der Vorstandsvergütung Beschluss vom 29.03.2007 – 5 HK O 12931/06 | AktG § 148 | AktG § 87' [2008] CCZ 157, <http://beck-online.beck.de/?vpath=bibdata%2fzeits%2fccz%2f2008%2fcont%2fccz.2008.157.1.htm> (accessed 1 July 2014).

141 Klaus Ulrich Schmolke, ' Die Aktionärsklage nach § 148 AktG – Anreizwirkungen de lege lata und Reformanregungen de lege ferenda' [2011] ZGR 398, 419–22; Hirt (n 21) 190ff.

admissibility of shareholders' claims/petitions in the other jurisdictions herein examined. The UK Companies Act and Greek Law 4548/2018 are more permissive in this regard, placing no restrictions upon the duties to be enforced, therefore compensating the company in more instances and deterring directors from breaching their duties in toto.

3.3.3 Ratification and equivalent means and possibilities for insulation of liability: The views of the body of shareholders

Ratification, as the word suggests, constitutes the expressed assent of the members to actions taken by the management, including some that would otherwise amount to a breach of duty or negligence. It is a competence of the GM that interlocks with those of the management, and, in effect, it is a way to legitimise the actions taken by the latter.

It is important to note that, as regards German law on public limited companies, ratification does not substantiate any sort of waiver for claims against the management.[142] As Wirth et al. conclude, 'ratification is only of symbolic significance'.[143] Nevertheless, if a proposed resolution to ratify the works of the management does not pass, there is an adverse consequence for the board. In Germany, a no-confidence vote is likely to follow such an incident, and this empowers the Supervisory Board to dismiss the *Vorstand*.[144] Similarly in Greece, following the introduction of article 22a to Law 2190/1920, article 35 adopted a quasi-ceremonial character and ratification does not constitute anything more than a vote of confidence.[145] Law 4548/2018 maintained this approach, in article 108, clarifying that such vote of confidence may be considered by a court hearing a lawsuit based on directors breach of duty. Therefore, 'ratification' in these two countries emulates the respective parliamentary procedures of reviewing the legitimacy of the serving government,[146] fortifying the observation that, indeed, company law often mimics constitutional and administrative law.[147] Of particular comparative interest are the similarities in wording between the Greek and the German text: in both cases the word 'discharge' is used as the equivalent of 'ratification'.[148]

However, one should not assume that the management boards in continental law jurisdictions cannot be excused under any circumstance their misfeasance by

142 AktG ss 119–120.

143 Gerhard Wirth, Michael Arnold, Ralf Morshäuser and Mark Greene, *Corporate Law in Germany* (2nd edn, CH Beck 2010) 133.

144 AktG s 84(3).

145 Similar wording in Hüffer (n 46) 661: 'a trust proclamation for the future management of the Company'.

146 Vote of confidence under art 84 of the Greek Constitution.

147 See Stephen Bottomley, 'Shareholder Derivative Actions and Public Interest Suits: Two Versions of the Same Story?' (1992) 15 UNSWLJ 127.

148 German, *Entlastung*; Greek, *apallagí*.

the body of shareholders. There is some discretion afforded to the GM to *waive* corporate claims against members of the management. Such discretion is more limited under German law, as the decision has to be taken three years after the claim arose (instead of two years under Greek law), by GM resolution excluding the prospective defendant's votes[149] and provided there is no disagreement (expressed by negative vote, abstention does not constitute disagreement)[150] by one tenth of the registered share capital (similarly to Greek law).[151] Intriguingly, there exists some disparity under German law regarding the percentages of capital contribution necessary to block a waiver of corporate claims and those needed to commence a derivative action.[152] The need for assembling a minority ten times bigger than that required by section 148 in order to block a waiver is problematic, but is limited by the condition that a respectable amount of time shall elapse before the latter can take place. What should be further noted is the antithetic position German law adopts regarding employees and their say in corporate matters regarding the issue of waiver. Contrary to the rule in Germany that it is the task of the Supervisory Board (and therefore employees' representatives, should there be codetermination) to assert claims for maladministration, waiver thereof is bestowed upon the stockholders. This can be viewed as a 'loophole' in the pro-stakeholder orientation of the German system. However, courts have explicitly provided that the Supervisory Board is under an *obligation* to investigate whether the company suffered damages and to assert claims respectively.[153]

Following the comparative approach adopted herein, the functionally equivalent continental law rule to that of ratification under UK Law is the discharge/ waiver rule. This assertion is made due to the fact that Law 4548/2018 article 102 and *Aktiengesetz* section 93 are effectively the solutions provided by law to the problem of whether and how management irregularities can be excused by the GM, whilst, under CA 2006 section 239, the GM is capable of providing an ex-post amnesty to mismanagement, effectively waiving the members' and the company's rights. Nevertheless, the difference in approach is substantial. Without any provision for a blocking minority, the UK CA 2006 adopts the pragmatic stance of disallowing members connected with the person whose conduct is to be ratified to vote, discarding the idea of statutorily set blocking minority thresholds.[154] Ratification can take place with no temporal constraint whilst, on the contrary, waiver of corporate claims under continental law cannot take place

149 AktG s 136(1).

150 Similarly under Greek law (Vassileios Antonopoulos, *Law of Societes Anonymes and Limited Liability Companies* (Sakkoulas 2011) 443).

151 cf AktG s 93; Law 4548/2018 art 102.

152 See the discussion in Walter Bayer and Philipp Scholz, 'Die Pflichten von Aufsichtsrat und Hauptversammlung beim Vergleich über Haftungsansprüche gegen Vorstandsmitglieder' [2015] ZIP 149, 150.

153 BGHZ 135, 244 (*ARAG/Garmenbeck*); see further Wirth et al. (n 143) 115.

154 CA 2006 ss 252, 254 offer some guidance as to who is an 'interested party'.

for a given amount of time; often sufficient for proceedings to be initiated. However, it would be completely incorrect for any student of law to claim that all wrongs are ratifiable under UK law.[155] On the whole, the rule reveals a totally different approach to the issue, much dependent on the court's judgment.

It can be concluded that the management of British companies is afforded a significant means of relief from misconduct. This evidences the importance of the role assumed by this corporate organ in the administration of the company's affairs, compared to what applies in the continental law jurisdictions. Therefore, shareholders have ample discretion to provide immunity for a board they trust: the right to object to such a motion should be considered a minority one and be read in conjunction with the provisions on derivative claims. Focusing on the Greek approach, it can be asserted that it adopts a somehow middle ground; the temporal threshold is lower than the German standards, whilst – in the absence of a Supervisory Board and any possibility for a derivative action – the only constituency that can bring a claim for mismanagement before court is mainly the board itself.

It follows that the provisions for waiver of corporate claims should be studied in conjunction with the possibilities for raising a derivative claim. In the absence of the latter, the proprietary interests of a minority might be frustrated by a majority resolution waiving the company's rights. On the other hand, ratification may limit the possibilities of bringing a derivative action successfully before court. Notably, the mechanics of many European statutory derivative actions focus on the General Meeting resolutions to waive corporate claims or exempt directors from liability, by granting the right to sue derivatively only to dissenting minorities (or parts thereof) or demanding that a (qualified) minority opposed the resolution, in order for such a claim to be filed by (a) shareholder(s).[156] The latter approach is followed by the EMCA, which, as was explained above, sets the relevant ownership threshold at one-tenth of share capital. It may be assumed that the rationale behind such provisions is to equip minorities with an enforcement mechanism, in addition to the right to block a waiver or ratification. However, by making the latter two the primary points of reference, such provisions become somewhat restrictive, as aspiring derivative litigants need a General Meeting to be convened, on a topic that often may extend beyond the grounds of the claim they want to pursue.

155 Len Sealy and Sarah Worthington, *Sealy's Cases and Materials on Company Law* (9th edn, OUP 2010) 406ff.

156 In fact, such provisos follow the setting of the early forms of the actio pro socio in Europe. Nowadays, this approach can still be found in the company law statutes of many EU jurisdictions, such as the Danish Companies Act § 364(3), Finnish Companies Act Ch. 22 s 7, Swedish Companies Act Ch. 29 and the Luxemburgish law on commercial companies of 10 August 1915 art 444–2.

Nevertheless, among the jurisdictions studied herein, only the UK CA 2006 expressly considers ratification a condition for a derivative claim to proceed, within the wording of the provisions on derivative claims. The statute adopts a two-fold approach in addressing the issues of ratification (or authorisation) and ratifiability. First, a resolution passed that ratifies (or authorises) the acts of the board absolutely bars any claim: the old common law principle in *Northwest Transportation v Beatty* remains good law.[157] However, ratifiability of the complained wrong, which under the pre-existing law would normally bar the derivative action,[158] remains relevant to the statutory derivative claim merely as a discretionary factor. Ratifiability, as an absolute bar to derivative actions, has been met with disdain by academics and considered significantly ambiguous regarding some of its facets.[159] In fact, this rule effectively limited derivative litigation to non-ratifiable actions; actions nowadays considered in section 239(7). It should be mentioned that section 239(3) and (4) arguably introduced some novelties to ratification, excluding 'connected' persons[160] from a vote on ratification and thus making the requirements stricter. The approach towards derivative claimants is (seemingly at least) further relaxed by the substitution of 'possibility' with 'likelihood'. Thus, a breach of duty has not only to be ratifiable but it must also be *likely* to be ratified by the members' resolution in order for the directors to be exculpated. Of course, ratifiability is also considered in the context of whether an effected resolution can be challenged. The problem inherent in ratifiability though, is that there is as yet no clear-cut answer as to what constitutes ratifiable behaviour and what does not.[161] Accordingly, despite the fact that ratification was rightly inserted as an absolute bar to derivative claims in order to facilitate commercial certainty, as it would make no sense to entangle parties in lengthy proceedings where no cause of action exists, the very content of the law on ratifiability entails for the moment some levels of legal (and commercial) uncertainty.[162] Some guidance is offered by references in several dicta to cases where a director cannot be excused in such a way for misfeasance.[163] Simpliciter, a rule of thumb accruing from the study of the majority of common law precedent would be that when dishonesty is involved, misfeasance is inherently non-ratifiable.

157 [1887] LR 12 App Cas 589.

158 As happened in *Edwards v Halliwell* [1950] 2 All ER 1064.

159 Arad Reisberg, 'Theoretical Reflections on Derivative Actions in English Law: The Representative Problem' (2006) 3 ECFR 69, 77.

160 As per CA 2006 s 252.

161 As acutely stated in *Gower and Davies* (n 21) 625, this issue 'has troubled a number of other writers'.

162 See Law Commission, *Shareholder Remedies* (Law Commission No 246, 1997) paras 6.83–6.86

163 See Mayson, French and Ryan (n 119) 564ff, referring to *Prudential Assurance Co Ltd v Newman Industries Ltd (No2)* [1981] Ch 257; *Taylor v National Union of Mineworkers (Derbyshire Area)* [1985] BCLC 237; *Regal (Hastings) Ltd v Gulliver* [1967] 2 AC 134.

It remains to be seen which stance the courts will adopt, as the line of relevant case law is up to now narrow. *Franbar* was one of the early post-2006 cases to consider the very concept of ratifiability[164] and strongly reflected the wrongdoer control-orientated[165] approach, in that emphasis was placed on disinterested votes. A similar rationale eventually followed in *Parry v Bartlett*.[166] The problem with this approach is that the disinterestedness of shareholders is difficult, lengthy and costly to ascertain.[167] In practice and law, 'interested persons' may extend well beyond those enumerated in CA 2006 section 252 (i.e. the wrongdoer's family members, partners, etc.) and any judgment on bias largely depends on a complex and painstaking process of considering the facts at hand.

Ratification is not the only context where the views of the shareholders are considered for permission to continue a derivative claim under British law. Another point, within the ambit of CA 2006, is where the views of disinterested members are considered by the court in exercising its discretion.[168] This is reminiscent of the rule in *Smith v Croft* regarding the 'majority of the minority'.[169] This rule, despite being based on a rationale that fully aligns with the exceptional nature of derivative claims, displays considerable ambiguity. For one, it is very difficult to ascertain what constitutes the majority of the minority. In the absence of a holistic approach, such as fixed percentages determining the requisite quora, attention may be shifted to those interested in the insulation of the directors: this might lead courts to the undesirable outcome of striking out meritorious claims, simply because they were misled that disinterested members did not favour such action. Furthermore, ascertaining from a multitude of shareholders who is interested and who is not is challenging, especially in traded companies. It remains to be seen whether courts will bar proceedings in public companies due to subsection 4. So far, there has been one case concerning allegations of mismanagement in a public company, where the factor of section 263(4) played a significant role in dismissing the application to continue a derivative claim.[170] Thereto, it was the company which sent a questionnaire to its major shareholders, regarding their view on the prospect of litigation.

164 [2008] EWHC 1534 (Ch); [2008] B.C.C. 885.

165 Other authors refer to this as 'voting theory'. The dichotomy in the theorisation of ratifiability depends on whether the focus is on the wrong itself (as according to the voting theory) or the wrongdoers. See KW Wedderburn, 'Shareholders' Rights and the Rule in *Foss v Harbottle*' (1957) CLJ 194.

166 [2011] EWHC 3146 (Ch) [2012] BCC 700 [81]. Note however, that in *Singh v Singh* [2014] EWCA Civ 103 the court focused more on the nature of the conduct.

167 Keay and Loughrey (n 11) 206.

168 S 263(4).

169 *Smith v. Croft (No. 2)* [1988] Ch 114; [1987] 3 WLR 405; [1987] 3 All ER 909; [1987] BCLC 206; *Smith v. Croft (No. 3)* [1987] BCLC 355, Ch D; (1987) 3 BCC 218.

170 *Bridge v Daley* [2015] EWHC 2121 (Ch).

In any case, it is to be noted that the judgment in *Smith v Croft* concerned a private company. The court dismissed the plaintiff's argument against the independence of the other minority shareholder's judgement (Wren Trust), on the grounds of a lack of evidence to ascertain that a biased decision to the detriment of the company was made.[171] In public companies however, where ownership is dispersed and sometimes hardly identifiable,[172] ascertaining the true view of the majority of the minority is complicated due to shareholders' apathy. This is a general phenomenon, and it is rather unfair to consider any abstention from expressing disagreement with the management's practices as affirmation or even tolerance. Even when apathetic shareholders express such assent, they may do so without considering the company's interests and without genuine consideration of the issue at hand, whilst their sheer numbers render it impossible for the court to examine if their views are biased. For these reasons the *Smith v Croft* criterion is more suitable for private companies; at least, it is a positive step that it was downgraded to a discretionary factor.

3.3.4 *Whether the action serves the corporate interest and is brought in good faith*

3.3.4.1 *The company's interests criterion*

A common criterion used to filter vexatious litigation in both the UK (including CA 2006 s 371) and Germany is whether the action is brought in the interests of the company.[173] Interestingly, such provisions constitute an attempt by the court to put shareholder-claimants into the shoes of directors who initiate proceedings in good faith and in accordance with their fiduciary duties: as we shall see, there are some qualifications. Given that ordinarily these standards apply to directors as the expressers of the corporate mind when they represent the company in litigating its claims, such a rationale is justified. Due to the very essence of the derivative action, claimants should thereto be expected to pursue the corporate interests in substituting for the directors within the ambit of corporate litigation and not to serve exclusively their individual interests.[174] The latter

171 (1987) 3 BCC 218, 258 (Knox J): 'there is no sufficient evidence that in relation to the present question whether these proceedings should continue Wren Trust has reached its conclusion on any grounds other than reasons genuinely thought to advance the company's interests'.

172 At least regarding the end owner/beneficiary.

173 See Zouridakis (n 2) 280–283.

174 In *Gower & Davies* (n 21) 662, it is rightly submitted that a quasi-agency relationship is created in derivative actions. The distinction between the claimant's interests and the company's interests, within the ambit of derivative claims, was clearly pronounced kin *Wilton UK Ltd v Shuttleworth and Others (No 2)* [2018] EWHC 911 (Ch) by Judge Davis-White QC sitting as a High Court judge (at [81]):

> On the face of things, a director acting in accordance with CA 2006 s 172 has to consider the interests of the company (even accepting that these are very wide). He or she does not have to consider the interests of the claimant seeking to bring the derivative claim.

point provides an extra justification as to the criterion posed; should litigants pursue their individual interests, in conflict with the corporate ones, the derivative action would in effect be a means of absolute circumvention of the no reflective loss principle.

In this vein, the UK CA 2006 poses the mandatory requirement that the claimant must satisfy the court that the action serves the corporate interests; if 'a person acting in accordance with section 172 (duty to promote the success of the company) would not seek to continue the claim', permission is refused.[175] The fact that, by design, a successful derivative claim may benefit all those involved with the company can justify consideration by the court of the interests of stakeholders other than shareholders in exercising its discretion under section 263. In particular, when applying the hypothetical director test, stakeholders interests become relevant, as they are encompassed in the 'enlightened shareholder value' approach permeating section 172.[176] Whereas, when the outcome of proceedings affects the interests of creditors, suppliers and so on, expecting to receive (indirectly) a share of the award through the company, this might be an indicator that the derivative claim is more appropriate than other alternative shareholder remedies not providing a possibility of such distribution.

However, the requirement as it stands in this subsection is anything but draconian. As Lewison J held in *Iesini*:

> In my judgment therefore (in agreement with Warren J. and Mr Trower QC) s263(2)(a) will apply only where the court is satisfied that *no* director acting in accordance with s.172 would seek to continue the claim. If some directors would, and others would not, seek to continue the claim the case is one for the application of s 263(3)(b). Many of the same considerations would apply to that paragraph too.[177]

It therefore appears that a claimant is unlikely to encounter difficulties satisfying the mandatory requirement, save for manifestly unfounded applications.[178] However, the dictum reveals that considerations on whether the claimant is acting in accordance with the duty under section 172 might eventually prove to restrict litigation significantly: the discretionary factor in section 263(3)(b) sets

175 S 263(2)(a).

176 in *Montgold Capital LLP v Ilska*, granting permission to continue the claim, Judge Simon Barker QC (sitting as a High Court judge) held that 'Mr Pay described the derivative action as a win-win situation for the company and its creditors irrespective of whether the person discharging the section 172 duty had regard to the members or to the creditors … . That submission is a powerful submission' (at [37]).

177 At 86. The 'hypothetical director test' can be said to have first appeared under the exceptions to the rule in *Foss v Harbottle*. See *Airey v Cordell* [2007] BCC 785.

178 In the UK, seven applications (out of almost 28 reported cases) have so far been dismissed on the mandatory ground of s 263(2)(a). See Annex I.

a higher threshold, by directing the court to additionally look into the importance attached to such a claim. In fact, an array of matters, many of which are factual,[179] can be considered in assessing the importance a person acting under section 172 would attach to the claim.[180] For instance, in *Kleanthous v Paphitis*,[181] Newey J was persuaded that the damaging effect the litigation would have on one of the defendants (Mr Paphitis, a well-known businessman and public figure) would also affect the reputation of the company, and thus it was not important for the company to continue the claim.[182] Case law so far shows that, in practice, the failure to satisfy the discretionary factor in section 263(3)(b) appears in most judgments dismissing an application.[183]

The German approach seems to be more permissive. Section 148(1)(4) makes reference to 'preponderant reasons opposing' the claim to be brought. Thus, it is submitted (and following the explanatory notes, purported) that this requirement would bar a claim only in exceptional circumstances:[184] that is, when balancing the arguments before it under the spectrum of the company's interests, the court becomes of the opinion that 'the arguments against the claim weigh significantly heavier against the shareholders' action'.[185] This proviso has its ancestry in the landmark *ARAG/Garmenbeck* decision, where it was held that the Supervisory Board, despite its general duty to assert corporate claims, might opt not to do so in view of overriding corporate interests. Nevertheless, the 'gross violations' restriction on the grounds upon which a derivative action may be brought (AktG s 148(1)(2) n 3) can also be held relevant to the company's interests criterion for a derivative action to proceed; it may be presumed that in such cases of misconduct it is always in the company's interests that shareholders bring a claim. Therefore, as in Britain, German courts treat shareholder-claimants as ad hoc substitutes for the corporate organ normally responsible for litigating corporate claims, levying similar duties upon them. In essence, by examining whether the derivative action accords with the corporate interests, both

179 In *Iesini* (n 137) [85], Lewison J enumerated factors to be considered in reaching a decision in accordance with the s 172 duty; including the size and strength of the claim, disruption of corporate business due to litigation etc. (see Chapter 5 for the full quotation). The strength of the claim comprised contributing factor also in the recent judgement in *Goodwin v Cook* (n 102). Interestingly, these factors were applied in *Bhullar v Bhullar* [2015] EWHC 1943 (Ch) [38] (Morgan J) regarding the criterion of the 'hypothetical director test', within the context of the common law exceptions to *Foss v Harbottle*.

180 See Keay & Loughrey (n 11) 199–200.

181 [2011] EWHC 2287 (Ch) [2012] BCC 676.

182 At 696.

183 See Annex 1. Consider that in *Iesini* (n 137) [102] (Lewison J) the application was mainly dismissed on the grounds of failing to meet the mandatory bar, yet the judge held that even if that was not the case, it would still fail to meet the s 263(3)(b) requirement; similarly in *Seven Holdings* (n 127) [45] (David Donaldson QC).

184 RegE-UMAG, BT-Drucks 15/5092 22.

185 Schmidt and Lutter (n 36) 2142.

jurisdictions rest permission to proceed with the claim on the discretion of the court.

Until recently, Greek law adopted a diametrically different approach. As per Law 2190/1920, not only were the board and the court not allowed to review, on such grounds, the petitions to bring a claim or to appoint special representatives, but special representatives were also under a duty to bring the claim irrespective of whether it promotes the company's interests or not.[186,187] It so appears that the General Meeting and the (then) 10% minority were the only arbiters of the desirability of litigation. This can only be explained by the legislator's confidence in these constituencies to voluntarily promote the interests of the company as a whole. However, this approach does not exclude the possibility that the 10% minority may use the company's action as a means of extortion or that special representatives are appointed, with a duty to bring a claim, on the frivolous initiative of this minority. The fact that costs for proceedings on appointment of special representatives are born by the company increases these possibilities. In such cases, the company's action ceases to be truly protective for shareholders en masse, allowing suits detrimental to their interests to be brought.

Interestingly, the EMCA does not mention the company's interests within the literary setting of its section 11.39 either. However, the latest reform of Greek company law, despite being subsequent to the EMCA, distanced itself from this approach. Under the new Law 4548/2018, the company's interests are for the first time explicitly required to be considered by the court in deciding whether to accept the shareholders' request to appoint a special representative. Article 105 now provides that a request may be dismissed if 'overriding interests of the company so demand'. The wording of the provision much resembles that of *Aktiengesetz* section 148(1)(4). Nevertheless, similarly to German practice, this filtering device is not expected to be of much practical significance. If anything, it may apply to situations that would be filtered out by the prima facie stage as per the UK CA 2006, such as claims without any good cause. In any case, this is one development that, from a shareholder protection and corporate governance perspective, is in the right direction and therefore is much welcome.

3.3.4.2 Good faith

This section does not purport to provide a comparative analysis of the general term 'good faith' and its functionally equivalent counterparts[188] as they operate

186 BGHZ 135, 244, NJW 1997 1926; Hüffer (n 46) 866.

187 Succinct review by Ioannis Delikostopoulos, 'Procedural Powers of a Minority Shareholder in AE' (2010) DEE 1282 para 10.

188 Greek, *kalí písti*; German, *Treu und Glauben*.

in each legal framework taken as a whole. The issue has been extensively discussed in comparative law literature, particularly concerning the families of German, Romanistic and common law. In my opinion, there is little to add to the exquisite analysis by Markesinis et al.[189] The aim here is instead to shed light on how and when a derivative or corporate action might be dismissed on the premises that it was brought in bad faith. Little effort has been made regarding the matter thus far in comparative company law studies whose domain includes non-common law jurisdictions. Good faith is of particular importance for the mechanics of such litigation, given that a common concern to legislators internationally is the prohibition of strike actions, an issue conceptually connected with the very essence of good faith in enforcing a right. It might be for this very reason why the British statute goes a step further by expressly pronouncing good faith as a criterion for derivative claims.[190] However, such criteria/requirements are bound to the uncertainty entailed in the application of the general term to corporate law.

As a requirement for an application to proceed, good faith featured in various cases under the common law regime, such as the decision in *Barrett v Duckett*, where it was submitted that personal interests (a 'family feud') that were disconnected from the purposes of the claim would infer lack of good faith: permission was therefore refused.[191] Good faith being a matter of motives, the question is raised as to whether the inclusion of collateral motives that do not conflict with those of the company should bar a claimant from proceeding with a derivative action. An identification of good faith exclusively with the intent to relieve damages to the company would stultify the social value and purpose of the derivative action. The Japanese experience shows that much of the litigation may be undertaken by activist shareholders who want to make an example of bad corporate governance.[192]

It is therefore suggested that collateral incentives in filing a claim should be considered as immaterial as long as they do not overshadow the purpose of benefiting the company: it should only be when the action contravenes this essential purpose of derivative actions that a claim is struck out on the grounds of (absence of) good faith. Lewison J was of that opinion in *Iesini*.[193] The primary issue at hand was that the company allegedly failed to defend diligently against rescission of a license contract. The defendants contended that the claim was brought so as to benefit the company (GGG) in the joint venture entered to exploit the license instead of the company where they were members

189 Basil S Markesinis, Hannes Unberath and Angus Johnston, *The German Law of Contract: A Comparative Treatise* (Hart 2006) 119–132.

190 CA 2006 s 263(3)(a).

191 [1995] BCC 362.

192 These activists can be environmental or other lobby groups. It is questionable to what extent such activism would lead to a successful derivative claim under CA 2006. See Puchniak and Nakahigashi (n 39) 7.

193 At 448.

(Westrip). They grounded their claim on the fact that the claimants had a costs indemnity provided by GGG, which was proved before the court to have terms aiming for a 'safe exit' from the joint venture. The claimants rebuked that continuance of the claim would benefit Westrip, even considering the indemnity terms and conditions. The learned judge concluded, relying on the decision in *Nurcombe*,[194] that 'it cannot, in my judgment, be said that but for the collateral purpose, the claim would not have been brought at all. The claim is, in my judgment, brought in good faith'.[195]Accordingly, a proper claimant in such litigation is expected not to use the mechanism of derivative actions (or claims) in a manner that constitutes abuse of process.

A subsequent case where good faith of the applicant was considered was *Hughes v Weiss*.[196] The judge followed the line in *Iesini* and negatively defined the requirement of good faith as not bringing the action exclusively for an ulterior purpose.[197] What can be concluded, regarding the application of the court's discretion to strike out a claim that is brought mala fide, is that the situation is not as bleak as feared in the early days of the statute. Despite the fact that good faith has been contended by defendants in many applications under Part 11 so far, courts have been parsimonious in ascertaining lack by claimants thereof: only one petition has been dismissed on such grounds.[198]

In the continental courts and under the applicable (quasi-)equivalent provisions, despite there being no express requirement for the claimant in derivative proceedings or the petitioner in proceedings to appoint special representatives to instigate them in good faith, the latter concept forms a general clause permeating much of the applicable private law. As regards Greece and Germany, however, allegations on such grounds were virtually inexistent in the cases herein examined (as they were reported). This is in contrast to the perceived 'animosity' of British litigants regarding good faith and illustrates how an already embedded concept in the British derivative claims culture retained its significance by being put on a statutory footing.[199] Of course, abuse of the right to sue on behalf of the company and the corresponding court procedure may lead a petition to be struck out even in Greece, yet only in limited circumstances:[200]

194 *Nurcombe v Nurcombe* (1984) 1 BCC 99, 269; [1985] 1 WLR 370.

195 At 449. Similarly in *Konamaneni v Rolls Royce Industrial Power (India) Ltd* [2003] BCC 790; [2002] 1 WLR 1269 (Collins J).

196 [2012] EWCH 2363 (Ch).

197 Ibid, 47 (Keyser QC).

198 *Stimpson and Ors v Southern Private Landlords' Association and Ors* [2009] EWHC 2072 (Ch) [2010] BCC 387, where it was held, regarding the weight which considerations on good faith carry, that: 'whether strictly this demonstrates a lack of good faith is not material – it is certainly relevant because s 263(3) is not exhaustive of the matters that require to be considered and in my judgment motivation of this sort is a negative factor so far as this application for permission is concerned' (per Pelling QC at 44).

199 Keay and Loughrey (n 11) 207.

200 GCC art 281; GrCivPrC art 116.

what could amount to abuse of right, is filing a petition (mala fide) when the defendant has the reasonable impression that the right would not be enforced.[201] All in all, the question of good faith is not that significant for the setting of the continental law rules on the herein examined types of shareholder litigation, nor has it been considered in the relevant case law or occupy any length of analysis in the relevant literature.[202]

3.3.5 The principle of subsidiarity and the 'demand rule'

A common denominator between derivative actions – in all their guises – and Law 4548/2018 article 105 is the requirement, in order for a shareholders' petition/application to proceed, that the company (through its competent organs) refrains from commencing proceedings itself ('subsidiarity principle').

Aktiengesetz, section 148 paragraph 1(2), sets the onus on shareholders to prove that their calls for the company to take action were ignored. This provision (together with paragraph 3 of the section) is an expression and facilitator of the principle of subsidiarity.[203] From certain viewpoints, it is reminiscent of the 'demand rule', as it is known in the US.[204] Its underlying rationale is that absent any rule limiting shareholders' litigation to cases where the company itself fails to assert its claims, corporate personality and boards' competences would be emptied of substance. The company retains the right to usurp (unconditionally and at any time) pending litigation for its claims against mismanagement.[205] This is again viewed as a means to constrain malicious litigants, as the company's power to overtake pending proceedings may act as a disincentive to them.[206]

Articles 104 and 105 of Law 4548/2018 ostensibly work in a similar vein: only following four month's inertia by the board to initiate litigation pursuant to a minority's demand, no prompt initiation of proceedings following a General Meeting resolution ordering the company to do so, rejection of the

201 See Greek Supreme Court 1844/2009, EllDni 2012 687. An agreement to waive the minority right under Law 2190/1920 art 22b which contravenes the law, cannot substantiate on its own such an impression according to Athens Multi-member Court of First instance 6881/2005, NOMOS Databank, DEE 2006 625. In the same judgment, an allegation of an 'ulterior purpose', behind the company's action, to circumvent a shareholders' agreement, was also dismissed.

202 As regards Greece, the exception confirming the rule is the work of Panagiotou (n 12).

203 Concurring view by Paul (n 38) 108.

204 For the application of the rule under the law of Delaware, see E Welch, A Turezyn and R Saunders, *Folk on the Delaware General Corporation Law* (Wolters Kluwer 2013) 17–1003.1. Supporting the view that the German legislator has 'borrowed heavily' from US law, see Ingo Saenger, 'The Best Interests of the Corporation, Procedural Questions of Enforcing Individual and Corporate Rights and Legal Actions against Board Members' (2015) 26 EBLR 13, 24.

205 Paul (n 38) 108.

206 ibid.

minority shareholders demand to the board to initiate proceedings (or non-compliance with the deadline set therefore), or the latter's inability to decide upon such demand are shareholders entitled to apply before court for the appointment of special representatives. The new provision reduced the time-frame, within which the company, via the board, should bring the claim when the minority so demanded, by two months – compared to its predecessor article 22b of Law 2190/1920 – adding shorter deadlines for the remaining cases permitting shareholders go to court.[207] The literary setting of the new provisions also avoids much of the ambiguity surrounding the old article 22b on how and when shareholders may file a petition to court, by removing the notorious 'fault exception'.[208] However, the wording of article 104 paragraphs 2 and 3 is rather unclear. In particular, ambiguity exists on whether notification of the inability to vote is mandatorily required per paragraph 3 and whether the shareholder-set deadline (as per paragraph 2) refers also to it. Paragraph 3 indicates that the board has to communicate its inability to vote upon the commencement of proceedings in any case ('the possible inability of the board of directors to decide is communicated to the applicants with diligence'). It therefore follows that the deadline of paragraph 2 also applies. If this is so, no proceedings to appoint a special representative may commence before two months passed since communication, should the board not refrain from notifying shareholders. That would mean a minimum three months since the request was filed.[209] However, paragraph 2 reads: 'shareholders have to set a reasonable deadline, within which the board of directors ought to assess the content of the request and *decide* whether the company will bring an action for the claims described in that request'. Since no decision may be made when so many members are accused and thus precluded from voting that the rest do not fulfil quorum requirements, it follows that either shareholders need just wait for their deadline to pass or that they can immediately apply for the appointment of a special representative. The latter view may be supported also by the fact that paragraph 3 pronounces that 'the provisions of article 105 apply' in such cases: this ambiguous reference may be read as establishing an exception that extends to paragraph 2 as well. From

207 Notably, under Law 2190/1920, the board's inertia to initiate proceedings has to be culpable, otherwise shareholders are not automatically entitled to request the appointment of special representatives when the six month's deadline expires (Athens Court of Appeal 1076/2006, NOMOS Databank, EpiskED 2006 248). It remains to be seen whether this approach will be followed by courts regarding Law 4548/2018 art 105.

208 It was ambiguous whether it only concerned the board's duty to file proceedings or the conditions for a shareholders' petition as well. See Nikolaos K Rokas, *Commercial Companies* (Sakkoulas 2006) 312; Filippos Doris, 'I schési ton árthron 69 AK, 22b § 3 n.2190/1920 kai 786 § 3 KPolD os rythmíseon gia tin apotropí tou kindýnou exypirétisis symferónton antithéton pros ta symféronta tou ekprosopoúmenou nomikoú prosópou' (2002) B' ChrID 865, 878, 883; Freris (n 84).

209 Art 105 para 1(e). Note that the same paragraph provides that proceedings may commence following the passing of the 'deadlines … of cases a and c'. This is believed to be a mistake in wording, since case a refers to the rejection of the request by the board, not a deadline.

a certain point of view, the adverse consequence of that would be the deprivation of the court to review the substantive justifications put forward by an ad hoc appointed committee.[210] It remains to be seen how case law interprets article 104 in this respect.

An intriguing feature of Law 4548/2018 regards the involvement of special independent committees in corporate litigation. Within the ambit of the business judgement rule, the new Law 4548/2018 provides – explicitly, for the first time in Greek company law – that the court *may* dismiss a claim against the management if the latter acted according to the recommendations of an independent committee operating in the company. Whilst the American influence on that provision is all too obvious,[211] the question arises of whether it will also result into the establishment of US-style special litigation committees (SLCs), in the context of shareholder-led litigation.[212] It is to be reminded here that the board may be liable against the company if it unduly refrains from enforcing the company's claims. Accordingly, in making a decision on whether to sue, following a shareholder's request as per article 104 or not, the board may consult such committee. This 'novelty' is expected to have several implications on the management's accountability.

If the American jurisprudence taught us anything, it is that the independence and unbiased judgment of such committees are not beyond question, to say the least.[213] American SLCs almost invariably opine against the claim being brought, concluding most often that the suit runs against the company's interests.[214] Structural bias aside, it is to be noted that such committees, as also per Greek law, are appointed and remunerated by the company, by virtue of board decision(s). The risk therefore exists that, when faced with the prospect of litigation, boards will turn to an amicable institution whose selection they control, billing the company for its services.

Besides independence and unfettered judgment of the committees, the other issue arising from their involvement to shareholder-led corporate litigation is that of judicial deference to their recommendations. It is reasonable to expect that, unless the independence of the committee is persuasively contested, courts will usually adopt their views: from a certain point of view, such deference to informed, business-specific opinions might even be desirable. However, such

210 Similarly John C Coffee Jr, 'New Myths and Old Realities: The American Law Institute Faces the Derivative Action' (August 1993) 48 Business Lawyer 1407, 1416.

211 It can be categorised as legal-institutional transplant.

212 SLCs have been operating in the USA since the 1970s. See concise review in Coffee (n 210) 1422–24.

213 Bryant G Garth, Ilene H Nagel and Sheldon J Plager, 'Empirical Research and the Shareholder Derivative Suit: Toward a Better-Informed Debate' (1985) 48 LCP 137.

214 'Although there have been more than a score of special litigation committee cases to date, in all but one the committee concluded that the suit in question was not in the corporation's best interests' (JD Cox, 'Searching for the Corporation's Voice in Derivative Suit Litigation: A Critique of Zapata and the ALI Project' [1982] Duke LJ 959, 963).

practice would eliminate the role of the court as a neutral arbiter regarding the substance of the dispute, to the benefit of a body whose judgment may well be biased. Yet, it might be counter-argued that, given that under article 104 the court has the power, not the obligation, to exculpate the board on the basis of the committee's prior consultation, such concerns are unwarranted and courts will not necessarily show disproportionate deference to the latter' views. For sure, consideration – not blindfolded espousal – of an independent view on the matter at hand would be much welcome a development. Time will tell if this is the case.

However, regardless of the stance courts adopt, the setting of the Greek provision remains problematic, for the very reason that a company's action will proceed, notwithstanding a negative response from the board, substantiated on a committee's recommendation or not, unless doing so would in the court's view gravely affect the company's interests. Hence, the committee's recommendations would in most cases be considered only within the ambit of a claim against the board's breach of duty in refusing to initiate proceedings, heard as part of the trial on the shareholder-led company's action or separately. Therefore, the outcome of the latter might well be that the claim(s) against the board is (are) eventually dismissed, following a lengthy and costly judicial dispute, despite the early warnings from the committee. From the same point of view, this proviso is further problematic due to the fact that the board cannot assign to the independent committee the power to decide upon the shareholders' request, when it is unable to vote upon the latter. As explained above, vexatious shareholders may be expected to unreasonably turn against the whole board, just to bypass the demand requirement; such abuse could be avoided if the committee's role was not so limited.

Notably, the EMCA does not require any sort of 'demand' to be made in order to file a derivative action. However, the shareholder's ability to raise the issue of board liability at the General Meeting can be considered to (partly) perform a functionally equivalent role, given that the General Meeting resolution, whereat exemption from liability or waiver of the right to take legal action was granted, constitutes both the forum where the shareholder's complaints are heard by the board and the point of reference in initiating the derivative proceedings' deadlines.

There is also little to be found in the wording of CA 2006 Part 11 regarding the company's inertia in bringing the claim before court.[215] It is only mentioned, within the non-exhaustive list of subsection 3,[216] that the court shall have particular regard of whether the company 'decided not to pursue the claim'.[217] Professor Kershaw considers that reference to 'the company' may

215 cf *Birch v Sullivan* [1958] All ER 56; [1957] 1 WLR 1247, 1250 (Harman J).

216 S 263; s 268(2)(e) for Scotland.

217 ibid. Paul (n 38) largely overlooks s 263(3)(e), possibly because of its discretionary character.

include the shareholders' meeting, yet this interpretation would only produce confusion and would call the importance of this subsection to question, as the criteria of ratification, ratifiability and the views of disinterested members have a similar effect.[218] Whatever the case may eventually prove to be before courts, this criterion should be understood as the only one among the discretionary factors listed in CA 2006 section 263(3), demanding courts to consider the board's views on litigation.

In fact, the UK CA 2006 adopts a different approach compared to its continental counterparts. As already explained regarding ratification, focus has traditionally been given to wrongdoer control. Where this is the case, the board cannot be expected to commence litigation with the intention of achieving an order against it, nor can it lawfully be insulated by manipulating the shareholders' resolution via associated votes.[219] However, this is not the only way for the wrongdoers to escape liability. Another strategy would be to make use of their capacity to initiate litigation in order to 'torpedo' (to borrow a term from private international law jargon) any potential derivative claim against them. Hence, pending proceedings would be carried out by the claimants with a view to acquit the defendants. Such abuse of procedure is considered by the company law statute, by enabling individual shareholders to take over proceedings initiated by the company in an abusive/negligent manner.[220] According to CA 2006 section 262(2):

A member of the company may apply to the court for permission (in Northern Ireland, leave) to continue the claim as a derivative claim on the ground that

a) the manner in which the company commenced or continued the claim amounts to an abuse of the process of the court,
b) the company has failed to prosecute the claim diligently, and
c) it is appropriate for the member to continue the claim as a derivative claim.

This is remarkably different to the continental rules and particularly the German provisions on derivative actions. Conceptually, the British sections can be characterised as a quasi-reversal of the demand rule and can be viewed as contrary to

218 David Kershaw, 'The Rule in Foss v Harbottle is Dead; Long Live the Rule in Foss v Harbottle' (2015) 3 JBL 274, 288–290.

219 The General Meeting may be unable to pursue a claim against (a certain) director(s) even when shareholders related to the complained misfeasance are prohibited to vote, leaving the derivative action as virtually the only viable solution to the impasse. This became all the more apparent in *Shandong Offshore Investment (HK) Co Ltd v Andresen* [2018] EWHC 2874 (Ch); [2018] 10 WLUK 245, where the company's shareholder agreement provided that it could not commence litigation without the other shareholder's (pa company controlled by the defendant) consent. The court, granting permission to proceed, considered, inter alia, the company's inability to have brought the claim in its own right.

220 CA 2006 s 262. See Zouridakis (n 2) 278.

and incompatible with the German approach on the principle of subsidiarity.[221] Indeed, there is no such provision in the German statute. However, considered in conjunction with the company's right to usurp pending litigation, the absence of such provisions can be seen as running contrary to the very essence of derivative actions, as it would increase the prospect of success for directors 'strategically' bringing an action in order to bar aggrieved shareholders from pursuing the corporate claims diligently. The only proviso against such abuse is the last sentence of *Aktiengesetz* section 148 paragraph 3, providing that shareholders who initiated proceedings shall be summoned to join if the company assumes action, as non-parties. However, joining the proceedings as such has little practical importance, as the claim initially brought is extinguished and shareholders' participation in the assertion of the claim is curtailed.

Similar conclusions are reached by examination of the Greek provision on corporate actions. There is nothing to prevent the incumbent administration and the acquiescent majority from blocking subsequent proceedings by bringing the action first or appointing the special representatives of their preference in order to frustrate a potential shareholders' petition.[222] Adding to this problem of accountability is the fact that the board is afforded ample time to 'torpedo' the shareholders' petition.

It is even ambiguous as to whether and how the special representatives could be substituted/replaced (by shareholders' petition) in cases where they do not perform their task diligently. In the absence of any express reference to the matter by Law 4548/2018 article 105, recourse to Civil Procedure Code article 786 (the procedural complement of Greek Civil Code article 69 on appointment and removal of interim administration) may provide such possibility should there be a 'good cause'. However, the procedure under article 105 is mandatory law, prescribing its particular requirements and restrictions regarding the appointment of special representatives by court. Therefore, strict interpretation of the applicable law would subject the replacement of special representatives that are negligent, culpable or in conflict of interests to all the procedural hurdles imposed to minorities under Law 4548/2018 article 105.[223] Adding to the complexity is the fact that the Civil Procedure rules address individual claimants ('anyone' having legal interest), in contrast to the shareholder 'minorities' prescribed by Law 4548/2018.[224] This is a confusing state of affairs, as, if the Civil Procedure Code's approach is applied by analogy, the objectives pursued by the quorum requirement in article 105 would be frustrated.[225] The new law also

221 CA 2006 ss 262, 267.

222 As happened in Patrai Court of Appeal 266/2011, NOMOS Databank, Armenopoulos 2013 293; see also Livada (n 12) 1019. Recall that a restriction to voting equivalent to the UK rule on 'disinterested votes' is not applicable to Greek company law.

223 cf the German approach under AktG s147; Hüffer (n 46) 862.

224 Livada (n 12) 1022–1023.

225 Concurring and proposing a teleological contraction of GrCivPrC art 786 is Doris (n 208) 884.

introduced the (discretionary) power of the appointed representative to communicate to the board, prior to filing a suit, that (s)he concluded that no liability appears to exist. In this case, the board of directors has the responsibility to notify the applicant minority accordingly, the latter being able to return with a new petition. This proviso might turn out to be problematic, if case law develops in a way demanding such communication to take place in order for a special representative to be substituted/replaced by shareholders' petition. The very real possibility that the board does not abide by their obligation to inform would aggravate this problem.

3.4 On accumulation of information and the need thereof

For litigation to be initiated and to have any prospect of success, the availability of information related to the management of corporate affairs is critical. The adequacy of the solutions provided by law has been repeatedly questioned in all three examined jurisdictions[226] and concerns have been expressed by the judiciary in recent decisions.[227]

A common point between the two selected continental European jurisdictions is that detailed inspection of corporate affairs is left for shareholder-appointed special auditors (*Sonderprüfer*). This mechanism has merits and demerits. For one, auditors are empowered to conduct thorough investigations relevant to the management of the company.[228] Except for contemporaneous/continuous ownership, the prerequisites for such an appointment by and large conform to those for legal standing and admissibility in a derivative action: facts have to raise suspicion for gross violation of law and a minority of at least 1% or 100,000 euros of registered capital can only apply.[229] In fact, the alignment of section 142 with section 148 was intentional, as it was the legislator's aim to facilitate fact-finding for derivative actions through this mechanism.[230] Greece's position is similar. Law 4548/2018 article 143 confers the right to the 'small' minority of 5% of registered share capital to ask for the appointment of special auditors, should there be suspicion of a breach/violation of the law, a General Meeting's resolution or the corporate by-laws. The rather restrictive approach regarding the scope of (suspected) misfeasance substantiating cause of action, compared to

226 Indicatively: Baum and Puchniak (n 37) 43–46; Reisberg, 'Shadows' (n 91) 234, regarding the UK and the US; Paul (n 38) 92–96, regarding UK and Germany; Mikroulea (n 84) 281, regarding Greece.

227 *Franbar v Patel* [2008] EWHC 1534 (Ch); [2008] BCC 885 [15] [22] (Trower QC).

228 AktG s 142(1).

229 See OLG Köln Beschl. v. 22.02.2010, Az. – 18 W 1/10, where it was held (in a decision where s 148 was considered) that 'suspicion in the meaning of § 142 para 2 AktG is only given if actual circumstances exist that make bad faith or gross violation seem not only possible, but probable' (at 28).

230 ibid, referring (at 26) to BR-Drs. 3/05, 44; see also Hüffer (n 46) 847.

that of articles 102–105, is mitigated by the fact that a larger minority (20%) may apply for a special audit when a breach of the duty of care and skill is suspected.[231] It is to be noted that petitions under both Greek and German provisions are adjudicated under the procedural rules on non-contentious jurisdiction.[232] The upshot is that in some respects, such as the requisite quorum, the German provisions are more permissive and in other respects the Greek provisions take the lead, such as the scope of suspected misfeasance covered. What really makes the difference is the matter of costs, as the default Greek rule is that they are borne by the applicant (including the remuneration of the auditors), whilst in Germany indemnification by the company can only be refused to applicants by the court in exceptional circumstances.[233]

Under the UK statute, the power to appoint special auditors rests primarily with the Secretary of State.[234] Therefore, a comparative disadvantage might be that shareholders, by virtue of their capacity as members, are afforded limited access to corporate information. However, within the ambit of the information available in the context of the proceedings is that, apart from the fact that section 261 subsection 3 provides the court with the power to order the company to provide evidence, shareholders have access to corporate documentation free from any cost, ranging from the annual accounts to the directors' and auditors' reports.[235] Accordingly, before bringing the claim, shareholders may resort to the provisions in CA 2006 to inform themselves about whether a cause of action exists and substantiate their prima facie case and, following the filing of the claim, courts are enabled to make an ad hoc discovery order.[236] In any case, shareholders can obtain an investigation order via their capacity as claimants, by virtue of the Civil Procedure Rules.[237] This pre-trial form of discovery attempts to bring litigation closer to American standards.[238]

Once again, the British approach stands as an outlier. Systematically, inspection of the corporate affairs is therein provided for the claimant in the capacity of plaintiff and individual shareholder, rather than that of a minority. From this viewpoint, British law seems to be less restrictive as to who obtains information of the corporate affairs, as the continental jurisdictions – conforming to the general considerations on derivative and corporate actions – follow a minority approach. This adds to the problem of collective action, as it necessitates that

231 Law 4548/2018 art 143 (3).
232 FamFG for Germany; Greek CivPrC arts 739f.
233 See also Paul (n 38) 155.
234 Similar state supervision is provided by Greek law, yet limited to the 'legality check' audit. See Law 4548/2018 art 143 (2).
235 CA 2006 ss 146, 431, 432, 1145; cf the approach under Greek law, as succinctly described by Mikroulea (n 78) 281, whereby shareholders have to indicate the specific page and even paragraph of the documentation to which access is requested.
236 Reisberg, 'Shadows' (n 91) 234.
237 CPR 31.16.
238 See Baum and Puchniak (n 37) 46.

shareholders satisfy the requisite quorum for two proceedings; that of the special audit and that of the derivative claim.

3.5 Restrictions regarding the claimant's discretion following success in the admission stage

If the shareholder-petitioner/claimant succeeds in the admission stage, the 'main' proceedings on the substantive action are by principle similar to proceedings between the company and the defendant wrongdoers in all three jurisdictions, given the representative nature of this form of shareholder-initiated litigation.[239] For the very same reason though, some intricacies exist.

In Germany, in a highly controversial manner, it is the company rather than the court who maintains control over the proceedings. The successful applicant under *Aktiengesetz* section 148(1) and (2) may bring a claim only if three months lapsed after the decision on the application became res judicata and is subject to the burden to request that the company brings an action for a second time (second 'demand'). The company's substitution right can be invoked any time.[240] As explained in Section 3.3, this is a disincentive for shareholders to enforce the company's claims, as it raises the possibility that all their efforts go back to ground zero. Their participation to the proceedings is, in such a case, limited to that of intervenor (*streitgenössischer Nebeninterventiente*), who may support the claimant corporation. The company, unless it substitutes the shareholder-claimant, in the way discussed above, is also called to join the proceedings in a similar capacity, given that under German Civil Procedure Law it cannot be a (nominal) defendant or claimant.[241]

Under Greek law, shareholders do not participate in the trial in their own name, by means of intervention or otherwise.[242] Proceedings are brought in the name of the company: the only difference with ordinary litigation on such issues lies in the representation of the corporate entity by the special representative(s), instead of the board or persons to whom this power is delegated. This difference matters, as their appointment took effect on the initiative of the minority shareholders. Consequently, if the minority waives their right to initiate a company's action, the special representatives lose their powers and proceedings are discontinued. Furthermore, settlement or waiver of the dispute is not entirely in the special representatives' hands, as it is the company's rights which are enforced: Law 4548/2018 article 102 paragraph 7 applies, as explained above (Section 3.3). Unless waiver or settlement of the company's claim takes place in the ways

239 It has to be noted that no particular guidance exists on the matter in German case law.

240 AktG s 148(3), (4).

241 Hüffer (n 46) 868.

242 cf the opinion in German academia regarding the pre-KonTraG s147 of AktG, on the ability of individual shareholders to intervene in certain circumstances (Hans Wilhelmi and Sylvester Wilhelmi, *Godin/Wilhelmi Aktiengesetz Kommentar*, vol. 1 (Walter de Gruyter 1967) 807.

prescribed by the latter article, the company retains full claim for the wrongs suffered, at least until a decision is reached at first instance. Aside from the tenets of article 102, ordinary rules of contract and procedural law apply as to the validity of settlements between the company and defendant directors.[243]

Given that in most jurisdictions a decision on the merits becomes res judicata between, on the one hand, the company and the shareholders and, on the other hand, the defendants,[244] termination of derivative proceedings by means of settlement raises significant issues and deserves attention. By itself, such a practice does not cause particular concern and speedy settlement of disputes is often preferable to lengthy court procedures. Yet, due to the very nature of the derivative action as a form of representative litigation, the risk emerges – for the company and the shareholders as a whole – that the derivative litigant reaches a settlement which is not in the best interests of the company, yet is binding for the latter. From a certain viewpoint, such practice would run contrary to the objectives of the derivative action as a mechanism of addressing agency problems – as an agency conflict would emerge between the derivative claimant and other shareholders/stakeholders – and would reduce their social value. American empirical studies confirm that this scenario is far from hypothetical.[245]

The studied jurisdictions, via ad hoc functionally equivalent and functionally alternative rules, attempt to minimise such risk, a risk already lowered in the UK and Germany, due to the determination needed by the prospective claimants to go through the filters of the respective admissions stages. The UK Companies Act considers settlement of claims mainly within the ambit of the permission stage, in section 261(4)(a), which pronounces that the court may 'give permission … to continue the claim on such terms as it thinks fit'.[246] Read in conjunction with CPR 19.9F, it follows that permission to continue proceedings may be on such terms, that further permission of the court is necessary to discontinue or settle the claim. According to this approach, review by the court of the conformity a settlement might have with the company's interests depends upon a decision at an early stage of the derivative claim and only on a case-by-case basis. The practical use of both provisions is doubtful, as one might not expect a court to grant permission to continue the claim at all if there are such doubts regarding the claimants' good faith[247] and pursuit of the company's interests[248] throughout the conduct of proceedings, as to result - at an early stage- in an order subjecting to the court's review the parties' discretion to discontinue or

243 C Calavros, *Civil Procedure-General Part* (2nd edn, Sakkoulas 2006) 444.

244 See Greek CivProC 329; German AktG s 148(5). This is the reason why the company is a defendant under UK derivative claims. See Joffe et al. (n 121) 43.

245 R Romano, 'The Shareholder Suit: Litigation without Foundation' (1991) 7 JL Econ & Org 61. European literature is lacking such studies on the topic of derivative litigation, probably due to lack of available data.

246 See Joffe et al. (n 121) 60; Paul (n 38) 109.

247 CA 2006 s 263(3).

248 CA 2006 ss 263(2)(a), 263(3)(b).

settle the claim. It comes as no surprise, therefore, that no such order has yet been made.

The other derivative action within the CA 2006 takes a different stance. Section 371(5) reserves to courts the power to permit or not a settlement (or discontinuation) of the claim in all cases and at any stage of the proceedings. This section reflects the recommendations of the Law Commission regarding the Part 11 derivative claim, as well as assimilating the wording of other jurisdictions' statutes.[249] It remains to be seen, with the growth of the number of cases that reach conclusion, whether the decision of the legislature not to follow the Law Commission with regard to Part 11 of CA 2006 proves to be regretful; supposing, of course, that the terms of the settlements are disclosed.

The German derivative action does not impose any form of judicial control upon discontinuation or settlement of the claim, but instead follows a 'name and shame' strategy in its effort to discourage hasty and unfair settlements. Section 149 was inserted into the *Aktiengesetz* by the UMAG to that effect, mandating public disclosure of both the application to pursue a claim derivatively and any agreement that brings proceedings to a close. The section goes further to demand that any agreement connected with the termination of proceedings is disclosed in the 'company's designated journals', as a condition for it to become binding. The rationale behind this rule is that, apart from notifying any third party with an interest in the proceedings of the pending or concluded litigation, public disclosure in the popular media foregrounds the names and strategies of predatory shareholders.[250] The German approach has the merit of providing a good amount of legal certainty and predictability.[251]

The German legislature decided to restrict the provision's scope of application to public listed companies only. This choice stands to reason, but at the same time betrays the unidimensional approach of the *Aktiengesetz* in ensuring that derivative claims do not run to the detriment of the company. Indeed, the German experience shows that professional litigants have wealthy corporations as their primary prey, where the stakes of litigation are particularly high and their greenmail may yield substantial returns. From this perspective and a practical point of view, placing such an obligation to disclose information about the proceedings upon small- or medium-sized companies would be unjustified, particularly considering that another layer of costs would be added to the companies in question.

The primary conclusion is that German and UK law pay more attention to the conduct of the main proceedings, compared to the approach followed by the Greek legislator and make greater efforts to ensure that derivative litigation runs to the interests of the company as a whole – and is thus truly protective of shareholders. This distrust of the shareholder-claimant can be justified on

249 As noticed by Joffe et al. (n 121) 59.
250 Hüffer (n 46) 873.
251 Baum and Puchniak (n 37) 60.

the presumption that he will place his individual interests over the company's, even though those sets of interests may not necessarily coincide. However, as explained, the institution of special representatives is not free of the risk of moral hazard either. Coupled with the convoluted procedure to replace incumbent special representatives, this is a problematic state of affairs. Mitigating the agency problem between the special representatives and the company is their liability for their actions and omissions in discharging their task of litigating, now (controversially) pronounced in the reformed Code of Civil Procedure.[252] Yet again, the only person capable of enforcing this liability is the company. This is frustrating for minority shareholders, as they need to initiate a separate claim to hold special representatives accountable, particularly in cases where the latter 'coordinate' with the interests of the wrongdoers. A further conclusion is that, for the time being, the UK provisions ostensibly take into account the complexity of derivative proceedings in the least controversial way, entrusting their supervision on courts and allowing them a fair amount of discretion in undertaking this task.

3.6 Conclusions

The preceding analysis identified several drawbacks to the Greek company's action. The problem with it lies partly in the institution of special representatives, as they are situated beyond the reach of the minority shareholders who initiated the procedure. They lack the incentives of procuring corporate interests with utmost diligence, being complete outsiders. Even worse, they themselves might be reproachable by the wrongdoers. But even when the court (in exercising its discretionary powers under Greek law) eventually appoints the petitioner shareholder(s) or their designated persons as special representative(s),[253] the further requirement that the latter's mandate is subject to the maintenance of the petitioners' shareholding up to the level required by law also renders the provision unappealing to shareholders and impractical.[254] From the outset, the very characteristic that distinguishes the company's action from derivative actions accounts for the ineffectiveness of the remedy.

The analysis showed that the very design of the company's action is controversial and inoperative in many respects. Availability of the remedy is severely restricted and is subject to a number of arbitrary conditions, as is the petitioners' ownership of their shares for six months preceding the filing of the petition. Furthermore, its narrow scope creates a sizeable leeway for wrongdoers to evade accountability. For instance, 'defrauding' a subsidiary company is a practice not considered by Law 4548/2018 article 103, nor is

252 Art 786 (4).

253 This was the case in Athens Single-Member Court of First Instance 4421/1970, EEmpD 1971 42 (with commentary by N Rokas (at 114)).

254 Concurring: Perakis, 'The Greek and International' (n 17) 3679, 3681.

wrongdoers' 'torpedoing' of the company's claim by initiating proceedings first. The law does little to facilitate the initiation of meritorious corporate claims, even when shareholders meet the demanding criteria of articles 104–105, as their access to information relevant to the wrongdoing is restricted in the first place. Ostensibly, the silver lining in the company's action apparatus is the matter of costs, which are assumed throughout the proceedings by the company. On a careful reading though, this approach may run to the detriment of the company's interests, when the 5% minority invokes article 104 in a frivolous or vexatious manner.

Overall, the comparative analysis illustrates that the Greek legal framework for shareholder litigation on behalf of the company, as encapsulated in the company's action, suffers – both as a whole and (especially) regarding most of its particular elements – from a comparative disadvantage in terms of shareholders' access to justice and protection of their proprietary interests. The question arises why did not Greece follow the example of its mother jurisdiction which, despite operating for a number of decades under the corporate action regime,[255] moved on more than a decade ago to introduce its statutory derivative action in an effort to enhance shareholder protection and the enforcement of directors' duties.[256]

The reluctance of the Greek lawmaker to render the law on public limited companies more permissive and protective of shareholders in this respect can be explained by the influence of block-holders (as a pressure group) and legislative status quo bias, resulting in the proliferation of a path-dependent trajectory. Officially, the Greek committee responsible for the reform of corporate law in 2007 opined that the introduction of 'any form of Derivative Action' would constitute an 'abrupt' and 'spectacular' amendment of the relevant law, pointing to a potential reluctance on the part of the directors to assume office, at least in the short term.[257] Twelve years and another reform later, not much has changed. Certainly, the new law on public limited companies did not revamp the law on shareholders enforcement of corporate claims. Despite the fact that numerous jurisdictions – both within Europe and overseas – either introduced or amended provisions on derivative actions in the past 15 years, the Greek legislature refrained, once more, from taking such a step. The preamble to Law 4548/2018 offers no explanation for opting to 'improve' and rationalise the long-existing company's action instead of enabling shareholders to sue derivatively. However, it is safe to assume that this alternative was considered at some

255 See Karsten Schmidt, 'Verfolgungspflichten, Verfolgungsrechte und Aktionärsklagen: Ist die Quadratur des Zirkels näher gerückt?Gedanken zur Reform der §§ 147–149 AktG vor dem Hintergrund der Juristentagsdiskussion des Jahres 2000' (2005) NZG 796: 'The dissatisfaction with AktG s147 accompanied the already 40-year old history of the 1965 Aktiengesetz'.

256 Janet Dine and Marios Koutsias, *The Nature of Corporate Governance* (2013) 286.

257 Livada (n 11) 1018.

point in the legislative process. The expert committee was led by a highly reputable academic who, like other members of the committee, had more than once advocated in favour of the remedy in his academic writings.[258] It can be adduced from those publications that the primary reason behind the reluctance to effectuate this legal transplant was, once again, the risk of abuse this remedy could entail: that is, the floodgates of litigation opening wide, with shareholders invoking their right (to sue on behalf of the company) frivolously or vexatiously. It is to be noted here that, as will be further analysed below in Chapter 4, most minority shareholder remedies under Law 4548/2018 are granted to qualified minorities, for the very same reason.[259] This distrust of 'small minorities' can also be identified in the fact that the reduction of the requisite qualified minority percentage per Law 4548/2018 (as compared to Law 2190/1920) was accompanied by additional requirements and conditions being set for a 'company's action' to proceed.

In view of the fact that derivative actions – on their own, as a concept – do not necessarily open wide the floodgates of litigation, as was made clear herein, this concern seems exaggerated, to say the least.

The laconic 'model' derivative action as per the EMCA was not followed by the Greek legislature in the latest reform and possibly rightly so. Despite the fact that its section 11.39 looks, prima facie, quite permissive as regards legal standing by allowing individual shareholders to sue, on a closer reading, it becomes clear that its availability is somewhat restricted. The condition it sets for an action to be brought, that dissent was expressed by a minority in a General Meeting on the topic of discharge of the company's directors, not only runs against the expediency of enforcing liability but also indirectly introduces high (10%) qualified minority thresholds to the mechanics of the remedy. Furthermore, the provision does little to incentivise shareholders to pursue corporate claims, as it only allows reimbursement of their litigation costs in the event that the claim is successful. Other than that, the analysis showed that the proviso does nothing to discourage frivolous and vexatious litigation: no judicial oversight or other safeguards are in place.

As for the comparison between the two jurisdictions conferring genuine derivative claims, it is not surprising to a lawyer familiar with common law that the UK Companies Act attempts to strike a balance between legal certainty and judicial flexibility. Legal certainty was indeed a matter considered by the reform committees.[260] However, this study confirms that some of the common law pathogens survived the advent of the statutory procedure, possibly 'swinging the

258 See Perakis, 'The Greek and International' (n 17).

259 Another reason could be that the adaptation of the remedy in Germany, a jurisdiction highly influential to Greece, was not an absolute success. Note that, conversely, in the early years following the German reform, several Greek academics advocated in favour of a proviso similar to that of UMAG being introduced to law 2190/1920.

260 Law Commission, *Shareholder Remedies* (Law Commission No 246, 1997), paras 6.73, 6.83, 6.85, 29.

pendulum' in the wrong direction.[261] The comparative analysis makes clear that the flexibility introduced by the 2006 statute did not completely eschew the complexity inherent in common law derivative actions, contrary to the clarity exhibited by the German provisions. Despite both statutes' provision for a judicial evaluative judgment to take place at the preliminary stage, only the UK statute provides a 'non-exhaustive' roadmap to the courts regarding what should be considered in allowing a petition to proceed. Undoubtedly, many of these factors are and will be taken into account by the German judiciary in the context of ascertaining whether the action serves the interests of the company.[262] However, the English judiciary has for long granted much weight on these considerations and thus, their application under the statutory provision will alone determine the levels of predictability and legal certainty offered by CA 2006 Part 11, as case law accumulates.

What can be said for the German derivative action is that, in fear that companies would be 'killed by kindness', eventually the provision itself was killed in its cradle. Up to now, the application of the rule in courts has largely been an uncharted area: relevant case law is very scarce. What is more, a survey based on statements of the chairs of the commercial courts (the courts having jurisdiction to hear derivative claims) on the application of section 148 illustrated that, in the very few cases judged on such grounds, no applicant was successful.[263] Therefore, what led to such an aversion from the part of shareholders to make use of this enforcement mechanism cannot be easily identified, as there is no sufficient evidence in judicial practice. At first glance, it could be the minority quorum requirement; however, much of the recent litigation in the UK was brought by shareholders owning a percentage of registered share capital well beyond that of 1%.[264] What also might have deterred shareholders is the restricted scope of misfeasance covered. It could also well be the double demand rule, as shareholders-claimants might find it frustrating that the company may assume litigation at will. Most likely, absence of litigation can best be understood by all the above explanations combined: whatever the case might be, German derivative actions have been of much less use than their (almost contemporaneous) British statutory counterparts. Considering that even British litigants have been so far rather parsimonious in the use of Part 11, it can be

261 Concurring: Paul (n 38) 115.

262 ibid 100, exemplifies low-value claims as a matter to be taken into account when examining a derivative action pursuant to s 148(1)(4). Such consideration can well fall under the ambit of CA 2006 s 263(3)(b): i.e. 'the importance' to be attributed to claims by a person acting under the duty of s 172.

263 The regional courts of Cologne, Berlin and Munich reported one case each. In all occasions petitions were dismissed. See Martin Peltzer, 'Das Zulassungsverfahren nach § 148 AktG wird von der Praxis nicht angenommen! Warum? Was nun?' in Ulrich Burgard, Walther Hadding, Peter O. Mülbert, Michael Nietsch and Reinhard Welter (eds), *Festschrift für Uwe H: Schneider zum 70. Geburtstag* (Otto Schmidt 2011) 955.

264 Concurring: Baum and Puchniak (n 37) 88.

argued that the German provisions, albeit of less ambiguous content, by and large perform disappointingly even regarding the deterrent role derivative actions have in the context of corporate governance.

A few words must be dedicated here to the 'law and finance' and 'leximetric' studies on private enforcement mechanisms. The comparison herein illustrates their inadequacies in providing evaluative conclusions. Consider first the work of LaPorta et al.[265] In their 'anti-director' index, private enforcement of directors' duties constitutes just one of the seven variables, whereas derivative actions were meshed with oppression remedies and appraisal rights. Thereto, just the possibility of enforcing any of those rights,[266] notwithstanding the procedural hurdles and the scope of the remedy in question, would equal a score of 1; absence thereof would equal zero. The 'refined' leximetric index by Siems and Lele follows a similar yet more meticulous approach, taking into account constraints on the availability of the remedy; again rather holistically, as presence of any such constraint would lower the score.[267] However, as already explained, a change on the screening mechanisms purportedly makes a significant impact on the availability and efficacy of the rules in question; not all constraints should rank equal. In general, none of these studies duly considered the scope of the remedies and factors important to their efficacy, such as rules on costs and accumulation of evidence available, to their full extent; astoundingly, none of them considered multiple derivative actions. The paradox then arises that, in this regard, the State of Delaware might score similarly to, say, Germany in leximetric indices.[268] Yet, in the former, this form of litigation is a major tool for shareholder activism and constitutes an economy in its own right, whilst in the latter, ten years after the introduction of *Aktiengesetz* section 148, the relevant case law is developing very slowly, if at all. Evidently, a comparison based on leximetric methodology might not always furnish an accurate picture of the protection afforded by the legal systems in question and might not capture the interaction among different legal rules. This observation is not dismissive of the relevant scholarship in its entirety; rather, it warns for a more detailed construction of the models and careful reading of the respective results by the academic readership.

265 'Law and Finance' (1998) 106 Journal of Political Economy 1113.

266 Unless it is allocated only to minorities representing more than 10% of share capital.

267 Priya P Lele and Mathias M Siems, 'Shareholder Protection: A Leximetric Approach' (2007) 7 JCLS 17.

268 As happens should we revise the LaPorta et al. index. See Sophie Cools, 'The Real Difference in Corporate Law between the United States and Continental Europe: Distribution of Powers' (2005) 30 Del J Corp L 697. Similarly regarding Lele and Siems (n 267).

4 The Greek framework for shareholder protection in a comparative context and the (in)existence of alternatives to derivative actions

4.1 Introduction

A scholarly comparative analysis on derivative actions should not stop at the comparison of provisions on shareholder litigation on behalf of the company, before reaching the conclusion that reform is necessary. The broader context of shareholder protection has also to be taken into account for two main reasons. First, to examine whether other forms of shareholder protection *do or may substitute* for derivative actions in their functions and purpose within the legal framework, thus filling in the lacuna left by the ineffectiveness of the company's action. The reason for doing so is that the necessity for an effective framework of shareholder derivative litigation depends on the absence of alternative means for shareholders to protect their interests from wrongs which the derivative action is designed to remedy. Second, it is important to provide a better picture of the overall level of shareholder protection provided by national law in order to understand the magnitude of the improvement in those levels a reform of shareholder remedies against maladministration may effect.

Hence, this Chapter comparatively examines shareholder rights and remedies which seemingly overlap with the derivative action in their function. Accordingly, the analysis considers not only the existing Greek framework but also foreign rules and practices which could be transplanted to or adopted by Greek law and corporate practice, evaluating at the same time whether such transplants would render the introduction of the derivative action redundant. The examination of British and German law not only avails a broader menu of alternatives to be considered but also provides an assessment of the overall level of shareholder protection under Greek law in relation with its foreign counterparts.

The Chapter analyses the core mechanisms of shareholder protection that are considered in the literature to have the potential to address the same problems as derivative actions. Accordingly, it first examines whether private contracting in a corporate context suffices as an alternative to derivative actions. It then looks into direct shareholder claims and whether they do or can fill the void left due to the inadequacy of the corporate action in protecting shareholders and disciplining management. Subsequently, it considers whether 'general clauses'[1] against oppressive or unfair treatment and shareholder suits against the validity of General Meeting resolutions constitute viable alternatives to derivative litigation. Furthermore, it is demonstrated that the right to exit the company can neither substitute for derivative actions as a means of shareholder protection, nor does it constitute a viable option for shareholders in Greek listed corporations, let alone non-listed companies. The Chapter continues with an assessment of the recent reforms of the Greek framework on shareholder protection, which focused mainly on rights connected with the General Meeting. It is illustrated that, despite ironing out some comparative disadvantages, the post-2007 amendments to the Greek statute on public limited companies reflect EU initiatives to a respectable extent. Section 4.8 summarises and concludes.

4.2 Contractual freedom as a means of shareholder protection[2]

It has been suggested that hard law rules and rights protecting (minority) shareholders are either of trivial importance or even redundant.[3] The argument goes that private initiative is not only sufficient but may even be more effective than hard law provisions in ensuring that corporate affairs are carried out to the benefit of all involved in the company.[4] This suggestion might call into question the very fabric of the derivative action as a means to address agency problems.

Nevertheless, unlike the UK, continental law jurisdictions – including Germany and Greece – restrict in their laws on public limited companies the ability of shareholders to 'write their own tickets'.[5] Focusing primarily on the most fundamental and enduring contractual arrangement within the corporation, its corporate constitution,[6] this Section investigates the implications of the Greek

1 This term, though not used by common law jurisdictions, is employed by A Spyridonos, *Minority Rights in the Company Limited by Shares* (Nomiki Bibliothiki2001), in reference to the unfair prejudice remedy

2 An expanded version of this section, titled 'Contractual Freedom and the Corporate Constitution; A Study on where Greek Law Stands in a Comparative Context and the Way Forward', appeared in David A Frenkel (ed), *Selected Issues in Public Private Law* (Athens Institute for Education and Research 2015) 69.

3 Bernard S Black, 'Is Corporate Law Trivial? A Political and Economic Analysis' (1989–1990) 84 Nw UL Rev 542.

4 ibid.

5 Frank H Easterbrook and Daniel R Fischel, 'The Corporate Contract' (1989) 89 Colum L Rev 1416, 1417.

6 Be that constitutional document the memorandum of association, the articles of association of CA 2006, the *Satzung* of AktG, or any akin document. See Andreas Cahn and David C Donald, *Comparative Company Law: Text and Cases on the Laws Governing Corporations in Germany, the UK and the USA* (CUP 2010) 261. Even though the only statute to expressly recognise the contractual nature of the corporate constitution is the UK CA 2006 s 33(1), the contractual nature of corporate by-laws is recognised under Greek and German law, despite the respective statutes being silent. Regarding Greek law, see M Varela in Evanghelos Perakis (ed), *Sociétés Anonyme's Law* (2nd edn, Sakkoulas 2010) 112ff; Rodopi Multi-Member Court

approach to shareholders' contractual freedom regarding shareholder protection, as well as considering whether a move towards a more enabling approach would render the need for a better framework on the enforcement of corporate claims less imperative.

Under English law and throughout its long historical course, the corporate constitution has been considered of paramount importance in providing shareholders with rights and protection, contractual in their nature.[7] Nowadays the contractual nature of the rights conferred by the articles of association is reflected in the UK CA 2006 section 33 subsection 1.[8] This approach is highlighted in early decisions such as *Borland's Trustee v Steel Brothers & Co Ltd*.[9] According to Farwell's J definition of (rights attached to) shares, 'a share is … an interest measured by a sum of money and made up of various rights contained in the contract, including the right to a sum of money of a more or less amount'.[10]

Despite the numerous legislative changes since *Borland's*, a paradigm shift has not yet materialised. Shareholders and founders of companies maintain the broad discretion to decide how they are going to conduct their business.[11] This freedom is only limited by what is regulated by hard law: whatever is not prohibited is permitted.[12] Party autonomy remains thus sacrosanct in Britain. As a starting point, parties are free to reach the agreement that suits their interests best and this agreement might only be constrained by the law.

Germany provides a contrasting case.[13] The starting point in formulating the German articles of association (*Satzung*) is the (statutory) law, which might in

of First Instance 29/1995 EEmpD 1997 722. Regarding German law, see Uwe Hüffer, *Aktiengesetz* (10th edn, CH Beck 2012) 105, stating that the nature of the by-laws is: 'sui generis, which can be considered as a debt contract and organization constitution'.

7 Section 12 CA 1862. See also *Wood v. Odessa Waterworks* [1889] 42 Ch D 636, 642 [Stirling J]: 'The articles of association constitute a contract not merely between the shareholders and the company, but between each individual shareholder and every other.' Its wording is not different from the preceding Joint Stock Companies Act 1856. For further discussion, see Richard C Nolan, 'Shareholder Rights in Britain' (2006) 7 EBOR 549, 550.

8 'The provisions of a company's constitution bind the company and its members to the same extent as if there were covenants on the part of the company and of each member to observe those provisions.'

9 [1901] 1 Ch 279.

10 ibid. 288.

11 See Nolan, 'Shareholder Rights' (n 7) 554. See also *Harben v. Phillips*, (1883) 23 ChD 14 [35]–[36] (Bowen LJ): 'When persons agree to act together in the conduct of a business, the way in which that business is to be carried on must depend in each case on the contract, express or implied, which exists between them as to the way of carrying it on.'

12 Len Sealy and Sarah Worthington, *Cases and Materials in Company Law* (9th edn, OUP 2010) 178; Paul Davies and Sarah Worthington, *Gower & Davies Principles of Modern Company Law* (9th edn, Sweet & Maxwell 2012) 64.

13 See Marcus Lutter and Herbert Wiedemann, *Gestaltungsfreiheit im Gesellschaftsrecht: Deutschland, Europa und USA: 11. ZGR-Symposion '25 Jahre ZGR'* (Walter de Gruyter 1998) 123–148, 187–215.

a few instances permit a level of party autonomy.[14] More specifically, German law on public limited companies is rigid: the vast majority of the provisions included in the *Aktiengesetz* are mandatory, leaving very little room for entrepreneurs to regulate corporate affairs themselves.[15] For this reason, the underlying principle of 'stringent law' (*Prinzip der Satzungstrenge*) is viewed by German scholars as one of the disadvantages the German public limited company has against its limited liability company counterpart.[16] The principle is said to be founded on the rationale of protecting unsuspicious investors from exploitative contractual arrangements.[17] However it appears that, to a great extent, the inflexibility of the provisions encapsulated in the *Aktiengesetz* fails to mirror the corporate reality in Germany. Many of the public limited companies are small and medium-sized businesses, more resembling the corporate model that the limited liability company (GmbH) is designed for, than the ideal corporate form of a big (public) capital company. In fact, the abolishment of the principle was proposed in the 67th German Jurists Forum in Erfurt in September 2008.[18] Unsurprisingly, the motion met with strong opposition. Participants – most notably practitioners – rejected the idea outright as being contrary to a well-established legal tradition and practice, by an almost unanimous consent.[19] Consequently, fundamental differences have persisted between the UK and Germany for more than a century, falsifying Hansmann and Kraakman's predicted convergence and vindicating the proliferation of a path dependent trajectory.[20]

Regarding Greece, there are indications that the trend is to move towards an intermediate stance between these two approaches: Greek law is steadily moving away from the German standards of contractual freedom. The reform of the law on public limited companies by enactment of Law 3604/07[21] introduced a broader system of optional ('opt-in' and 'opt-out') rules than the pre-existing ones[22] scattered across the body of Law 2190/1920. Working to the same,

14 As observed by Evanghelos Perakis, *The New Law of the Société Anonyme* (Nomiki Bibliothiki 2007) 5. Contrary to what applies to common law jurisdictions (such as the law of Delaware, where 'everything is permitted, unless expressly prohibited'), in continental law jurisdictions 'everything that is not permitted is prohibited'.

15 AktG s 23(5) sentence 2: 'the Constitution can derogate from the rules of this statute only when it is so expressly permitted'. The similarity with the Greek law on the matter is also identified by Perakis, *The New Law* (n 14) 4, referring to GCC art 3.

16 Martin Schulz and Oliver Wasmeier, *The Law of Business Organisations* (Springer 2010) 40.

17 See also Gerhard Wirth, Michael Arnold and Ralf Morshäuser, *Corporate Law in Germany*, tr Mark Greene (2nd edn, CH Beck 2010) 67.

18 It is doubtful if the problem can be addressed by 'more or less relaxing ... the principle' (Hüffer (n 6) 115).

19 For further discussion on the minutes of the 67th forum, see Jessica Schmidt, 'Reforms in German Stock Corporation Law: The 67th German Jurists Forum' (2008) 9 EBOR 637, 638–656.

20 Henry Hansmann and Reinier Kraakman, 'The End of History for Corporate Law' (2001) 89 Geo LJ 439.

21 FEK 189/A'/8.8.2007.

22 Vassileios Antonopoulos, *Law of Societes Anonymes and Limited Liability Companies* (Sakkoulas 2011) 41.

enabling effect is Law 2190/1920 article 2 paragraph 1a (inserted by virtue of the 2007 amendment), which prescribes that, unless a derogation from the default statutory provisions is instituted, the corporate constitution does not have 'to include provisions that merely constitute repetition of the legal provisions in force' in order to be considered valid and therefore binding inter partes (including provisions conferring rights to shareholders).[23] This proviso is now repeated verbatim in the new law (Law 4548/2018 article 5), which further extended the scope of optional provisions within statutory company law. It appears that Greece had its own version of *Satzungstrenge*,[24] founded upon the same (underlying) principles (e.g. legal and commercial certainty) but employing different levels of strictness. The legislator recognised the alienation of the law from the commercial reality and the recent reforms produced a more enabling statute. However, the strict and typical nature of Greek law on public limited companies still leaves little room for contractual freedom, at least compared to Britain. Regarding corporate actions, for example, Law 4548/2018 article 104 permits that the corporate constitution is able to decrease freely the prescribed quorum for a minority to file a petition. However, reducing the quorum is as far as contractual freedom can get in this respect. Shareholders cannot litigate derivatively and have instead to petition for the appointment of special representatives, even in cases where quorum is (contractually) set at one share.[25]

A move towards a more enabling law on public limited companies may realise some substantial benefits for Greek companies. The most obvious one is flexibility. Flexibility is essential, especially for small and medium enterprises. Indeed, the stringency of a law designed for large corporations runs against the benefit of smaller companies that are subject to the same statute. This one-size-fits-all approach cannot be justified in a corporate environment where the majority of corporations take the form of public limited companies and the vast majority of the latter are SMEs. The reported calls in Germany for the abandonment of *Satzungsstrenge*[26] may be viewed as exaggerated, because the private limited company is the most common corporate form and successfully serves its purpose as a flexible vehicle for small and medium businesses: this is not exactly the case in Greece though. In fact, the flexibility necessary for small corporations was a driving force for the introduction of more enabling provisions in the Greek statute; renowned authors refer to the introduction of a 'small SA'[27] by virtue of the by-laws, following the 2007 reform.[28] However, the point of reference for the statute remains the ideal form of

23 Art 2 para 1a can be said to reflect the interpretation given to the law in the past. See Greek Council of State 1861/1993 DForN 1994 41; Antonopoulos (n 22) 40.

24 For a concurring view, see Nikolaos K Rokas, *Commercial Companies* (Sakkoulas 2006) 218.

25 Alexandra Mikroulea, *Scope of Corporate Managers' Duties and Liability* (Nomiki Bibliothiki 2013) 273.

26 Lutter and Wiedemann (n 13) 123–148, 187–215.

27 In German scholarship there has been a longstanding similar discussion of *kleine AG*. See Schmidt (n 19) 640.

28 Perakis, *The New Law* (n 14) 14.

the 'Big Capital Company': the 'small SA' and the flexibility inextricably connected with its existence constitute exemptions. I believe that a shift towards the UK paradigm, where the point of reference is the 'small' plc, would be a (belated) pragmatic response to the existing corporate reality.[29]

Importantly in terms of this book, a more enabling approach could have a positive impact on shareholder protection. From a shareholder's point of view, it would allow the ability to offer rights and for the respective protection to be tailored to the business in question, even beyond the (default) level offered by hard law. There is another important dimension of such flexibility: the discretion to formulate rights and duties not anticipated in the time of formation of hard law, especially when the latter largely depends on statute.[30] For instance, the European Directive on Shareholder Rights cannot be said to have resulted in a paradigm shift in the English corporate reality, as many of the elements it harmonised regarding voting in GMs were already implemented in practice by virtue of the corporate by-laws.[31] Arguably, an alert legislature may equally mitigate the deficiency entailed in an outdated statute by regularly updating it.[32] In any case, an enabling statute may capture the benefits of fostering innovation in corporate matters, including shareholder protection, by allowing parties to privately regulate issues not predicted by the legislator.

However, contractual freedom in the corporate context, be it within the ambit of the corporate constitution or shareholder agreements, suffers from a similar problem of unpredictability. Contract cannot cover every potential conflict of interests that may arise in the course of corporate business, due to the latter's long-term nature.[33] This is a reason why the law imposes open-ended standards of conduct on directors, in the form of statutory duties.[34] Derivative actions, as a means of the latter's enforcement, retain thus their importance, even in an enabling corporate law environment. Enforcement of directors' duties by means of shareholder suits may also help clarify their precise content, in a dynamic fashion. It would lead to accumulation of precedent, delimiting which conduct is permissible and which is not.[35]

29 For similar views see Christina Livada, 'Introductory Comments to Articles 18–22B' in Perakis Evanghelos (ed), *Sociétés Anonyme's Law* (3rd edn, Sakkoulas 2013) 863–879, 867.

30 Alessio M Pacces, 'Corporate Governance and the Coase's Legacy: A Reply to Henry Manne' in Alessio M Pacces (ed), *The Law and Economics of Corporate Governance: Changing Perspectives* (EE 2010) 210.

31 See Nolan for further discussion, 'Shareholder Rights' (n 7) 583.

32 For the effect that changes on default rules had on CG, see Henry Hansmann, 'Corporation and Contract' (2006) 8 ALER 1.

33 Arad Reisberg, *Derivative Actions and Corporate Governance: Theory and Operation* (OUP 2007) 53.

34 Reinier Kraakman, John Armour, Paul Davies, Luca Enriques, Henry Hansmann, Gerard Hertig, Klaus Hopt, Hideki Kanda and Edward Rock, *The Anatomy of Corporate Law: A Comparative and Functional Approach* (2nd edn, OUP 2009) 40; Reisberg (n 33) 53; John Coffee Jr, 'The Mandatory/Enabling Balance in Corporate Law: An Essay on the Judicial Role' (1989) 89 Colum L Rev 1618.

35 Reisberg (n 33) 53–54.

Furthermore, it is questionable whether an enabling approach would alone suffice to contractually protect parties whose bargaining power is meagre. In the corporate context, the majority has the decisive say in negotiating and re-negotiating the terms of corporate membership. Therefore, the importance of an enabling approach is qualified, regarding the majority–minority agency problem, by the majority's willingness to make concessions. But even when such concessions are made in the design of the corporate constitution, they will not necessarily concern all minority shareholders, as would be the case in a minority shareholders' right to appoint the director of his or her preference. A fortiori this applies to shareholders' agreements, due to their binding force being primarily inter partes.[36] From that perspective, provisions on the protection of minorities' interests by mandatory law, such as the derivative action, are essential, as they disconnect protection from bargaining power. Furthermore, as explicated in Chapter 2, derivative actions aim to protect the interests of the company, not exclusively those of the claimant. Protection thus is afforded not only to shareholders as a group, but also to all corporate stakeholders.

Finally and congruent with the last argument, derivative actions, being a means of enforcement of directors' duties and a check on majority abuse, constitute a public good.[37] For this reason, rendering derivative litigation a matter of private bargaining is ill-advised, as it would exclude those unable to reach an agreement due to their lack of bargaining power.[38] Even granting permission to individual or minority shareholders to litigate on behalf of the company, in lieu of the provisions in the corporate constitution, would be undesirable from this perspective, due to the possibility of frivolous or vexatious suits being brought before court. Conversely, the right to sue on behalf of the company should not be negotiable, as this would frustrate the objectives of minority protection and the deterrence of corporate misconduct.[39] From this point of view, the line consistently followed by Greek case law in not permitting minorities to forfeit their right to petition for a corporate action, is absolutely justified.[40]

In conclusion, private bargaining cannot substitute for the weaknesses of shareholder suits on behalf of the company under statute, not only because contractual

36 See Evanghelos Perakis, *Contractual Restrictions of the Shareholder's Voting Right* (1976). Under Greek law, a shareholders' agreement becomes 'part' of the corporate bylaws if all members are signatory parties. See Athens Single-Member Court of First Instance 5079/2002, EEmpD 2002 572; Rokas *Commercial Companies* (n 24) 217.

37 See Chapter 2; see also Reisberg (n 33) 69, 70.

38 Reisberg (n 33) 69, 70; IH Chiu, 'Contextualising Shareholders' Disputes: A Way to Reconceptualise Minority Shareholder Remedies' [2006] JBL 312, 338.

39 Reisberg (n 33) 70.

40 See Greek Supreme Court (in plenary session) 5/2015 ChrID 2015 610, Greek Supreme Court 350/2011 ChrID 2011 691; Athens Court of Appeal 3494/2007 DEE 2007 1193; Athens Multi-Member Court of First Instance 6881/2005 DEE 2006 625. However, after a claim of the company comes into existence, minorities may opt (contractually) not to enact or even waive their right to file a petition regarding this claim, as the exercise of the right is a matter of private initiative.

freedom is restrained in the context of national corporate law but also because of the different functions and objectives served by each instrument of shareholder protection. An enabling approach allowing for more contractual freedom would of course be welcome, for the reasons delineated above. Derivative actions should in any case be understood as adopting a complementary function to private contracting, providing substance to the provisions in the corporate constitution by enforcing a claim which belongs to the company as a separate legal person. [41]

4.3 Collective litigation

It is often highlighted in the literature that derivative actions in the US, where the remedy has thrived for decades, are losing ground to other forms of collective shareholder redress and, in particular, securities class actions.[42] The question therefore arises as to whether the need to enhance shareholders' derivative litigation under Greek law is qualified by the existence of such or similar alternatives.

Considering the applicable Greek law, this question is answered in the negative. Such alternatives cannot be said to exist, despite the fact that some forms of collective redress are procured, within the statutory legislation on consumer protection.[43] Regarding consumer protection, Greek jurisprudence is still unclear as to whether shareholders fit the definition of 'consumer'.[44] From a certain point of view, issuers and stockbrokers provide services that fall within the ambit of the Treaty on the Functioning of the European Union and thus their clients, the end-owners of shares, may enjoy the benefit of a declaratory judgment for damages. Following such a judgment, the only further action they have is to execute the res judicata decision within a reasonable timeframe set by the statute. No case law exists so far though, and the discussion remains academic. Furthermore, it is doubtful whether conferral to shareholders of consumer status would alone be of any help towards better board accountability, as

41 A violation of the corporate constitution may constitute a cause of action for the company, as long as the rights affected are the company's, in all three jurisdictions. Regarding the enforceability of rights conferred to members, even under the pro-contractarian approach of English law, the law is riddled with uncertainty. See Janet Dine and Marios Koutsias, *Company Law* (8th edn, Palgrave MacMillan 2014) 31ff; Ben Pettet, John Lowry and Arad Reisberg, *Pettet's Company Law* (3rd edn, Pearson 2009) 85ff. Both discuss the lines of case law set by the decisions in *Eley v Positive Government Security Life Association Co. Ltd* (1876) 1 Ex D 88; *Hickman v Kent or Romney Marsh Sheep-Breeders Association* [1915] 1 Ch 881; *Quin & Axtens Ltd v Salmon* [1909] AC 442.

42 See Kenneth B Davis, 'The Forgotten Derivative Suit' (2008) 61 Vand L Rev 378.

43 Elisa Alexandridou and Magdalini Karypidou, 'Evaluation of the Effectiveness and Efficiency of Collective Redress Mechanisms in the European Union: Country Report Greece', <http://ec.europa.eu/consumers/archive/redress_cons/finalreportevaluationstudypart1-final2008-11-26.pdf> (accessed 2 November 2014); Stelios N Kousoulis, 'Ta apotelésmata apófasis epí syllogikís agogís. Idíos epí chríseos katachristikón GOS, en ópsei tis AP 1219/2001' [2002] 11 DEE 1097.

44 Alexandridou and Karypidou (n 43) 1.5.2.

this objective can only be attained by sophisticated regulation of securities law. This situation is problematic. Compensation for corporate wrongs, in companies with significant dispersion of share ownership, cannot be easily facilitated by means of the ordinary Civil Procedure Rules, as the numbers of prospective claimants in such cases are usually dazzling. If the ordinary procedure is followed, then courts face a daring threat to their workload.

Once again, Greek law appears less developed on the issue of shareholders' access to judicial redress, as other countries explicitly allow for shareholders' collective litigation. German law considered collective securities litigation mechanisms in the introduction of the KapMuG (Capital Markets Model Case Act), which was initially provisional in force, being a response to the extraordinary number of claims, by German standards, against Deutsche Telekom between 2000 and 2003. The statute provides that for certain violations of the Law on Capital Markets, the pending individual claims may be merged into one, to be adjudicated as a 'model' case,[45] should certain requirements be fulfilled.[46] Thereafter, having a model decision on the merits in common, the stayed proceedings may continue, making use of the decision in the collective claims procedure. In any case, this mechanism lacks the attractive element of the opt-out rule, as well as the element of time efficiency, given that the claims have to proceed individually. Furthermore, its scope is limited strictly to certain forms of securities fraud, thus narrowing the remedial avenues for shareholders in group litigation.

The UK undertakes a position similar to Germany. Apart from the long-existing representative action, the Civil Procedure Rules (CPR Part 19III) provide for the so-called Group Litigation Order (GLO) whereby, when similar claims reach a certain number, group litigation proceedings may be triggered. The attractive feature of this procedure, from a shareholder perspective, is that it is available for any kind of dispute. However, there is no evidence yet of shareholders availing themselves of this mechanism in order to achieve redress against losses to their investment, such as losses accruing from misstatements under the Financial Services and Markets Act 2000 (FSMA 2000) sections 90 and 90A, where application of the mechanism seems appropriate (securities class actions), if we are to follow the US paradigm.[47]

However, even if Greek law improves its mechanisms of collective redress for shareholders,[48] the need for an effective framework of derivative litigation

45 'Model case' should not be confused with 'test case': the decision of the former is binding for the individual claims. See Stefan Wrbka, Steven Van Uytsel and Mathias Siems, *Collective Actions: Enhancing Access to Justice and Reconciling Multilayer Interests?* (CUP 2012) 35.

46 For more detailed analysis, see Mathias Reimann, *Cost and Fee Allocation in Civil Procedure: A Comparative Study* (Springer 2011) 160ff; Paul G Karlsgodt, *World Class Actions: A Guide to Group and Representative Actions Around the Globe* (OUP 2012) 246ff.

47 Jonathan Cary and Jo Rickard, 'Section 90 of FSMA: Time for Collective Action?' (2012) 23 PLC 23–29.

48 There has been some EU initiative on the matter recently. See Commission Recommendation 2013/396/EU of 11 June 2013 on common principles for injunctive and compensatory

would not be eclipsed. Class actions certainly have great potential in addressing agency problems and costs, similarly to derivative actions. By virtue of collective litigation, easier access to justice is purported, as a single court award benefits all participants. Thereby, the investment risk is minimised for micro-shareholders, who cannot afford to individually initiate litigation, have negligible bargaining power and whose property fortunes effectively rest on the benevolence of the investee's management. Most importantly, compensation for their losses is direct and certain, contrary to what applies with derivative actions. For the same reason, however, derivative actions should be understood as complementary to other forms of collective redress.[49]

Firstly, the cause of action in derivative litigation does not necessarily overlap with that in class actions. Collective litigation refers to the representative means of enforcement of shareholders' direct claims, en masse, in cases where a plethora of shareholders share the same cause of action against corporate wrongdoers and/or the corporation. Such a shared cause of action usually concerns cases where the company and/or its management is directly liable to shareholders, particularly when the veracity of statements regarding quoted securities is disputable.[50] It follows that their scope of application does not coincide with that of derivative actions, nor is it meant to. Secondly, their relevance to non-listed companies, particularly closely held ones, is somewhat limited, for the very reason that the regulatory design of class actions is intertwined with securities law and does not cover other forms of misfeasance. Thirdly, they are devoid of the derivative actions' 'public policy' effect described in Chapter 2, as it is principally shareholders who benefit from the outcome of litigation, not the company's coffers. Against this background, my opinion is that even if class actions or similar mechanisms of collective redress become available in Greece (as they should), by virtue of extension of the 'consumer' status to accommodate shareholders as claimants or otherwise, they will not be able to satisfy the same needs and achieve the same objectives as the derivative action.

4.4 Remedies against oppression, abuse and unfair prejudice

Spyridonos, author of the leading monograph on minority shareholders' protection in Greece, considered the absence of a 'general clause' on minority protection the most significant caveat of Greek shareholder law.[51] The 'general clause'

collective redress mechanisms in the Member States concerning violations of rights granted under Union Law [2013] OJ L201 60–65. For a comparative analysis see John C Coffee Jr, 'Litigation Governance: Taking Accountability Seriously' (2010) 110 Colum L Rev 288.

49 See also Robert B Thompson and Randall S Thomas, 'The New Look of Shareholder Litigation: Acquisition-Oriented Class Actions' (2004) 57 Vand L Rev 133, 168–69.

50 For a succinct overview of the UK and German law on the matter, see David Greene (ed), *Shareholder Claims* (Jordans 2012) 12–29 (report on UK by David Greene), 89–116 (report on Germany by Klaus Rotter and Thomas Ertl).

51 Spyridonos (n 1).

he envisaged in 2001 is meant to remedy majority oppression, giving the courts significant discretion as to the appropriate order and award. Even though such a rule does not exist under Greek or German law, it has long been a key component of UK law To a great extent, Spyridonos drew his inspiration from UK Companies Act 1985 section 459.[52] Times have changed and judicial practice, along with article 35a of Law 2190/1920 and its successor, article 137 of Law 4548/2018 (which, by and large, repeats the former provision), have rendered the need for such a clause less imperative.

Extensive analysis of the statutory provisions and precedent relevant to the unfair prejudice remedy falls beyond the scope of this book and the purpose of this Chapter, yet, in order to understand the current position of Greek law compared to the UK model, we shall briefly explain what it is all about. Sections 994 and 996 UK Companies Act 2006 go beyond the other provisions in statute and in the articles of association, to remedy conduct which may not be 'in any way unlawful'.[53] The term refers to a somewhat open-ended category of conduct, leaving courts with much discretion as to how to apply the statutory remedy and thus formulate a precedent clarifying what exactly amounts to unfair prejudice.[54] To date, case law has been clear in identifying that the sections are meant to protect the 'legitimate expectations' of members or 'equitable considerations'.[55] This again is a rather broad criterion, despite the fact that limitations accrue from the study of case law. For instance, 'sophisticated investors' are presumed to be capable of reaching formal arrangements in order to protect their interests and therefore fall outside the protection afforded by section 994.[56] Furthermore, not every member expectation is protected. Unless there is a breach of law or the by-laws or an informal arrangement among members, protection is unlikely to be afforded.[57] In fact, the unfair prejudice remedy has proven particularly useful in protecting members from having the informal arrangements on their participation in the company frustrated. That is, arrangements and mutual understandings that

52 The position of UK law has not changed significantly since then. 'Although Pt 30 is set out somewhat more expansively than was its predecessor, the aim was not to reform the substance of the unfair prejudice provisions'. See Geoffrey Morse (ed), *Palmer's Company Law* (Sweet & Maxwell 2015) 8.3801.

53 *Gower & Davies* (n 12) 722.

54 See Joseph EO Abugu, 'A Comparative Analysis of the Extent of Judicial Discretion in Minority Protection Litigation: The United Kingdom and United States' (2007) 18 ICCLR 181, 190–193.

55 In many cases, such as in *Re Saul D Harrison & Sons Plc* [1995] 1 BCLC 14 [19] (Lord Hoffmann) the term 'legitimate expectations' was endorsed. Recent cases refer instead to equitable considerations, following Lord Hoffmann's statement that use of the former term was 'probably a mistake' (*O'Neill v Phillips* [1999] 1 WLR 1092, 1102).

56 *Gower & Davies* (n 12) 733.

57 In *Re Blue Arrow Plc* (1987) 3 BCC 618, 623 (Vinelott J): 'Outside investors were entitled to assume that the whole of the constitution was contained in the articles, read, of course, together with the Companies Acts. There is in those circumstances no room for any legitimate expectation'.

go beyond the content of the corporate constitution or other contractual agreements.[58] Overall, the remedy bears relevance mostly to closely held company situations, as it is easier to identify the existence of informal arrangements in such cases.[59] Of particular significance is also the courts' discretion in making an order, should a claim be successful. Despite the fact that most often the order sought is that the petitioner's shares are bought out by the company or other members at a fair price,[60] the courts may make any order they may think 'fit for giving relief in respect of the matters complained of'.[61]

Is Greek law completely devoid of such protection? Certainly not. Equitable considerations may not be developed in Greece in the same way as in the UK. However, the general principles of the Civil Code, performing functions similar to equitable considerations, do apply to public companies. Accordingly, any 'exercise of right is prohibited, if it obviously goes beyond the limits set by good faith, bona mores or the social or economic purpose of the right'.[62] If there is abuse, damages may be awarded.[63] The Greek company law statute now further clarifies that abuse on the part of the majority, under the conditions of Civil Code article 281, may also constitute the ground for a 2% share capital minority to challenge a GM resolution.[64] This provision pays significant resemblance to the French remedy of *abus de majorité* against abusive resolutions.[65] Law 4548/2018 goes further to provide that, in case shareholders do not reach the requisite minority threshold, they may be compensated for the *direct* damages they suffered because of the adopted resolution (article 137 paragraph 4).[66] However, the Greek approach should not be understood as coinciding with the UK one.

To a certain extent, the grounds upon which a resolution may be challenged overlap with the definition of the UK Companies Act concept of 'unfairness': the latter may 'consist in a breach of the rules or in using rules in a manner

58 *O'Neill v Phillips* at 1102 (Lord Hoffmann); see also *Ebrahimi v Westbourne Galleries Ltd* [1973] AC 360, 379 (Lord Wilberforce).

59 'In the case of larger companies a legitimate expectation based upon an informal understanding supplementing the articles will be more difficult to establish' (*Palmer* (n 52) 8.3816).

60 CA 2006 s 996(2)(e). Regarding the valuation of shares, see *Re Bird Precision Bellows Ltd* [1986] Ch 658 (Oliver LJ); under CA 2006, see *Sunrise Radio Ltd, Re* [2009] EWHC 2893 (Ch); [2010] 1 BCLC 367 [276]–[309] (Purle QC); *Shah v Shah* [2011] EWHC 1902 (Ch) [44]–[55] (Roth J).

61 CA 2006 s 996(1).

62 GCC art 281.

63 GCC arts 914, 919; cf the German BGB art 826, according to which: 'anyone who intentionally causes injury to another person in a manner contrary to public policy shall be held liable for damages' (as translated by Rotter and Ertl (n 50) 108).

64 Art 137(2)(b). It is questionable whether this limitation is appropriate, as minorities may also be abusive in the exercise of their rights. See Giovannopoulos, 'Void General Meeting Resolutions' in Perakis, *Sociétés Anonyme's Law* (n 29) 1348, with further references on the German treatment of 'binding minorities' (*Sperrminoritäten*)

65 ibid. 1346.

66 ibid. Reflective loss is not compensated.

which equity would regard as contrary to good faith'.[67] However, Law 4548/ 2018 article 137 confers a right exercisable *against the company* only.[68] This is in contrast with the unfair prejudice remedy under the UK Companies Act, where defendants may also be fellow shareholders and directors. Furthermore, the scope of the Greek remedy has only recently begun to crystallise. Particularly, in Greek literature it is supported that there are matters which, under Greek law, fall under the exclusive competence of the GM and where the majority rule is not subject to review by court; an example being the appointment and removal of directors.[69] The contrary view has also been expressed and was endorsed by the Supreme Court in 2006,[70] a decision which, rather disappointingly, did not go to great lengths of analysis.[71] The number of reported subsequent cases on the matter is very limited and therefore the precise scope of what is covered by the term 'abuse' cannot be defined with much certainty yet. Additionally, the remedy under article 137 paragraph 2(b) is considered to be subject to the criterion of the company's interests, thus adding another hurdle for petitioners to overcome.[72] In contrast, the UK courts have entertained a number of claims on similar facts and case law on frustration of shareholders' expectations regarding participation in the management.[73] Furthermore, the test of unfairness under the UK Companies Act is an objective one, disconnected from the intentions of the controllers.[74] In any case, 'abuse' is a narrower concept than 'fairness' under Part 30 of CA 2006.[75] What could complement the notion of abuse and work towards better minority protection, would be the imposition of fiduciary duties on the majority, against the company and fellow shareholders. This has been the case for some decades in Germany. Following the doctrine set by the Federal Supreme Court, fiduciary duties were imposed on controlling shareholders, whose scope and content depends on particular circumstances.[76] Recently Greek academia became receptive to the German

67 *O'Neill v Phillips* [1999] 1 WLR 1092, 1099A.

68 I Dryllerakis, 'Abusive Exercise of the Right to Vote in a GM of a S.A. Regarding the Election of a Member of the B.o.D.' [2008] DEE 435.

69 ibid. 439.

70 Greek Supreme Court 1121/2006 DEE 2007 583, with commentary by M Varela.

71 Notably, the issue as to whether the understandings inferred by a shareholder's agreement can form the basis of abuse on the part of the majority was referred to the plenary session of the Supreme Court: for procedural reasons, the latter never decided on the matter.

72 Giovannopoulos (n 64) 1350–6.

73 *Gower & Davies* (n 12) 725–729.

74 See ibid 733, referring to *Re Saul D Harrison & Sons plc* [1995] BCLC 14 [17] (Hoffman LJ); cf the Greek approach as described by Varela 'commentary' (n 70) 592, according to which abuse is constituted where 'the subjective element of the majority's intent purports to either pursue the majority's interests, or to weaken or damage the interests or rights of the minority'.

75 See Evanghelos Perakis, *Rights of Minority Shareholders* (Bruylant 2004) 41ff.

76 BGH, BGHZ 103, 184, 194–5 (*Linotype*); BGH, BGHZ 142, 167, 170 (*Hilgers AG*); see Hüffer (n 6) 258–260.

doctrine and there is growing support of the idea of shareholders' duties,[77] particularly within the context of closely held companies.[78] The fiduciary duties are determined in the literature on a sliding scale: the more control exerted, the greater the responsibility to the company and/or other shareholders.[79] However, to date the discussion has been confined to academic circles and neither statute nor contemporary judicial practice can be said to endorse this approach. In fact, introducing such a provision was considered 'too complicated' a task by members of the expert committee.[80]

Regarding the use of the provisions in the Civil Code for conduct outside the ambit of GMs, the situation is still somewhat unclear concerning their application to factual situations within a corporate context. The leading decision on the matter is Greek Supreme Court 1298/2006, concerning a closely held company.[81] The company had five shareholders, of which some held a position in the board and were executives (except for the minority claimant). [82] The company (K) had as its single asset stocks in another company (A), which was about to make an initial public offer (IPO) in the Athens Stock Exchange. This move would be presumably profitable, as the Greek stock-market was then thriving.[83] In view of this prospect, three of the shareholders requested that the claimant sell them his shares, or they would divert the company's shareholding to a company of their ownership, registered in Luxemburg. Following the claimant's refusal, they sold the shares to their company, at a value significantly lower than the value expected by the IPO. The claimant succeeded in establishing that such conduct was contrary to good faith and caused damage to his shareholding. The Supreme Court upheld the Court of First Instance decision, asserting that such actions resulted to direct damage of the claimant, that the defendants intended to damage the claimant's proprietary interests and that their actions were contrary to bona mores. The decision raises questions as to what is considered direct and what is considered reflective loss under Greek company law. It also raises the question whether recourse to article 914 and, predominantly, article 919 of the Greek Civil Code may render the requirement to sue derivatively, in cases where the shareholders-litigants suffered losses in their investment, an empty letter of law.

77 Following the decision in BGH BGHZ 129, 136, ZIP 1995 819 (*Girmes*), the German doctrine places duties upon minorities as well; cf Greek Supreme Court 432/2016, DEE 2017 354.

78 For extensive discussion, see Eleni Karamanakou, *Shareholders' Fiduciary Duties* (Nomiki Bibliothiki 2013).

79 Georgios Trantafillakis, 'Business Failure and the Response to It: The Role of the Duty of Loyalty' (2014) DEE 204, 211.

80 Evanghelos Perakis, *The New Law of Limited Companies* (5th edn, Nomiki Bibliothiki 2018) 10.

81 Trantafillakis (n 79); see also Giovannopoulos (n 64) 1349.

82 Three shareholders, all defendants in the case at hand, shared family connections.

83 Ironically, several months after the wrongdoing took place the stock exchange crashed spectacularly (September 1999).

The decision is, as a matter of legal reasoning, not perfectly sound.[84] In fact it is problematic in most of its assumptions. To begin with, a fundamental mistake in its opening paragraphs would strike even an undergraduate student of company law. It conceives that shareholder rights include a 'co-ownership right to the proprietary assets or the property (as a whole) of the company'.[85] Furthermore, the decision relied heavily on the finding that the aggrieved shareholder suffered direct loss. However, the law as it now stands does not examine to whom the intent of the wrongdoing was directed: it rather focuses on the recipient of the wrongful act or omission to distinguish between direct and indirect (reflective) loss.[86] Here, the recipient was clearly the holding company, which had absolute and exclusive ownership of the shares in A: the claimant's shares would only reflect the increase in K's market value. The Supreme Court erred in ascertaining that the damaged person was the claimant.

Despite some subsequent decisions following the rationale of this decision and, surprisingly, repeating these obvious mistakes,[87] it cannot be held to have formulated a clear precedent for direct shareholder claims. However, the factual circumstances in this case, wherefrom liability against fellow shareholders arose, have been referred to obiter by subsequent decisions as examples for grounds on which direct claims may be brought.[88] Much uncertainty remains, as evident in decisions of the Athens Court of First Instance Nos. 12468/2012 and 9669/2014.

Both decisions concerned a multi-million euros case which received much media attention, namely the collapse of Proton Bank. Petitions concerned the same facts and sought freezing orders regarding the company's assets; however, the results were diametrically different. The main issue was whether shareholders suffered direct loss from the company's mismanagement. The factual background of the case is highly complex, involving a series of allegations for misfeasance and criminal activity (including fraud and embezzlement).[89]

The multitude of the alleged wrongdoers can be grouped into two categories, namely those who – in violation of the law and the established credit procedures – were issuing loans to companies connected with the controller of the bank (majority shareholder and president of the board of directors) and those

84 G Sotiropoulos, 'Comments on Supreme Court 1298/2006' (2006) NZ' EEmpD 601, 605, graphically refers to the reasoning of the judgment as an 'interpretative coup d'état'.

85 Sotiropoulos (n 84) 601 attributes this mistake to a misprint in copying the wording of an earlier decision.

86 ibid. 603.

87 Athens Single-Member Court of First Instance 12468/2012, EEmpD 2012 275 reads: 'The Societe Anonyme … has its own property independent of that of its shareholders. The latter have, as shareholders, only the rights provided by law … including the right of co-ownership of the assets of the company or the corporate property as a whole.'

88 See for instance Athens Court of Appeal 4960/2012, DEE 2013 248; Athens Court of Appeal 6900/2013, DEE 2014 136; cf Athens Court of Appeal 877/2014, DEE 2014 505.

89 Athens Single-Member Court of First Instance 9669/2014, DEE 2014 1055, 1057.

who were receiving illegal credit, either directly or through third parties acting on behalf of them, with the intention to achieve illegal benefit.[90] This activity, largely unbeknownst to shareholders, led to high leverage and eventually to insolvency (at the time the company went into liquidation losses exceeded 862,000,000 euros).[91]

Petitioners in both cases based their claims on the grounds of diminution of their share property because of serious misconduct that 'went beyond the limits of ordinary management'.[92] In the 2012 decision, the court found that the petitioners, two institutional investors, enjoyed legal standing and that the directors, one of them notably the major shareholder, were jointly and severally liable to both the company and its shareholders. The decision met with immediate academic criticism, as violating the no reflective loss principle.[93] The embezzlement and fraud involved corporate assets, not the shareholders' property, given the company's distinct legal personality. This outcome was expected, as decision No. 1298/2006 Supreme Court, on which the court of first instance based much of its rationale, was already seen as problematic. The 2014 decision, issued by the same court of first instance (different composition), dismissed the claim of other minority shareholders, despite it being brought on the same grounds: the principle of separate corporate personality effectively deprived petitioners from legal standing. The previous decision (No. 12468/2012) was considered as being contrary to the prevailing line of case law on reflective loss.[94] The controversy could have been avoided if applicants (holding 5% of the company's capital) in the 2012 decision could bring a company's action or had coalesced with others (including those of the 2014 decision) in order to be able to do so, a point illustrative of the problems entailed in quorum thresholds and collective action.

The freezing order cases do not bear the (persuasive) authority of a Supreme Court decision. Still, they evidence the confusion surrounding direct shareholder claims under Greek law. They also show that the Supreme Court, in its 2006 decision, did not establish a precedent identical to an unfair prejudice remedy at least as the latter is understood under UK law. The facts of these Greek cases could possibly fit those behind the English court decisions on serious mismanagement, amounting to unfair prejudice against shareholders,[95] yet there is no

90 Athens Single-Member Court of First Instance 12468/2012, EEmpD 2012 275.

91 ibid; Athens Single-member Court of First Instance 9669/2014, DEE 2014 1055, 1057.

92 ibid.

93 Isaak Gerontidis, 'I atomikí axíosi apozimíosis tou metóchou apó 'synchrónos énanti tis etairías kai ton metóchon' adikopraktikí symperiforá tou DS stin anónymi etairía. Anaskópisi kai sképseis me aformí ti MPrAth 12468/2012' (2013) EpiskED 237.

94 (n 89) 1057.

95 See for instance *Re Elgindata Ltd. (No. 2)* [1992] 1 WLR 1207, 1219 (Beldam LJ): 'mismanagement may amount to conduct unfairly prejudicial and it may be so even if those responsible for the mismanagement suffer equally with the minority shareholders the same or even greater prejudice'.

such remedy under Greek law; resorting to ordinary tort law is no guarantee for achieving results similar to section 994 UK Companies Act. Indeed, the factual background of the Proton Bank cases is familiar to the reader of UK company law, as it resembles the *Cutland* case.[96] In both instances, misappropriation of corporate money took place at board level and abuse/unfair prejudice was complained for. As summarised by Lady Arden:

> without Mr Clark's knowledge, Mr Cutland had misappropriated from the company sums totalling £517,734. The exact method of his misappropriation is not material for present purposes.[97]

However, the claimant and petitioner, Mr Clark, availed himself of two remedies, which he could not have sought if the Greek law on public limited companies was applicable: he brought an unfair prejudice action and a derivative action. Despite succeeding in the unfair prejudice petition, the court ordered that the company should be compensated and not the shareholder. This raises the question of whether, in order to remedy their reflective loss, shareholders may by-pass CA 2006 Part 11, by filing a petition under sections 994 and 996. There are compelling arguments why this should not be the case, ranging from the purpose of the statutory derivative claim to achieve redress for the benefit of the company as a whole to the difference between the two remedies regarding the nature and scope of misfeasance they are meant to address.[98] We should bear in mind that in *Cutland* the petitioner had already filed a derivative claim – which was eventually consolidated with the unfair prejudice proceedings – and had presumably succeeded in satisfying the standing requirements under the common law derivative action. But for rare and exceptional circumstances, as the law now stands, shareholders may achieve redress on behalf of the company by filing a petition under the unfair prejudice provisions only if they succeed in obtaining an order that they bring proceedings 'in the name and on behalf of the company … on such terms as the court may direct', under section 996(2)(c). Yet, there seems to be little reason for shareholders to seek such an order to start a new round of proceedings, if they are to succeed in their petition in the first place.[99] Anyway, the decision in *Cutland* evades much of the criticism that the decision of the Greek Supreme Court 1298/2006 (deservedly) withstood, because the court (and particularly Lady Arden) maintained the orthodoxy of providing a remedy *to the company* for losses suffered directly *by the company.*

It can be stated that a more nuanced (and accurate) conclusion as to the comparative disadvantage of Greek law regarding oppression remedies would be that they are more limited in scope compared to the British 'unfair prejudice'

96 *Clark v Cutland and Others* [2003] EWCA Civ 810 [2004] 1 WLR 783.
97 [2004] 1 WLR 783, 785.
98 Reisberg (n 33) 280–291.
99 See *Gower & Davies* (n 12) 735–738.

remedy. A move towards the latter could thus be beneficial, as it would render protection of minorities more effective, because such an 'umbrella' remedy accommodates the resolution of a broad range of minority–majority disputes. However, even such a move would not render derivative actions unnecessary. The UK model of unfair prejudice actions applies mostly to quasi-partnership situations, where the 'personal' element of membership is dominant. As such, its relevance to public limited companies, the subject of this book, is limited. Furthermore, the discretion afforded to courts regarding the orders to be made is necessary for the operation of such a 'general clause'. Even if Greece were to introduce such a clause, the deciding court should be able to make an order that does not frustrate the no reflective loss principle: as explained in Chapter 2, there is good reason to not compensate directly shareholders' reflective loss. In any case, as persuasively argued by Reisberg on the point of the relationship between derivative claims and unfair prejudice petitions:

> The derivative action is simply a different apparatus: under a derivative action the issue for the court is doing justice to the company, i.e. the shareholders as a whole in a solvent company, and not to the petitioning shareholder.[100]

As Greek law stands, there is an obvious need to improve shareholders' derivative litigation, in the light of the unavailability of an 'unfair prejudice' remedy and the application of the provisions in the law of obligations to the context of public limited companies. For the framework of shareholder protection to be truly effective, both personal and derivative remedies are equally important. The provisions in the Greek Civil Code may only remedy shareholders' direct loss, a loss difficult to establish when the complained of behaviour took place at board level, as shown in the preceding analysis. In fact, these provisions cover a specific kind of misfeasance, which does not coincide with that covered by derivative actions. For example, it is inconceivable that shareholders may bring, under the provisions of the Civil Code, a direct claim for breach of directors' duty of care. Furthermore, due to the different nature of the remedies, the recipients of redress are not the same: derivative actions are collective in their nature[101] and provide redress for the company and its shareholders as a whole, whereas personal actions provide only for the claimant. An enabling and shareholder-friendly framework for litigation on behalf of the company is thus necessary. Otherwise, disgruntled shareholders will persist, to their eventual frustration, in resorting to direct claims in order to remedy their reflective loss and controversial decisions such as the Athens Court of First Instance No 12468/2012 will continue to surface.

100 Reisberg *Derivative Actions* (n 33) 298.
101 ibid 281.

4.5 Remedies for improprieties related to General Meeting resolutions

Continental European legislations are much concerned with the validity of General Meeting resolutions.[102] Such concern is reflected in the voluminous provisions in the Greek and German statutes, the immense amount of litigation on such grounds in those jurisdictions and the review of the relevant framework by the Greek legislator in the 2007 reform. Even though common law is not devoid of protection against defective resolutions, the UK statute does not put any emphasis on the matter nor has it gained any significant importance in court practice.[103]

There are quite a few explanations for this phenomenon of divergence. First, the influence of the differences in ownership structures on the relevant law cannot be overstated. The primary forum for members is, by design, the GM, and disputes between the minority and majority shareholders are likely to emerge therein. Furthermore, grievances minorities may have against influential or controlling shareholders are more likely to emerge in concentrated ownership structures. Therefore, it is expected that a remedy designed to address the minority–majority agency problem within the GM will be more frequently used in jurisdictions where these structures constitute the rule rather than the exception.

Furthermore, it can be argued that differences in contract law and the general law of obligations existing between the continent and common law play their part in formulating such a divergence in approach. The nature of General Meeting resolutions is perceived to be contractual or, at least, quasi-contractual. Accordingly, Greek and German legal doctrines apply the rules on contractual validity by analogy to relevant parts of company law. Such an application is not without difficulties. The 2007 reform of Law 2190/1920 brought a variety of grounds to challenge a resolution under the scope of voidability. The legislator in fact followed the Italian paradigm in this case (mostly as it stood following the Draghi reforms of the 1990s). Accordingly, defects which, by application of ordinary contract law principles or the versions of Law 2190/1920 previous to Law 3604/2007, would render a resolution (or contract) void (such as the content of the resolution being contrary to the prohibition on abusive exercise of rights), now only result in voidability of the latter, as Law 4548/2018 follows the route set by Law 3604/2007 in this respect.[104]

102 See Maria Isabel Saez and Damaso Riano, 'Corporate Governance and the Shareholders' Meeting: Voting and Litigation' (2013) 14 EBOR 343, 355–356.

103 A relevant decision is *Edwards v Halliwell* [1950] 2 All ER 1064.

104 Giovannopoulos (n 64) 1346–1349. The reason for this development was predominantly the avoidance of conferring locus standi to third parties for claims stemming from internal corporate affairs. Void resolutions, as happens with ordinary contract law principles, can be challenged by anyone having legal interest.

These explanations are not sufficient to appreciate properly this form of doctrinal and functional divergence. A significant number of closely held companies do exist in the UK. Therefore given the minority–majority agency problem, aggrieved minorities would be expected, all other things being equal, to resort to such a form of remedy more often than practice shows. The reason for not doing so might be the existence of more attractive alternatives. Of particular relevance is the unfair prejudice remedy, overlapping to a significant extent with the grounds available for challenging GM resolutions, as explained in Section 4.4.

Closer examination of the law on the validity of GM resolutions reveals divergence between Greece and Germany which is relevant to the legislative and practical focus and, more specifically, the scope and availability of the remedy. German law recognises an individual shareholder's right to have the court review the propriety of resolutions,[105] whilst Greek law constrains legal standing mainly to a qualified minority, depending on the grounds of the action. The Greek legislator, in attempting to decrease the likelihood of frivolous and vexatious litigation, followed the practice – common in continental jurisdictions – of restricting the availability of the remedy to a qualified minority that is presumed to have its interests more closely intertwined with those of the company's. The dubious doctrinal appropriateness – from a variety of perspectives – and efficiency of this approach in achieving its goals, are discussed in detail in Subsection 5.3.1.2.

The strategy adopted in Germany is different. Actions to set aside resolutions had been a frequent, disturbing phenomenon for corporate business. The motives behind litigation reportedly contravened the company's interests in many cases.[106] The German legislator decided to address the problem in a two-way fashion. First, the scope of the remedy was reduced by means of exceptions (also recently attempted by Greek law, as now evidenced by Law 4548/2018 article 137 paragraph 5): if a procedural irregularity does not result in frustrating the interests of shareholders or of the company, then it is excused.[107] Second, courts are now enabled to register resolutions (a mandatory requirement for resolutions to come into effect) pending litigation on their validity, removing much of the shareholders' actions potential as a means of blackmail.[108]

105 *Anfechtungsklage* (AktG ss 246, 246a).

106 T Baums, 'Empfiehlt sich eine Neuregelung des aktienrechtlichen Anfechtungs- und Organhaftungsrechts, insbesondere der Klagemöglichkeiten von Aktionären?'" in *Gutachten für den 63. Deutschen Juristentag* (JC Beck 2000).

107 This is the 'relevance theory' (*Relevanztheorie*) promulgated by Zöllner. Greek law provides only for limited exceptions for irregularities, under the more demanding criterion of causality (i.e. in order for the resolution to be set aside, the claimant has to show that the irregularity complained for materially affected the conduct and outcome of the resolution). See Giovannopoulos (n 64) 1336. The irregularity principle under common law is reminiscent of the Greek approach on causality, at least in its effects.

108 AktG s 246a.

The relevance of such remedies for addressing wrongs against the company is interesting to consider. In common law jurisdictions, the primary remedy for wrongs suffered by the company has historically been the derivative action. However, this has been statutorily or practically unavailable in continental law jurisdictions. Consequently, the only avenue of litigation that could address (ex post or ex ante) wrongs suffered by the company is challenging the validity of GM resolutions, where and to the extent appropriate. The operation of the latter remedy as a substitute to claims on behalf of the company is illustrated by the commentary on the decision No. 1298/2006 of the Greek Supreme Court (discussed above). It is therein suggested that resorting to a review by the court of the resolutions would (partially) address the problematic situation of a minority unable to invoke the Greek functional equivalent of the derivative action.[109]

There is an element of truth in this assertion. In cases where law requires authorisation by the shareholders prior to action taken by the board, in particular, challenging the respective resolution may prove an effective means of addressing corporate wrongdoing at board level. However, the two remedies differ significantly in their nature and scope, despite some circumstantial overlap. The derivative action is designed to champion the company's claims, particularly in cases where the board is unwilling to do so (in its capacity as the authorised body) or is in conflict of interests. Its function is mainly to compensate (the company and indirectly shareholders) and deter future misfeasance. On the other hand, challenging GM resolutions is a remedy designed to ensure the legality of a certain decision-making corporate organ. Contrary to the derivative action, it is not concerned with remedying the losses a company has suffered on behalf of the company: shareholders-petitioners are acting on their own behalf, in an effort to set aside or declare invalid a resolution unduly taken. The damage sustained by the company and – reflectively – by the shareholders remains, unless the company sues the wrongdoers or shareholders are enabled to initiate litigation on its behalf. For instance, if the company resolved to enter a transaction with its CEO, and, following a shareholders' suit under article 137, this resolution was declared void, then normally the company (not shareholders) may recover monies paid to the CEO (under ordinary contract law or on the basis of unjust enrichment).[110] The fact that actions challenging the validity of resolutions are not designed to provide recovery to shareholders is all the more apparent in view of the construction of Law 4548/2018, article 137, which allows members falling below the 2% threshold to bring a claim to recover their losses, against the company, *as long as their losses are direct*. It follows that derivative actions and actions against the validity of GM resolutions constitute two mechanisms which should be understood as complementary in their function.

109 Further supporting this argument is the analysis in Cahn and Donald (n 6), where the two remedies are grouped together, and Mikroulea (n 25) 287.

110 GCC arts 904f.

4.6 The market for corporate control: Exit as an option?

Before continuing, we should briefly consider the market of corporate control as a disciplinary mechanism and its potential to operate as an alternative to derivative actions. This idea has occupied much of the scholarly thought on the topic of corporate governance, particularly in the Anglo-Saxon jurisdictions.[111]

This comes as no surprise. An active market for corporate control first emerged in these regions and, for a variety of reasons, continues to proliferate. Nevertheless, any discussion on whether it may discipline management or lead managers to increase short-term shareholder value in order to defend their positions in corporate offices, loses relevance in the continental European context. Certainly, takeover activity has received only modest support by the relevant EU directive,[112] with its problematic structure and the optional character of board neutrality and breakthrough rules.[113] But more generally, on the continent, very few firms showcase large levels of dispersed share ownership at present, despite the recent growth of share dispersion in some countries.[114] This applies particularly for Greece, where share concentration maintains high levels, as explained in Chapter 2. The reluctance of block-holders, such as founding families, to cede control over their company is therefore a more frequent phenomenon.

Even for the few firms that exhibit some level of share dispersion, the market for corporate control does not function as a perfect substitute for derivative actions.[115] First and foremost, it lacks any compensatory value for the corporation. The only benefit to the company may only accrue from the promise of the incoming management, a rather uncertain possibility and one disputed by empirical studies.[116] These considerations leave deterrence as the only potential for the market of corporate control. Similarly to derivative actions, the latter assumes an ex post and ex ante function in disciplining managers. Another thing these forms of 'voice' and 'exit' shareholder activism mechanisms have in common is that they deter mismanagement by leaving the stigma of incompetence on the incumbent directors and officers. But similarities end there. The first fundamental difference lies in the fact that the market for corporate control

111 See Frank Easterbrook and Daniel Fischel, *The Economic Structure of Corporate Law* (Harvard University Press 1996).

112 Directive 2004/25/EC on takeover bids [2004] OJ L142/12. For thorough analysis, see Thomas Papadopoulos, *EU Law and the Harmonization of Takeovers in the Internal Market* (Kluwer Law 2010).

113 Greece has transposed the board neutrality rule, applying reciprocity. See Greek Law 3461/2006.

114 Regarding Germany, see Wolf-Georg Ringe, 'Changing Law and Ownership Patterns in Germany: Corporate Governance and the Erosion of Deutschland AG' (2015) 63 Am J Comp L 493, 508–17, providing detailed statistical data.

115 This argument has been persuasively advanced by Reisberg (n 33) 42–45.

116 Chrispas Nyombi, Tom Mortimer, Rhidian Lewis and Georgios Zouridakis, 'Shareholder Primacy and Stakeholders' Interests in the Aftermath of a Takeover: A Review of Empirical Evidence' (2015) 2 IBLJ 161, 173.

only incidentally serves as a disciplinary mechanism. Shareholders may hold the almighty position of plaintiff, judge, jury and executioner when using their right to exit, yet dissatisfaction with the incumbents is not an exclusive motive in selling their shares. It is highly unlikely that one-off violations of the law and breaches of duty would spur a takeover, for instance, whereas (law permitting) they would attract litigation-oriented types of activism such as derivative suits. At the end of the day, the market for corporate control may even provide all the wrong incentives to the management, such as empire-building and short-termism.[117]

In any case, the stock market and the market for corporate control are not meant to perform the same functions as the derivative action. Instead of a remedy, they provide a means to keep losses at a low level. Even regarding the mitigation of agency problems, their function is controversial and different in scope. But most importantly for this book, the discussion on the role of the market of corporate control in Greek corporate governance and shareholder protection is out of pace with economic reality. If the law and finance theorists got it right, legislative focus on shareholder protection may change this situation.

4.7 Recent measures to improve the Greek framework on shareholder protection: Big steps, not leaps

4.7.1 Overview

As explained in Chapter 2, the level of shareholder protection in Greece has long been perceived to be particularly low, not only by international studies and leximetric indices but also by Greek academia. Given the argument of this book, that a reform of the provisions on shareholder suits on behalf of the company would strengthen shareholder protection, it is pertinent for two reasons to examine the efforts of the Greek legislator to bolster shareholder protection during the past decade. First, it is necessary to check the veracity of the findings that shareholder protection in Greece is low and their relevance to the law as it now stands. Apart from the World Bank's 'investor protection' index, which is updated annually, most comparative studies referring to Greek shareholder law are not up to date. If then a weak Greek framework for protection is not the case nowadays, the argument that a move towards an efficient model for derivative actions would be a significant step towards better shareholder protection is qualified as to its strength (without being overturned though). Second, a study of the recent reforms will highlight fact that they were exhaustively focused to a particular aspect of shareholder protection that is not meant, nor has the potential to address the same problems as shareholder suits.

This Section's title succinctly reflects the mentality of the Greek legislator, as depicted in the wording of the preamble to the 2007 reform Act. As regards the

117 See Nyombi et al. (n 116).

'betterment of shareholders' position' under the law of public limited companies, it reads:

> This betterment cannot be abrupt and intense, because otherwise lurks the danger of overturning existing balances and expectations in business, with adverse results. Thus, the reform of minority rights is pursued, without being radical.[118]

Despite the explicit focus of the 2007 reform on strengthening shareholder protection, the attempt to facilitate such a change was, by and large, limited within the confines of the law on General Meetings.[119] Reform was based primarily on three axes of legislative action.[120] First, making rights and remedies available to a wider number of shareholders, by decreasing the percentages of voting power or share capital ownership ex lege required for invocation and enforcement of statutory rights. Secondly, correcting inconsistencies and obscurities in the literary and systemic setting of existing provisions within the Greek company law statute. Thirdly, alignment of Greek law with European Union law provisions was sought. However, further steps were necessary in this last respect, as the EU legislator has been quite prolific lately regarding company law.[121] Notably, full implementation of the Shareholder Rights Directive (SRD) resulted in numerous changes in Greek law, amending in some instances provisions shortly afterwards they were introduced/reformed by Law 3604/2007.

At the time of publication, the new law on public limited companies (Law 4548/2018) will have come to force (as of 1 January 2019), replacing a statute (Law 2190/1920) that lasted for almost a century. As happens with most of the recent Greek acts of parliament, passing a reform on company law comprised one of the 'memoranda' obligations: in particular, it was included in the 'Supplemental Memorandum of Understanding' within the ambit of the fourth review.[122] This may have expedited the legislative process, given that

118 Preamble to Law 3604/2007 Pt I.

119 Other matters included deregulation of incorporation requirements and liberalising the content of the Corporate Constitution. See I Dryllerakis, 'The Most Significant Recent Amendments of L 2190/1920 (A Brief Overview)' (2007) 30 Epiheirisi 1199; A Sinanioti-Maroudi, 'Oi vasikés paremváseis tou nómou 3604/2007 ston n. 2190/1920' (2008) 1 PeirN 5; M-T Marinos (ed), *Issues from the New Law of the Societe Anonyme* (Sakkoulas 2009).

120 Law 2190/1920 art 39. All the rights falling under the title 'minority protection' (inserted by Law 3604/2007) are connected with participation within the GM.

121 Indicatively: European Commission, 'Action Plan: European Company Law and Corporate Governance:A Modern Legal Framework for More Engaged Shareholders and Sustainable Companies', Brussels, 12 December 2012, COM(2012) 740/2; Directive 2012/30/EU, OJ 2012 L 315/74, recasting the second company law directive; Green Paper 'Corporate Governance in Financial Institutions and Remuneration Policies', COM(2010) 284 final; Commission Recommendation 2009/384/EC of 30 April 2009 on remuneration policies in the financial services sector [2009] OJ 2009 L 120/22.

122 Perakis, *The New Law* (n 80) 4.

the first expert committee appointed to prepare the new law produced an interim draft not long before Law 4548/2018 was passed, whereas new members were added to the committee just few months before the final draft was submitted.[123] Some of the – admittedly very few – mistakes in wording, such as those in articles 104–105 on shareholders enforcement of directors duties (the focus of this book), may be attributed to the aforementioned setting and amendment of timeline. Passing a new law, instead of amending the long-lasting Law 2190/1920 was preferred due to the fact that the latter statute was amended already many times,[124] becoming a 'patchwork' that could not be patched anymore. Whereas, the required number of amendments in details would entail a cumbersome process.[125] Law 4548/2018 introduced few reforms that could be considered as major, such as the abolishment of bearer shares, the single-member board of directors and the method to certificate capital subscription. Notwithstanding the introduction of few new shareholder rights,[126] Law 4548/2018 attempted to improve shareholder protection following the same threefold strategy as that of the 2007 reform.[127] The following paragraphs investigate these three distinct courses of reformative action.

4.7.2 Making rights more accessible

The 2007 reform did not intend to increase the menu of shareholder rights under Law 2190/1920: this is clear from the preamble to Law 3604/2007, which reads 'the catalogue of rights in articles 39 and 40 Law 2190/1920 was not widened. ... However, it was deemed necessary to lower the percentages for enacting minority rights'.[128] The law in fact reconsidered its position regarding what is a minority in a modern legal context. Prior to 2007, many of the minority rights were given to holders of 30% of registered share capital. This travesty stemmed from the fact that most of the provisions of Law 2190/1920 on shareholder protection dated back to the early 1960s[129] and,

123 ibid.

124 Not that this would be an unsurmountable burden to overcome: the German AktG shows otherwise.

125 Perakis, *The New Law* (n 80) 6.

126 Those are the minority (20% of capital) right to block the adoption of a members resolution without a meeting taking place (art 167 para. 6); the shareholder right to be sent information relevant to the General Meeting by email (art 122 para. 4); and the shareholder right to be informed regarding the capital of the company and ownership thereof (art 141 paras 10, 11). The first one should only be viewed as the trade-off for the reduction of minority shareholder influence in corporate decision-making that the absence of a shareholder meeting (whereat the majority of 'voice' rights may exclusively be exercised) may entail, whereas, the latter two should be considered as increasing the scope and availability of minority shareholder information rights.

127 See Preamble to Law 4548/2019 paras i, ii.

128 Preamble to Law 3604/2007 Pt I.

129 e.g. Law 2190/1920 art 22b originated from Law 4237/1962.

in some cases, the early twentieth century.[130] In modern day practice, 30% of registered share capital is in most instances a controlling percentage, being more than sufficient a participation in share capital in order to pass a resolution by majority.[131] Furthermore, this percentage comes very close to the mandatory bid threshold of one-third of voting shares, as set by Law 3461/2006. Not only is this further evidence of such share ownership being very close to representing control of the company in a modern business context, but also the Greek law on takeovers could lead to complications for groups of shareholders invoking such minority rights, by obliging them to launch a mandatory bid.[132] Law 4548/2018 further reduced the requisite ownership thresholds regarding few minority rights; however, it did so in a much less radical fashion than Law 3604/2007.[133]

The approach followed by Law 3604/2007 was that of placing minority rights within three basic categories: individual rights, 'minor minority' rights (one-twentieth minority),[134] and 'major minority' rights (one-fifth minority).[135] Law 4548/2018 maintained this approach, despite 'moving' some minority rights from one category to another. There are exceptions of course to this grouping, such as the right to challenge voidable resolutions, which is provided for one fiftieth of registered share capital.[136] Overall, Law 4548/2018 still employs a 'qualified minority strategy' regarding most shareholder rights, in the sense that it allocates rights to minority shareholders representing a given percentage of share capital or voting, yet the requisite thresholds are significantly lower compared to the ones applicable a few decades ago.

One, if not the only, innovation brought by Law 4548/2018 within the ambit of Greek shareholder protection was the institutionalisation of shareholder associations in the company law statute. Of course, this is another (belated)

130 As is art 39, on the right to information, where ownership thresholds stayed put for more than seven decades.

131 Unless deviations existed within companies regarding the one-share-one-vote paradigm.

132 It could evidence that shareholders are 'acting in concert'. See Pavlos Masouros, 'Is the EU Taking Shareholder Rights Seriously? An Essay on the Impotence of Shareholdership in Corporate Europe' (2010) 7 ECL 195, 200; Djioufas, '"Acting in Concert" and Calculation of Voting Rights in the Public Offer for Securities' (2005) DEE 918; Law 3461/2006, implementing Directive 2004/25/EC of the European Parliament and of the Council of 21 April 2004 on takeover bids (OJ L 142, 30.4.2004).

133 However, as stated in the statute's preamble (part ii[2][h]), the (rather small) increase of the availability of minority shareholder rights was somewhat counterbalanced by the 'requirements of proper and prompt payment of capital becoming stricter'.

134 Such as the right to request information on the GM (art 39(4)), to request from the chairman of the GM to adjourn the adoption of the resolution (art 39(3)), to add items to the GM's agenda (art 39(2)) and to be bought out in case a majority shareholding reaches the level of 95% of registered share capital (art 49b).

135 Such as the 'enhanced' right to information under art 39(5) (see below) and to request a special audit under art 40(3) (see Chapter 3).

136 Law 2190/1920 art 35a(3); now Law 4548/2018 art 137(3).

legal transplant, originating from Germany.[137] The proviso (article 144) is quite brief (at least compared to its German counterpart), delineating the basic structure, competencies and functions of the associations: its paragraph 3 assigns detailed regulation to a presidential decree to be issued following proposal of the Minister of Finance and Development. More specifically, article 144 provides that minority rights under Law 4548/2018 may be enacted by shareholder associations, acting in their name but on their members behalf, excluding, at the same time, individual shareholder rights from the definition of minority rights. Paragraph 2 of the article further provides that such associations may put information on the available shareholder rights on the internet and operate an online shareholders' forum in order to facilitate 'eponymous communication' among members ahead of a General Meeting.

As pronounced in the explanatory notes, this article aspires to 'facilitate the enactment of shareholder rights and supervision of corporate management'. However, there are good reasons not to expect much from it. To begin with, the associations instituted thereby are ostensibly targeted for shareholders with small stakes in listed companies ('wide free float'), who better fit the profile of the shareholder-consumer, even though the article does not expressly say so. This becomes all the more apparent by the requirement that shareholders associations are registered in the consumer unions registry. Yet, contrary to consumer unions, such associations may only represent their members regarding qualified minority rights. Thereby, representation in cases of direct claims against corporate management, a primary form of shareholder-led liability enforcement, is excluded from their scope. That being said, we can hold that the institutionalisation of shareholders' associations offers only a marginal contribution to the shareholder rights apparatus. The proviso on the competence to represent notwithstanding, article 144 merely reproduces the constitutionally protected freedom of association. But even as regards qualified minority rights, the success and popularity of Greek shareholder associations is nothing but guaranteed. Addressing the shareholder-consumer or shareholder-investor, they may find it hard to overcome their addressee's rational apathy and convince them to become members and/or actively participate: certainly, a membership fee and operational charges (as expected for them to be financially sustainable) do not help towards that end.[138] Of course, a much more direct – and cheaper – form of communication would be shareholders forums operated by the associations. Sadly though, the wording of article 144 restricts their scope to the rights relevant to the General Meeting, thereby excluding the company's action, among

137 This is safely adduced by the explanatory notes to the respective article 144 of Law 4548/2018, using German terminology (*Aktionärsforum*) and making express reference to AktG s 127a.

138 Ulrich Noack, 'Aktionärsforum im Bundesanzeiger: ein Flop' [18 March 2013] Handelsblatt Rechtsboard, https://blog.handelsblatt.com/rechtsboard/2013/03/18/aktionarsforum-im-bundesanzeiger-ein-flop/ (accessed 20 June 2019): 'apparently €25 per entry in view of the resolution is too much'.

other rights. Even setting such restrictions aside, online forums are not expected to be frequently used for seeking allegiances in suing the management, liability being a delicate issue to openly discuss.

That being said, it is most peculiar that the Greek legislator envisages the institution of fora similar to the German *Aktionärsforum*. Not only due to the fact that the latter is operated by the state operator (*Bundesanzeiger*), in contrast to the Greek proviso allocating this task to the associations, but also due to the fact that the German experience showed that it is very difficult to develop a functioning shareholders forum. The survey by Bayer/Hoffmann from the Jena Institute for Legal Facts Research succinctly summed up the (in) activity of the forum as per section 127a, by calling it a 'Sleeping Beauty'.[139] It is therefore hard to see how the effected and the envisaged legal transplants may have any substantial effect on shareholders collective action.

The 2007 reform and the new law on public limited companies did eventually make rights available to a greater audience of shareholders, but did those reforms give a comparative edge to Greek shareholder law? It is worth comparing the Greek approach to the British and German approaches, from the perspective of availability of rights. Despite the generous lowering of ownership thresholds by Law 3604/2007 and, subsequently, Law 4548/2018, the same or functionally equivalent rights are available to smaller minorities in Germany and the UK. For instance, the right to challenge defective or oppressive resolutions under Greek law is given to a 2% minority, whereas it is an individual right in the other two jurisdictions.[140] Even considering the system of qualified minority rights as a whole, Greek law adopts a one-size-fits-all approach that is less favourable to small investors than those of its fellow jurisdictions. To clarify, in the UK and in Germany qualified minorities are determined not only on the basis of participation in registered share capital and/or voting rights but also, alternatively, according to the financial value such participation represents or the number of shareholders forming the minority group. In particular, in German companies with large capitalisation, it is possible for shareholders falling well below the usual threshold of one-twentieth of registered share capital to invoke the respective right, if they satisfy instead the nominal value threshold. According to the UK model of minority thresholds on the other hand, an aggregation of a certain number of members would suffice for the qualified minority right to be evoked, even if the sum of their shares falls short of the participation in share capital or voting rights thresholds.[141]

The upshot is that the Greek market offers significantly more 'voice premia' to shareholders of 5%, compared to individual ones. They constitute 'premia' because, in effect, when a single shareholder reaches such levels of participation in capital, eventually he or she obtains more rights compared to the aggregate

139 According to Noack (n 138): 'The abolition of the so-called shareholder forum (deletion of § 127a AktG) is obvious from the experience so far, because nothing more will come of it.'
140 Ever since the 2007 reform. See Section 4.5.
141 e.g. CA 2006 ss 338, 370(3).

of persons holding an equivalent percentage of share capital. Any such right then can be viewed as a control premium, making the shareholding exponentially more valuable compared to those falling short of the requisite thresholds for the right to be conferred to them. Conversely, such groups of individual shareholders need to undertake the additional costs of coordinating their actions in order to enjoy such rights.[142] Under the prism of the bundle of rights theory, these considerations translate into individual shareholders owning a property of disproportionately lower value compared to their counterparts who reach the qualified minority thresholds.

Of course, this observation applies, to different extents, to every jurisdiction where corporate decision-making depends upon majority rules, whereby majority is calculated on the basis of participation in capital.[143] However, it is evident that Greek law is more demanding regarding qualified minority rights, compared at least to its German and British counterparts. It therefore follows that a shareholding of 1.5% in, say, a German company carries more rights than an equal participation in the capital of a Greek company and thus bestows more control to its holder over corporate affairs and is, ultimately, more valuable.

The desirability of a 'qualified minority strategy' regarding certain shareholder rights is questionable, not only from a practical but also from a doctrinal perspective. As argued in Chapter 5, this is the case particularly for shareholder-initiated litigation on behalf of the company. Qualified minority thresholds are impractical, because of their failure to reflect the differences in terms of shareholding structures between listed and non-listed companies and due to the problems entailed in collective action.[144] Furthermore, the doctrinal bases behind this approach are shaky. On the one hand, the presumption that block-holders have their interests more closely connected with those of the company is contestable and should not preclude smaller minorities from redress on behalf company; on the other hand, large thresholds have the potential to frustrate the purpose of shareholders' (derivative) litigation as an accountability mechanism for the benefit of the company as a whole.

4.7.3 Alignment of statute with academic and judicial interpretation: Re-wording of provisions and gap-filling

The 2007 reform in Greece was a unique opportunity to address long-standing issues regarding the literary setting of the century-old statute. The terminology used therein was convoluted and troubling both for business and lawyers,

142 On the problem of collective action, see Lucian A Bebchuk, 'The Myth of the Shareholder Franchise' (2007) 93 Va L Rev 675, 688ff; Frank H Easterbrook and Daniel R Fischel, *The Economic Structure of Corporate Law* (Harvard University Press 1996) 66.

143 Regarding 'shareholder democracy', see Arman Khachaturyan, 'Trapped in Delusions: Democracy, Fairness and the One-Share-One-Vote Rule in the European Union' (2007) 8 EBOR 335.

144 Problems not adequately solved by 'shareholder unions/associations', such as those instituted by Law 4548/2018, as argued in Chapter 3.

conceivably due to the direct translation of foreign provisions in the course of legal transplants. Ambiguity was also caused by the very structure of certain provisions, unintentionally leaving space for a variety of interpretations. The literary setting of Law 2190/1920 had also significant caveats, leaving important issues to be addressed by statutory interpretation. The Greek legislator proceeded to a number of changes, providing the statute with renewed, yet by no means absolute, clarity.

These 'corrective' interventions did not substantially improve the level of shareholder protection, nor were they designed to. In the context of shareholder rights, the most significant addition in the course of such statutory 'gap-filling' can be held to be the introduction to Law 2190/1920 of a provision on the right to place items on the GM agenda: a proviso that was transferred verbatim to Law 4548/2018.[145] Such a shareholders' right existed prior to the enactment of Law 3604/2007, by virtue of teleological interpretation of the statutory provision on the right to call for a GM.[146] Academics had reached the consensus that, given the right to call for a GM (and therefore to set the stage for discourse over particular aspects of corporate affairs), it follows a majori ad minus that a similar ability existed to influence the setting of the agenda of an already convened GM, as the activist minority would otherwise attend a discussion which may or may not include their concerns regarding the course of corporate business.[147] Case law did not contradict the views of academics in that instance, yet the legislator decided to clarify the position and application of the law by introducing a statutory provision to that end. The initiative undertaken by Law 3604/2007 was welcome therefore, from the perspective of legal certainty. The law now provides details as to the deadlines to be met by the minority and the duty of the board to publish or communicate the inserted items. Nevertheless, the Greek statutory provision on the shareholders' right to add items to the GM's agenda should also be understood as an early alignment with the EU mandates. By the time Law 3604/2007 was voted by Parliament, the draft version of the SRD explicitly provided for such a right, which eventually became the subject of the directive's article 4.[148] It therefore can be concluded that the motives behind the reform of Law 2190/1920 article 39 paragraph 2 had more to do with legal certainty and transposition of the SRD rather than genuine shareholder empowerment on the Greek legislator's initiative.[149] Anyway, the case of the statutory right to add items to the GM's

145 Law 2190/1920 art 39(2); now Law 4548/2018 art 141(2).

146 The right to call for a GM existed since the early versions of Law 2190/1920. Regarding which types of GMs this right refers to, see E Perakis, 'Danger to Frustrate the Minority's Right to Call for a GM (art 39 par. 1 CL 2190/1920)?' [2010] DEE 1133.

147 See preamble to Law 3604/2007. The leading work is I Markou, 'I sýnklisi tis genikís syneléfseos tis AE apó ti meiopsifía' [1978] EEN 774, 776.

148 See Drakopoulos, 'Minority Rights' in Perakis *Sociétés Anonyme's Law* (n 29), 1498, 1499.

149 cf GN Michalopoulos, 'Genikés Grammés tou néou Dikaíou tis anónymis etaireías' (2008) 1 PeirN 12.

agenda shows that the occasional 'gap-filling' effected by Law 3604/2007 purported and resulted only in incremental, if any, improvement of shareholder protection.

The recent reforms touched upon an array of provisions which were problematic due to their wording. The editors of the only available Greek to English translation of Law 2190/1920 make no overstatement by observing that

> the fact that Law 3604/2007 was not drafted from zero basis but includes parts of various past laws, going back to 1920, with the addition of several new provisions, makes the Greek text rather cumbersome and, on occasion, conflicting.[150]

This is particularly true regarding shareholder protection, where Law 2190/1920 article 22b on company's actions maintained, until its replacement, its highly criticised setting. It is worth recapitulating and expanding on the relevant observations raised in Chapter 3, given that – as explained above – article 22b of Law 2190/1920 was modelled after the German *Aktiengesetz* and bears significant resemblance to legislation in force in other jurisdictions, such as Austria. Paragraph 1 of the article made reference to a right of a minority of 10% of registered (paid) share capital to demand that the board enforces the company's claims against its members, going further to impose a duty of the directors to assert such claims, if the minority or the GM so demanded. However, the same paragraph contained an exception to the aforementioned conditions for the duty to assert corporate claims to arise, if the claim at question is grounded on fault.[151] Furthermore, the third paragraph referred to a 'minority's right' to petition before court for appointment of special representatives with a mandate to initiate proceedings, in case the board did not do so within the period specified in paragraph 2 of the same article, despite the 10% minority's demand. There existed, therefore, ambiguity as to the content of the Greek functional equivalent to derivative actions. Firstly, it was disputed that the minority in paragraph 3 referred to the same minority of 10% in the first paragraph, even though no other minority was mentioned in the article.[152] Furthermore, the opinion has been expressed that the exception of fault regarding the directors' duty to assert corporate claims

150 Lambadarios Law Firm (tr and ed), *Law 2190/1920 on Companies Limited by Shares (Sociétés Anonymes); Law 3190/1955 on Limited Liability Companies: Greek and English Text* (Nomiki Bibliothiki 2011), VIII.

151 This exception was inserted into Law 2190/1920 art 22b(1), by virtue of Law 2339/1995 art 10(5).

152 cf Filippos Doris, 'I schési ton árthron 69 AK, 22 v § 3 n.2190/1920 kai 786 § 3 KPolD os rythmíseon gia tin apotropí tou kindýnou exypirétisis symferónton antithéton pros ta symféronta tou ekprosopoúmenou nomikoú prosópou' (2002) B' ChrID 865, 873; see AI Freris, 'Judicial Enforcement of Corporate Claims against the Members of the Board of Directors' in VG Antonopoulos and S Mouzoulas, *Sociétés Anonymes*, vol. 2 (Sakkoulas 2013) 208.

expanded to the conditions to petition for appointment of special representatives, possibly under the rationale fraus omnia corrumpit.[153] Lastly, the phrase in paragraph 3 – 'if pursuit of the claim is demanded by the minority or in case that the deadline set in the above paragraph lapses without any action being brought' – has led some commentators to hold that a minority-led corporate action is not subject to the deadline set in paragraph 2, despite the fact that paragraph 3 went on to provide that 'the Chair of the Court of First Instance … may, upon application of the minority submitted within one month from the expiration of the deadline set in the above paragraph … appoint special representatives'.[154] Nevertheless, case law of the higher courts had been rather consistent in the interpretation of article 22b, thereby mitigating the uncertainty created by the convoluted literary setting of a poorly translated legal transplant.[155] The successor of Law 2190/1920 article 22b paragraph 3, article 105 of Law 4548/2018, put a definite end to the aforementioned ambiguities. It is now abundantly clear that, by default, shareholders can only apply for the appointment of special representatives as part of a qualified minority and that no exceptions whatsoever apply to the deadlines set for the minority's 'demand' and petition before court. This is not to say, of course, that the new provisions are perfectly unambiguous as a whole. For instance, its wording is not clear on whether the shareholders majority needs to prove ownership of shares for six months prior to demanding the enforcement of the company's claims.[156] In any case, the literary corrections effected by Law 4548/2018 may have bolstered legal certainty, yet they cannot be held to have otherwise improved shareholder protection. On the contrary, it can be argued that the additional detail sometimes runs against the latter. A good example is the demand requirement, applicable even in case the board is unable to decide. As will be further argued in Chapter 5, this requirement is rather redundant in such cases, resulting only to the postponement of the special representative's appointment, in this case by several months. However, the new proviso is very detailed and specific on the matter, leaving no room for such exceptions to be formed by judicial interpretation of the statute.

153 G Triantafillakis, 'Duty of a Shareholder Exerting Influence on the Management of a Public Limited Company' in 12th Panhellenian Conference of Greek Corporate Lawyers, *Contemporary Issues of Corporate Responsibility* (2003) 281, 311; Spyridonos (n 1) 170; cf Mikroulea (n 25) 252; Chrysanthis, 'Comments on Single-Member CFI of Agrinio 177/2009' (2009) EEmpD NI' 563; SA Mouzoulas,*L.3604/07 for the Reform and Amendment of CL 2190/1920 on Societes Anonymes, Annotated*(Sakkoulas 2008) 364; Themis K Skouras, 'Appointment and Replacement of Special Representatives in the Societe Anonyme' (1983) EEmpD 553, 556.

154 Doris (n 152) 873; cf Freris (n 152) 209; G Sotiropoulos, 'Sýnkrousi symferónton metaxý ton melón tou DS kai tou nomikoú prosópou tis anónymis etairías. Schési tou árthrou 69 AK kai tou árthrou 22b N.2190/1920. Antikatastástasi ton eidikón ekprosópon tis par. 3 tou árthrou 22b N.2190/1920' (1997) 12 DEE 1145.

155 See also Ioannis Passias, *To Díkaion tis Anonýmou Etaireías* (1969) 696–699.

156 Achilleas Christodoulou, 'Remarks on Articles 103–105 of Law 4548/2018 Regarding the Filing of the Company's Action' (2018) 11 DEE 1267, 1271.

4.7.4 European union influence

The transposition of EU directives has led over time to an augmentation of the catalogue of shareholder rights under Greek law. The vast majority of the EU-driven amendments to Greek company law are related to the law on shareholders meetings.[157] European harmonisation did not have identical effects on the national legislations examined, primarily in the sense that differences exist regarding the scope of application of the now European-wide shareholder rights between listed and non-listed companies.

The most influential piece of EU secondary legislation on shareholder law in the recent years is undoubtedly the SRD.[158] Its predominant focus was the shareholders' exercise of the right to vote, with particular reference to the issues of proxy and distance voting (voting by correspondence), in an effort to bolster cross-border shareholder voice.[159] The outcome of the transposition of the SRD was the amendment of a variety of the existing statutory provisions, along with the introduction of new ones.

To begin with, proxy voting, even though permissible under the pre-existing Greek provisions, was never a matter seriously considered by the company law legislator; it was left to be addressed by the general provisions of the Civil Code on representation.[160] Unsurprisingly, the national legislator heavily relied upon the provisions of the carefully drafted directive.[161] The more sophisticated new framework on proxy voting was also welcome by Greek academia, as it better addresses the complexity of corporate decision-making, the conflicts of interests entailed therein and the difficulties involved in getting the GM resolutions to reflect the genuine will of the shareholders.[162]

Another significant effect of the SRD on Greek shareholder law, again related to shareholders' participation in the GM, was the abolition of share-blocking. Prior to the directive, share-blocking in Greece consisted of the requirement to

157 The exception being the sell-out right, introduced to Law 2190/1920 by implementation of Directive 2004/25 on takeover bids [2004] OJ L142/12 art 16

158 Directive 2007/36 on the exercise of certain rights of shareholders in listed companies [2007] OJ L184/17. The deadline for transposition of the SRD was 3 August 2009. Greece, having failed to meet it, was handed a reasoned opinion by the commission in 2010. See, regarding Germany, F Ochmann, *Die Aktionärsrechte-Richtlinie: Auswirkungen auf das deutsche und europäische Recht* (Walter dWalter de Gruyter 2009); regarding Greece, Christina I Tarnanidou, 'Reform of the Law on Listed Companies Following the Amendment of L 2190/1920 by virtue of L 3884/2010' (2010) 2 ChriDik 154.

159 SRD, Recital 2.

160 A. Kouloridas, 'Entitlement to Participate in the General Meeting' in Perakis *Sociétés Anonyme's Law* (n 29) 1234.

161 European Commission, 'Action Plan: European Company Law and Corporate Governance: A Modern Legal Framework for More Engaged Shareholders and Sustainable Companies', Brussels, 12 December 2012, COM(2012) 740/2.

162 Kouloridas (n 160) 1235; cf M Rapti, 'Amendments of the Greek law on Societes Anonymes for theImplementation of Directive 2007/36 on the Exercise of Certain Rights of Shareholders in Listed Companies' (2012) 23 ICCLR 24, 30.

deposit shares for a substantial amount of days prior to the GM, the underlying rationale being that resolutions should be adopted by legitimate voters, meaning by persons whose membership is beyond doubt. However, the collateral intention of share-blocking and its most drastic effect upon shareholders was the prohibition of transferring shares prior to the GM.[163] The EU legislator saw such provisions as problematic, hindering not only active shareholder participation but also the free flow of capital.[164] Consequently, SRD article 7 abolished share-blocking within the EU and resulted in the introduction of article 28a paragraph 1 to Law 2190/1920 (now Law 4548/2018 article 124). As a means of shareholder status' verification, the directive introduced the 'record date' mechanism.[165] Notably, regarding Greek law, contrary to the approach followed in relation to other means of shareholder protection within the SRD, share-blocking was abolished only regarding listed companies.[166]

Nevertheless, the facilitation of participation in the GM, the principal matter of the EU legislator's focus when it comes to shareholder rights and protection so far, is addressing just part of the problem of effective shareholder protection. Although it constitutes a means to align shareholders' views with those of the management, thereby reducing the respective agency costs, it does little to address the minority–majority agency problem.[167] Therefore, the significance of the SRD and the respective transposed provisions in the protection of shareholders in Greek companies is qualified. As explained in Chapter 2, share ownership in Greece is highly concentrated, and, therefore, the majority of votes in Greek GMs are predetermined, as they ultimately rest in the hands of few individuals who have intersecting interests within the company. Accordingly, even if minorities make best use of all their rights within the GMs in such ownership structures, they have to bow to the will of the majority sooner or later (save for the instances where a super-majority is needed, such as resolutions approving board remuneration). This is regardless of whether the majority's position is creating value or not for the company and thus for shareholders as a whole.[168] Voting cannot substitute shareholder remedies such as the derivative action in their function. It constitutes a whole different form of shareholder activism. The GM is a decision-making body with an

163 Rapti (n 162) 27.

164 Preamble to SRD (3).

165 SRD art 7(2), (3).

166 See Law 2190/1920 art 28. The new Law 4548/2018 abolished blocking for non-listed companies but allows the articles of association to provide for it.

167 See also Reisberg (n 33) 29. It has to be noted that even in cases where the discharge of members of the board of directors from liability is discussed in the GM, the latter members are not precluded from voting by Law 4548/2018 art 108, if it so happens that they hold shares.

168 According to Reisberg (n 33) 29, it is only the right to ask questions that has (slight) potential of deterrence, as the question may affect the reputation of the board members or executives in question.

authority distinct from that entrusted to directors. The right to vote becomes therefore of minuscule importance for minority shareholders in such circumstances, as a significant part of corporate decision-making takes place outside the GM. Even if the German doctrine of the 'unwritten competences'[169] of the GM were to be applied to Greek law, as advocated by some Greek academics,[170] in order to extend the scope of matters upon which the board needs shareholders' authorisation to act, this situation would not substantially change: in concentrated ownership, the American-style activism of proxy solicitation is of little relevance, as minority shareholders cannot subdue the will of a GM where their opponents hold the vast majority of shares.[171] What minorities would be left with, is the option of exiting the company, which is not an optimal option, given the effects that maladministration might have on the value of their shares. In any case, the GM's monitoring potential of the decision-makers rests in the hands of the majority and in situations where the 'ownership and control' agency problem gives way to the minority–majority one, participation rights for minority shareholders usually are, on their own, nothing more than a weapon loaded with blanks.

Furthermore, despite its efforts to minimise the costs involved in minority shareholders' voting and thus encourage participation, the SRD was not devoid of practical problems,[172] now attempted to be addressed by the new directive (SRD II).[173] The issue of empty voting was early detected as being left unaddressed,[174] and now the amended directive seeks to tackle it by article 3a. The idea behind the amendment is that, despite facilitating vote by proxy, the SRD did little before to ensure that the intermediaries do not obstruct communication between the company and the shareholders, because identification of the owners remained a matter largely left to national laws.[175] The

169 *Ungeschriebene Hauptversammlung-Kompetenz*, as established by BGH, BGHZ 83, 122, NJW 1982 1703 (*Holzmüller*); see Hüffer (n 6) 610, 655, for succinct analysis on the doctrine.

170 Maria Milathianaki, *I katanomí ton exousión metaxý tis Genikís Synélefsis kai tou Dioikitikoú Symvoulíou tis A.E.* (Nomiki Bibliothiki 2013).

171 It has to be noted that, possibly for this reason, the first 'proxy fight' evidenced in a German 'blue-chip' company (Infineon) took place in 2010, led by Hermes (a UK-based investment fund). See Richard Milne, 'Hermes Bid to Oust Next Infineon Chairman' (18 January 2010) Financial Times <www.ft.com/cms/s/2/e085c90a-045e-11df-8603-00144feabdc0.html#axzz3cijYNIhf> (accessed 11 June 2015).

172 See Masouros (n 132).

173 Directive 2017/828 amending Directive 2007/36/EC as regards the encouragement of long-term shareholder engagement [2017] OJ L 132 art 1. See also Commission, 'Proposal for a Directive Amending Directive 2007/36 on the Encouragement of Long-Term Shareholder Engagement and Directive 2013/34 on Certain Elements of the Corporate Governance Statement' COM(2014) 213 final.

174 Masouros (n 132) 198.

175 cf A Alexandropoulou, 'The New Proposal for a Directive Regarding the Strengthening of the Shareholder's Position, Board Remuneration and Transparency of the Role of Proxy Advisors and Intermediaries' (2014) 10 DEE 940, 941.

amendment[176] follows the UK paradigm,[177] whereby the company becomes the sole recipient of information regarding shareholders' identity, to the extent allowed by the fundamental right to privacy,[178] in order to communicate with them directly.

SRD II further tries to address, by means of the new article 3j, the issue of the conduct of proxy advisers and other service providers in a similar fashion (comply or explain) to the UK Stewardship Code,[179] imposing certain duties and transparency requirements.[180] The effects of this approach remain to be seen, as the new directive's deadline for transposition was set for 10 June 2019.[181] It is noteworthy that in another matter of shareholder protection the EU has followed (to an extent) the UK approach.

Evidently, the EU impact so far on the Greek law on shareholder meetings is positive, from the perspective of shareholder empowerment and protection, yet the applicable EU secondary legislation does not fully address agency problems of particular significance for Greek company law. In particular, the agency problem between minority and majority shareholders, a matter that the derivative action is designed to remedy, cannot be satisfactorily addressed within the ambit of the GM. It remains to be seen if in the future the EU proceeds with the harmonisation of shareholder suits.

Lastly, given that transposition of EU secondary law is mandatory for all member states, one should not expect Greek shareholder law to now enjoy a comparative edge over its European counterparts. In fact, apart from some divergence regarding the extent of implementation of the directive's provisions and the use of the default options provided therein, the directive can be said to have achieved a good level of harmonisation regarding significant components of the law on GMs. It is therefore understood that, due to the SRD(s), Greek law has caught up with its European counterparts in some respects, rather than surpassed them. This is all the more evident by the fact that in a variety of matters the directive effected an approximation of laws towards well-established Anglo-Saxon standards and practices. An example is the abolition of share-blocking prior to GMs in favour of the introduction of 'record dates'.[182] Similar

176 Art 3A.

177 CA 2006 s 793.

178 Art 16 TFEU; art 8 Charter of Fundamental Rights of the European Union.

179 FRC, UK Stewardship Code 2012, <www.frc.org.uk/Our-Work/Publications/Corporate-Governance/UK-Stewardship-Code-September-2012.pdf> (accessed 10 August 2015).

180 ibid. 4.

181 Notably, the directive is partly transposed by Law 4548/2018, regarding the provisos on board remuneration and on transparency and approval of related party transactions.

182 David Milman, 'Ascertaining Shareholder Wishes in UK Company Law in the 21st Century' (2010) 280 Co LN 1, 4. See Peter Bateman and Simon Howley, 'Legislative Comment. Shareholder Rights Directive: New General Meeting Requirements for Traded Companies' (2009) 256 Co LN 1, 4: 'the Directive ... mandates a record date system very similar to the one already used in the UK. As a result, investors in UK traded companies will see little change, but those with holdings in some continental overseas companies should find it

observations apply to the focus of the SRD on proxy voting. In the Anglo-Saxon jurisdictions,[183] proxy voting has been a particularly important element of shareholder participation and thus was therein regulated more extensively than in continental law countries such as Greece.[184] The SRDs moved Greek law closer to the Anglo-Saxon paradigm, a move also dictated by modern corporate practice and the growing influence of institutional investors internationally.[185]

4.8 Concluding remarks

The Greek legislator has exhibited some activity lately, modestly enriching and rationalising the framework of shareholder protection. A material aspect of shareholder protection that was left unaddressed during the latest reforms, however, was that of shareholder remedies. Contrary to its counterparts, Greek law has not yet introduced a form of derivative action and the company's action remains a rather restrictive remedy and cumbersome to invoke. This often leads to inconvenient results. Exemplifying the unsatisfactory state of the law, is the case of the Proton Bank collapse, where shareholders who could not avail themselves of the company's action brought – in one case unsuccessfully – direct claims against the management.

The existing framework of protection focuses primarily on the GM and the respective resolutions. Shareholders are bestowed an ensemble of rights, with the objective that resolutions represent decision-making free from abuse and conform to legal requirements. However, rights connected with the convening of GMs do not offer a complete or optimal form of protection for individual and minority shareholders, nor do they compensate for the shortcomings of the

easier to vote'. On the situation in Germany, see Till Naruisch and Fabian Liepe, 'Latest Developments in the German Law on Public Companies by the Act on Corporate Integrity and Modernisation of the Right of Resolution-Annulment (UMAG) – Shareholder Activism and Directors' Liability Reloaded' (2007) JBL 225, 233.

183 Differences within this legal family existed and persist. Proxy voting is more heavily regulated in the US than in the UK, a phenomenon possibly explained by the market for corporate control as an alternative to proxy contests in the shareholders' struggle to affect the constitution of the board of directors. See Mathias M Siems, *Convergence in Shareholder Law* (CUP 2008) 105. For the position in the UK prior to CA 2006 and the SRD, see RC Nolan, 'The Continuing Evolution of Shareholder Governance' (2006) 65 CLJ 92, 100, 101, 105.

184 See Kouloridas (n 160) 1234; cf the position in Germany, where rules on proxy voting are 'more detailed and systematically arranged than in the case in most other European jurisdictions' according to Frank Wooldridge, 'Voting Rights in German Public Companies' (2013) 34 Comp Law 51, 55.

185 Germany offers itself as a case study for this phenomenon. Since 2001, the German idiosyncratic model of reserving voting by proxy mainly to the banks where shares were deposited began to lose significance in law and business practice, giving way to models of proxy voting that resembled established practices in the US and the UK. See Siems, *Convergence* (n 183) 105, 107; for a succinct analysis of the German law on shareholder voting, see Wooldridge (n 184) 55.

company's action. This consideration also applies to the existing mechanism of challenging GM resolutions. To the extent misfeasance takes place outside the confines of the assembly, the shareholders' right to challenge its resolutions is by and large insignificant. It is therefore understood to fit the purpose of dealing with the minority-majority agency problem, assuming therefore a complementary function to derivative litigation within a shareholder protection framework.

Other mechanisms of shareholder protection cannot compensate for the ineffectiveness of the company's action either. Contractual freedom, already restricted by Greek law, is unable to provide shareholders with a complete and fair bargain, leaving gaps which the law attempts to fill by the imposition of duties and their enforcement. The market of corporate control, on the other hand, has a controversial effect on corporate governance and its relevance to the contemporary Greek corporate landscape is minuscule anyhow.

Analysis has illustrated that the level of shareholder protection under Greek law has not changed radically during the past decade, remains relatively low in a comparative context and can be further improved. The EU influence on the matter has provided a level playing field, yet its effect on shareholder remedies is minimal so far.[186] Contrary to the harmonisation of key rules on the conduct of GMs, shareholder remedies have not held a prominent position in the EU legislator's agenda ever since the proposed and now abandoned fifth company law directive. Against this backdrop, some prima facie extrema arise in juxtaposing the laws of Germany, Greece and the UK. The UK poses as the only jurisdiction providing an 'umbrella' remedy for oppression, whilst Greece is alone in not providing for a derivative action.

Even a move towards the foreign standards will not be optimal, unless the problems of the company's action are addressed. Class actions, a mechanism largely unknown to Greek law, may perform a role similar to derivative actions as a tool for collective redress. Further similarities concern their compensatory and deterrent functions. However, similarities end there, as their scope cannot cover the misfeasance the derivative action is designed to remedy. Regarding the prospect of broadening the scope of Greek remedies against abuse, by introduction of a UK-styled unfair prejudice remedy, the following points have been concluded. Firstly, the latter are limited regarding their application in practice, bearing relevance predominantly in closely held companies. Furthermore, they are rightfully classified as personal claims.[187] The distinction between personal claims and corporate claims remains important, even in jurisdictions with a long-standing tradition on shareholder litigation. The view that classification should be based on the person suffering direct loss from a corporate wrongdoing is doctrinally sound. Accordingly, if

186 The exception is the sell-out right provision of Law 4548/2018 art 46 (triggered when the majority holds 95% or more of the company's share capital).

187 Reisberg (n 33) 298: 'fundamentally s 994 is a remedy for shareholders who have suffered personal harm amounting to unfair prejudice'.

a wrong is done to the company and only the company suffers a direct loss, then the claim should be a corporate one and pursued by the company or the shareholders on its behalf. This rationale follows the no reflective loss principle and is based on the justifications analysed in Section 2.2. Therefore, they do not and should not function as a perfect substitute to derivative actions.

Against this background, shareholder suits to enforce corporate claims emerge as a pressing issue and reform on that matter may lead to a genuine upgrade of the national levels of shareholder protection. Reform would not only address the problems inherent in the company's action, but it would also compensate, to a certain extent, for the ineffectiveness of other mechanisms of shareholder protection, such as the (in)existing means of collective redress. The task of the ensuing Chapter is set accordingly.

Part III

Derivative actions de lege ferenda

Suggestions based on comparative considerations

5 Proposals for a functioning and truly protective derivative action

5.1 Introduction

The previous Chapters identified an ongoing issue in shareholder protection under Greek law. The company's action is fraught with problems in its construction and application. It was further shown that many of these problems are not encountered in jurisdictions where derivative actions exist. Moreover, it was illustrated that the levels of shareholder protection offered by Greek company law – particularly viewed in a comparative context – cannot compensate as a system for the defects of the company's action.

This Chapter advances proposals for reform, for the law *as it should be*. The conclusions reached from the preceding comparative analysis shall be implemented in order to form the appropriate recommendations. Specifically, this part of the study attempts to incorporate into the existing Greek legal framework the elements, existing in the other jurisdictions that can render it more protective. Furthermore, throughout this Section the works of other academics on the matter are scrutinised. The proposals are not only based on comparative law considerations de lege lata but also de lege ferenda: the views of the British and German scholarship on how the law on shareholder protection *should be* provide valuable insights for this Chapter.[1]

The ensuing Sections thus undertake to suggest a revision of mandatory legal provisions that are specifically intended for the protection of shareholders, with the aim of reasserting the effectiveness and competitiveness of Greek shareholder law. The recommended rules are crystallised and systematised. Furthermore, apart from procuring legal certainty,[2] it is essential that the reform proposals

1 Klaus Ulrich Schmolke, 'Die Aktionärsklage nach § 148 AktG – Anreizwirkungen de lege lata und Reformanregungen de lege ferenda' [2011] ZGR 398. Martin Peltzer, 'Das Zulassungsverfahren nach § 148 AktG wird von der Praxis nicht angenommen! Warum? Was nun?' in Ulrich Burgard, Walther Hadding, Peter O. Mülbert, Michael Nietsch and Reinhard Welter (eds), *Festschrift Für Uwe H. Schneider zum 70. Geburtstag* (Otto Schmidt 2011) 763, 764–65; Arad Reisberg, *Derivative Actions and Corporate Governance: Theory and Operation* (OUP 2007).

2 Interesting insights on the subject by Carsten Paul, 'Derivative Actions under English and German Corporate Law: Shareholder Participation between the Tension Filled Areas of Corporate Governance and Malicious Shareholder Interference' (2010) 115 ECFR 81.

strike the right balance between the availability of derivative actions and their exceptional character. The proposals have to reflect the subsidiary nature derivative actions have vis-a-vis claims brought by the company.

This Chapter proceeds as follows: first, an inquiry takes place regarding the desirability of the introduction of derivative actions to Greek law, with particular reference to the German experience. Then, the study addresses the question of whether an individual shareholder right is preferable compared to the alternative of a qualified minority one. Continuing, this Chapter adopts a position in the debated issue of what kinds of misfeasance are to be covered by shareholders' litigation. Furthermore, mechanisms for filtering unmeritorious litigation are considered. The proposals also consider regulation of costs for derivative proceedings and access to claim-related information. Section 5.7 concludes.

5.2 Is the transition from company's actions to derivative actions desirable? Insights from Germany

Is a genuine derivative action necessary, or would another reform of the company's action suffice? Until 2005, German law on public limited companies shared many similarities, already identified in Chapter 3, with the Greek legal order regarding the matter of shareholders' suits. Thus, the examination of the opinions given by the German legislator and academics, on why the regime of company's actions had to change and what were the purposes of the reform, has useful implications for this Chapter. We should thus avail the privilege of having the German *experience* on the matter at hand.

The commentaries and explanatory notes to the Reforming Act (UMAG) pinpoint the betterment (*Verbesserung*) of enforcement of corporate claims as the preponderant reason for the introduction of derivative actions; within the limits of non-abusive litigation.[3] Consequently, the pre-existing arsenal of claims against mismanagement (i.e. AktG s 147, as it stood before UMAG) – with all its commonalities to the Greek one – was considered inefficient and/or inadequate. The new Section 148 of *Aktiengesetz* can be perceived as a first step towards the forge of a shareholder-friendly environment in Germany, a belated response to a cross-border trend described in Chapter 2.[4] Among other reasons for taking more incisive steps, the failure of the KonTraG amendments to prevent corporate scandals arising from breaches of fiduciary duties in 1999–2000 boosted the reconsideration of the 'special representatives' regime on company's actions.[5]

To briefly recapitulate the relevant parts of the discussion in Chapter 3, prior to the enactment of UMAG, one could hardly distinguish between the Greek and German statutory company's actions. Both jurisdictions followed the special

3 Uwe Hüffer, *Aktiengesetz* (10th edn, CH Beck 2012) 865.

4 Concurring: Janet Dine and Marios Koutsias, *The Nature of Corporate Governance* (EE 2013) 287–288.

5 RegE-UMAG, BT-Drucks 15/5092 20.

representatives model, the only material difference between the two adaptations of the latter being the discretion of the appointed representatives to decide not to pursue the claim under German law. Special representatives may be anyone with capacity to act in law, appointed to replace the board, but only with regards to the issue of litigation of corporate claims.[6] Therefore, the possibility exists in that model of corporate litigation that the persons selected by the court to act on behalf of the company may have no motive to exhibit any zeal in championing the company's interests, enjoying only a short-term and issue-specific interim appointment and having secured compensation for their services.

Nevertheless, almost 15 years ago Germany introduced genuine derivative actions to its law on public limited companies. Greece however, has retained the former model, despite some changes (in 2007 and 2019) on ownership thresholds, court review and cost rules in the admission proceedings.[7] Surely, the preparatory committees for company law reforms in both jurisdictions have both considered the introduction of derivative actions during the past two decades, yet only one materialised the thought of strengthening shareholder protection and management accountability in such a way. It may also be true that German law prior to 2005 was marginally lacking, from a shareholder protection point of view, compared to the then contemporary Greek regime on company's actions: the discretionary powers of the *besondere Vertretern* being the main reason, alongside the high liability thresholds.[8] The German legislators went a few steps beyond eliminating this disadvantage and merely providing 'enhancements' analogous to those of the Greek 2007 amendment and 2019 reform: a genuine derivative action was introduced. The derivative action was preferred to proposals to 'enhance' shareholder control over special representatives, such as a right of shareholders to nominate their preferred persons to assume the tasks and duties of special representatives – a right already existing under Greek law, as we saw above.[9] The rationale behind this attempted 'betterment' of German law thus provides some insight and argumentation against Greek parsimony in instituting private mechanisms of directors' accountability.

6 The plural used by the Greek statute has led many to interpret it as demanding more than one representative to be appointed always, but the correct opinion supports that one person may suffice. See AI Freris, 'Judicial Enforcement of Corporate Claims against the Members of the Board of Directors' in VG Antonopoulos and S Mouzoulas, *Sociétés Anonymes*, vol. 2 (Sakkoulas 2013) 208. In practice, attorneys whose offices are close to the company's offices are preferred for this task by the courts. See Patrai Court of Appeal 266/2011 NOMOS Databank, Armenopoulos 2013 293.

7 Law 3604/2007 art 31(2), (3).

8 Note that, by virtue of the latest reform, similar discretionary powers are bestowed to Greek special representatives.

9 Jens Koch, 'Das Gesetz zur Unternehmensintegrität und Modernisierung des Anfechtungsrechts (UMAG)' [2006] ZGR 769, 778: 'Compare Krieger who had proposed in view of these difficulties, basically to keep with the figure of the special representative, but significantly reshape their legal position. In particular, the minority shareholder should be given a right of proposal as to the person of the representative.'

One of the starting points for the German legislator was that the threshold of 5% for legal standing in company's actions and 10% in special audit requests was too high.[10] The coincidence of numbers with the Greek approach makes any further elaboration on the similarities redundant. Furthermore, the absence of judicial supervision on the admissibility of such actions was viewed as 'absurd'.[11] Now, this is another point in common with article 22b of Greek Law 2190/1920: as long as the quorum requirements and 'demand' are satisfied, anyone could file an application under the old version of Section 147 III of *Aktiengesetz*, for whatever the reason.[12]

A critical departure from the old regime concerned the institution of the special representatives. Despite the 'compromise' made by KonTraG, as admitted by the explanatory notes to UMAG, the 'discussion on board liability never came to rest'.[13] Soon after the enactment of KonTraG, the 63rd German Jurists Forum resolved that change was necessary and, eventually, the German government-appointed commission on CG and ultimately the legislature espoused Professor Baums' recommendations to the forum.[14] The idea was proposed accordingly, that it is preferable that minorities pursue the claim themselves. UMAG thus attempted to alleviate the concerns raised over the motives and representation by the special representatives. Prior to the amendment, the very concept of shareholders representing the company in corporate claims was dismissed as contrary to the tenet that, within the 'corporate democracy', corporate powers are distributed by statute.[15] Despite the fact that the very regime of special representatives was in itself a deviation from those principles,[16] as the latter constituted an ad hoc corporate organ (appointed by the court or the GM), the German legislator found it easier to justify from a theoretical perspective than a genuine derivative action.[17] However, the institution (*Rechtsinstitut*) of special representatives was in various ways unattractive for minorities: not only the latter ran the risk of costs, but also they were limited to the admission procedure and had thus no control over the claim

10 Nikolaos Paschos and Kay-Uwe Neumann, 'Die Neuregelungen des UMAG im Bereich der Durchsetzung von Haftungsansprüchen der Aktiengesellschaft gegen Organmitglieder' (2005) 33 DB 1779, 1780.

11 RegE-UMAG, BT-Drucks 15/5092 20.

12 Procedure under s 147 II was slightly different in this respect, as it left some discretion to the court to decide whether the special representative was preferable an option to the ordinary corporate organs capable of bringing the claim.

13 RegE-UMAG, BT-Drucks 15/5092 20.

14 See, for an overview of the events leading to the UMAG, Hans C Hirt, The Enforcement of Directors' Duties Pursuant to the Aktiengesetz: Present Law and Reform in Germany: Part 2' (2005) 16 ICCLR 216, 220.

15 Hans C Hirt, *The Enforcement of Directors' Duties in Britain and Germany: A Comparative Study with Particular Reference to Large Companies* (Peter Lang 2004) 188.

16 ibid.

17 The institution of special representatives may be viewed as an ad hoc appointed administration of the company, something common in the general commercial and company law of civil jurisdictions in cases of conflicts of interest.

itself. Various academics voiced concerns in this respect,[18] and the German quest for an effective accountability mechanism culminated in the introduction of a minorities' right to sue in their own name but on behalf of the company.

Overall, derivative actions should be considered an important element of shareholding.[19] They constitute in most of the advanced economies a significant part in the bundle of rights that is share ownership and, as such, any jurisdiction not providing a functioning legal mechanism to that end should be perceived as having shares of a comparative lower value traded in its market(s).[20] The German legislator realised that in 2005 and did not hesitate to amend the company law statute. There are already voices in Greek academia supporting the introduction of derivative actions. Apart from the unsuccessful attempt to include a relevant provision in the Law on Corporate Governance for Listed Companies in the beginning of the previous decade, several authors have recently expressed their support for change in shareholder litigation mechanisms.[21] The similarity some proposals have with the German model is rather intriguing. A quick perusal of the relevant papers suffices to show that the contemporaneous ownership rule, the demand rule, litigation costs allocation (as a deterrent to 'predatory' litigation) and limitations on the scope of misfeasance remedied are all enshrined in the minds of Greek academics as necessary elements of an efficient framework for derivative actions. However, it was explained herein that the German provisions are (still) far from perfect. Therefore, the ensuing analysis will consider both German and UK law in its quest for the optimal framework for derivative litigation.

The proposals advanced in the following Sections are most suitable for statutory reform. The reason is that the applicable Greek (company) law leaves little room for judicial gap-filling by means of interpretation and,[22] in any case, cannot respond to

18 See Theodor Baums, 'Personal Liabilities of Company Directors in German Law' (1996) 7 (9) ICCLR 318, 322; Hans C Hirt, 'The Enforcement of Directors' Duties Pursuant to the Aktiengesetz: Present Law and Reform in Germany: Part 1' (2005) ICCLR 179, 189–190; Peter Ulmer, 'Die Aktionärsklage als Instrument zur Kontrolle des Vorstands- und Aufsichtsratshandelns' (1999) 163 ZHR 290, 334–336.

19 Concurring: Marcus Lutter, 'Theorie der Mitgliedschaft: Prolegomena zu einem Allgemeinen Teil des Korporationsrechts' (April 1980) 180 AcP 84 144.

20 Quality of corporate governance affects market value. See John C CoffeeJr, 'Racing towards the Top: The Impact of Cross-Listing and Stock Market Competition on International Corporate Governance' (2002) 102 Colum L Rev 1757, 1786.

21 Indicatively: Georgios Triantafillakis, *From the Protection of the Minority to the Protection of the Shareholder*, in Minutes of the 18th Panhellenian Conference on Commercial Law (Collaborative Work), *Trends and Prospects of the Law of the Public Limited Company* (Nomiki Bibliothiki 2009) 117ff; Christina Livada, 'Filing of Company Claims against the Members of the Board of Director' in Perakis Evanghelos (ed), *Sociétés Anonyme's Law* (3rd edn, Sakkoulas2013) 1017–1018, reproduced in Alexandra Mikroulea, *Scope of Corporate Managers' Duties and Liability* (Nomiki Bibliothiki 2013) 284.

22 Nikolaos K Rokas, 'Corporate Organisation and Shareholders' Individual Action' [2007] NH' EEmpD 1, 18: 'the recommended solution for Greek law would be the statutory regulation of the matter' (of the 'minority's protection against abuses on the part of the management and the controlling shareholder'). It has to be noted that, according to the prevailing

the challenges posed by the complexity of derivative litigation.[23] As explained in Chapter 3, for derivative actions to be truly protective of shareholder interests, regulatory safeguards against undesirable litigation have to be in place alongside incentives for shareholders to assume the stewardship role of the derivative claimant.

Lastly, the de lege ferenda suggestions herein articulated do not necessarily envisage the replacement of the company's action by a derivative action. Depending on the construction of the respective legal provisions, both can work in parallel within a legal system.

In Germany, the introduction of *Aktiengesetz* Section 148 abolished the *exclusivity* of the institution of special representatives as a means of shareholder protection against mismanagement, not the institution itself.[24] With the necessary amendments in the wording of Law 4548/2018 articles 104 and 105, the company's action and the proposed derivative action can co-exist. In fact, some of the ensuing proposals may even benefit the company's action in such co-existence. In particular, the ability of shareholders to take over or join pending litigation may work towards the prudent and loyal discharge of special representatives' duties. Such participation of shareholders in the proceedings would mitigate any agency problem arising between the appointing minority and the appointed representatives. Moreover, the extension of liability to controlling shareholders will also make the enforcement of corporate claims via special representatives more likely. This is evidenced in Germany where, despite the fact that the appointment of special representatives (even by court decision following a 10% minority petition) is subject to the condition that a General Meeting resolution is taken to that effect by simple majority,[25] the exclusion of the accused shareholders from voting has resulted, occasionally, in the appointment of special representatives.[26]

In any case, by virtue of the herein proposed framework minority shareholders would have two options in their armoury. Accordingly, if a minority's petition to appoint special representatives is likely to be dismissed, because they fall short of the quorum threshold or six months did not lapse since they demanded that the board brings the action, shareholders may resort to suing derivatively under the

opinion in Germany, the company's action under the old AktG s 147 – with all its similarities to Greek Law 2190/1920 art 22b and Law 4548/2018 art 105 – rendered any interpretation allowing for a derivative action or actio pro socio unjustified (Uwe Hüffer *Aktiengesetz* (2nd edn, CH Beck 1995) 622).

23 Evanghelos Perakis, 'The Greek and International Discussion on Acceptance and Restriction of the Derivative Action brought by a Shareholder of a Public Limited Company' in Hideo Nakamura, Hans Fasching, Hans F Gaul and Apostolos Georgiades (eds), *Festschrift für Kostas E Beys dem Rechtsdenker in Attischer Dialektik* (5th edn, Eunomia 2003) 3687.

24 See AktG s147(2).

25 Barbara Mayer, 'Geltendmachung von Ersatzansprüchen' in Albert Schröder, Barbara Mayer, Gerhard Manz, Hendrik Thies and Stefan Lammel, *Die Aktiengesellschaft: Umfassende Erläuterungen, Beispiele und Musterformulare für die Rechtspraxis* (7th edn, Haufe 2014) 289–290; Hüffer 2012 (n 3) 862.

26 Uwe Schneider, 'Der mühsame Weg der Durchsetzung der Organhaftung durch den besonderen Vertreter nach § 147 AktG' [2013] ZIP 1985, 1986.

more permissive (from the viewpoint of legal standing) proposed framework. That said, we shall move to the discussion on which minority should be afforded legal standing in derivative proceedings.

5.3 Who should be allowed to sue?

5.3.1 Individual right instead of qualified minority one[27]

5.3.1.1 Introduction

The first question to be posed in proposing the introduction of derivative actions is 'to whom should the right to petition for leave to bring a derivative action be conferred?' As explained in the previous Chapters, there are two approaches: either construing a minority ownership threshold (qualified minority strategy/approach) or considering the right to sue on behalf of the company as inherent in share ownership.

Greek law (through its latest general reform) attempted to make company actions available to a wider range of shareholders by lowering the share ownership thresholds required for standing to sue. So did the UMAG, though the reform there was more substantial. These developments beg the question of whether the 'qualified minority strategy' should be maintained. It is hereinafter argued that it is not only doctrinally inconsistent with the nature and rationale of derivative actions to confer the relevant right to a qualified minority but also impractical and ineffective in restricting malicious litigation, as such a quantitative restriction may also bar meritorious claims.

5.3.1.1.1 THE PROBLEMS ENTAILED IN AN EX LEGE QUALIFIED MINORITY APPROACH

It is a rather challenging task to construe appropriate ownership thresholds. The civil law experience shows that the required percentages have been constantly revised by the legislator, downwards, in most cases. The reason for such amendments has been the fact that (presumably high) ownership thresholds proved to be a stumbling block for litigation and often rendered statutory provisions 'empty shells' with no practical value.[28]

The previous Chapter identified regarding such criteria that, by logical necessity, they reflect a one-size-fits-all approach. Considering the German threshold of 1% of registered share capital, it may amount to hundreds,[29] or millions of

27 See Georgios Zouridakis, 'Introducing Derivative Actions in the Greek Law on Public Limited Companies: Issues of Legal Standing and Lessons from the German and UK Experience' (2015) 26 ICCLR 271, 274–80.

28 In different kinds of litigation, the qualified minority approach did not have such adverse effects. This is the case of the special audit procedure in the Kingdom of the Netherlands: Martin Gelter, 'Why do shareholder derivative suits remain rare in continental Europe?' (-2011–2012) 37 Brook J Int'l L 843, 889ff.

29 Given that minimum capital rules apply across the EU, 1% stake at a Greek company would be 260 euros minimum.

euros in market value of shareholdings.[30] This is a significant limitation of the availability of the right to sue to rich members only. Thus, many jurisdictions (including Germany and the UK) set supplementary criteria in determining the proportion of corporate capital necessary to enact the right to sue.[31] Accordingly, some focus on the financial value of the shareholding and set the alternative threshold according to it,[32] whilst other focus on the numbers of claimants, so as to make sure that in dispersed shareholdings there is no need to summon hundreds of petitioners for admission proceedings to be initiated.[33]

If the Greek legislator wants to maintain the qualified minority approach, the second solution is the safest one.[34] The nominal share value is a misleading concept, as the trade value may be (and usually is) much bigger. The number of members willing to initiate proceedings is more in line with the anti-predatory-suits rationale: in other words, it would be hard for a single shareholder to convince a number of his/her counterparts to file a strike suit.

Nevertheless, even this 'solution' is incompatible with the Greek business reality. Suppose that derivative actions are availed to 5% of share capital or at least 50 members of the company (as happens with CA 2006 s 370), it is hard to find any non-listed corporation which actually has this number of members altogether, yet I can think of many that have loyal shareholders owning less than 5% of the registered share capital.

In any case, the default minimum of 5% as now applicable in Greece is high from a comparative and practical perspective.[35] Furthermore, the pretence that

30 Consider that among ten listed companies in the Athens Stock Exchange (Eurobank, Hellenic Petroleum, Minoan Lines, Motor Oil Hellas, National Bank of Greece, OLP, OPAP, Piraeus Bank, Titan and Viohalco), the lowest market capitalisation was 213,960,100 euros (Minoan Lines), while the largest was 3,388,290,496.13 euros (National Bank of Greece) in April 2015, even following a protracted nosedive of the general index (values as of 17 April 2015; data retrieved from the official website of Hellenic Exchanges <www.helex.gr/el/web/guest/companies-map>).

31 AktG s 148 I; CA 2006 s 370.

32 In Germany, regarding AktG s 148, it is submitted that the dual threshold attempts to strike a balance on the availability of derivative actions in both listed and non-listed companies; the proposal to set the threshold according to 'listed' value did not materialise. See Koch, 'Das Gesetz' (n 9), 772; Karsten Schmidt, 'Verfolgungspflichten, Verfolgungsrechte und Aktionärsklagen: Ist die Quadratur des Zirkels näher gerückt? Gedanken zur Reform der §§ 147–149 AktG vor dem Hintergrund der Juristentagsdiskussion des Jahres 2000' [2005] NZG 796, 799.

33 CA 2006 s 370.

34 Dario Latella, 'Shareholder Derivative Suits: A Comparative Analysis and the Implications of the European Shareholders' *Rights Directive* (2009) 6 ECFR 307, 320, suggested that an alternative would be to introduce ownership thresholds according to the free float of (listed) companies; despite addressing practical concerns, this solution does not fit with the arguments in Subsection 5.3.1.2.2, as it still constitutes a qualified minority approach.

35 Apart from Germany and the UK, nine more member states prescribe lower shareholding thresholds for derivative actions than Greece within the EU. See Carsten Gerner-Beuerle, Philipp Paech and Edmund Philipp Schuster, 'Study on Directors' Duties and Liability'

the by-laws may lower the percentage to the minimum of one share[36] should not be understood as having any practical significance at all: given the concentrated ownership structure of Greek companies, it is hard to see why the founders or the GM would decide to make use of such discretion.[37] A look at the published articles of association of major listed Greek companies supports this argument: among ten companies listed in the Athens Stock Exchange, none of them had lowered the default ownership threshold under Law 2190/1920.[38] Even though it is still too early to check for responses under the new law, there is nothing to suggest that a change of heart will take place anytime soon. Anyhow, any aspirations that, since the 2007 reform of Law 2190/1920, Greek law provides for the possibility of contractually (by virtue of the company's by-laws) rendering the right to sue on behalf of the company an individual one, are wishful thinking, as (1) it is the institution of special representatives, not shareholders, who are afforded legal standing in the main proceedings, and (2) there is little reason for companies to avail themselves of the option to lower the quorum thresholds, especially in the absence of considerable safeguards against predatory suits other than legal standing restrictions.

<http://ec.europa.eu/internal_market/company/docs/board/2013-study-analysis_en.pdf> (accessed 1 May 2015) 201.

36 Livada, 'Company Claims' (n 21) 1016.

37 Alongside the ensuing argumentation, consider the insightful behavioural economics study of Russell Korobkin, 'The Status Quo Bias and Contract Default Rules' (1998) 83 Cornell L Rev 608. By means of controlled experiments, it supported the thesis that contracting parties exhibit a status quo bias in favour of default rules. From this viewpoint, a default of, say, one share to initiate the corporate action with a maximum set at 5% of registered share capital (i.e. the exact reverse of Law 4548/2018 arts 104–105) would most likely be in favour of minorities, as majorities would be less inclined to move away from the statutorily-set status quo, all things being equal.

38 Namely, Eurobank Ergasias SA, Hellenic Petroleum, METKA, Motor Oil Hellas, National Bank of Greece, OLP, OPAP, OTE SA, Piraeus Bank and Terna Energy SA. The sample represents 40% of the companies comprising the FTSE/XA Large Cap index. The respective by-laws are readily available online at the companies' websites (accessed 1 May 2015):

<www.eurobank.gr/Uploads/pdf/katastatiko_en_12.04.2014.%20eng.pdf>, <www.helpe.gr/userfiles/8a53b155-76e9-4d45-9773-a27000e44a36/katastatiko.pdf>, <www.metka.com/Uploads/parousiaseis-entypa/entypa/COMPANY_STATUTE_eng.pdf>, <www.moh.gr/media/PDF_inside_texts/Etairiky_diakivernisy/Company%20Memorandum%20(Gr).pdf>, <www.nbg.gr/greek/the-group/corporate-governance/regulations-principles/Documents/GR_ARTICLES%20OF%20ASSOCIATION_22.07.2014.pdf>, <www.olp.gr/en/the-port-of-piraeus/organization-statute>, <www.opap.gr/documents/11503/3551006/%CE%9A%CE%91%CE%A4%CE%91%CE%A3%CE%A4%CE%91%CE%A4%CE%99%CE%9A%CE%9F%20%CE%A4%CE%97%CE%A3%20%CE%95%CE%A4%CE%91%CE%99%CE%A1%CE%95%CE%99%CE%91%CE%A3.pdf>, <www.ote.gr/documents/10280/42094851/AOI_EGM_30_12_2013_eng_v2.pdf/445013f9-36fc-423f-9937-fb8245149246>, <www.piraeusbankgroup.com/en/investors/corporate-governance/board>, <www.terna-energy.com/userfiles/5a12449c-be9f-43ce-9e75-ba74180074b6/TENERG_ARTICLES_OF_ASSOCIATION_13-05-2014_EN.pdf>

Last but not least, we must consider a further problem created by such requirements. Even though dispersed ownership is largely unknown on the continent, few listed companies do exhibit quite high rates of 'free float'. There, the only viable way for a derivative action to be brought is for a good number of shareholders to ally with the view of bringing a claim. The legislators are thus at pains to ensure that the right to sue is available to minor investors by arguing that the law accommodates, through various mechanisms, collective action in this regard.[39] Ideally, minorities would not be deprived of protection, whilst predatory claimants would be isolated by the other members, acting rationally and for the benefit of the company: all this achieved by just picking the right numbers in devising an ownership threshold.

Reality comes at odds with those presumptions. Collective action in respect of shareholder engagement remains problematic in general: in the EU context, it has been a matter of focus for the European Commission for some time.[40] Communication amongst shareholders involves additional costs and the hardship of discovering who the fellow members are.[41] Doing away with the qualified minority strategy will render the need for effective collective action mechanisms within the ambit of derivative actions redundant.

The upshot is that ownership thresholds cannot ensure that potential champions of the corporate interest are not deprived of the right to sue on behalf of the company. Any of the available thresholds in the comparative study leaves significant minorities disenfranchised: a problem unlikely to be resolved by collective action mechanisms. The next paragraph suggests that it is not only impractical, but also doctrinally inconsistent to adopt a qualified minority strategy.

5.3.1.1.2 A CONTESTATION OF THE RATIONALE BEHIND THE QUALIFIED MINORITY APPROACH FROM A DOCTRINAL PERSPECTIVE

An oft-produced justification for the adoption of the qualified minority strategy is that the interests of members holding a substantial investment in the company coincide with those of the latter.[42] The problem with this rationale is that it is to a large extent probabilistic. There is nowadays a fervent discussion on how to incentivise institutional investors within the context of corporate governance.[43] Such investors are the most significant block-holders in Europe nowadays, but their passivity thus far defeats much of the argument's strength.

39 In Germany an on-line 'shareholders' forum' exists to that end. See Paschos and Neumann (n 10) 1786, 1780.

40 See Subsection 4.7.4.

41 See, on the matter, Dirk A Zetzsche, 'Shareholder Passivity, Cross-Border Voting and the Shareholder Rights Directive' (2008) 8 JCLS 289; Pavlos Masouros, 'Is the EU Taking Shareholder Rights Seriously?: An Essay on the Impotence of Shareholdership in Corporate Europe' (2010) 7 ECL 195.

42 Livada, 'Company Claims' (n 21) 1017; concurring: Begr. RegE UMAG, BT-Drs. 15/5092, Explanatory notes, 21.

43 Dine and Koutsias, *The Nature* (n 4) 234.

When the need for block-holders' 'voice' arose, the latter remained silent in the comfort of their 'splendid isolation'.[44] Apart from shareholder apathy, an explanation for the latter phenomenon within the continental European context could be that block-holders, being limited in numbers, are more readily approachable by the wrongdoers. An agreement between them and the management not to sue in return for a considerable counter-performance, although not judicially enforceable under the laws of most of Western jurisdictions, is a realistic option for both the board and the block-holders.[45] After all, given that except for jurisdictions like New Zealand and the US, pursuing a derivative claim is not quite a profitable enterprise in general,[46] such an agreement would most often strike the economically rational equilibrium. Potentially, block-holders may in such situations use their right to sue as a means of extortion: either the board succumbs to their demands or they initiate proceedings.

The adverse effect of this strategy is that, by expressly basing the capital thresholds on the rationale that members satisfying the latter have interests more closely intertwined with those of the company, the latter assumption becomes the effect: the two aforementioned sets of interest equate in practice and the company eventually operates for the sole benefit of the block-holders.

Overall, it may be true that shareholders with a material stake in the company's capital are more likely to have their interests intertwined with those of the company, as long as they bear more risk. However, entrusting the corporate claims upon them excludes minorities which may have the incentive to act for the benefit of the company. The subtext in those arguments is that a quorum may deflect the threat of predatory shareholders, or, more profoundly, that block-holders are more trusted and thus more desirable investors. On the contrary, the judicially based approach strikes at the heart of the problem, without disenfranchising members with a small financial stake in the company. If the alignment with corporate interests is to be ensured, the legislator should not leave it to share capital participation to decide. What should be instituted

44 See Roman Tomasic and Folarin Akinbami, 'Shareholder Activism and Litigation against UK Bank' in Joan Loughery (ed), *Directors' Duties and Shareholder Litigation in the Wake of the Financial Crisis* (EE 2013) 143–172.

45 Game theory models have been deployed to explain why the qualified minority approach accommodates misappropriation of corporate wealth. An insightful and pioneering paper on this subject is Kristoffel Grechenig and Michael Sekyra, 'No Derivative Shareholder Suits in Europe: A Model of Percentage Limits, Collusion and Residual Owners' (2007) The Center for Law and Economic Studies Columbia University School of Law, Working Paper No. 312 <http://papers.ssrn.com/sol3/papers.cfm?abstract_id=933105> (accessed 29 August 2014). A crucial element of this rationale is that when the right to bring a suit is an individual one, wrongdoers find it more difficult to 'bribe' every each one of the shareholders not to initiate proceedings and thus be deprived of the proceeds of misfeasance and suffer damage on their reputation as managers. This argument hits at the core of the derivative actions' function as anti-block devices addressing the majority-minority agency problem.

46 See Section 5.5 on litigation costs.

instead, is the courts' discretion to judge ad hoc whether a claimant acts in accordance with the corporate interests or not.

It is therefore more appropriate doctrinally to perceive derivative actions as an individual right accruing from membership. In essence, it is the right of every member to champion the corporate interests by substituting ad hoc the board in corporate decision-making.[47] When entering the company via shares purchase, every shareholder expects that the company is managed in a lawful and diligent manner. By deriving the right to sue for maladministration from the company, the claimant seeks judicial enforcement of such shareholders' expectations. It is hard thus to see why, for a procedure designed to benefit the company as a whole, an elite of block-holders and minority groups should prevent the individual acting in accordance with the corporate interests to seek accountability of wrongdoers. In such a way, members with a higher stake in the corporate capital are privileged with additional rights, arguably disturbing the equal treatment of equity ownership.

Constructing the Greek derivative action as an individual right of members may serve *two purposes.*

First, it ensures that accountability of the management may be judicially enforced by a wide range of constituencies that are unaffected by the views of the board. Block-holders can exercise de facto monitoring over the board, but, on the other side of the coin, they might partake in damaging decision-making for the company. The question in situations where the ones entrusted with the right to sue derivatively are block-holders of, say, 5% share ownership is ultimately: 'who will monitor the monitors'?[48]

Second, it nurtures a shareholder-friendly culture. Within the bargain for shares, the right to protect the equity investment from mismanagement will be in place. If the Greek legislator wanted to foster a more disperse ownership culture, such an arbitrary threshold would not exist. On the contrary, it can be said that the high threshold (significantly higher even than the German one) has two implications: first, it reflects the perception of the national legislator that the interests of the company are closely intertwined with those of block-holders of significant voting power and the belief that this is the way things should remain, and, second, shareholder actions are thus limited to closely held companies, where dissident minorities can easier satisfy the given threshold.

A similar rationale of making rights available to smaller minorities was followed in Germany where a low threshold of 1% of registered capital was instituted, yet the quorum approach was maintained despite the otherwise drastic steps of the 2005 reform.[49] My opinion is that the Greek legislator should look

47 What Hirt (*The Enforcement* (n 13) 46ff) calls 'decision rights strategy'.

48 The phrase appeared in a different context in John C Coffee Jr, 'Litigation and Corporate Governance: An Essay on Steering Between Scylla and Charybdis' (1983–1984) 52 Geo Wash L Rev 789, 798.

49 Begr. RegE UMAG, BT-Drs. 15/5092 21. See also Christoph H Seibt, 'Die Reform des Verfolgungsrechts nach § 147 AktG und des Rechts der Sonderprüfung' [2004] WM 2137, 2145ff.

beyond the statutory provisions of the otherwise familiar German legal order and consider the growing opinion in the German academia that such thresholds have no place in derivative actions.[50]

5.3.1.2 Summary and further remarks

The above paragraphs propose that the qualified majority strategy should not be followed in the introduction of genuine derivative actions in Greece. The justifications of such an approach are, at least, shaky and outweighed by the arguments in favour of an individual right. An individual shareholders' right to litigate on behalf of the company is more shareholder-friendly, unambiguous, reducing agency problems and free from the impracticalities entailed in collective action.

In tandem with this study's focus, only shareholders were considered as eligible for locus standi. Given that the derivative action purports to enforce the corporation's rights, it could be submitted that other entities having a stake at the company should be able to avail them. The proposals in this Section and the rationale behind them do not necessarily refute this proposition (occasionally, they may be perceived to support it), but further analysis would fall outside the scope of this study.

5.3.2 Contemporaneous and continuous ownership of shares

A further point to be addressed in the introduction of a genuine derivative action is that of contemporaneous and continuous ownership. As explained, due to the requirement that petitioners in a company's action or claimants in a derivative action were members when the wrongful behaviour took place (contemporaneous ownership rule) or even several months prior to and for the complete duration of the proceedings (continuous ownership rule), civil law jurisdictions substantially limit the availability of the right to sue on behalf of the company.

As a matter of policy, such rules provide favourable treatment to (presumably) long-term investors and purport to relieve management from unnecessary judicial interference. The rationale for such rules – as illustrated by their proponents – is that shareholders satisfying these thresholds are more likely to have their interests aligned with those of the company: what is further proposed is that in such a way an 'automated' filter of predatory actions is established.[51] Neither of these suggestions is conclusive. Long-standing shareholders may well bring an action contrary to the corporate interests, so as to satisfy ulterior personal motives or due to lack of proper appreciation of the litigation's effects on the company and its members, whilst buying shares only to embroil a company

50 Schmolke (n 1) 425; G Bezzenberger and T Bezzenberger, 'Section 148' in K Hopt and H Wiedemann (eds), *Großkommentar AktG* (De Gruyter 2008); Peltzer (n 1) 954, explaining the arbitrary determination of the quorum; see also Gelter (n 28) 879, 856ff.

51 See Ioannis Passias, *To Díkaion tis Anonýmou Etaireías* (1969) 695.

in litigation is a rather expensive and exclusive sport, whose popularity is unlikely to be seriously affected by such requirements.

On the contrary, such rules may lead to injustice in certain situations. Suppose that, following the issue of new shares, tunnelling of assets takes place, and the company is rendered an 'empty shell', to the detriment of the new members. Under Greek law, the aggrieved shareholders might have some luck pursuing a personal claim for damages, on the basis of general tort law (Civil Code articles 914–919); however, the principle that only the company may enforce its claims will most likely prove to be a stumbling rock. Furthermore, due to the temporal shareholdership threshold of six months prior to filing the claim set by Greek law, members will be unable to exercise the right to appoint special representatives. Redress would thus be unavailable both for shareholders (reflectively) and for the company for some time and the protracted initiation of claims may run to the latter's detriment. Such a threshold is of questionable value, even from an anti-predatory-suits perspective, as 'professional' litigants may well be patient. In any case, this threshold cannot always reflect the claimant's intentions and is out of pace with modern commercial practice.[52] Consider now the situation where, following a successful merger or acquisition, shareholders that brought a claim lost their membership status.[53] The continuous ownership rule would debar them from continuing with the action:[54] this is hardly an equitable outcome, as claimants lost their member status involuntarily, having already assumed the risk of litigation.[55] In view of the above, it is unsurprising that in countries where contemporaneous or continuous ownership used to be required for a derivative action to proceed, the respective legislators soon realised the redundancy of such rules and reformed accordingly.[56]

In any case, such temporal thresholds are inconsistent doctrinally with the very essence of the derivative action.[57] Its purpose is to provide redress for a wrong done to the company, not necessarily to select shareholders let alone long-term ones, by assigning members with a stewardship role to promote the corporate interests. It should therefore be immaterial whether the claimant was part of the company when the wrong to the latter occurred, provided bringing an action fulfils this stewardship role.

52 See Fang Ma, 'The Deficiencies of Derivative Actions in China' (2010) 31(5) Comp Law 150, 152, explaining that the respective temporal threshold under Chinese law does not correspond to the average shareholding period.

53 This would be the effect of a squeeze-out under Law 4548/2018 art 46.

54 The applicable Greek continuous ownership rule aggravates the problem, by requiring that the requisite ownership threshold of shares exceeding 2.5% of share capital is maintained by applicants. See Chapter 3.

55 Similar was the factual background in the American (California) case of *Gaillard v Natomas Company* 173 Cal App 3d 410, 219 Cal Rptr 74 (1985).

56 An example is Italy. See Latella, 'The Implications' (n 34) 320.

57 For further elaboration on this argument see Travis Laster, 'Goodbye to the Contemporaneous Ownership Requirement' (2008) 33 Del J Corp L 673, 673–694.

From a certain viewpoint, contemporaneous and continuous ownership rules seem to reflect the rationale that only those who suffered loss may litigate. Notwithstanding the contestability of the argument that a loss suffered by the company is a loss always suffered by the shareholders,[58] relevance of such considerations with the legitimacy of the derivative claimant is questionable. It would of course be myopic to deny that there is a relationship in litigation practice between reflective losses and damage suffered by the company; indeed, should no loss be suffered by the members, the latter would probably be uninterested in bringing an action. However, it is hardly reconcilable with the rationale of derivative actions as a corporate governance mechanism to demand – even covertly – that reflective loss is suffered by the derivative claimant as a condition for locus standi. The reason is that the purpose of the derivative action is to provide redress for the company (directly) and shareholders en masse (indirectly/reflectively). It is this uniquely 'representative' nature of the remedy which distinguishes it from personal claims, whose primary purpose is instead to provide redress for the shareholder-claimant. Focus within the ambit of the procedure on derivative actions should therefore be exclusively on recovery of losses suffered by the company and any detraction of focus towards the effects of the wrongdoing on the shareholder-claimant's wealth would render procedural stewardship an uncertain incident rather than a purpose of the remedy.

5.3.3 Legal standing in (de facto)[59] groups of companies situations: The case for multiple derivative actions

The problem of legal standing is further exacerbated in situations where the company may suffer injuries by mismanagement at a lower level within a corporate group chain. Modern-day business is often organised in parent–subsidiary structures, whereby the subsidiary may be fully owned by the parent. Therefore, the practical situation arises that it is only up to the board of the subsidiary or the parent company (acting through its board) to enforce the company's claim. Due to the control exerted by the holding company, it is highly unlikely that any claim will be pursued at subsidiary level, in case damage was incurred due to its directions.

The solution given to such problems by common law countries is the mechanism of multiple derivative actions, whereby a member of one juridical entity has standing to sue on behalf and for the benefit of a related (usually subsidiary corporate) entity.[60] As the case is under common law, standing is allowed

58 Such an argument largely depends on methods of firm valuation and market (im)perfection.

59 Greece and UK do not have any legislation remotely similar to that of the German *Konzernrecht*. See Janet Dine, *The Governance of Corporate Groups* (CUP 2000) 44, talking about the British 'failure to develop a law of the enterprise'.

60 It is not always necessary that both entities are limited liability companies: in *Universal Project Management Services Ltd v Fort Gilkicker Ltd and others* [2013] EWHC 348 (Ch); [2013] Ch. 551 the parent company (Askett Hawk Properties) was an LLP.

subject to the same conditions applicable to single derivative actions.[61] The non-inclusion of multiple derivative actions in CA 2006 Part 11, may come as a surprise to the reader of UK company law, given that other common law countries provide for such actions, if no attempt to understand the law on shareholder actions in the broader context is made.

The problem that would arise in such an inclusion would be that the statute should normally also determine the cases in which a member of a holding company should enjoy locus standi in a dispute concerning the subsidiary, a completely separate legal entity de lege.[62] The other statutory derivative action,[63] shows one way around this conundrum: there, if the persons liable to the company are the directors of its holding company, both the shareholders of the holding and of the subsidiary may bring an action. Such claim may be brought on the grounds of Section 369, which pronounces that the directors of the parent may be held liable if they 'failed to take all reasonable steps' to prevent an unauthorised donation to be made. Negligence, even though largely excluded from the common law rules on multiple derivative actions, finds its way through Section 370, in one of the few instances where the law expressly prescribes a duty of care in parent–subsidiary structures. However, the UK legislature opted to provide such a relaxed requirement for multiple derivative actions to proceed for a very limited range for misfeasance, connected with the public policy objectives surrounding political donations.

Therefore, the problem remains: should the members of the parent company enforce the claims of the subsidiary and, if yes, when? Common law addressed this issue by taking the position that when the subsidiary acted (de facto) dependently by being subject to the same wrongdoer control as the parent an action pursued by a member of the parent but on behalf of the subsidiary may be allowed. Given though that 'wrongdoer control' is not to be found anywhere in CA 2006, a statutory pronunciation of this criterion could give rise to further problems and inconsistencies. The solution was provided by courts. As explained, recent judgments in the UK accepted that the common law derivative action was superseded by statute, only to the extent of single actions.[64] Therefore, 'wrongdoer control' and 'fraud (on the minority)' still survive within the ambit of multiple derivative actions.[65]

61 In a simple parent–subsidiary situation reference is made to 'double derivative actions': if another entity stands in between the two aforementioned entities (e.g. parent–subsidiary–subsidiary of the subsidiary structure) the term usually is 'multiple derivative actions'. For the sake of convenience, the latter is used as an umbrella term for both cases hereafter.

62 It is to be noted that statutory provisions on derivative actions in New Zealand (s 165(1)(a) CA 1993) and Australia (s 236 1(a)(i) CA 2001) confer the right to sue derivatively to shareholders of the company and its 'related' companies/bodies corporate.

63 CA 2006 s 370.

64 *Gilkicker* (n 60) 173 (Briggs J); followed by *Abouraya v Sigmund* [2014] EWHC 277 (Ch) at [16] (Richards J).

65 Both come part and parcel as the exceptions to the rule in *Foss*. See David Kershaw, 'The Rule in Foss v Harbottle is Dead; Long Live the Rule in Foss v Harbottle' [2015] 3 JBL 274, for an interesting view on their relevance with the statutory derivative claim.

Nevertheless, wrongdoer control may be hard to establish.[66] Given the particular reference to the interests of the shareholders as a corporate organ, it is difficult to ascertain the amount of votes that are controlled indirectly by the wrongdoers when ownership is dispersed. It is even difficult to identify a conflict of interests such dispersed shareholders may have vis-à-vis the company as a whole. Control of the votes in the GM may be easy to ascertain in certain parent–subsidiary situations; establishing that the same wrongdoers are in control of both companies is not. The accompanying requirements of 'fraud' and direct benefit for the wrongdoers (excluding thus negligence) render the common law position incompatible with the herein proposed framework, as is shown below.

German jurisprudence offers some valuable insights. For liability to exist within an intra-group corporate framework, control of a particular kind has to be exerted by the parent. But, for the cases where an express agreement exists to that end,[67] (de facto) control can be inferred in cases where interlocking membership in the boards of the parent and the subsidiary exists when both companies act as an economic unit or when the composition of the subsidiary's board is dependent on the parent's (major shareholder) discretion the presumption is refutable.[68] What German law identifies in such a way is the 'common direction' of both the parent and the subsidiary. This is a good starting point for identifying the instances where multiple derivative actions should be allowed.

On its own, however, de facto control over the subsidiary should not suffice for a multiple derivative action to be pursued. Something more is needed to ensure that, in the face of such litigation, the different parts of the group chain remain separate and directors do not face intervention in their decision-making by shareholders other than those of their company's without good cause. Going back to the rationale behind multiple derivative actions, we identify their objective of remedying mismanagement that is detrimental to the (shareholders of the) parent company but, due to the separate corporate personality doctrine, cannot be brought before court by anyone else than the subsidiary itself, which, in turn, may be unable to litigate by being subject to the will of the parent's administration and/or controllers. Multiple derivative actions thus make good of two, usually interconnected, wrongs: first, expropriation of corporate wealth attempted to be sheltered from litigation by (ab)using the separate corporate

66 These concerns have been expressed by Lord Wedderburn (KW Wedderburn, 'Shareholder Rights and the Rule in Foss v Harbottle' (1957) CLJ 194, 200); for a detailed review of His Lordship's position and Vinelott J's views on the matter as expressed in *Prudential*, see Hirt, *The Enforcement* (n 14) 185–199.

67 Under German law, corporate groups may be formed by agreements. The law governing the latter encourages greater transparency of intra-group business and incentivises the assumption of such obligations by expressly permitting that (subject to conditions and compensation) the directions of the holding company may work to the detriment of the subsidiary.

68 AktG s 18. See Gerhard Wirth, Michael Arnold and Ralph Morshäuser (eds), Mark Greene (tr), *Corporate Law in Germany* (2nd edn, CH Beck 2010), 210.

personality doctrine and, second, situations where injustice cannot be remedied by means of company or shareholder (of the subsidiary) litigation. This book proposes that, instead of providing the parent's shareholders with an unqualified decision right to litigate on the subsidiary's affairs, the law has to address the specific problems expressly.

We can identify specific occasions where it is pragmatic to allow for multiple derivative claims. First, such claims should be permitted where overarching influence is exerted by the administration of the holding company to the subsidiary. Indications of such influence may be the (near) absolute dependence of the subsidiary's board composition on the parent's board and associated persons (as the latter are statutorily defined), interlocking directorates, absence of members other than the parent company and lack of independent business as evidenced by the annual accounts. Such criteria should be used in order to establish a rebuttable presumption of dominance over the subsidiary's affairs, alleviating therefore the claimant from much of the burden of proof, as these facts are relatively easy to ascertain even in the light of the informational asymmetry existing between members of the company and corporate administration. The merit in this approach is that it identifies the occasions where a subsidiary is not acting independently, without the complexity of 'wrongdoer control' under English law. Overall, this proposal is shareholder-friendly, providing legal certainty and ensuring that no undue intervention by means of litigation threatens genuine and unfettered business decision-making.

Second, and subject to the aforementioned criterion, detrimental effect of the subsidiary's mismanagement to *both* the subsidiary's *and* the parent's business has to be ascertained.[69] This criterion is fully in line with the compensatory function of derivative actions: it sets the minimum standard of compensating damage to both the parent and the subsidiary, accruing from a wrong caused to the latter. Furthermore, such a requirement is consistent with the rationale that a shareholder may champion (exceptionally) the interests of *her/his* company.

Lastly, if the latter condition is not met but the first one is, the court has to be satisfied that there is no rational expectation for the *board* of the subsidiary *or its shareholders* to bring the claim themselves. The reason for this additional (alternative) condition is that the deterrent effect of multiple derivative actions may be compromised in cases where detriment to the business of the parent or the subsidiary cannot be supported by evidence. Admittedly, focus on the emphasised constituency of shareholders may render it very difficult to bring

69 Contrary to the common law approach, the herein proposed framework purportedly avoids the wrongdoers' benefit criterion. See *Abouraya* (n 64) [24] (Richards J) regarding the application of this common law criterion within the ambit of multiple derivative actions. See also Trevor Mascarenhas, 'Case Comment Multiple Derivative Actions under English Law' [2013] 24 ICCLR 336, 337.

a multiple derivative action in cases where the subsidiary has a multiplicity of shareholders other than the controlling company. Nonetheless, the members of the parent company should be able to intervene to the subsidiary's affairs in limited, exceptional circumstances, to prevent injustice, otherwise the argument of violating the separate corporate personality by virtue of the multiple derivative action mechanism would prove to be a strong opposition to its introduction.

In effect, the proposed criteria for bringing a multiple derivative action reflect some elements of the common law rule of wrongdoer control in its most relaxed form (de facto wrongdoer control). The purported differentiation from the latter adds clarity and legal certainty. From a German perspective, such criteria emulate the rules of the *Konzern*, at least regarding the definition of 'common direction' (*einleitliche Leitung*)[70] and the cause of action under the *Konzernrecht*'s regime on shareholders' claims (damage caused to the company that is not compensated).[71] Overall, the proposal attempts to strike a balance between, on the one hand, a permissive regime on multiple derivative actions that covers a wide spectrum of liability to the company and, on the other hand, respect for the separate corporate personality of the subsidiary. In doing so, a mechanism for multiple derivative actions that accords to the underlying principles of and works in conjunction with the proposed procedure for single derivative actions is suggested. Therefore, satisfaction of these requirements should not suffice eo ipso for a double derivative claim to proceed. Shareholders should further meet the requirements applicable to single derivative actions under the proposed framework (i.e. claim in the company's interests and worthy to pursue, 'demand', etc.) at subsidiary level.

Extending legal standing to the shareholders of a parent company is not a step too far for the Greek legislator if derivative actions are to be introduced to Greek law. The parent company's shareholders comprise the constituency whose interests are the next closest to the one capable of bringing a single derivative action (that is, the parent company) in such situations. At least compared to creditors, who are allowed locus standi in the German Konzernrecht derivative proceedings, shareholders of the parent company do not seem so remote from the wronged company, its interests and decision-making.[72] Accordingly, if the law permits that the parent represents the subsidiary in court, by litigating on its behalf, there is little reason not to permit the parent's shareholders to do so.[73]

70 See, regarding the *einleitliche Leitung*, Wirth et al. (n 68) 210ff; cf the Greek perception of 'connected companies' as reflected in Law 4308/2014 art 32.
71 Wirth et al. (n 68) 210ff.
72 See AktG ss 309, 310, 317, 318, 323.
73 Assuming a stewardship role for the benefit of the wronged company as a *gesetzliche Prozessstandschafter*.

5.4 Constraints to frivolous/vexatious litigation: The admission stage

5.4.1 Introduction

The comparative analysis in Part 2 illustrated the different approaches the UK and the German legislators took in restraining malicious and frivolous litigation. Some common denominators were identified, such as express statutory requirements that the shareholder-litigant acts in the corporate interests in bringing the claim. The variety of the devices used to weed out unmeritorious suits illustrated their importance in the mechanics of derivative actions, providing also useful material for normative suggestions.

Having said that, we can now move to the substance of the issue at hand: the conditions under which a derivative action may proceed according to the proposed model, tailored for the Greek legal order, and further constraints on non-meritorious litigation. The ensuing paragraphs envisage the criteria for admissibility of a derivative claim to be considered at a preliminary 'admissions' stage. As the UK and German experience show, the preliminary/admission stage (*Klagezulassungsverfahren*) is a method to weed out unmeritorious claims early on and save the parties to the proceedings from much of the costs and time involved in a hearing on the merits.

Accordingly, under the proposed model, the court would be called at preliminary/admission proceedings, before the trial on the merits commences, to determine the legitimacy of the shareholder to act as a procedural steward and bring proceedings in his own name on behalf of the company. Only if the applicant – at this stage – fulfils the substantive and procedural criteria to litigate on behalf of the company, convincing the court of the importance that enforcement of the company's claim has in promoting the corporate interests, s/he would be permitted to proceed to the next stage ('main proceedings') and seek such enforcement, as a (derivative) claimant, at a trial on the merits (of the company's claim) and achieve a court order on behalf and for the benefit of the company, if successful. Defendants may be the alleged wrongdoers, not the company. The company may participate in the proceedings as a third party, given that under Greek law there is simply no such thing as a 'nominal' defendant.

Therefore, the 'preliminary stage' procedure could fall (under Greek law) either under the contentious (iurisdictio contentiosa) or under the non-contentious jurisdiction (iurisdictio voluntaria). The German law-maker opted for the former, 'addressing the critique on old Section 147(3)'.[74] The main practical implication in the choice between either of jurisdictions is that, contrary to the contentious jurisdiction, the non-contentious one is inquisitory in character and allows the court significant discretion (thereby being closer to the English procedure). For

74 Karsten Schmidt and Marcus Lutter, *Aktiengesetz: Kommentar* (Otto Schmidt 2010) 2137. The old AktG s147 fell under the Act on Proceedings in Family Matters and Matters of Non-Contentious Jurisdiction (FamFG).

this reason, many disputes, adversarial in their nature, were located by the legislature to the non-contentious jurisdiction.[75] In the context of derivative actions, the non-contentious jurisdiction's further advantage would be the fact that lis pendens excludes other shareholders from petitioning. However, a carefully drafted special summary procedure could make the best of both worlds.

5.4.2 Restrictions on the scope of misfeasance

A major point of discussion within the context of US corporate governance was the shareholders' ability to enforce the duty of due care (and skill). In the mid-1980s, a vibrant discourse on the topic culminated in the publication of three papers, authored by an equal number of academics with the highest of reputation and input on the field: Professor John 'Jack' Coffee Jr, Professor James Cox and Professor Kenneth Scott.[76] Read together, these articles constitute a good starting point for any inquiry as to what extent the law and its enforcement should intrude on management decisions, compensate, deter and educate. Constructing the proper boundaries for the *cause of action* in derivative litigation is a matter seriously contemplated therein and relevant to this book, as it has also been a focal point in the setting of the relevant provisions in the jurisdictions herein examined.

Indeed, it has been observed that filtering derivative litigation by restrictions on the cause of action was a rather common strategy among EU states.[77] As explained in Chapter 3, *Aktiengesetz* still limits admissibility of shareholder claims to those arising from dishonesty and gross violations of the law and/or the corporate constitution; also restrictive was the pre-CA 2006 common law 'fraud on the minority' ground for derivative actions.[78] Now the position of UK law is different: every breach of duty and/or the law can be litigated against, including negligence. This approach is closer to the EMCA, the existing Greek rules on company's actions and is the right one.

Let us first consider whether a German-like limitation to 'gross' misconduct is appropriate a filter. We identified that *Aktiengesetz* Section 148 paragraph 1(2) and (3) is a reason why Germany does not experience any shareholder activism

75 Kostas Beys, *Politikí dikonomía: genikés archés kai ermineía ton árthron. 14/, V. - Asfalistiká métra* (articles 682–738) (Sakkoulas 1983) 885. For a similar approach under German law, see Leo Rosenberg and Karl-Heinz Schwab, *Zivilprozessrecht* (14th edn, CH Beck 1986) 53.

76 Respectively: John C Coffee Jr, 'Litigation and Corporate Governance: An Essay on Steering Between Scylla and Charybdis' 1983–(1984) 52 Geo Wash L Rev 789; James D Cox, 'Compensation, Deterrence, and the Market as boundaries for Derivative Suit Procedures' (1984) 52 Geo Wash L Rev 745, 749–752; Kenneth E Scott, 'Corporation Law and the American Law Institute Corporate Governance Project' (1983) 35 Stan L Rev 927; see Marjorie Fine Knowles and Colin Flannery, 'The ALI Principles of Corporate Governance Compared with Georgia Law' (1996–1997) 47 Mercer L Rev 1, 4.

77 Li Xiaoning, *A Comparative Study of Shareholders' Derivative Actions* (Kluwer 2007).

78 'Fraud', on its own, included breach of directors' duties under common law (*Estmanco (Kilner House) v Greater London Council* [1982] 1 WLR 2).

of this sort. Intuitively, this is an early sign why the Greek legislator should avoid the introduction of any similar provision. Given that further reasons were identified for the relative failure of the German provisions, we should consider the appropriateness of such a rule in detail.

The 'German approach' swings the pendulum of excused liability too far in favour of the management. It is one thing to exclude momentary lapses of judgment – within the course of decision-making – from the possibility of litigation, on the grounds of letting corporations be run smoothly (something that the business judgment rule does anyway), and completely another thing to demand a high level of misconduct for a claim to proceed. To be sure, such a provision practically excludes liability for (mere) negligence and goes even further than the business judgment rule in insulating directors and other potential defendants.[79] Section 148 commits thus two sins: first, it does not learn from the mistaken common law position under the exceptions in *Foss*, which,[80] by limiting permissible shareholder litigation to 'fraud on the minority', worked to a similar effect; second, it frustrates much of the compensatory and deterrent effect derivative actions have, by requiring a high standard of misconduct. Ordinary breaches of law and the by-laws may amount to massive losses for the company: not being able to be compensated for under the existing regime, their impact is to be felt by both shareholders and the society as a whole.[81] Furthermore, good corporate governance is not only about avoiding gross violations of mandatory and soft-law rules: legality of decisions, skill and diligence are required to that end. In the absence of even the threat of accountability (in terrorem), for misconduct falling outside such requirements, it is hard to see how the board is to be deterred from exercising bad governance. German academia has already voiced support towards lowering this burden of proof in the preliminary stage to gross negligence: as stated by Peltzer, 'die Hürde ist zu hoch'.[82] It has to be noted, that the 70th *Deutscher Juristentag* (the 70th German Jurists Forum) decided that the most appropriate measure to enhance the existing framework for derivative actions, is to relax the requirements under Section 148 paragraph 1(2) and (3): the resolution on this issue was passed by a marginal majority (27 votes for, 26 against).[83] In the context of the special audit, such

79 Gross negligence falls outside the catch of the business judgment rule, at least according to the American standards. We read in J Cox, 'Litigation and the Deterrence of Corporate Misconduct' (1997) 60 LCP 1, 29: 'gross negligence and reckless behavior, though within the coverage of the standard D&O policy, are not protected under the business judgment rule'.

80 *Foss v Harbottle* (1843) 67 ER 189.

81 Peltzer (n 1) 958ff.

82 ibid. 958–959.

83 *70. Deutscher Juristentag Hannover 2014 – Beschlüsse, Abteilung Wirtschaftsrecht* (70th German Jurists Forum Hannover 2014: Resolutions, Business Law Section), <www.djt.de/fileadmin/downloads/70/140919_djt_70_beschluesse_web_rz.pdf> (accessed 20 August 2015) resolution 12(c).

relaxation did not amount to eliminating the 'gross violations' criterion.[84] Instead, such a hurdle was resolved to be removed, if the company suffered material financial losses or the applicant minority represents one tenth of registered share capital.[85] The effects of the above resolutions on the setting of Sections 148 (and 142) remain to be seen. Notably, at the time of publication of this book, a draft law amending Section 148 was proposed by the AfD fraction. The proposal removes 'gross violations' from the wording of the proviso, acknowledging the adverse role this criterion plays in the effectiveness of enforcement proceedings. It further attempts to increase the availability and attractiveness of the remedy to shareholders by reducing the ownership threshold and awarding successful claimants with a share of the proceeds.[86]

Definitely, the German approach of raising the bar of misfeasance is to be avoided. As explained, it scares off potential claimants, as 'grave violations' of the law or the corporate constitution is a rather ambiguous term, showing a legislative proclivity towards insulating negligent boards. The UK approach looks more substantiated and doctrinally consistent with the derivative action's *raison d'être*. Nevertheless, the German idiosyncrasy of the two-tier system may excuse, to an extent, the strategy taken by Section 148 paragraph 1(3). Such a constraint does not apply for the board-claimant and the German legislators have long put much confidence on the monitoring exerted by one board on the other.[87] In the absence of such a structure, as happens in Greece, could the same be said for the analogous (in its function) body of independent directors?[88] Hardly, given the record of their behaviour.[89]

Nevertheless, one should not forget that, while the UK statute has nothing in its wording resembling *Aktiengesetz* Section 148 paragraph 1(3), the 'ratification' condition may work to similar results: wrongs that are ratified cannot be remedied by court,[90] and the latter, in exercising its discretion, considers whether the wrongs complained for are likely to be ratified.[91] Potentially, a dichotomy arises regarding the ease of litigation between ratifiable and non-ratifiable wrongs.[92] As explained in Chapter 3, the ratification/ratifiability conditions are not free of controversy, and British scholars have advocated against

84 ibid. resolution 14(a).
85 ibid. resolution 14(b).
86 BT-Drucksache 19/8233 of 12 March 2019, referred to the committees.
87 See Jean Du Plessis, 'Reflections On Some Recent Corporate Governance Reforms In Germany: A Transformation of the German Aktienrecht?' (2003) 8(2) Deakin LR 381.
88 Klaus J Hopt in Klaus J Hopt, Hideki Kanda, Mark J Roe, Eddy Wymeersch and Stefan Prigge, *Comparative Corporate Governance: The State of the Art and Emerging Research* (Clarendon Press 1998), 227–259.
89 See Chapter 2.
90 CA 2006 s 263(2)(2).
91 CA 2006 s 263(3)(c)(ii).
92 Harald Baum and Dan W Puchniak, 'The Derivative Action: An Economic, Historical and Practice-Oriented Approach' in Dan W Puchniak, Harald Baum and Michael Ewing-Chow (eds), *The Derivative Action in Asia: A Comparative and Functional Approach* (CUP 2012) 54.

them as running contrary to the purposes of derivative actions.[93] Given that ratification does not work in the same way in Greek law, there is no reason to introduce a rather problematic feature of the UK law into it.

Turning back to negligence, let us consider its propriety as a ground for derivative actions. Within the confines of ALI, this has been an intense discussion topic. The question, simply put, was: should liability for breaches of the duty of care be on an equal footing with those of the duty of loyalty, in light of the particularities entailed in the former duty?

The duty of care has attracted special attention in all three jurisdictions herein examined. Setting minimum standards of diligence in business decision-making is not easy. Modern business requires the (regular) assumption of good levels of risk. An ex-post review of corporate management's diligence by the judiciary is perceived to threaten profitable risk-taking and to fend off capable managers. Definitely, the law purports to keep business decisions as far away from the courtroom as possible in the examined countries. What was acutely stressed by Lord Eldon in *Carlen v Drury* in the beginning of the nineteenth century still applies well beyond the jurisdictional boundaries of the UK: 'this Court is not to be required on every Occasion to take the Management of every Playhouse and Brewhouse in the Kingdom'.[94] Directors' duties have been recently revised, regarding the discretion afforded in managing the corporation in Greece; the highlight being the introduction of the US-derived business judgment rule.[95]

The positions American academics took in anticipation of the ALI principles varied. Some considered immunity from shareholder-initiated litigation regarding breaches of the duty of care;[96] others advocated an overall cap on liability (whether enforced by shareholders or otherwise).[97] Apparently, the rationale in the US was that, in view of the growing amount of litigation, the board should be left with some assurance that risky decisions would not necessarily lead them to personal financial disaster.

I cannot be persuaded that a liability cap should form part of a set of provisions on derivative actions. In short, what applies for the examination above of the 'gross violations' threshold under the compensatory and deterrence perspectives, applies pari passu for suggestions to limit liability for negligence. Accordingly, there is a lot of potential for compensation in holding directors accountable for such behaviour. Professor Cox identified severe economic effects endemic in negligent management decisions.[98] Not that liability for negligence

93 Reisberg, *Derivative Actions* (n 1) 198, referring to the view expressed by Boyle prior to the enactment of CA 2006 (A Boyle *Minority Shareholders' Remedies* (CUP 2002) 76–8).

94 (1812) 1 Vesey & Beames 154, 158.

95 A comprehensive monograph on the matter is Harris E Apostolopoulos, *The Business Judgment Rule and the Challenge of the Firm's Insolvency* (Nomiki Bibliothiki 2014).

96 Scott (n 76) 940–947.

97 Coffee, 'Scylla and Charybdis' (n 76) 823.

98 Cox, 'Compensation' (n 76) 786ff.

is devoid of 'deterrence' value: the fact that a good deal of corporate scandals arose from overtly risky decision-making,[99] makes deterrence of such behaviour an imperative objective for the law.

Possibly, a well-constructed liability cap could make the best of both worlds: maintain good compensatory and deterrence levels whilst, at the same time, protect directors from unwarranted threats to their wealth. However, such a cap should not be fixed: the arbitrariness of this approach is to be avoided in any case.[100] Nor should it be confined to the provisions on derivative actions. There is no persuasive reason why the company should be compensated up to a ceiling when the proper claimant is permissibly substituted by a shareholder, while no such restriction applies if the claim is brought by the company's usual representatives. As this book does not intend to propose a wholesale change of the recently reformed Greek company law, general ceilings on liability should be left for discussion elsewhere.

In any case, directors enjoy the 'safe harbour' of the Greek Business Judgment Rule, qualifying the duty of care and excusing liability for negligence if they acted in good faith, in the interests of the company and based on sufficient information.[101] The rule originates in American law and found its way to Greek law through the German *Aktiengesetz* Section 93,[102] as evidenced by the fact that the burden of proof is placed upon the (defendant) directors in both jurisdictions (contrary to the mainstream approach in the US). The rationale behind the rule is basically that the court should not review genuine business decisions, ex post, substituting thus the management of the company with the benefit of hindsight.[103] However, in view of this, and considering the state of enforcement mechanisms, the balance between directors' accountability and their discretion is disturbed in favour of the latter as Greek law stands.[104] The herein proposed framework attempts, by increasing the possibilities of enforcement of directors' duties and facilitating thus their accountability, to reach an equilibrium. True, genuine derivative actions may add some extra 'bite' against misfeasance ex parte the directors. However, they do not affect the content of the director's duties and their purpose is not to make corporate decision-making overly cautious; instead, they are destined to operate in exceptional circumstances, where the company's organisational structure fails to remedy a wrong. To put simply,

99 See Joan Loughrey, 'The Director's Duty of Care and Skill and the Financial Crisis' in Joan Loughrey (ed), *Directors' Duties and Shareholder Litigation in the Wake of the Financial Crisis* (EE 2013) 12–14, 33–40.

100 Coffee, 'Scylla and Charybdis' (n 76) 822: 'Concededly, a serious problem with the approach … is that any fixed ceiling is necessarily arbitrary and lacks a conceptual foundation'.

101 BJR cannot excuse breaches of the duty of loyalty. See Coffee, 'Scylla and Charybdis' (n 76).

102 Which in turn was inspired from 'Anglo-Saxon law' and the *ARAG/Garmenbeck* decision. See RegE-UMAG, BT-Drucks 15/5092 11.

103 A *Praesumptio Similitudinis* in this case is justified regarding English law, considering the attitude of the courts towards adjudication of business decisions.

104 See Lia Athanasiou, *Shareholders' Activism and Corporate Monitoring* (Nomiki Bibliothiki 2010) 101.

if directors behave within the broad boundaries of discretion afforded by their statutory duties, then they have little to fear, particularly in lieu of the 'English rule' on litigation costs. As succinctly put by Antiphanes' maxim: 'he who does no wrong has no need of the law'.[105]

Therefore, the grounds on which a claim may be brought should include any breach of the duties and obligations the directors are subject to: nothing less. Narrowing the scope of these grounds would endanger the provision of becoming obsolete. Greek law must learn from the German and English (under common law) mistakes, if rigor mortis of their mechanisms for derivative suits is to be avoided. However, it is proposed herein that the only influence that the cause of action may have on the procedure, should be related to the extent that the court is allowed to consider the board's views when granting permission (i.e. the instances where demand may be excused): we shall revisit this topic in Subsection 5.4.4.

As the law on the appointment of special representatives stands, any breach of duty may be brought before a court upon application for a company's action. This relaxed approach works as a counterweight to the restrictions posed by the other facets of the relevant law on shareholders' litigation. Following the preceding argumentation, there seems to be no reason in moving away from this paradigm, should derivative actions be introduced into Greek law. Any contrary argument, endorsing the restrictive German approach, fails to consider duly the idiosyncrasies of the dual board system. As observed, the applicable liability threshold in Germany is very high, discouraging claimants from bringing an action from the very beginning. However, corporate claims against the management are an otherwise exclusive capacity of the Supervisory Board.[106] Therefore, as explained, in drafting the statutory derivative action the German legislator had to consider the judgment of the Supreme Court in *ARAG/Garmenbeck*, according to which the Supervisory Board may be under no duty to bring an action in situations where no grave violation of the law or the articles of association took place. Apparently, the rationale was that shareholders can substitute the *Aufsichtsrat* only where the latter fails to perform such a duty. However, given the absence of a corporate body with a similar function under Greek law, imposing such a high threshold cannot be justified.

It is not unlikely (it may even be a welcome policy, but this is a discussion beyond the scope of this book) that directors' duties may be widened as to whom they are owed to. Arguably, the statutory duty of loyalty now obliges the UK boards to consider the interests of 'stakeholders' other than shareholders.[107] Such an 'inclusive' trend in corporate governance might eventually reach Greece. It thus may be possible for members – that is shareholders in the studied jurisdictions – as legitimate right-holders to privately enforce, in the name of the company, an infringement of the corporate interests in this, somewhat post-modern,

105 The quote is often misattributed to Plato.

106 Similar observation in Rokas, 'Corporate Organisation' (n 22) 14.

107 See, among others, Andrew Keay, 'Tackling the Issue of the Corporate Objective: An Analysis of the United Kingdom's Enlightened Shareholder Value Approach' (2007) 29 Syd LR 577.

broader sense: i.e. including the interests of, say, the community as part of the corporate interests. This might sound as wishful thinking, given the conventional wisdom that shareholders are Hobbesian-minded, individualistic actors, motivated exclusively by the prospects of returns on their investments.[108] However, the Japanese experience has proven this tenet wrong in a number of instances.[109] Should derivative actions be introduced to Greek law and the duty of loyalty become more inclusive, time will tell whether Greece affords any place for such kind of activism.

In any case, constraining the scope of remediable misfeasance is not an appropriate strategy to repel unwanted litigation. On the contrary, extending that scope recommends itself as a means of improving shareholder protection. As we saw in Chapter 3, the company's action is available for corporate claims against directors or persons to whom powers are delegated. However, in the UK and Germany, derivative actions can be brought also against other persons involved in misfeasance taking place at board level. In fact, the amendment of *Aktiengesetz* Section 117 in order to accommodate suits against those intentionally exerting their influence in order to induce the board(s) to 'act to the detriment of the company or its shareholders', in conjunction with prohibiting controlling shareholders to vote against their liability (AktG s 136), have resulted in an increase of the number of suits against major shareholders, in the past few years.[110] A move towards that direction is recommended for Greek company law. Given the ownership structure of Greek companies, the possibility of majority shareholders and block-holders causing damage to the company by using their influence on the board is higher than in other ownership structures. Facilitating the enforcement of their accountability is therefore essential for a Greek derivative action. This step is already taken within the context of the recently amended Greek insolvency code, in order to protect creditors against wrongful and fraudulent trading.[111] There is good reason to afford shareholders with similar protection, particularly in the light of the discussion in Section 2.4.3, on the increasing importance of equity finance for Greek companies nowadays. An express provision, worded similarly to *Aktiengesetz* Section 117(1) or CA 2006 Section 260(5) could work to that end.

108 Kent Greenfield, *The Failure of Corporate Law: Fundamental Flaws and Progressive Possibilities* (UCP 2008) 84.

109 See Chapter 3.

110 See discussion and analysis of case law in Andreas Fabritius, 'Der Besondere Vertreter gemäß § 147 Abs. 2 AktG' in Theodor Baums and Stephen Hutter (eds), *Festschrift für Michael Gruson* (Walter de Gruyter 2009) 138–140; Yaron Nili, 'Missing the Forest for the Trees: A New Approach to Shareholder Activism' (2014) 4 Harv Bus L Rev 157, 195.; see also LG München I v. 6.9.2007–5 HK O 12570/07, ZIP 2007 1809; OLG München, Urt. v. 28.11.2007–7 U 4498/07, ZIP 2008 73; BGH 27.9.2011, ZIP 2011 2195 (*HVB/Unicredit*).

111 Art 98(1), (2).

5.4.3 The company's interests and derivative litigation[112]

Chapter 3 identified a common position between the herein studied jurisdictions about the criteria on which leave proceedings are judged: whether the action serves the interests of the company.[113] As explained, despite the differences in wording, the directors' duty of loyalty in the examined jurisdictions consists of acting bona fide in the corporate interests.[114] Consequently, this criterion puts the shareholder-claimant in the shoes of the management, calling the court to adjudicate on the admissibility of the claim on the same (or at least similar) loyalty standards applicable to the management. In fact, this criterion is used by many influential jurisdictions.[115] Therefore, it appears that one of the primary questions to be asked, when recommending the introduction of derivative actions to a jurisdiction, is whether the action should not be contrary to the company's interests. Remarkably however, under Law 2190/1920, courts were not supposed to review the interests which the petition to appoint special representatives intends to promote.[116] The reform effected in 2019 brought some change, yet it set the bar for admissibility of petitions quite low. It is worthy for the Greek lawyer and legislator to draw some comparative insight, regarding how such a statutory criterion for the admission of derivative actions may be formed and the objectives it may serve.

The UK Law Commission, in its consultation paper, advocated the introduction of such a filter for vexatious litigation. In doing so, it reviewed the approaches taken by a number of common law countries.[117] The position it took is summarised at 16.33:

> Given, however, the essential nature of this action it could be strongly argued that courts in any jurisdiction would not permit such actions to proceed unless they were satisfied on this point, whether or not it appears in the statute.[118]

It is hard to disagree with this. By looking at the applicant's compliance with the director's duty of loyalty, the court effectively undertakes the task of

112 Zouridakis (n 27) 281–83, regarding pp. 192–93 in this Subsection and 198–200 in the next Subsection.

113 According to the unanimous position in German literature, this is the case regarding AktG s 148. See Baum and Puchniak (n 92) 53; Schmolke (n 1) 420. For the UK, see Julia Tang, 'Shareholder Remedies: Demise of the Derivative Claim?' [2012] UCL JL and J 178; David Gibbs, 'Has the Statutory Derivative Claim Fulfilled its Objectives? A Prima Facie Case and the Mandatory Bar: Part 1' (2011) 32(2) Comp Law 41.

114 See Chapter 2.

115 Including Australia, Canada and New Zealand.

116 The similar absence of judicial supervision on the admissibility of actions under s 147 III AktG was viewed as 'absurd'; RegE-UMAG, BT-Drucks 15/5092 20.

117 Law Commission, *Shareholder Remedies: A Consultation Paper* (Law Commission Consultation Paper No 142, 1996).

118 ibid.

adjudicating whether it has before it a 'strike suit' or not. Should the claim be brought for the sole reason of paralysing the company's business or constitute some form of 'greenmail' to the corporate executives, it should definitely fall outside the ambit of the duty of loyalty and be dismissed. Furthermore, such a rule expressly acknowledges the nature (or, as the Law Commission put it, 'essence') of derivative actions as being brought on behalf and for the benefit of the company. As such, it constitutes an unavoidable question for the court regarding inter partes admission proceedings. Lastly, this criterion aligns the position of the shareholder-litigant with that of the constituency substituted ad hoc in derivative actions: the corporate organ entrusted with the authority to litigate. A deviation from the standards applicable to the board's litigation-related decision-making would create an inconsistency within the company law statute from the perspective that litigation is, among other things, a corporate decision, derivative actions exceptionally allocate the competence to make such decisions to shareholders.

However, it might be argued that as a threshold it is too low to keep the floodgates of litigation shut. Indeed, it is not unlikely that petitioners satisfy the court of their loyalty to the 'corporate purpose' and success, but their claim eventually proves to be detrimental to the overall business profile of the company or wasteful regarding money and resources. Furthermore, the British experience shows that, as an absolute bar, the criterion under Section 263(2)(2) is far from being the exclusive ground upon which permission has been refused in the reported cases, even when this was the case, courts stated that the application would be unsuccessful under the discretionary grounds. The reason is that UK courts would refuse leave only in cases where '*no* director acting under the duty of Section 172 would bring a claim'.[119] However, the British experience itself shows a way out of this conundrum.

In most of the UK reported cases under the statutory regime on derivative claims, the decisive question for the court was: 'would the hypothetical director acting under the duty of Section 172 attach considerable importance to the claim?'[120] Qualifying the 'company's interests' criterion with the importance attached to the claim intuitively appeals as a good formula of letting through the judicial filter only meritorious shareholders' actions that honest and diligent directors would bring before court. Let us thus bring this consideration under closer scrutiny.

A prima facie problem for the court is finding the appropriate grounds on which to evaluate the importance the claim has regarding the company's

119 *Iesini v Westrip Holdings Ltd* [2009] EWHC 2526 (Ch) [2010] BCC 420, 422 (Lewison J).

120 e.g. decisions in *Iesini,* (n 119) 441–442 (Lewison J); *Franbar v Patel* [2008] EWHC 1534 (Ch); [2008] BCC 885 [27]–[29] (Trower QC); *Wishart v Castlecroft Ltd & Ors* [2009] CSIH 65 [43] (Lord Nimmo Smith, Lord Reed, Sir David Edward QC); see review by Andrew Keay and Joan Loughrey, 'An Assessment of the Present State of Derivative Proceedings', in Loughrey (n 99) 197–202.

interests. In search for a rationale to be followed, we have to look at each jurisdiction's perception of the public limited company and its purpose as a business vehicle within the society. Should the company be perceived as a wealth maximising entity and within the confines of questioning whether litigation is in the corporate interests,[121] the judicial filters to derivative litigation should go no further than attesting whether the outcome of the litigation is likely to add to corporate wealth or, in case it does not and does not result in a grave financial detriment, whether litigation is likely to deter future misconduct.[122]

Nevertheless, determining whether litigation will be economically beneficial may be challenging. Certainly, courts assess with relative ease whether recovery, if the claim is successful, outweighs expenses, or how it compares to the cost of losing. Such a risk/benefit analysis was applied in *Zavahir v Shankleman*, where John Baldwin QC sitting as a deputy judge said:

> In my judgment, any prudent director carrying out a normal risk/benefit analysis would not seek to continue this claim. In the circumstances of a company such as YSL in the position it finds itself in with few assets and no future prospects, the downsides and costs of losing far outweigh the benefits of winning even if there is factored in a significantly greater chance of winning than losing.[123]

However, this is not the full picture regarding the cost/benefit analysis of shareholder litigation. Other factors are economically relevant and sometimes more important than the expected recovery. First, it is one thing to look at recovery, which by definition is a short-term return for the company, and another to look at the long-term profitability of a management decision, against which the claim stands. Second, regarding listed companies and their market value, the response of the stock market will not necessarily be favourable to pending litigation. At least preceding a judgment on the merits, the adverse effect of alleged mismanagement on the corporate goodwill is likely to trigger the exit of existing shareholders and a fall on the stock's price.[124]

121 Livada, 'Company Claims' (n 21) 981. This is a common position among the examined jurisdictions: some deviations exist though, as explained earlier on. As observed by Keay, despite decisions on the statutory derivative action in the UK touching upon s172 in their entirety, they provide little guidance as to what the interests of the company are; the reason is that litigation forms a small part of decision-making in the corporate interests (Andrew Keay, 'The Duty to Promote the Success of the Company' in Loughrey (n 99) 64–65).

122 Painted with a broad brush, this is the rationale of the 'Functional and Focused Model' proposed by Reisberg. See also Section 2.3.2.

123 [2017] BCC 500 at [38]. This approach was followed by Judge Mark Raeside QC in *Goodwin v Cook* [2018] 6 WLUK 425.

124 Indicatively: Jonathan R Macey and Geoffrey P Miller, 'The Plaintiffs' Attorney's Role in Class Action and Derivative Litigation: Economic Analysis and Recommendations for Reform' (1991) 58 U Chi L R 1; Paul Davies and Sarah Worthington *Gower & Davies' Principles of Modern Company Law* (9th edn, Sweet & Maxwell 2012) 667.

Continuing, the deterrence argument in favour of derivative litigation, sound as it may be, is not so easy to clearly define, let alone form expressly a legal provision on its own. As admitted by Reisberg:

> Although the decision about the *likelihood* of deterrence cannot be made with mathematical precision, it is expected that courts will learn over time that some types of action, even if uneconomic in the sense that they fail to recover their immediate costs, ultimately result in beneficial deterrence of harmful misconduct.[125]

Deterrence, as an express criterion for leave of derivative actions, seems therefore well suited for courts enjoying a good deal of discretion in their decisions, as are the common law courts and Greek courts under the non-contentious jurisdiction.

Balancing the deterrence and compensation effects of litigation will be the task for the court in assessing the importance of bringing the claim. The 'functional and focused model' (FFM) proposed by Reisberg sets these exact two overriding criteria for judiciary discretion; whether the action is to benefit economically the company and/or whether the action is likely to deter future misfeasance.[126] The rationale behind the FFM is, to an extent, already endorsed by courts. Particularly regarding recent UK decisions, it is worth remembering Lewison J's enumeration of relevant factors to be considered when attesting a litigation decision under Section 172:

> The size of the claim; the strength of the claim; the cost of the proceedings; the company's ability to fund the proceedings; the ability of the potential defendants to satisfy a judgment; the impact on the company if it lost the claim and had to pay not only its own costs but the defendant's as well; any disruption to the company's activities while the claim is pursued; whether the prosecution of the claim would damage the company in other ways (e.g. by losing the services of a valuable employee or alienating a key supplier or customer) and so on.[127]

These lines provide a roadmap on how to attest the compensatory facet of derivative litigation, useful for the purposes of this Section. The considerations of the learned judge go beyond the criterion of 'recovery net of litigation costs' and approximate a transaction cost efficiency test.[128] However, as such, this test might fall outside the court's willingness to substitute the board in decision-making, at least when the case before it is not clear. Such cases constitute the exception rather than the rule however. Under the proposed criterion, and as it

125 Reisberg *Derivative Actions* (n 1) 210.
126 ibid.
127 *Iesini* (n 119) 441.
128 Similar to Reisberg *Derivative Actions* (n 1) 208.

applies already in the UK,[129] the task of the judiciary is not to make a business decision on behalf of the company; rather, it is to adjudicate between the competing views of the claimant and the board. Nevertheless, deference to the board's decision-making is not an aphorism: this is the spirit of the Greek Business Judgment Rule and it is the task of the court to strike a good balance between desirable deference and undesirable insulation from liability in corporate litigation generally, including shareholder-initiated one.[130]

In fact, as will be further elaborated upon below, regarding the subsidiarity of the derivative claim, the court ought to have particular regard to the views of the disinterested members of the board regarding the decision to litigate. Disinterestedness would of course be contestable. In such a way, the arguments for and against litigation, from the perspectives of persons having intimate knowledge of corporate affairs, will be better illustrated during the proceedings. This can be facilitated by having the company involved in the action as a mandatory non-party.[131]

Complementing the aforementioned factor(s) are considerations on deterrence of misfeasance. It can be submitted that, at least regarding the 'deterrent' effect of derivative litigation, grave violations (breaches) of law, by-laws or duty should be presumed important enough to litigate in borderline – from the perspective of compensation – cases.[132] The solution here proposed, adopts as a rule of thumb the German criteria of *Aktiengesetz* article 148 paragraph 1(3) and (4), in formulating a *presumption* of importance based on the rationale of deterrence.

Another real challenge when it comes to derivative actions is to construe legal provisions for the admission proceedings that do not touch disproportionately on the merits of the main proceedings. To begin with, the proposals herein would not result in a paradigm shift in Greek company law from this perspective. In petitions for the convening of a special audit under Law 2190/1920 article 40, which normally precede litigation under article 22b, Greek courts consider whether damage is suffered by the company or is to be suffered, whether maladministration occurred and finally whether the aforementioned two are in a causal relationship.[133] I cannot see how the existing procedure touches upon the merits of the main proceedings less than the herein proposed procedure for derivative actions does.

Practically, by attesting the importance to be attached to pursuing the claim, the court reviews the dispute between the shareholder-litigant and the board on the topic of litigation. The court, as a neutral arbiter, is in the advantageous

129 Keay and Loughrey (n 120) 202.

130 Apostolopoulos (n 95) 36–37.

131 Similarly to AktG s148(2). The respective provisions in the GrCivProC are arts 80ff.

132 The rationale aligns, to a good extent, with that in Reisberg, *Derivative Actions* (n 1) 212: 'a deterrence rationale should be constrained by a compensatory ceiling'.

133 Lucas Kokkinis, 'Auditors and Minority Right' in Evanghelos Perakis (ed), *Sociétés Anonyme's Law* (3rd edn, Nomiki Bibliothiki 2013) 1559–1561; see also Thessaloniki Single-Member Court of First Instance 15126/2001, NOMOS database.

position of considering both views and evaluating the credibility of evidence before it; this is the task entrusted on the judiciary after all.[134]

Overall, no overriding problems emerge from granting the court the discretion of adjudicating whether the action is brought in compliance with a duty of loyalty similar to those of directors. On the contrary, this criterion accords to the characteristic of derivative actions as mechanism of ad hoc substitution of the board in matters of corporate litigation. Furthermore, its objective is to grant leave only to claims which, if successful, are likely to benefit the company. As such, it is fit for purpose and should form part of a future Greek legal framework on derivative actions.

5.4.4 Subsidiarity of the claim: Making the company the first option

A method of filtering out unmeritorious claims and ensuring the board's primacy in asserting the company's claims is the 'demand rule'.[135] If it is to be adopted, as it currently applies in Germany,[136] the demand rule has to be supplemented by additional safeguards ensuring that 'demand' does not result in entrenching the board's position as the final arbiter of litigation. Rules permitting shareholders to take over pending claims and to contest ab initio the effectiveness of demand in a given situation have to be in place. The position adopted here bears some similarities to that of Reisberg's and fewer similarities regarding Hirt's proposals. This is expected, due to the fact that the direct or indirect source of inspiration to that matter, the law of Delaware (DGCL), is common. However, the ensuing paragraphs consider the Greek and German provisions as they now stand in their quest for insight, making (limited) reference to American law only where necessary.

To begin with, what has to be clear in the law is what constitutes 'demand'. Three possible alternatives emerge.[137] First, that of a 'draft suit', in the sense of a detailed exposition of the facts giving rise to the claim, with clear substantiation on legal grounds and valuation of the claim. Second, that of a notice of facts giving rise to the suspicion that the company suffered or will suffer damage of a particular kind, accompanied by a statement of intention to initiate derivative proceedings in absence of action assumed by the corporate representatives. The third option is that of a general complaint for suspected maladministration, without providing any detailed exposition of the damage suffered by the company. The preferable approach is the second one, as it neither prohibitively restrains petitioners nor it is inappropriately vague. The position of the Greek law as it

134 Concurring Keay and Loughrey (n 120) 202.

135 See Baum and Puchniak (n 92) 49–52; Chapter 3.

136 AktG s 148(1)(2); see also Hirt, *The Enforcement* (n 14) 60.

137 See Reisberg, *Derivative Actions* (n 1); Filippos Doris, 'I schési ton árthron 69 AK, 22 v § 3 n.2190/1920 kai 786 § 3 KPolD os rythmíseon gia tin apotropí tou kindýnou exypirétisis symferónton antithéton pros ta symféronta tou ekprosopoúmenou nomikoú prosópou' (2002) B' ChrID 865, 877.

now stands on company's actions is closer to this solution.[138] Maintaining it in an introduced derivative action would thus be consistent an approach with the broader company law framework and established corporate practice. But we should not stop there.

The Greek legislators did revisit the timeframe for the board to respond to the shareholders' demand. Six months comprises a considerable amount of time in business, thus the respective threshold not only ran to the detriment of the company from an economic perspective but also allowed the wrong-doers to dispose of any evidence of their misfeasance.[139] Law 4548/2018 replaced it with a more reasonable timeframe that better reflects modern corporate practice. The approach followed is similar to the German one, the latter setting the threshold at two months.[140] However, it is somewhat ambiguous whether the court deciding upon the application may review the reasonableness of the deadline set by the shareholders: there is no such reference in article 105. For sure, it is for the best to allow courts some discretion in judging what is reasonable and what is not, following consideration of the company's size, organisational structure (for instance whether the company has an in-house legal department), business environment and other factors. In such a way, the reduced threshold would not disproportionately burden small corporations. What needs be further clarified are the consequences of premature demand. It is recommended that courts, rather than dismissing the application, stay proceedings, in order to afford more time for the board to respond and act. Thereby, in the case of a board's negative response, shareholders would not need to re-initiate the whole procedure, avoiding thus an unnecessary delay that would run against the company's best interests.

Futility of demand in certain circumstances is a further matter to consider. Temporal thresholds, such as that of Law 4548/2018 article 104, become too onerous when demand is presumed to fall on deaf ears or when litigation is a matter of urgency. It is an understatement to hold that there is no bright-line rule. The American jurisprudence has an extensive (yet controversial and mostly state-specific) line of case law and scholarship to provide to that end.[141] Painting the US experience with a broad brush, demand is mainly excused in cases of

138 Doris (n 137) 877; cf Patrai Court of Appeal 266/2011, Armenopoulos 2013 293, where specification of the value of the claim was considered (obiter) to be a necessary element for the admissibility of the application.

139 The danger of loss of evidence has been highlighted in Greek academia since the early days of art 22b. See Leonidas Georgakopoulos, *To Díkaio ton Etaireión* (Sakkoulas 1974) 142.

140 See Explanatory Notes: RegE-UMAG, BT-Drucks 15/5092 22; Paul (n 2) 99.

141 Richard M Buxbaum, 'Conflict-of-Interests Statutes and the Need for a Demand on Directors in Derivative Actions' (1980) 68 CLR 1122; Victor Arnell DuBose, 'Whose Corporation is It, Anyway? Abolishing the Futility Exception in Derivative Litigation' (1991–1992) 12 Miss CL Rev 197; Jessica Erickson, 'Corporate Misconduct and the Perfect Storm of Shareholder Litigation' (2008–2009) 84 Notre Dame L Rev 75.

conflicts of interests between, on the one hand, the board as a whole and, on the other hand, the company.[142]

This book proposes that futility (or redundancy) of demand can be established under two broad criteria: when demand is reasonably presumed to be rejected by the board no matter the merit of the case to be made and when it is a matter of absolute urgency that litigation is initiated.[143] The first criterion could be fulfilled in cases where the composition of the board is involved in the wrongdoing to an extent that does not (and should not, under Greek Civil Code article 66) permit an unbiased decision on litigation.[144] The second criterion could be of relevance in claims running the risks of imminent prescription or further damage to be suffered by the company. In any case, shareholders pleading for demand to be excused should run the risk of their claim being rejected as inadmissible if they do not meet either of the aforementioned criteria.

A clear-cut rule on how 'demand' should operate would entail a number of benefits. First, it ensures that the primacy of the board, as the corporate body entrusted with representation of the company, is not compromised. The board of directors would be called to take action or substantiate the choice not to do so to the concerned shareholders within a reasonable amount of time. In such a way, multiplicity of proceedings is avoided[145] and broader communication between the board and the company's members is encouraged.[146]

Second, a properly constructed 'demand' rule would provide the court with the board's view on the decision not to litigate. The position here adopted is that the board's opinion should not be preclusive; rather, the court, in adjudicating whether the action fosters the corporate interests and its significance justifies the continuance of a claim as a derivative one, should have particular regard to the views of *disinterested* decision-makers.[147] Otherwise, the risk emerges that shareholders will always attempt to devise an

142 Buxbaum (n 141) 1124.

143 This proposition deviates from Greek law as it now stands. See Supreme Court 1256/2011, DEE 2012 29.

144 Art 66 pronounces: 'member of the management is not entitled to vote, if the decision concerns … the initiation of court proceedings … between the legal person and the member or its spouse or its relative by blood up to the third degree'.

145 Similarly Paul (n 2) 101.

146 Without the need to call for an extraordinary resolution and place the item of suspected misconduct in the agenda.

147 In the US (particularly Delaware), the effect of the business judgment rule makes pursuit of derivative claims following rejection of demand almost impossible, as courts review the decision of the board under this 'filter' and the claimant might find it hard to prove that the defendants fell foul of the rule; however, were the American approach be transposed to Greek law, the outcome would be different, because of the reversal of the burden of proof to the defendants (directors).

argument of futility (e.g. by suing the entire board), so as to increase their chances of having their case heard.[148]

The effect of the demand requirement and the accompanying discretion of the court to have particular regard to the views of *disinterested* directors on the matter of litigation will most probably filter out much of the unmeritorious litigation. The court will be provided with a useful roadmap on whether an honest director – with knowledge of the company's business – would bring litigation or not, particularly where, by virtue of the 2002 law on corporate governance, (truly) independent directors are in place.[149] A problem endemic in this approach is that courts may defer to the views of the board too often in reaching a decision. Nevertheless, it is better for the law on derivative actions to emphasise the views of disinterested directors than be silent on the matter. It is an ostrich's approach to deny that courts are inherently reluctant to review management decisions: express rules and guidelines on the matter address the problem rather than aggravate it.

Before concluding, let us consider whether demand should be addressed to shareholders ('universal demand'). As we saw, the UK, being a shareholder-centric jurisdiction, has historically put much emphasis on the views of disinterested shareholders on prospective litigation, even though it does not pose universal demand as a procedural requirement for derivative litigation. Such a requirement, in my opinion, adds an unnecessary layer of criteria in the court's decision-making.[150] Notably, most US state jurisdictions have abolished such rules.[151] What the majority of the shareholders think fit may be relevant in judging whether a suit is brought in good faith and for the benefit of the company, but establishing that the majority rule should preclude a claim from being brought may lead to unfair results for both the company and minority shareholders.

A 'universal demand' requirement could be of use only if shareholders disinterested in the alleged misfeasance and the decision (not) to litigate exist at the time the claim is brought, with clear and informed views on the proposed litigation. In closely held companies such shareholders would be a handful at best, whilst in listed companies with high ownership dispersion it can be expected that they would reach high numbers. Given, however, that shareholders may be easily reproachable by the wrongdoers (particularly in the first case), whilst disinterested shareholders may also be apathetic in their majority (particularly in the second case), such universal demand rule would pose a task for claimants and courts that is either futile or overly difficult to discharge, save for the cases of few closely held companies. A further problem with 'universal demand' is

148 As happens in the US. See Ralph C Ferrara, Kevin T Abikoff and Laura Leedy Gansler, *Shareholder Derivative Litigation: Besieging the Board* (Law Journal Press 2013) 6.03f; Erickson (n 141) 1772.

149 Law 3016/2002 art 3, FEK 110/2002: 'among non-executive members there shall be at least two independent members'.

150 See also Hirt, *The Enforcement* (n 14) 349ff.

151 Arnell Du Bosse (n 141) 202.

that it lacks practicality and adds significantly to the costs of the derivative suit, because of the sheer numbers the addressees may reach. Addressing demand to shareholders collectively, even within the ambit of the shareholders' meeting, does not solve this problem, as it involves the difficulties of convening a GM on the minority's initiative or placing a motion in an already convened GM.

Overall, the proposed framework acknowledges the primacy enjoyed by the board in initiating litigation. A 'demand rule' makes the board the first option among corporate organs in asserting the company's claims, and, together with the accompanying rule that the court should consider the views of disinterested directors, they deter and limit the volume of frivolous and vexatious litigation. Nevertheless, the law has also to consider the fact that directors might purportedly bring proceedings before court, even with the blessings of the majority, with the sole objective of frustrating a shareholders' action by application of lis pendens: this is the 'dark side' of board primacy in corporate litigation. The following paragraphs elaborate further on this issue.

5.4.5 The ability to take over a pending claim[152]

For shareholders' derivative litigation to be effective, it is important that a claim is not brought for the same cause of action by the company in bad faith, so as to prohibit members from pursuing the claim diligently. Indeed, the possibility that the wrongdoers sabotage the procedure in such a way, in order to insulate themselves, is very real and such incidents have been complained of before Greek courts even under the regime of special representatives, as explained in Chapter 3. The proposals shall thus provide for ways to combat the phenomenon, taking into account the procedural complexities associated with such a rule.

Let us first consider whether it should be permissible for shareholders to bring a suit whilst an action, brought directly by the company or derivatively by other shareholders, is pending. The literature on the procedurally similar actio pro socio, within the ambit of the law of partnerships and associations, supports the position that if the company brings a suit, shareholders cannot litigate derivatively and vice versa.[153] The explanatory notes to Law 4548/2018 article 104 repeat this position. The rationale is that the defendant(s) should not sustain the burden of standing in separate proceedings.[154] Ceteris paribus, the same rationale may apply to derivative actions, under the herein proposed

152 See Zouridakis (n 27) 278–79.

153 Panagiotis I Kolotouros, *Actio Pro Socio: i Dikonomikí Diástasis tis Etairikís Agogís* (Sakkoulas 2006) 41–42; concurring, regarding private limited companies (EPEs): the later Greek Supreme Court 1280/2012, EEmpD 2013 616. Actio pro socio is herein perceived in its 'ut singuli' form, similar to the derivative action in that it allows shareholders to sue on behalf of the company. Similar the German literature and case law. See OLG München, Beschl. v. 21. 10. 2010 – 7 W 2040/10, ZIP 2010 2202.

154 Kolotouros (n 153) 41.

framework. However just and fair this approach may be for defendants, it leaves the problem identified in the previous paragraph unresolved.

An important facet of the UK provisions on derivative claims is the ability of members to take over pending proceedings, in certain circumstances.[155] Arguably, such a rule stems from and conforms to the pro-shareholder attitude that English law traditionally had. However, should the examination of such a substitution rule focus exclusively on the nature of derivative actions and their purpose, an argument against it is hard to substantiate. Substitution rules are in place to ensure that proceedings brought in bad faith do not block meritorious litigation.

They essentially constitute a procedural mechanism. As explained, such a right is unavailable to shareholders as Greek law now stands: should the board initiate proceedings, there is no legal avenue of replacing them (as claimants) with special representatives.[156] The matter was brought before the court under the regime of special representatives, but the judgment dismissed the claim that the proceedings were initiated with the view of never achieving redress against the wrongdoings of incumbent managers on the basis that there is no statutory provision to that effect. The court went further to ascertain that corporate claims are by statute a capacity of the board.[157] Accordingly, cases where the claimant needs to be substituted are not part of a purely hypothetical scenario. I doubt that in cases where Greek courts enjoyed the discretion afforded to common law ones such injustice would be excused. It is therefore suggested that this caveat is finally filled within Law 4548/2018, and, to that end, the Companies Act 2006 has some insight to offer.

UK law provides a roadmap as to how Greek law should be reformed on the matter. Claimants should be permitted to take over proceedings by the company or fellow shareholders, if they can prove that pending litigation amounts to an abuse of process. Doctrinally, as long as the provision in the Company Law statute expressly permits, a substitution rule is not inconsistent with the broader Greek legal context: a similar procedure can be found in the Civil Procedure Code regarding substitution of interim corporate management by court decision.[158] However, this procedural rule has apparently limited scope, referring explicitly to representatives of the company and express provision to that end is preferable, if not necessary. To explain, even if derivative actions are introduced into Greek law on public limited companies, its wording cannot be easily understood as permitting members to take over proceedings initiated by the company. Furthermore, it could be interpreted as allowing members to take over proceedings from fellow members,

155 CA 2006 s 264 (269 for Scotland).

156 A Spyridonos, *Minority Rights in the Company Limited by Shares* (Nomiki Bibliothiki 2001) 628, also views the board's and majority's ability to block shareholder-instigated proceedings as one of the major flaws of art 22b.

157 Patrai Court of Appeal 266/2011, NOMOS Databank, Armenopoulos 2013 293.

158 786 GrCivPrC.

only under the perception that a derivative claimant acts in a formally representative capacity. A derivative claimant acts in his own name and on his own right to sue derivatively though, thus the existing article 786 of the Civil Procedure Code cannot be literally interpreted to extend to derivative actions.

A similar effect could be achieved by enabling shareholders to join pending proceedings, whether initiated by the company or otherwise by means of intervention.[159] Under the Greek Law of Civil Procedure, if a claim is brought to enforce the company's rights, such intervention can only be in support of the existing claimant or defendant, unless the intervenor has a cause of action against both existing parties to pending litigation. The latter case is not readily applicable to the enforcement of directors' duties, as derivative claimants enforce the company's claims and would normally not have a(n) (independent) cause of action against the company. The former case on the other hand, allows substitution of the claimant by the intervenor only upon agreement of all parties. Anyhow, regarding both alternatives, an express provision would be necessary, as Greek law does not allow shareholders to intervene as it now stands.[160] Such provision may be placed in Law 4548/2018 instead of the Civil Procedure Code, in a similar fashion to the German *Aktiengesetz* Section 148(3).[161]

It is to be noted that Greek academics have advocated the introduction of a 'substitution rule' in favour of the company, following the German prototype, should a Greek derivative action come to existence.[162] The obvious rationale for such a rule is to ensure that the company has the first say in the litigation throughout the course of proceedings. The German experience, however, shows that this substitution rule not only proved to be of no use in practice but also rendered *Aktiengesetz* Section 148 an irrational option for potential claimants: it has been suggested that the provision is removed from the statute.[163] A 'substitution rule' in favour of the company is a rather catastrophic idea unless the intent is to frustrate the function of derivative actions in practice and merely use the introduction of such a shareholders' right merely as a 'signal' to the international market. However, this is not the intent of the proposals this book offers.

5.4.6 *Summary and further remarks*

The expression of the company's will and interests normally lies with the board of directors. However, derivative actions should be conceived as a mechanism

159 This position has long been advocated by Rokas, 'Corporate Organisation' (n 22) 17.

160 See ibid.

161 However, shareholders are allowed to intervene under German law only up to conclusion of admission proceedings for a derivative claim. See Schmidt and Lutter (n 74) 2133.

162 Triantafillakis (n 21) 128.

163 Peltzer (n 1) 959.

through which the board is substituted, in exceptional circumstances, regarding the capacity to assert corporate claims. Under this prism, the proposed model attempts to strike a balance among various competing factors, such as access to justice and excessive litigation, deterrence of managerial misconduct and business-making discretion. In doing so, the proposed rules endorse the 'decision rights' strategy and the 'trusteeship strategy', whereby the court acts as the (external) trustee of the company by being the arbiter of whether the derivative action is meritorious or not.[164] Among a variety of alternatives considered, the conclusion was that the court should primarily attest whether the action serves the corporate interests and is important enough for the company to proceed. However, all considerations were made on the grounds that the proposed criteria would be applicable in a single inter partes stage.

Therefore and for the sake of completeness, as a final point let us consider the desirability of a multi-staged admissions procedure. Chapter 3 showed that this approach was endorsed in the UK by a last-minute inclusion of the 'prima facie' ex parte procedure to the bill.[165]

The reasons put forward by the UK Law Commission in rejecting the idea of a preliminary stage for the permission process was that such an option would increase the likelihood of a mini trial on the merits taking place in the ex parte stage; involving thus more costs and time than desirable.[166]

Setting aside any elucidation on the motives of the legislator in introducing this stage in proceedings, practice so far has illustrated that the 'prima facie case' stage is, to the greatest extent, redundant. Courts have examined the applications pending before them ex parte, often using the same criteria (i.e. those of CA 2006 s 263) as in the inter partes hearings.[167] Interestingly, in the latter stage, whether the claim represents a prima facie case on the merits is to be considered again.[168] In essence, the only undisputed difference between the two stages in practice relates to the defendants' standing, putting thus the necessity of such a procedural duality to question. Furthermore, as illustrated before, courts are willing to allow the merger of the stages into one; on the rationale of time and cost efficiency.[169]

Some British academics have put forward the idea of limiting the first stage to an examination, on paper, of whether the applicant satisfies the formal requirements for legal standing and the claim is appropriate for the derivative claims procedure.[170] However, even if we are to consider such construction of a dual stage admission procedure for a proposed model of derivative claims under Greek

164 Detailed explanation of these strategies in Hirt, *The Enforcement* (n 14).

165 Keay and Loughrey (n 120) 194; see also Hansard, HL 9 May 2006, vol. 681, col. 883.

166 ibid.

167 ibid., 195; *Bridge v Daley* [2015] EWHC 2121 (Ch) [8], [75]–[76] (Hodge QC).

168 *Stainer v Lee* [2010] EWHC 1539 (Ch) [29] (Roth J).

169 *Franbar v Patel* [2008] EWHC 1534 (Ch); [2008] BCC 885 [24] (Trower QC); see also commentary by Julia Tang, 'Shareholder Remedies (n 113) 178.

170 Keay and Loughrey (n 120) 195.

law, strong arguments against such duality remain. Under the viewpoint of the need for expeditious resolution of disputes, such an addition of a judicial layer may work to the detriment of meritorious litigation. Even though the Greek judicial system does not face problems – pressing in other jurisdictions – regarding the quality of the judges' legal background and expertise, the slow rhythm under which Greek justice operates has been an issue for decades and only a miracle will extinguish it overnight.[171] At its heart lies the disproportionality between the numbers of judges and the volumes of litigation,[172] as well as the very design of certain procedures (for instance, lengthy deadlines for the parties to submit particulars). The recently passed Law 4334/2015, reforming 319 articles of the Greek Civil Procedure Code and taking effect in January 2016, constitutes an effort to re-distribute work among courts and speed up justice, but we should not expect too much of it at such an early point in time. If derivative actions are to be introduced, experience with the reformed Civil Procedure Code will tell whether an 'extra judicial layer' is a reasonable, let alone desirable, option.

5.5 Removing the disincentives of litigation costs

It is a common concern among comparative studies on derivative actions, that the costs entailed in the litigation often fend off meritorious claims.[173] As explained, the strategies adopted by the studied jurisdictions attempt to curb the disincentive of the 'loser pays' principle by imposing, with qualifications, the shareholder-claimant's/petitioner's litigation costs on the company. This Subsection adds to the proposed framework the important dimension of costs indemnity and the appropriate exceptions to it, particularly when the claim is brought in a frivolous or vexatious manner.

The crucial point for determining the allocation of the costs of the proceedings should be the *admission stage*. It is then that the shareholder-claimant should be judged as appropriate to substitute for the board in its function and as acting in the corporate interests. It should be thus mandatory that the company assumes the costs from that point on. Otherwise, the adverse result of incurring massive costs in the main proceedings may work as a disincentive. Notably, the German literature has identified that, despite the low costs of the admission proceedings by virtue of the statutory cap in place, an action may reach millions of euros in litigation costs in the main proceedings, as no such cap applies.[174]

171 For Greek justice in a comparative context, see the 'Rule of Law' index of the World Justice Project, <http://data.worldjusticeproject.org/> (accessed 1 November 2015).

172 CEPEJ 'Report on 'European Judicial Systems – Edition 2014 (2012 data): Efficiency and Quality of Justice', <www.coe.int/t/dghl/cooperation/cepej/evaluation/2014/Rapport_2014_en.pdf> (accessed 20 August 2015).

173 Baum and Puchniak (n 92) 35ff.

174 T Baums, 'Die Prozesskosten der aktienrechtlichen Anfechtungsklage' in Uwe Schneider (ed), *FS Marcus Lutter zum 70 Geburtstag* (Otto Schmidt 2000) 283, 284.

As Greek law stands, the rule that the company assumes the costs of the admission proceedings has only the merit of counterweighing important restraints on legal standing, found elsewhere in the relevant provision. Should, however, Greek law move from redress on paper to actual and efficient redress, this practice cannot be maintained. The reason is simple: up to obtaining clearance to proceed, it is just the member's decision whether to file a petition or not. The motives can be good or vexatious. Why then encourage 'pirate' litigation by removing any financial risk?

In other provisions within Greek company law, a different standard applies: the court can decide that costs are borne by the company, the claimant or both. This seems to be a more pragmatic and suitable approach for admission proceedings on derivative claims, particularly considered in conjunction with the fact that Greek law follows the loser-pays principle.[175] In the context of company's actions and derivative litigation, there is real risk for the company to assume the directors' expenses, them being winning defendants.

Furthermore, the examination of the other two jurisdictions showed their desire to relieve shareholders of the risk of incurring extensive litigation costs,[176] yet with considerable parsimony, so as to keep the floodgates of litigation closed. The Greek legislator should be cautious enough not to permit suits brought in a (at least) vexatious manner to become a financial detriment to Greek companies. Some qualifications should be put in the admissions procedure.

The discretion of the court should be limited in imposing costs upon litigants that failed to show any level of loyalty to the 'corporate purpose' in bringing the action: that is, when no person acting under the duty of loyalty (as defined in the Greek company law statute) would bring the action.[177] Effectively, this criterion covers much of the definition of what 'vexatious litigation' is. The proposed rule is thus issue specific and clear cut. Furthermore, it limits itself to only a subset of dismissed claims: litigants who honestly believed their claim to be in the company's interests but failed to persuade the court of its importance will be reimbursed by the company despite their claim being dismissed.

A final point concerns the allocation of costs when the shareholder applicant sought to have demand excused. For the demand rule to have any prospect of attaining the goals set in the previous paragraphs, namely to give priority to the company in decisions on corporate litigation and to provide the court with a substantiated opinion on the matter, shareholder-litigants should run a risk in their effort to by-pass the company's ordinary decision-making processes. It is therefore suggested that any claimant whose petition before the court to have demand declared futile is eventually dismissed should bear the costs of litigation.

175 GrCivPrC art 176; exceptions to the principle in arts 177, 179, 184, 185, 186.

176 Indemnification via a '*Wallersteiner* order' in the UK and AktG s148(6) in Germany.

177 The English reader is familiar with such criterion: case law under the statutory derivative claims procedure defined it as the benchmark of failure/success to satisfy the mandatory requirement of CA 2006 s 263(2)(a). See Subsection 3.3.4.

This approach does not weigh disproportionately against shareholder-claimants. Rather, such allocation of costs effectuates the exceptionality of the 'demand excused' rule under the proposed framework.

Indemnity of costs is, of course, not the only strategy available to remove disincentives or provide incentives for derivative claimants to enforce the corporate claims. Many view the American 'success story' as the outcome neither of a litigation culture nor of relaxed rules on the admission of shareholder suits but instead of the ability to conduct contingency fees arrangements.[178] The rationale is simple: these arrangements alleviate the burden of the costs from the claimant and place it on the shoulders of the attorney(s). If the claim is successful, the latter retain part of the proceeds or a fixed sum, as agreed upon at their appointment.

Oftentimes, contingency fees arrangements are hard to reconcile with the broader legal context. English law and the common law tort of champerty had for long provided such an example.[179] Yet, absence of such tort or any other rule to that effect under Greek law, evidences an approach less suspicious to such arrangements and renders the examination of such argumentation redundant for the purposes of this Section.[180]

In view of the beneficial effects of contingency fees – as is obviously the enhanced access to justice for the economically weak – the latter are gradually gaining ground in the continent, overriding concerns that litigation may become the playground for opportunist practitioners.[181] In fact, under Greek law, contingency fees have long been allowed: the system in place has a statutory cap on the arrangement of the proceeds and rules determining whether the outcome of litigation was successful or not.[182] However, despite their doctrinal compatibility with the loser pays principle, it is hard to see how such arrangements may become popular in jurisdictions where the 'English rule' applies. Particularly within the context of derivative litigation, it is expected that the financially weaker party will often be the shareholder-claimant. Unless his/her attorney is very confident of having a strong case at hand, the assumption of the winning party's litigation fees, with or without a cap, is a risk very few rational actors would be willing to take.

178 M Siems, 'Private Enforcement of Directors' Duties: derivative Actio ns as a Global Phenomenon' in Stefan Wrbka, Steven Van Uytsel and Mathias Siems (eds), *Collective Actions: Enhancing Access to Justice and Reconciling Multilayer Interests?* (CUP 2012) 93–116; Gelter (n 28) 866; Hirt, *The Enforcement* (n 14) 132–133; Baum and Puchniak (n 92) 41; Reisberg *Derivative Actions* (n 1) 262–264.

179 See commentary on *Wallersteiner* by Reisberg, *Derivative Actions* (n 1) 265.

180 It has to be noted that the Greek Attorneys' Code (art 1) stipulates that lawyers provide 'social service', a 'fundamental' element for the 'rule of law'.

181 Ever since the decision BVerfG 12.12.2006, 1 BvR 2576/04, NJW 2007 979, on the unconstitutionality of an absolute ban on contingency fees arrangements, Germany has become more receptive of the latter.

182 Attorneys' Code art 60.

Another well-discussed topic in academia[183] concerns the strategy of 'rewarding' shareholders who are successful in championing the corporate interests (award/incentive strategy).[184] This strategy is a step too far for a country which has not experienced derivative litigation before. It is furthermore hard to see any room for compatibility of this rule with the existing Greek legal framework, as in such a case the court substitutes for the corporate will in distributing the proceeds of litigation.

But, fundamentally, a reward strategy may create all the wrong incentives in pursuing a derivative action. Sure, it is hard to conceive how an economically rational actor would undertake a procedure that would potentially give trifles in return or, even worse, diminish (in the short term) the value of the company's shares. On the other hand, it is not difficult to imagine investors with minor and/or short-term interests in the company, taking the opportunity to make a profit out of litigation, if a reward strategy is in place.

It may be that in the conceptual space between the short-term irrational option of pursuing a derivative action and rational apathy is where the appropriate filter for frivolous litigation actually lies. Instead of construing arbitrary percentages for legal standing in order to 'ensure' that members with a close connection to the corporate interests bring the action, the legislator should realise that there is such a filter already in place: that is, the minor benefit the members enjoy from successful litigation in the short term.

5.6 Access to (claim-related) information

A well-cited author within the European scholarship on derivative actions is Latella. In my opinion, his major contribution to the study of derivative actions in Europe is his view that access to claim-related information is one of the most significant drawbacks European jurisdictions showcase regarding shareholder litigation.[185] Although I consider other factors to be more significant in explaining the imperfections of the relevant law in the herein studied countries, I equally believe that, should the Greek legislator want to provide a working framework for corporate litigation, information has to be disseminated to the shareholders effectively. After all, how would it ever be possible to bring a claim successfully, if evidence is unavailable and nobody but the wrongdoers knows of the misfeasance occurred? For the shareholders' claim to have potential for success, it is important that they have access to corporate information, particularly prior to filing the claim.[186] However, the mandatory disclosure regimes may not be (and usually are not) adequate to disseminate the information necessary for

183 See particularly Reisberg, *Derivative Actions* (n 1) 246.

184 As happens in Australia. See Section 3.2.

185 Latella (n 34) 321: 'the theme I consider really fundamental to allow a full and effective exercise of shareholder derivative action, is that of information rights'.

186 See also Chapter 3.

court proceedings. Greek law has already in place a (qualified) minority right to request a special audit: as explained, the equivalent German provision is regarded as complementary to the derivative action. However, the British approach allows for a court order to be made for case-specific investigations of corporate affairs. Both approaches are considered hereinafter.

The first way to achieve anything towards the desirable end of adequate information is granting 'information rights' to shareholders.[187] This is a matter harmonised to an extent at EU level, as reviewed earlier on this study.[188] The problem is that the harmonisation focused exclusively on information to be furnished within the ambit and for facilitation of the GM. No significant harmonisation exists (yet) regarding records and registries of the company.[189] Importantly, board meetings are secluded from the monitoring of shareholders. Mitigating the information asymmetries and agency costs involved is, potentially, a block-holder structure. However, only block-holders have access to sensitive information in this case, principally by virtue of their special relationship with the appointed directors. Greece has not come up with an effective solution regarding this matter. As explained, the national legislator did not go much further than the Shareholder Rights Directive.

Nevertheless, what constitutes a mechanism for pre-trial investigation is the special audit procedure. On that matter, Greek law much resembles the German provisions.[190] UK law does not provide the respective right of auditors' appointment to shareholders. There have been studies identifying this difference in approach as a comparative disadvantage.[191] There is good reason to maintain a rule addressing the intra-corporate information asymmetry and adjust it with the prerequisites for what is supposed to follow such discovery (unless the misfeasors voluntarily make good the damage they caused): shareholders' litigation.[192]

In suggesting the introduction of rules on derivative actions and their complementarity with the right to call for a special audit, the first point to consider is legal standing, regarding both procedures. The German legislature decided to eliminate disparities in quorum requirements, yet in Greece differences remain as to who may call for a special audit and who may petition for the appointment of special representatives. Having asserted that accumulation of information and evidence constitute a significant gear in the corporate litigation mechanism, it is rather absurd to

187 Dissemination of information on demand is called 'push system' of information rights. See Masouros (n 41) and Zetzsche (n 41).

188 Chapter 4.

189 The Transparency Directive (2004/109/EC (OJ L 390, 31.12.2004 38)) mandates that significant shareholdings are disclosed. Aside from the imperfections of the directive's objectives (no particular reference to end-investors), its significance within the ambit of derivative actions is limited to the extent that it facilitates collective action.

190 See Chapter 3.

191 Reisberg *Derivative Actions* (n 1) 218–219; Paul (n 2) 95–96.

192 As explained, the UMAG considered *Sonderprüfung* to be a procedure independent from but auxiliary to the exercise of the AktG s148 right.

restrict legal standing disproportionately between the respective procedures.[193] At least regarding the 'legality check' audit of article 40 paragraph 1, my opinion is that shareholder claimants in derivative actions should avail themselves of the latter right prior to litigation, without the need to seek allies to meet quorum requirements. Greece should learn by others' mistakes on this issue.[194]

The special audit under paragraph 3 is another case altogether. Being designed to investigate the diligence and loyalty of corporate management, it touches upon business-sensitive information. Its availability to shareholders has to be therefore more parsimonious than the cases of legality check. In recognition of this, the Greek legislator rightly imposed stricter (quorum) requirements.[195]

The further question to ask is whether the UK approach of pre-trial discovery procedure is incompatible with the special audit procedure or redundant because of the latter. There are good reasons to hold that neither is the case. In France, the donor country of fundamental Greek company law rules, both rights exist in parallel. Reportedly, the investigation procedure is more popular in view of litigation.[196] However, quasi-equivalent investigation procedures under the Greek Civil Procedure Code are restricted to circumstances where evidence is in danger of being lost or when expert advice is expedient.

The Greek legislator should follow the UK and French paradigms. If a derivative action is introduced, the right to request an investigation under the Civil Procedure Rules should be conferred on the prospective shareholder claimants, provided that they can reasonably show that a cause of action may exist on a summary of facts substantiating their suspicions.[197] That will constitute significant progress from a shareholder protection perspective, compared to the current regime of special representatives. As the law stands, special representatives have access to corporate information, yet their (vaguely defined) right to have recourse to corporate documentation is bound by their mandate to bring a claim within the limits set by the shareholders' petition for their judicial appointment.[198] This is problematic, as the petition's content is determined by the limited information available to shareholders. Allowing thus shareholders ample access to information, prior and following the filing of their derivative claim, will work towards holding wrongdoers accountable for misbehaviour that

193 Concurring: Suzanne Kalss, 'Shareholder Suits: Common Problems, Different Solutions and First Steps towards a Possible Harmonisation by Means of a European Model Code' (2009) 6 ECFR 324, 342.

194 France and Switzerland, despite conferring an individual right to derivative litigation, set ownership thresholds for the enactment of the right to call for a special audit; this position has been criticised in the literature. See Gelter (n 28) 875.

195 Kokkinis (n 133) 1555.

196 Bernard Grelon, 'Shareholders' Lawsuits against the Management of a Company and its Shareholders under French Law', (2009) 6 ECFR 205, 208.

197 cf Latella (n 34) 323.

198 See Themis K Skouras, 'Appointment and Replacement of Special Representatives in the Societe Anonyme' [1983] EEmpD 553, 563.

might fall under the shareholders' radar pursuant to the now applicable ordinary company, civil and procedural law provisions.

5.7 Concluding remarks

The suggestions advanced by this Chapter envisage a meaningful framework which facilitates the protection of shareholders' interests and the accountability of corporate wrongdoers whilst, at the same time, minimises the risk of litigation detrimental to the company's interests. A further, collateral objective was to construe a working framework which does not necessitate a revision of core principles of Greek law. To that effect, several departures from the status quo are proposed in order to make shareholder litigation on behalf of the company a reasonable and available option. The most striking ones are the marginalisation of the institution of special representatives, the recalibration of the minority right to petition as an individual right to sue and the remedy of wrongs done to connected companies. Simultaneously, the proposed constraints on shareholders' frivolous and vexatious litigation focus on the decision to litigate instead of on the contribution of the shareholder to the company's capital, as is now the case.

The suggested reforms followed comparative considerations. The methodology adopted ensures, on the one hand, that the competitiveness of the Greek legal framework on shareholder protection is reasserted in the European context, while, on the other hand, limiting the comparative advantages the reform proposals may have to the given cross-jurisdictional context. Other legal orders may also provide for alternative frameworks with considerable merit.[199]

It may be true that the proposed framework resembles, to different extents, existing provisions in jurisdictions other than those examined; such as the Australian derivative action.[200] This is expected. Under the tenet of praesumptio similitudinis in comparative law, legal orders are likely to give similar solutions to functionally equivalent legal problems.[201] Furthermore, Western jurisdictions adopt and apply common legal principles and strategies, such as the proper plaintiff rule, the subsidiarity of the shareholders' action, the strategy of filtering out unmeritorious litigation in an admissions stage and the separate corporate personality doctrine. It is in the details where the comparative scholar should look for differences. Divergence in the weighting of regulatory objectives may result in significant disparities in the practical value of legal provisions, depending on the point of view one assumes. From a shareholder's perspective and within the ambit of derivative actions, for instance, a qualification of the cause of action may result

199 e.g. the American attorney-based corporate litigation model and the Federal Disclosure Rules. See, regarding both, Coffee 'Scylla and Charybdis' (n 76) 800.

200 Corporations Act 2001 ss 236–242.

201 Konrad Zweigert and Hein Kötz, *An Introduction to Comparative Law*, tr Tony Weir (3rd edn, OUP 1998), 40.

in the provision becoming inaccessible, compared to the respective law on shareholders' remedies in another jurisdiction, where functionally equivalent rules exist but no such qualification applies.

Overall, the proposed framework is designed to improve shareholder protection under Greek law and reassert its competitiveness. In conformity with the argument made in Chapter 2, that stronger protection facilitates investment and growth, this is a timely and important task.

6 Conclusion

6.1 Synopsis

The derivative action, a beast largely unknown to Greek law to date, is an ingenious and highly complex apparatus. As explained in this book, it has – as a concept – scintillating potential in addressing the domestic law's problems in protecting shareholders from wrongs done to the company. By suing derivatively, they can remedy their reflective loss in an indirect, yet doctrinally acceptable, way. In fact, derivative actions serve the broader purpose of protecting the interests of shareholders in globo against the opportunistic behaviour of those in control of the company. They thus advance the fair and efficient administration of corporate affairs.

The analysis highlighted the inadequacies of Greek law regarding this matter of shareholder protection. The company's action, a surprisingly resilient relic from the early days of Greek company law, falls short of the challenges it has to meet. On the other hand, other mechanisms of shareholder protection cannot compensate for the shortcomings of the company's action. Overall, the second Part of this book showed that Greek law cannot protect effectively the (minority) shareholder from the opportunism derivative actions aim to deter and remedy. The law is strict and the hurdles are often insurmountable. In some instances, problems of shareholder protection are not even considered.

Undoubtedly, the most significant contribution of the comparative approach to the objectives of this study is the exposition of existing alternatives to the Greek status quo. The analysis showed that other jurisdictions provide more effective responses to problems that are significant and common. Yet, as an exercise of seeking differences in the law, it showed that there is no silver bullet solution. On the contrary, laws on the matter remain quite divergent, a phenomenon best explained by the complexity of derivative litigation. The design of legal rules on the matter necessitates the consideration of various and often conflicting objectives. The law aims to encourage such litigation in order to facilitate the accountability of corporate wrongdoers and the consequent protection of shareholders' interests, yet, at the same time, it attempts to deter derivative litigation to the extent that the latter does not promote the company's interests. The legal framework on derivative actions, being a spoke in the wheel of shareholder protection and part of the system of checks and balances on the administration of corporate affairs, has to strike a delicate balance between use and abuse, incentives and restrictions. All this is very challenging. Within the scope of this research, no jurisdiction proved to discharge this task flawlessly: still, some do perform better than others. However, the comparative considerations show the way forward.

The de lege ferenda suggestions in Chapter 5 concluded the search for the 'better law'. The proposed framework attempts to distil the insights Germany and the UK have to offer to Greek law. The end result aspires to delineate a derivative action that protects the company's interests. Concordantly, it calls for a shift of focus from the protection of minorities to the protection of the shareholder as a member and investor. This is a timely task for the Greek law-maker and, possibly, long overdue.

6.2 Derivative actions beyond the jurisdictional focus of this book

The arguments put forward and the conclusions reached herein may concern primarily the examined jurisdictions, yet they also suggest themselves for the broader study of shareholder law and shareholder remedies. The selection of a study area covering both common law and civil law traditions worked to that effect. Incidents of convergence and divergence among jurisdictions belonging to each legal family, similar to those identified in this book, are likely to be found to exist.

As happens with most comparative studies though, the applicability of the conclusions and normative implications of this study to other jurisdictions should be considered with caution. Jurisdictions may be similar in many respects, yet they are hardly ever identical. The comparison between Greece and Germany evidences the fact. Readers should carefully consider the line of reasoning and how this was herein affected by the broader legal context in which the studied rules operate, as well as the limitations of this study, before espousing (or dismissing) the output of this research for their jurisdiction(s). For instance, the herein considered means of redress of shareholders' reflective loss and enforcement of directors' duties – alternative to derivative actions – correspond to the law as it now stands in Germany, Greece and the UK, and the conclusion on the necessity for the introduction of the derivative action to Greek law was partly reached on the premises of the insufficiency of those alternatives.[1] I expect this conclusion to bear different strength in other jurisdictions – after all, human reason should never be underestimated and derivative actions are not its only product in the effort to address issues of shareholder protection and corporate governance.

1 Chapter 4.

That being said, some of the book's conclusions may be readily applicable to jurisdictions falling outside its study area. This is particularly the case regarding the problems of legal standing in 'corporate actions'. There remain jurisdictions who follow this path up to date and where the preceding analysis may offer valuable insight. To illustrate, Austria provides for a, rather obsolete, version of the corporate actions that much resembles the Greek one, particularly in its pre-2019 setting.[2] In fact, both descend from the German *Aktiengesetz* of 1937. Historically, the Austrian provisions remained closer to the original template of the donor jurisdiction though.[3] In both cases, the remedy bestows the power to enforce the company's claims to special representatives, not shareholders. Therefore, the concerns raised herein about the special representatives' moral hazard and the dis-incentivisation of shareholder activists can be held to also apply to Austrian law. Another common feature between the two jurisdictions is the imposition of qualified minority thresholds as requirement for legal standing in petitions to appoint a special representative: notably, under certain circumstances, the applicable thresholds coincide. The arguments advanced by this book against such rules are therefore relevant to Austrian corporate governance, where block-holders' prominence is also observed. Ownership thresholds are arbitrary, disenfranchising, doctrinally questionable and obstruct D&O liability enforcement. This can be said regarding other jurisdictions that set such requirements for corporate actions and derivative actions,[4] the weight of each argument depending on the size of the applicable thresholds and the shareholding

2 Section 134 of the Austrian AktG ('Obligation to Assert Claims') reads: '(1) The claims of the company ... must be asserted if the General Meeting so resolves by a simple majority of votes. The same applies if it is so required by a minority whose shares together reach ten per cent of the share capital, and if the claims asserted by it are not manifestly unfounded. If in the audit report ... facts were established that substantiate claims for compensation ... a minority whose shares together reach 5% of the share capital shall suffice. (2) The general meeting may appoint special representatives to conduct the legal dispute. If the minority demands the assertion of the claim and the claim asserted by it is not manifestly unfounded, the court shall appoint the persons designated by it as the representative of the company for the conduct of the dispute, if its appointment does not preclude an important cause. Apart from that, the representation of the company is based on § 97, even if the minority has requested the assertion of the claim.'

3 The Greek remedy also suffered from ambiguity due to inaccurate translation of the German wording. Notably, the recent reform of Greek law approximated its Austrian counterpart regarding the (narrow) discretionary power of the court to dismiss such a shareholder's petition; however, the Austrian proviso remains stricter, since it only allows the court to check if the claim is manifestly unfounded in considering such petition. In any case, in both jurisdictions corporate interests assume a minor role in filtering frivolous and vexatious litigation. I trust that Austrian corporate governance could benefit from the approach herein proposed, of putting the company's interests at the forefront of derivative litigation, consigning arbitrary and ultimately unfair filters of unmeritorious litigation – such as ownership thresholds – to the dustbin.

4 Such as Belgium, Bulgaria, Croatia, Czech Republic, Italy, Latvia, Luxemburg, Slovakia, Slovenia, Spain and Sweden, within the EU. Other notable examples are Brazil and China.

structures in question though.[5] Furthermore, multiple derivative actions, despite not being on a statutory footing anywhere in Europe yet, have been allowed by English courts, as explicated in Chapter 3, under the common law regime. Given that in Cyprus and Ireland derivative actions operate as exceptions to the rule in *Foss*,[6] multiple derivative actions may also be allowed there, at least in theory. It is interesting to see what stance the courts will adopt when presented with such a case and whether other jurisdictions will follow this example and address this loophole in shareholder protection and enforcement of directors' duties.

As regards the scope of misfeasance covered by the derivative action (and its functional equivalents), useful parallels can be drawn between this book's study area and other common law and civil law jurisdictions. Regarding the former legal family, the derivative action has yet to be put on a statutory footing in several of its members. Within the EU, the remedy still applies in Cyprus and Ireland under the narrow constraints set by the 'fraud on the minority' rule.[7] As happened with England prior to CA 2006, this rule largely accounts for the scarcity of derivative litigation there.[8] Accordingly, the analysis of how the statutory derivative action has fared in the UK provides a guide for them on how a move away from the common law regime may revive the practical significance of the remedy. It also offers a good point of reference for comparisons with other common law jurisdictions that recently proceeded to such reform. As for civil law countries, some (e.g. Croatia) impose the 'gross violations' restriction, in a fashion similar to that of German law.[9] I expect that the arguments made herein against it would have comparable strength there too.

The analysis of further aspects of shareholders' enforcement of corporate claims, such as the rules on shareholders' demand for the management to take action prior to filing a derivative suit (or functionally equivalent remedy), may also be relevant to jurisdictions outside the scope of this research,[10] due to the commonality of problems national law-makers are called to address. It is worth recalling though that, as stated in Chapter 3, the scarcity of derivative litigation in Europe is often attributed to only one such common problem: the allocation

5 See Chapter 2.3 on a discussion on the interrelation between ownership structures and minority protection.

6 *Foss v Harbottle* (1843) 67 ER 189.

7 Derivative actions also operate as exceptions to the rule in *Foss* in Malta, yet case law offers little to no guidance as to how the remedy applies. See Carsten Gerner-Beuerle, Philipp Paech and Edmund Philipp Schuster, 'Study on Directors' Duties and Liability', <http://ec.europa.eu/internal_market/company/docs/board/2013-study-analysis_en.pdf> (accessed 1 May 2015) 200.

8 See John Quinn, 'The Companies Act 2014 and the Absence of the Derivative Action' (2016) 23 CL Pract 102.

9 Croatian Companies Act 273.a.

10 The Czech Republic (Business Corporations Act s 373), Latvia (Commercial Law clause 172), Slovakia (Commercial Code s 182).

of litigation costs and the financial disincentives involved.[11] However, similarly to the conclusions reached in Chapter 3, this is rarely the only factor responsible for such scarcity. There are jurisdictions that provide for possibilities for reimbursement, yet they still experience a drought when it comes to derivative litigation.[12] Looking closer at each jurisdiction individually, the expected conclusion would be that it is the mixture of rules, such as the ones in the paragraphs above, to blame for the lack of shareholders' suits.[13]

6.3 The prospects of convergence within the EU

Given that this research considered European jurisdictions, it is worth switching focus from the national to the supranational EU level and reflect, in brief, on the prospects of regulatory action thereat regarding derivative actions. As mentioned in the introductory Chapter, the EU recently commissioned two studies relevant to shareholders enforcement of directors' duties. Improving shareholder protection and corporate governance are among the commission's stated goals within the framework of company law and corporate governance.[14] However, at the moment of publication, measures other than harmonising shareholder remedies seem to have priority.[15] It is worth recalling here that the proposal for a fifth company law directive included a form of derivative action. Even though disagreement among member states on this proviso was not the reason why the directive never came into force, it is safe to say, following the comparative analysis, that a 'European derivative action', despite being a meaningful task,[16] will not be an easy one. The remedy's dual – procedural and substantive law – nature, the dependence of its success on other provisions of company law, such

11 Several reporters within the TGS Baltic Study on Minority Shareholders Protection (Gintautas Bartkus, Daina Belicka, Mindaugas Civilka, Pierre-Henri Conac, Christoph Teichmann, Tineke Lambooy and Brenda Hannigan, 'Study on Minority Shareholders Protection', <https://publications.europa.eu/en/publication-detail/-/publication/1893f7b8-93a4-11e8-8bc1-01aa75ed71a1/language-en> (accessed 1 March 2019)), expressed such concerns, including those of Austria, Belgium, France, Hungary, Lithuania and Poland.

12 The Czech Republic and Latvia have rules on assumption of costs similar to the Greek ones, whereas Cyprus and Ireland assimilate the English approach regarding reimbursement.

13 Similar conclusion reached by Martin Gelter, 'Why do Shareholder Derivative Suits Remain Rare in Continental Europe?' (2011–2012) 37 Brook J Int'l L 843, 891, regarding influential European jurisdictions.

14 EU Company Law and Corporate Governance, <https://ec.europa.eu/info/business-economy-euro/doing-business-eu/company-law-and-corporate-governance_en> (accessed 10 March 2019).

15 Company Law Package, <https://ec.europa.eu/info/publications/company-law-package_en> (accessed 10 March 2019).

16 For instance, as I have argued elsewhere (Georgios Zouridakis, 'Shareholders' Derivative Suits against Corporate Directors, Following Cross-Border Mergers: A Functioning Remedy within the EU?' in Thomas Papadopoulos (ed), *Cross-Border Mergers Directive: EU Perspectives and National Experiences* (Springer, forthcoming), approximation of laws may provide solutions in derivative actions involving the cross-border element.

as those on shareholders information rights, and the need to strike the perfect balance between incentivising shareholders' enforcement of corporate claims and preventing frivolous and vexatious litigation, not only result in high levels of complexity but also require a harmonious relationship between the remedy and the broader company law and corporate governance framework. In other words, for the harmonisation of this remedy to have any prospect of practical significance, not only further harmonisation of other, related provisions may be required but also the divergence among member states must be seriously taken into account and the objectives that the remedy should serve must be clearly set before such a proviso is introduced into EU company law.

The difficulty of doing that is evident by the only notable step towards that direction in the European context up to now, the EMCA. The minimalistic form of derivative action it provides can be understood as mainly serving the purpose of providing a common point of reference, as it mostly contains the very basic elements of the remedy, shared among most jurisdictions: it seems as if the group would have difficulty in reconciling anything more detailed with the addressee national frameworks. Even though it is too soon to assess or predict its impact on legislation at national level, it is not expected to be substantial: at most, it may serve as the 'derivative action starter pack' for jurisdictions introducing the remedy to their statutory law for the first time. So far, Greece did not follow this route. It remains to be seen if Austria, Estonia or the Netherlands will.

This is not to say that the EMCA should be replaced by the derivative action proposed in Chapter 5 nor to propose that the latter should be followed by every jurisdiction in Europe, let alone globally. Given that the decades-long discussion of derivative actions has not culminated in a conclusion in statutory law or in academic scholarship, it would be hubris to claim that this book advances a universal understanding of how all derivative actions should be. This has never been its purpose. What it does, though, is communicate a substantiated argument on why and how they may assume an important role in a given temporal and jurisdictional context, from a particular perspective. This objective is precise, worthy and, most importantly, realistic.

Bibliography

Authored books

Amos MS, Walton FPand Anton AE, *Amos and Walton's Introduction to French Law* (Clarendon Press 1963).

Antonopoulos V, *Law of Societes Anonymes and Limited Liability Companies* (Sakkoulas 2011).

Apostolopoulos HE, *The Business Judgment Rule and the Challenge of the Firm's Insolvency* (Nomiki Bibliothiki 2014).

Athanasiou L, *Shareholders' Activism and Corporate Monitoring* (Nomiki Bibliothiki 2010).

Baums T, 'Empfiehlt sich eine Neuregelung des aktienrechtlichen Anfechtungs- und Organhaftungsrechts, insbesondere der Klagemöglichkeiten von Aktionären?' in *Gutachten F zum 63. Deutschen Juristentag Leipzig 2000* (CH Beck 2000).

——— 'Die Prozesskosten der aktienrechtlichen Anfechtungsklage' in Uwe Schneider (ed), *FS Marcus Lutter zum 70 Geburtstag* (Otto Schmidt 2000).

——— and Hutter S (eds), *Festschrift für Michael Gruson* (Walter de Gruyter 2009).

Berle A and Means G, *The Modern Corporation and Private Property* (first published 1932, Macmillan 1962).

Beys K, *Politikí dikonomía: genikés archés kai ermineía ton árthron. 14/, V. Asfalistiká métra* (articles 682–738) (Sakkoulas 1983).

Bezzenberger G and Bezzenberger T, 'Section 148' in K Hopt and H Wiedemann (eds), *Großkommentar AktG* (Walter de Gruyter 2008).

Bitter G, Lutter M, Priester H-J, Schön W and Ulmer P (eds), *Festschrift für Karsten Schmidt zum 70. Geburtstag* (Otto Schmidt 2009).

Boele-Woelki K, *Perspectives for the Unification and Harmonisation of Family Law in Europe* (Intersentia 2003).

Bogdan M, *Comparative Law* (Kluwer 1994).

Boyle A, *Minority Shareholders' Remedies* (CUP 2002).

Brach-Thiel D, *Le Guide juridique du créateur d'entreprise* (Heures de France 2007).

Burgard U, Hadding W, Mülbert OP, Nietsch M and Welter R (eds), *Festschrift Für Uwe H. Schneider zum 70. Geburtstag* (O. Schmidt 2011).

Bürgers T and Körber T (eds), *Heidelberger Kommentar zum Aktiengesetz* (CF Müller 2008).

——— *Heidelberger Kommentar zum Aktiengesetz* (3rd edn, CF Müller 2013).

Cahn A and Donald DC, *Comparative Company Law: Text and Cases on the Laws Governing Corporations in Germany, the UK and the USA* (CUP 2010).

Calavros C, *Civil Procedure-General Part* (2nd edn, Sakkoulas 2006).
Casper M, *German Corporate Governance in International and European Context* (Springer, 2012).
Chen W, *A Comparative Study of Funding Shareholder Litigation* (Springer 2017).
Clark R, *Corporate Law* (Little, Brown 1986).
David R and Brierley JEC, *Major Legal Systems in the World Today: An Introduction to the Comparative Study of Law* (Simon & Schuster 1978).
Davies P and Worthington S, *Gower and Davies' Principles of Modern Company Law* (9th edn, Sweet & Maxwell 2012).
De Cruz P, *Comparative Law in a Changing World* (3rd edn, Cavendish-Routledge 2007).
Dine J, *The Governance of Corporate Groups* (CUP 2000).
——— and Koutsias M, *Company Law* (8th edn, Palgrave MacMillan 2014).
——— and ——— *The Nature of Corporate Governance* (EE 2013).
Douglas Z, Pauwelyn J and Viñuales JE, *The Foundations of International Investment Law: Bringing Theory into Practice* (OUP 2014).
Easterbrook FH and Fischel DR, *The Economic Structure of Corporate Law* (Harvard University Press 1996).
Ferrara RC, Abikoff KT and Leedy Gansler L, *Shareholder Derivative Litigation: Besieging the Board* (Law Journal Press 2013).
French D, Mayson S and Ryan C, *Mayson, French & Ryan on Company Law* (31st edn, OUP 2014).
Galanis M and Dignam A, *The Globalization of Corporate Governance* (Ashgate 2013).
Georgakopoulos L, *To Díkaio ton Etaireión* (Sakkoulas 1974).
——— *To Díkaio ton Etaireión* (4th edn, Sakkoulas 1991).
Greene D (ed), *Shareholder Claims* (Jordans 2012).
Greenfield K, *The Failure of Corporate Law: Fundamental Flaws and Progressive Possibilities* (UCP 2008).
Haar B, Merkt H, Mülbert PO, Wellenhofer M, Baum H, von Hein J, von Hippel T, Pistor K, Roth M and Schweitzer H (eds), *Festschrift für Klaus J. Hopt zum 70. Geburtstag am 24. August 2010: Unternehmen, Markt und Verantwortung* (Walter de Gruyter 2010).
Guest AG (ed), *Oxford Essays in Jurisprudence* (OUP 1961).
Gutteridge HC, *Comparative Law, An Introduction to the Comparative Method of Legal Study and Research* (CUP 1946).
Hirt CH, *The Enforcement of Directors' Duties in Britain and Germany: A Comparative Study with Particular Reference to Large Companies* (Peter Lang 2004).
Hirte H and Teichmann C, *The European Private Company: Societas Privata Europaea (SPE)* (Walter de Gruyter 2012).
Holmes WO Jr, *The Common Law* (1881), www.gutenberg.org/files/2449/2449-h/2449-h.htm (accessed 15 May 2015).
Honoré AM, 'Ownership', in AG Guest (ed), *Oxford Essays in Jurisprudence* (OUP, 1961).
Hopt KJ, Kanda H, Roe MJ, Wymeersch E and Prigge S, *Comparative Corporate Governance: The State of the Art and Emerging Research* (Clarendon Press, 1998).
Hüffer U, *Aktiengesetz* (2nd edn, CH Beck 1995).
——— *Aktiengesetz* (10th edn, CH Beck 2012).
Joffe V, Drake D, Richardson G, Lightman D and Collingwood T, *Minority Shareholders, Law, Practice and Procedure* (4th edn, OUP 2011).

Karamanakou E, *Shareholders' Fiduciary Duties* (Nomiki Bibliothiki 2013).

Karlsgodt PG, *World Class Actions: A Guide to Group and Representative Actions Around the Globe* (OUP 2012).

Kolotouros PI, *Actio Pro Socio: i Dikonomikí Diástasis tis Etairikís Agogís* (Sakkoulas 2006).

Kraakman R, Armour J, Davies P, Enriques L, Hansmann H, Hertig G, Hopt K, Kanda H and Rock E, *The Anatomy of Corporate Law: A Comparative and Functional Approach* (2nd edn, OUP 2009).

Lambadarios Law Firm (tr and ed), *Law 2190/1920 on Companies Limited by Shares (Sociétés Anonymes) Law 3190/1955 On Limited Liability Companies, Greek & English text* (Nomiki Bibliothiki 2011).

Legrand P and Munday R (eds), *Comparative Legal Studies: Traditions and Transitions* (CUP 2003).

Levantis E, *Commercial Law: Companies with Limited Liability* (Sakkoulas 1998).

Liakopoulos A, *Zitímata emporikoú dikaíou IV* (Sakkoulas 1997).

Loughrey J (ed), *Directors' Duties and Shareholder Litigation in the Wake of the Financial Crisis*, (EE 2013).

Lutter M and Wiedemann H., *Gestaltungsfreiheit im Gesellschaftsrecht: Deutschland, Europa und USA: 11. ZGR-Symposion '25 Jahre ZGR'* (Walter de Gruyter, 1998).

McCahery JA, Moerland P, Raaijmakers T, and Renneboog L (eds), *Corporate Governance Regimes: Convergence and Diversity* (OUP 2002).

Margaritis M and Margariti A (eds), *Commentary on the Code of Civil Procedure* (Sakkoulas 2012).

Marinos M-T (ed), *Issues from the New Law of the Societe Anonyme* (Sakkoulas 2009).

——— (ed), *The Public Limited Company among Company: Insolvency and the Law of Capital Markets* (Sakkoulas 2011).

Markesinis BS, *Foreign Law and Comparative Methodology* (Hart, 1997).

———, Unberath H and Johnston A, *The German Law of Contract: A Comparative Treatise* (Hart, 2006).

Mentis G, 'Liability of Corporate Administrative Organs for Investor's Loss' in Minutes of the 11th Panhellenian Conference of Greek Corporate Lawyers (Collaborative Work)," *The Societe Anonyme and the Stock Market: The Protection of the Investor* (Sakkoulas 2003).

Mikroulea A, *Scope of Corporate Managers' Duties and Liability* (Nomiki Bibliothiki 2013).

Milathianaki M, *I katanomí ton exousión metaxý tis Genikís Synélefsis kai tou Dioikitikoú Symvoulíou tis A.E.* (Nomiki Bibliothiki 2013).

Morse G (ed), *Palmer's Company Law* (Sweet & Maxwell 2015).

Mouzoulas SA, *L.3604/07 for the Reform and Amendment of CL 2190/1920 on Societes Anonymes, Annotated* (Sakkoulas 2008).

Nakamura H, Fasching H, Gaul FH and Georgiades A (eds), *Festschrift für Kostas E Beys dem Rechtsdenker in Attischer Dialektik* (5th edn, Eunomia 2003).

Ochmann F, *Die Aktionärsrechte-Richtlinie: Auswirkungen auf das deutsche und europäische Recht* (WWWAWalter de Gruyter 2009).

Olson M, *The Logic of Collective Action: Public Goods and the Theory of Groups* (Harvard University Press 1965).

Pacces AM, 'Corporate Governance and the Coase's Legacy: A Reply to Henry Manne' in Pacces AM (ed), *The Law and Economics of Corporate Governance: Changing Perspectives* (EE 2010).

Papadopoulos T, *EU Law and the Harmonization of Takeovers in the Internal Market* (Kluwer Law 2010).
——— (ed), *Cross-Border Mergers Directive: EU Perspectives and National Experiences* (Springer, forthcoming).
Passias I, *To Díkaion tis Anonýmou Etaireías* (n.p. 1969).
Perakis E, *Contractual Restrictions of the Shareholder's Voting Right* (n.p. 1976).
——— (ed), *The New Law of Limited Companies* (5th edn, Nomiki Bibliothiki 2018).
——— (ed), *The New Law of the Société anonyme* (Nomiki Bibliothiki 2007).
——— (ed), *Rights of Minority Shareholders* (Bruylant 2004).
——— (ed), *Sociétés Anonyme's Law* (Nomiki Bibliothiki 2010).
——— (ed), *Sociétés Anonyme's Law* (3rd edn, Nomiki Bibliothiki 2013).
Pettet B, Lowry J and Reisberg A, *Pettet's Company Law* (3rd edn, Pearson 2009).
Posner R, *Economic Analysis of Law* (3rd edn, Little, Brown 1986).
Puchniak WD, Baum H and Ewing-Chow M (eds), *The Derivative Action in Asia: A Comparative and Functional Approach* (CUP 2012).
Rathenau W, *Vom Aktienwesen: Eine Geschäftliche Betrachtung* (Fischer 1917).
Reimann M, *Cost and Fee Allocation in Civil Procedure: A Comparative Study* (Springer 2011).
Reisberg A, *Derivative Actions and Corporate Governance: Theory and Operation* (OUP 2007).
Rokas NK, *Commercial Companies* (Sakkoulas 2006).
Rosenberg L and Schwab K, *Zivilprozessrecht* (14th edn, CH Beck 1986).
Sanford DH, 'Determinates vs. Determinables' in EN Zalta (ed), *The Stanford Encyclopedia of Philosophy* (Spring 2013) http://plato.stanford.edu/archives/spr2013/entries/determinate-determinables (accessed 15 May 2015).
Schlessinger RB, Baade HW, Damaska MR and Herzog PE, *Comparative Law, Cases-Text-Materials* (5th edn, Foundation Press 1988).
Schmidt K and Lutter M (eds), *Aktiengesetz: Kommentar* (Otto Schmidt 2010).
Schröder A, Mayer B, Manz G, Thies H and Lammel S, *Die Aktiengesellschaft: Umfassende Erläuterungen, Beispiele und Musterformulare für die Rechtspraxis* (7th edn, Haufe 2014).
Schulz M and Wasmeier O, *The Law of Business Organisations* (Springer 2012).
Schwab M, *Das Prozeßrecht gesellschaftsinterner Streitigkeiten* (Mohr Siebeck 2005).
Sealy L and Worthington S, *Sealy's Cases and Materials on Company Law* (9th edn, OUP 2010).
Siems, MM, *Convergence in Shareholder Law* (CUP 2008).
——— and Cabrelli D (eds), *Comparative Company Law* (Hart 2013).
Smith A, *An Inquiry into the Nature and Causes of the Wealth of Nations*, ed RH Campbell, AS Skinner and WB Todd (first published 1776, Clarendon Press 1976).
Smits, MJ (ed), *Elgar Encyclopedia of Comparative Law* (EE 2012).
Spyridonos A, *Minority Rights in the Company Limited by Shares* (Nomiki Bibliothiki 2001).
Triantafillakis G, 'Duty of a Shareholder Exerting Influence on the Management of a Public Limited Company' in Minutes of the 12th Panhellenian Conference of Greek Corporate Lawyers (Collaborative Work), *Contemporary issues of Corporate Responsibility* (Nomiki Bibliothiki 2003).
——— 'From the Protection of the Minority to the Protection of the Shareholder', in Minutes of the 18th Panhellenian Conference on Commercial Law (Collaborative

Work), *Trends and Prospects of the Law of the Public Limited Company* (Nomiki Bibliothiki 2009).

——— *To Symféron tis Epicheírisis os Kanónas Symperiforás ton Orgánon tis AE* (Sakkoulas 1998).

Van Hoecke M (ed), *Epistemology and Methodology of Comparative Law* (Hart 2004).

VVon Gierke O, *Das Deutsche Genossenschaftsrecht*, vol. 11 (first published 1868, Wissenschaftliche Buchgemeinschaft 1954).

Welch E, Turezyn A and Saunders R, *Folk on the Delaware General Corporation Law* (Wolters Kluwer 2013).

Wilhelmi H and Wilhelmi S, *Godin/Wilhelmi Aktiengesetz Kommentar*, vol. 1 (Walter de Gruyter 1967).

Wirth G, Arnold M and Greene M, *Corporate Law in Germany* (CH Beck, 2004).

——— Arnold M, Morshäuser R and Greene M (trs), *Corporate Law in Germany* (2nd edn, CH Beck 2010).

Wrbka S, Van Uytsel S and Siems M, *Collective Actions: Enhancing Access to Justice and Reconciling Multilayer Interests?* (CUP 2012).

Wright M, Siegel DS, Keasey K and Filatotchev I, *The Oxford Handbook of Corporate Governance* (OUP 2013).

Xiaoning L, *A Comparative Study of Shareholders' Derivative Actions* (Kluwer 2007).

Xuereb P, *The Rights of Shareholders* (BSP 1989).

Zouridakis G, 'Contractual Freedom and the Corporate Constitution: A Study on where Greek Law Stands in a Comparative Context and the Way Forward' in David A Frenkel (ed), *Selected Issues in Public Private Law* (Athens Institute for Education and Research 2015).

Zweigert K and Kötz H, *An Introduction to Comparative Law*, tr. T Weir (3rd edn, OUP 1998).

Academic articles

Abugu JA, 'Comparative Analysis of the Extent of Judicial Discretion in Minority Protection Litigation: The United Kingdom and United States' (2007) 18 ICCLR 181.

Ahern D, 'Directors' Duties: Broadening the Focus Beyond Content to Examine the Accountability Spectrum' (2011) 33 DULJ 116.

Albuquerue R and Wang N, 'Agency Conflicts, Investment, and Asset Pricing' (2008) 63 Journal of Finance 1.

Alexandropoulou A, 'The New Proposal for a Directive Regarding the Strengthening of the Shareholder's Position, Board Remuneration and Transparency of the Role of Proxy Advisors and Intermediaries' (2014) 10 DEE 940.

——— '«Squeeze-out» kai nomiká zitímata pou anakýptoun apó tin efarmogí tou' (2008) 4 DEE 404.

Arlen J, 'Symposium: The Legal Implications of Psychology: Human Behavior, Behavioral Economics, and the Law: Comment: The Future of Behavioral Economic Analysis of Law', (1998) 51 Vand L Rev 1765.

Armour J, Lele P, Deakin S and Siems M, 'How Do Legal Rules Evolve? Evidence From a Cross-Country Comparison of Shareholder, Creditor and Worker Protection' (2009) ECGI Law Working Paper 129/2009, http://papers.ssrn.com/sol3/papers.cfm?abstract_id=1431008 (accessed 12 April 2014).

Arnell DuBose V, 'Whose Corporation is It Anyway? Abolishing the Futility Exception in Derivative Litigation' (1991–1992) 12 Miss CL Rev 197.

Arthur WB, 'Competing Technologies, Increasing Returns, and Lock-In by Historical Events' (1989) 99 Economic Journal 116.
Bainbridge SM, 'Independent Directors and the ALI Corporate Governance Project' (1992–1993) 61 Geo Wash L Rev 1034.
Bateman P and Howley S, 'Legislative Comment: Shareholder Rights Directive: New General Meeting Requirements for Traded Companies' (2009) 256 Co LN 1...
Baums T, 'Ersatz von Reflexschäden in der Kapitalgesellschaft' [1987] ZGR 554.
——— 'Personal Liabilities of Company Directors in German Law' (1996) 9 ICCLR 318.
——— and Scott KE, 'Taking Shareholder Protection Seriously? Corporate Governance in the United States and Germany' (2005) 53 Am J Comp L 31.
——— Drinhausen F and Keinath A, 'Anfechtungsklagen und Freigabeverfahren: Eine empirische Studie' [2011] ZIP 2329.
Bayer W and Scholz P, 'Die Pflichten von Aufsichtsrat und Hauptversammlung beim Vergleich über Haftungsansprüche gegen Vorstandsmitglieder' [2015] ZIP 149.
Bebchuk LA, 'The Myth of the Shareholder Franchise' (2007) 93 Va L Rev 675.
Black BS, 'Is Corporate Law Trivial? A Political and Economic Analysis' (1989–1990) 84 Nw UL Rev 542.
Borg-Barthet J, 'Free at Last? Choice of Corporate Law in the EU Following the Judgment in Vale (Case Comment)' [2013] ICLQ 503.
Bottomley S, 'Shareholder Derivative Actions and Public Interest Suits: Two Versions of the Same Story?' (1992) 15 UNSWLJ 127.
Boyle AJ, 'The Minority Shareholder in the Nineteenth Century' (1965) 28 MLR 317.
Braendle UC, 'Shareholder Protection in the USA and Germany: "Law and Finance" Revisited' (2006) 7(3) German Law Journal 257.
——— and Noll J, 'On the Convergence of National Corporate Governance Systems' (2006) 17 Journal of Interdisciplinary Economics 57.
Buxbaum RM, 'Conflict-of-Interests Statutes and the Need for a Demand on Directors in Derivative Actions' (1980) 68 CLR 1122.
Cary J and Rickard J, 'Section 90 of FSMA: Time for Collective Action?' (2012) 23 PLC 23.
Cheffins BR, 'Law as Bedrock: The Foundations of an Economy Dominated by Widely Held Public Companies' (2003) 23 OJLS 1.
——— and Black SB, 'Outside Director Liability Across Countries' (2006) 84 Tex L Rev 1385.
Chen KCW, Chen Z and Wei JKC, "Agency Costs of Free Cash Flow and the Effect of Shareholder Rights on the Implied Cost of Equity Capital" (2011) 46 Journal of Financial and Quantitative Analysis 171.
Chiu IH, 'Contextualising Shareholders' Disputes: A Way to Reconceptualise Minority Shareholder Remedies' [2006] JBL 312.
Christodoulou A, 'Remarks on Articles 103–105 of Law 4548/2018 Regarding the Filing of the Company's Action' (2018) 11 DEE 1267.
Chrysanthis C, 'Comments on Single-Member CFI of Agrinio 177/2009' [2009] EEmpD 563.
Coffee JC Jr, 'The Future as History: The Prospects for Global Convergence in Corporate Governance and its Implications' (1998–1999) 93 Nw U L Rev 641.
——— 'Litigation and Corporate Governance: An Essay on Steering Between Scylla and Charybdis' (1983–1984) 52 Geo Wash L Rev 789.

——— 'Litigation Governance: Taking Accountability Seriously' (2010) 110 Colum L Rev 288.
——— 'The Mandatory/Enabling Balance in Corporate Law: An Essay on the Judicial Role' (1989) 89 Colum L Rev 1618.
——— 'New Myths and Old Realities: The American Law Institute Faces the Derivative Action' (1992–1993) 48 Bus Law 1407.
——— 'Racing towards the Top: The Impact of Cross-Listing and Stock Market Competition on International Corporate Governance' (2002) 102 Colum L Rev 1757.
——— 'Rescuing the Private Attorney General: Why the Model of the Lawyer as Bounty Hunter is Not Working' (1983) 42 Md L Rev 215.
——— 'The Rise of Dispersed Ownership' (2001) 111 Yale LJ 1.
——— 'The Unfaithful Champion: The Plaintiff as Monitor in Shareholder Litigation' (1985) 48 LCP 5.
Cools S, 'The Real Difference in Corporate Law between the United States and Continental Europe: Distribution of Powers'' (2005) 30 Del J Corp L 697.
Cox JD, 'Compensation, Deterrence, and the Market as boundaries for Derivative Suit Procedures' (1984) 52 Geo Wash L Rev 745.
——— 'Litigation and the Deterrence of Corporate Misconduct' (1997) 60 LCP 1.
——— 'Searching for the Corporation's Voice in Derivative Suit Litigation: A Critique of Zapata and the ALI Project' [1982] Duke LJ 959.
Cross ML, Davidson WN and Thornton JH, 'The Impact of Directors and Officers' Liability Suits on Firm Value'' (1989) 56 Journal of Risk and Insurance 128.
Dahan F and Dine J, 'Transplantation for Transition: Discussion on a Concept around Russian Reform of the Law on Reorganisation' (2003) 23 Legal Stud 284.
Dasilas A and Leventis S, 'Corporate Governance, Dividend Status, Ownership Structure, and the Performance of Greek Seasoned Equity Offerings' (2013) 20 International Journal of the Economics of Business 387.
Daskalakis N, Jarvis R and Schizas E, 'Financing Practices and Preferences for Micro and Small Firms'' (2013) 20 Journal of Small Business and Enterprise Development 80.
Davis KB, 'The Forgotten Derivative Suit' (2008) 61 Vand L Rev 378.
Delikostopoulos I, 'Procedural Powers of a Minority Shareholder in AE' (2010) 12 DEE 1282.
——— and Sinaniotis LD, 'Mi peraitéro stírixi ton eidikón ekprosópon anónymis etaireías sto 1/3 tou metochikoú kefalaíou tis' [2000] Diki 990.
Dine J, 'Fiduciary Duties as Default Rules: European Influences and the Need for Caution in the Use of Economic Analysis' (1999) 20 Co Law 190.
Dine J, 'Implications for the United Kingdom of the EC Fifth Directive' (1989) 38 ICLQ 547.
——— and Cheffins BR, 'Shareholder Remedies: Lessons from Canada' (1992) 13 Co Law 89.
Djankov S, La Porta R, Lopez-de-Silanes F and Shleifer A, 'The Law and Economics of Self-Dealing' (2008) 88 Journal of Financial Economics 430.
Djioufas K, '"Acting in Concert" and Calculation of Voting Rights in the Public Offer for Securities' [2005] DEE 918.
Dodd ME Jr, 'For Whom are Corporate Managers Trustees' (1932) 45 Harv L Rev 1145.
Doris F, 'I schési ton árthron 69 AK, 22 v § 3 n.2190/1920 kai 786 § 3 KPolD os rythmíseon gia tin apotropí tou kindýnou exypirétisis symferónton antithéton pros ta symféronta tou ekprosopoúmenou nomikoú prosópou' (2002) B' ChrID 865.

Drylllerakis I, 'Abusive Exercise of the Right to Vote in a GM of a S.A. Regarding the Election of a Member of the B.o.D.' [2008] DEE 435.

Drylllerakis I, 'The Most Significant Recent Amendments of L 2190/1920 (A Brief Overview)' (2007) 30 Epiheirisi 1199.

Du Plessis J, 'Reflections on Some Recent Corporate Governance Reforms in Germany: A Transformation of the German Aktienrecht?' (2003) 8(2) Deakin LR 381.

Easterbrook FH and Fischel DR, 'The Corporate Contract' (1989) 89 Colum L Rev 1416.

Elston J and Rondi L, 'Shareholder Protection and the Cost of Capital: Evidence from German and Italian Firms'(2007) 18(2) Statistica Applicata 153.

Erickson J, 'Corporate Misconduct and the Perfect Storm of Shareholder Litigation' (2008–2009) 84 Notre Dame L Rev 75.

Fama EF, 'Agency Problems and the Theory of the Firm' (1980) 88 Journal of Political Economy 288.

Fang M, 'The Deficiencies of Derivative Actions in China' (2010) 31 Comp Law 150.

Ferris SP, Jandik T, Lawless RM and Makhija A, 'Derivative Lawsuits as a Corporate Governance Mechanism: Empirical Evidence on Board Changes Surrounding Filings' (2007) 42 Journal of Financial and Quantitative Analysis 143.

Fleischer H, 'Act on Corporate Integrity and Modernization of Rescission Law' [Das Gesetz zur Unternehmensintegrität und Modernisierung des Anfechtungsrechts] [2005] NJW 3525.

Garth BG, Nagel IH and Plager SJ, 'Empirical Research and the Shareholder Derivative Suit: Toward a Better-Informed Debate'(1985) 48 LCP 137.

Gelter M, 'Why do Shareholder Derivative Suits Remain Rare in Continental Europe?' (2011–2012) 37 Brook J Int'l L 843.

——— and Helleringer G, 'Lift not the Veil! To Whom are Directors' Duties Really Owed?' [2015] U Ill L Rev 1069.

Gerontidis I, 'I atomikí axíosi apozimíosis tou metóchou apó "synchrónos énanti tis etairías kai ton metóchon" adikopraktikí symperiforá tou DS stin anónymi etairía. Anaskópisi kai sképseis me aformí ti BrAth 12468/2012' [2013] EpiskED 237.

Giannetti M and Simonov A, 'Which Investors Fear Expropriation? Evidence from Investors' Portfolio Choices' (2006) 61 Journal of Finance 1507.

Gibbs D 'Has the Statutory Derivative Claim Fulfilled its Objectives? A Prima Facie Case and the Mandatory Bar: Part 1' (2011) 32(2) Comp Law 41.

Giudici P, 'Representative Litigation in Italian Capital Markets: Italian Derivative Suits and (If Ever) Securities Class Actions' (2009) 6 ECFR 246.

Goo S, 'Multiple Derivative Actions and Common Law Derivative Action Revisited: A Tale of Two Jurisdictions' (2010) 10 JCLS 255.

Grantham BR, 'The Doctrinal Basis of the Rights of Company Shareholders' (1998) 57 CLJUK 554.

Grechenig K and Sekyra M, 'No Derivative Shareholder Suits in Europe: A Model of Percentage Limits, Collusion and Residual Owners' (2007), The Center for Law and Economic Studies Columbia University School of Law, Working Paper No. 312, http://papers.ssrn.com/sol3/papers.cfm?abstract_id=933105 (accessed 29 August 2014).

Grelon B, 'Shareholders' Lawsuits against the Management of a Company and its Shareholders under French Law' [2009] 6 ECFR 205.

Hannigan B, 'Altering the Chapters to Allow for Compulsory Transfer: Dragging Minority Shareholders to a Reluctant Exit' [2007] JBL 471.

——— 'Board Failures in the Financial Crisis: Tinkering with Codes and the Need for Wider Corporate Governance Reforms: Part 2' (2012) 33 Comp Law 35.

——— 'Drawing Boundaries between Derivative Claims and Unfairly Prejudicial Petitions' [2009] JBL 606.

Hansmann H, 'Corporation and Contract' (2006) 8 ALER 1.

——— and Kraakman R, 'The End of History for Corporate Law' (2001) 89 Geo LJ 439.

Hirt CH, 'The Enforcement of Directors' Duties Pursuant to the Aktiengesetz: Present Law and Reform in Germany: Part 1' (2005) 16 ICCLR 179.

——— 'The Enforcement of Directors' Duties Pursuant to the Aktiengesetz: Present Law and Reform in Germany: Part 2' (2005) 16 ICCLR 216.

Hohfeld WN, 'Fundamental Legal Conceptions as Applied in Judicial Reasoning' (1916) 26 Yale LJ 710.

Hopt KJ, 'Die Verantwortlichkeit von Vorstand und Aufsichtsrat: Grundsatz und Praxisprobleme – unter besonderer Berücksichtigung der Banken' [2013] ZIP 1793.

Jensen MC, 'Value Maximization, Stakeholder Theory, and the Corporate Objective Function' (April 2002) 12 Business Ethics Quarterly 235.

——— and Meckling WH, 'Theory of the Firm: Managerial Behavior, Agency Costs and Ownership Structure' (1976) 3 Journal of Financial Economics 305.

Johnston A and Syrpis P, 'Regulatory Competition in European Company Law after Cartesio' (2009) 34 EL Rev 378.

Kahan DM, 'Social Influence, Social Meaning, and Deterrence' (1997) 83 Va L Rev 349.

Kalss S, 'Shareholder Suits: Common Problems, Different Solutions and First Steps towards a Possible Harmonisation by Means of a European Model Code' (2009) 6 ECFR 324.

Kapopoulos P and Lazaretou S, 'Corporate Ownership Structure and Firm Performance: Evidence from Greek Firms' (2007) 15 Corporate Governance: An International Review 144.

Keay A, 'Tackling the Issue of the Corporate Objective: An Analysis of the United Kingdom's Enlightened Shareholder Value Approach' (2007) 29 Syd LR 577.

Kershaw D, 'The Rule in Foss v Harbottle is Dead; Long Live the Rule in Foss v Harbottle' (2015) 3 JBL 274.

Khachaturyan A, 'Trapped in Delusions: Democracy, Fairness and the One-Share-One-Vote Rule in the European Union' (2007) 8 EBOR 335.

Knowles MF and Flannery C, 'The ALI Principles of Corporate Governance Compared with Georgia Law' (1996–1997) 47 Mercer L Rev 4.

Koch J, 'Das Gesetz zur Unternehmensintegrität und Modernisierung des Anfechtungsrechts (UMAG)' (2006) ZGR 769.

Kokkinis L 'Comments on Patrai Court of Appeal 226/1997: Maladministration, Conflict of Interests and Pursuit of the Corporate Action in the SA' (1997) 6 DEE 592.

——— 'I apokatástasi tis émmesis zimías ton metóchon ferengyos AE' (1997) 3 DEE 256.

——— 'I zimía ton metóchon kai i apokatástasí tis. Sképseis me aformí tis AP Ol 14/1999 kai AP 795/2000' (2002) 6 DEE 574.

Korobkin R, 'The Status Quo Bias and Contract Default Rules' (1998) 83 Cornell L Rev 608.

Kousoulis SN, 'Ta apotelésmata apófasis epí syllogikís agogís. Idíos epí chríseos katachristikón GOS, en ópsei tis AP 1219/2001' (2002) 11 DEE 1097.

Lanoo K and Khachaturyan A, 'Reform of Corporate Governance in the EU' (2004) 5 EBOR 37.

LaPorta R, Lopez-De-Silanes F and Shleifer A, 'Corporate Ownership Around the World' (1999) 54 Journal of Finance 471.

LaPorta R, Lopez-De-Silanes F and Shleifer A, 'The Economic Consequences of Legal Origin' (2008) 46 Journal of Economic Literature 285.

LaPorta R, Lopez-De-Silanes F, Shleifer A and Vishny WR, 'Investor Protection and Corporate Governance' (2000) 58 Journal of Financial Economics 3.

LaPorta R, Lopez-De-Silanes F, Shleifer A and Vishny WR, 'Law and Finance' (1998) 106 Journal of Political Economy 1113.

Laster T, 'Goodbye to the Contemporaneous Ownership Requirement', (2008) 33 Del J Corp L 673.

Latella D, 'Shareholder Derivative Suits: A Comparative Analysis and the Implications of the European Shareholders' Rights Directive' (2009) 6 ECFR 307.

Lele PP and Siems MM, 'Shareholder Protection: A Leximetric Approach' (2007) 7 JCLS 17.

Lutter M, Theorie der Mitgliedschaft: Prolegomena zu einem Allgemeinen Teil des Korporationsrechts' (April 1980) 180 AcP 84.

McCahery JA, Vermeulen EPM, Hisatake M and Saito J, 'Traditional and Innovative Approaches to Legal Reform: The "New Company Law"' (2007) 8 EBOR 7.

Macey JR and Miller GP, 'The Plaintiffs' Attorney's Role in Class Action and Derivative Litigation: Economic Analysis and Recommendations for Reform (1991)58 U Chi LR 1.

Markou I, 'I sýnklisi tis genikís syneléfseos tis AE apó ti meiopsifía' [1978] EEN 774.

Mascarenhas T, 'Case Comment Multiple Derivative Actions under English Law' (2013) 24 ICCLR 336.

Masouros P, 'Is the EU Taking Shareholder Rights Seriously? An Essay on the Impotence of Shareholdership in Corporate Europe' (2010) 7 ECL 195.

Michalopoulos GN, 'Genikés Grammés tou néou Dikaíou tis anónymis etaireías' (2008) 1 PeirN 12.

Milman D, 'Ascertaining Shareholder Wishes in UK Company Law in the 21st Century' (2010) 280 Co LN 1.

——— 'Shareholder Ltigation in the UK: The Implications of Recent Authorities and Other Developments' (2013) 342 Co LN 1.

Naruisch T and Liepe F, 'Latest Developments in the German Law on Public Companies by the Act on Corporate Integrity and Modernisation of the Right of Resolution-Annulment (UMAG): Shareholder Activism and Directors' Liability Reloaded' [2007] JBL 225.

Nili Y, 'Missing the Forest for the Trees: A New Approach to Shareholder Activism' (2014) 4 Harv Bus L Rev 157.

Nolan RC, 'The Continuing Evolution of Shareholder Governance' (2006) 65 CLJ 92.

——— 'Shareholder Rights in Britain' (2006) 7 EBOR 549.

Nyombi C, Mortimer T, Lewis R and Zouridakis G, 'Shareholder Primacy and Stakeholders' Interests in the Aftermath of a Takeover: A Review of Empirical Evidence' (2015) 2 IBLJ 161.

Pampoukis KG, 'Liability of Corporate Directors for Shareholders' Reflective Loss' (1995) A' EpiskED 333.

Panagiotou KP, 'Actio pro socio and the principle of fiduciary duty as a means to limit the latter in company law' (2013) 2 EEmpD 291.

Papadimopoulos I 'Ta dikaiómata tou squeeze-out kai tou sell-out ypó to fos tis Odigías 2004/25/EK schetiká me tis dimósies prosforés exagorás' [2005] DEE 396.

Paredes T, 'A Systems Approach to Corporate Governance Reform: Why Importing U.S. Corporate Law Isn't the Answer' (2003–2004) 45 Wm & Mary L Rev 1055.

Paschos N and Neumann K-U, 'Die Neuregelungen des UMAG im Bereich der Durchsetzung von Haftungsansprüchen der Aktiengesellschaft gegen Organmitglieder' (2005) 33 DB 1779.

Paul C, 'Derivative Actions under English and German Corporate Law: Shareholder Participation between the Tension Filled Areas of Corporate Governance and Malicious Shareholder Interference' (2010) 115 ECFR 81.

Perakis E, 'Danger to Frustrate the Minority's Right to Call for a GM (Art. 39 par. 1 CL 2190/1920)?' (2010) 11 DEE 1133.

Platsas AE, 'The Functional and the Dysfunctional in the Comparative Method of Law: Some Critical Remarks' (December 2008) 12(3) *Electronic Journal of Comparative Law*, www.ejcl.org/123/art123-3.pdf (accessed 12 September 2014).

Potter J and Thompson J, 'Government Responses to the Impact of the Global Crisis on Finance for Young and Small Enterprises' (2011) 20 Strat Change 145.

Puchniak DW and Nakahigashi M, 'Japan's Love for Derivative Actions: Irrational Behavior and Non-Economic Motives as Rational Explanations for Shareholder Litigation' (2012) 45 Vand J Transnat'l L 1.

Quinn J, 'The Companies Act 2014 and the Absence of the Derivative Action' (2016) 23 CL Pract 102.

Rapti M, 'Amendments of the Greek law on Societes Anonymes for the Implementation of Directive 2007/36 on the Exercise of Certain Rights of Shareholders in Listed Companies' (2012) 23 ICCLR 24.

Reisberg A, 'Shadows of the Past and Back to the Future: Part 11 of the UK Companies Act 2006 (In)action' (2009) 6 ECFR 219.

——— 'Theoretical Reflections on Derivative Actions in English Law: The Representative Problem' (2006) 3 ECFR 69.

——— and Prentice DD, 'Multiple Derivative Actions' (2009) 125 LQR 209.

Ringe W, 'Changing Law and Ownership Patterns in Germany: Corporate Governance and the Erosion of Deutschland AG' (2015) 63 Am J Comp L 493.

——— 'Independent Directors: After the Crisis''' (2013) 14 EBOR 401.

Roe MJ, 'Corporate Law's Limits' (2002) 31 J Legal Stud 233.

Rokas NK, 'CComments on Athens Multi-Member Court of First Instance 4831/1992' [1993] EEmpD 596.

——— 'Comments (on Cases 7476/1980 & 1285/1980)' (1981) LB EEmpD 402.

——— 'Corporate Organisation and Shareholders' Individual Action' (2007) NH' EEmpD 1.

Romano R, 'The Shareholder Suit: Litigation without Foundation' (1991) 7 JL Econ & Org 61.

Saenger I, 'The Best Interests of the Corporation, Procedural Questions of Enforcing Individual and Corporate Rights and Legal Actions against Board Members'' (2015) 26 EBLR 13.

Saez MI and Riano D, 'Corporate Governance and the Shareholders' Meeting: Voting and Litigation' (2013) 14 EBOR 343.

Schmid RH and Spindler G, 'Path Dependence, Corporate Governance and Complementarity' (2002) 5 International Finance 311.

Schmidt J, 'Reforms in German Stock Corporation Law: The 67th German Jurists Forum' (2008) 9 EBOR 637.

Schmidt K, 'Verfolgungspflichten, Verfolgungsrechte und Aktionärsklagen: Ist die Quadratur des Zirkels näher gerückt?Gedanken zur Reform der §§ 147–149 AktG vor dem Hintergrund der Juristentagsdiskussion des Jahres 2000' (2005) NZG 796.

Schmolke KU, 'The Shareholder Derivative Action according to § 148 of the German Stock Corporation Act: Incentives of Current Law and Proposals for Reform' ('Die Aktionärsklage nach § 148 AktG – Anreizwirkungen de lege lata und Reformanregungen de lege ferenda') [2011] ZGR, http://ssrn.com/abstract=1716929 (accessed 15 May 2015).

Schneider U, 'Der mühsame Weg der Durchsetzung der Organhaftung durch den besonderen Vertreter nach § 147 AktG' [2013] ZIP 1985.

Scott EK, 'Corporation Law and the American Law Institute Corporate Governance Project', (1983) 35 Stan L Rev 927.

Seibt CH, 'Die Reform des Verfolgungsrechts nach § 147 AktG und des Rechts der Sonderprüfung' [2004] WM 2137.

Shleifer A and Vishny RW, 'A Survey of Corporate Governance' (1997) 52 Journal of Finance 737.

Siems MM, 'Shareholder Protection around the World (Leximetric II)' (2008) 33 Del J Corp L 111.

——— 'What does not Work in Comparing Securities Laws: A Critique on La Porta et al's Methodology' (2005) 16 ICCLR 300.

Sinanioti-Maroudi A, 'Oi vasikés paremváseis tou nómou 3604/2007 ston n. 2190/1920' (2008) 1 PeirN 5.

Skouras TK, 'AAppointment and Replacement of Special Representatives in the Societe Anonyme' [1983] EEmpD 553.

Sotiropoulos G, 'Comments on Supreme Court 1298/2006' (2006) NZ' EEmpD 601.

——— 'Sýnkrousi symferónton metaxý ton melón tou DS kai tou nomikoú prosópou tis anónymis etairías. Schési tou árthrou 69 AK kai tou árthrou 22b N.2190/1920. Antikatastástasi ton eidikón ekprosópon tis par. 3 tou árthrou 22b N.2190/1920' (1997) 12 DEE 1145.

Spamann H, 'The "Antidirector Rights Index" Revisited' (2009) 23 Review of Financial Studies 467.

Spanos LJ, 'Corporate Governance in Greece: Developments and Policy Implications" (2005) 5 Corporate Governance: The International Journal of Business in Society 15.

Spiekermann A, 'LG München: Zur Frage der Angemessenheit der Vorstandsvergütung Beschluss vom 29. 03.2007-5HK O 12931/06 | AktG § 148 | AktG § 87' [2008] CCZ 157.

Sullivan G R, 'Restating the Scope of the Derivative Action' (1985) 44 CLJ 236.

Tang J, 'Shareholder remedies: demise of the derivative claim?' [2012] UCL JL & J 178.

Tarnanidou CI, 'Reform of the Law on Listed Companies Following the Amendment of CL 2190/1920 by virtue of L 3884/2010' (2010) 2 ChriDik 154.

Thompson RB and Thomas RS, 'The New Look of Shareholder Litigation: Acquisition-Oriented Class Actions' (2004) 57 Vand L Rev 133.

Triantafillakis G 'Business Failure and the Response to It: The Role of the Duty of Loyalty' [2014] DEE 204.

Ulmer P, 'Die Aktionärsklage als Instrument zur Kontrolle des Vorstands- und Aufsichtsratshandelns' (1999) 163 ZHR 290.

VVan Aaken A, 'Shareholder Suits as a Technique of Internalization and Control of Management: A Functional and Comparative Analysis' (April 2004) 68 RabelsZ 288.

Van der Elst C, 'Law and Economics of Shareholder Rights and Ownership Structures: How Trivial are Shareholder Rights for Shareholders?', Tilburg Law and Economics Center (TILEC) Law and Economics Discussion Paper No. 2010-009 and Tilburg Law School Legal Studies Research Paper No. 008/2010 15 February (2010).

Varela M, 'Comments on Supreme Court 1121/2006' [2007] DEE 583.

——— 'I kálypsi tis améleias sti genikí asfálisi tis astikís efthýnis' [2008] DEE 412.

Wedderburn KW, 'Shareholders' Rights and the Rule in Foss v Harbottle' (1957) CLJ 194.

West MD, 'Why Shareholders Sue: The Evidence from Japan' (2001) 30 JLS 351.

Williamson O, 'Corporate Governance' (1983–1984) 93 Yale LJ 1197.

Wooldridge F, 'Voting Rights in German Public Companies' (2013) 34 Comp Law 51.

Worthington S, 'Shares and Shareholders: Property, Power and Entitlement: Part 1' (2001) 22 Comp Law 258.

Zetzsche AD, 'Shareholder Passivity, Cross-Border Voting and the Shareholder Rights Directive', (2008) 8 JCLS 289.

Zouridakis G, 'Introducing Derivative Actions in the Greek Law on Public Limited Companies: Issues of Legal Standing and Lessons from the German and UK Experience' (2015) 26 ICCLR 271.

——— 'Tortious Liability of Parent Companies: Some Thoughts in Light of the Recent English Case Law and a Comparative Law Overview' [2015] DEE 990.

Articles in the press

Kollia E, 'Areios Págos gia metochés- foúskes: Oi dikastés den ángixan tin ypóthesi «Chastoúki» to skeptikó tis aítisis anaíresis apó to anótato dikastírio' [15 March 2014] To Vima, www.tovima.gr/society/article/?aid=577096 (accessed 1 October 2015).

Mandrou I, 'Se díki 35 átoma gia ta dáneia ekatommyríon evró tou T.T' [30 September 2015] Kathimerini, www.kathimerini.gr/832828/article/epikairothta/ellada/se-dikh-35-atoma-gia-ta-daneia-ekatommyriwn-eyrw-toy-tt (accessed 1 October 2015).

Milne R, 'Hermes Bid to Oust Next Infineon Chairman' [18 January 2010] Financial Times, www.ft.com/cms/s/2/e085c90a-045e-11df-8603-00144feabdc0.html#axzz3cijYNIhf (accessed 11 June 2015).

'Recapitalising Greek Banks: The Damage' [7 November 2015] The Economist, 79.

'Why Volkswagen's Share Price has Fallen so Far' [21 September 2015] The Economist, www.economist.com/news/business-and-finance/21665452-18-billion-fine-not-car makers-only-worry-why-volkswagens-share-price-has-fallen-so (accessed 25 September 2015).

Other secondary sources

'70. Deutscher Juristentag Hannover 2014: Beschlüsse, Abteilung Wirtschaftsrecht' [70th German Jurists Forum Hannover 2014: Resolutions, Business Law Section], www.djt.de/fileadmin/downloads/70/140919_djt_70_beschluesse_web_rz.pdf (accessed 20 August 2015).

Alexandridou E and Karypidou M, 'Evaluation of the Effectiveness and Efficiency of Collective Redress Mechanisms in the European Union: Country Report Greece', http://ec.europa.eu/consumers/archive/redress_cons/finalreportevaluationstudy part1-final2008-11-26.pdf (accessed 2 November 2014).

Bartkus G, Belicka D, Civilka M, Conac P-H, Teichmann C, Lambooy T and Hannigan B, 'Study on Minority Shareholders Protection', https://publications.europa.eu/en/publication-detail/-/publication/1893f7b8-93a4-11e8-8bc1-01aa75ed71a1/language-en (accessed 1 March 2019).

Commission, 'Proposal for a Directive amending Directive 2007/36 on the Encouragement of Long-Term Shareholder Engagement and Directive 2013/34 on Certain Elements of the Corporate Governance Statement' COM(2014) 213 final.

Company Law Reform White Paper (Cm6456), DTI, London, March 2005.

Deutscher Bundestag: Drucksachen und Protokolle [BT] 16/181, 7 October 2008.

European Central Bank 'Survey on the Access to Finance of Small and Medium-Sized Enterprises in the Euro Area' (ECB 2013). www.ecb.europa.eu/pub/pdf/other/accesstofinancesmallmediumsizedenterprises201304en.pdf?bb16b7e4d7d49e53249f2be976653b18 (accessed 20 November 2014).

European Commission, 'Action Plan: European Company Law and Corporate Governance: A Modern Legal Framework for More Engaged Shareholders and Sustainable Companies', Brussels, 12 December 2012, COM(2012) 740/2.

Gerner-Beuerle C, Paech P and Schuster E, 'Study on Directors' Duties and Liability', http://ec.europa.eu/internal_market/company/docs/board/2013-study-analysis_en.pdf (accessed 1 May 2015).

Green Paper 'Corporate Governance in Financial Institutions and Remuneration Policies', COM (2010) 284 final.

Hansard, HL 9 May 2006, vvol. 681, col. 883.'The Kay Review of UK Equity Markets and Long-Term Decision Making' (2012), http://lawcommission.justice.gov.uk/docs/kay-review-of-equity-markets-final-report.pdf (accessed 30 August 2015).

Law Commission, 'Shareholder Remedies' (Law Commission No 246, 1997).

—— 'Shareholder Remedies: A Consultation Paper' (Law Commission Consultation Paper No 142, 1996).

Noack U, 'Aktionärsforum im Bundesanzeiger: ein Flop' (Handelsblatt Rechtsboard 18 March 2013), https://blog.handelsblatt.com/rechtsboard/2013/03/18/aktionarsforum-im-bundesanzeiger-ein-flop (accessed 20 June 2019).

Websites and other online sources

Bank of Greece, www.bankofgreece.gr/Pages/en/Statistics/externalsector/balance/transactions.aspx#portfolio (accessed 15 October 2014).

ECB statistics, www.ecb.int/stats/money/surveys/sme/html/index.en.html (accessed 5 October 2015).

Eurobank Ergasias SA, Articles of Association, www.eurobank.gr/Uploads/pdf/katastatiko_en_12.04.2014.%20eng.pdf (accessed 1 May 2015).

Greek Business Portal, www.businessportal.gr/search_1.php (accessed 21 November 2015).

Hellenic Exchanges, www.helex.gr/el/web/guest/companies-map (accessed 17 April 2015).

Hellenic Petroleum, Articles of Association, www.helpe.gr/userfiles/8a53b155-76e9-4d45-9773-a27000e44a36/katastatiko.pdf (accessed 1 May 2015).

METKA, Articles of Association, www.metka.com/Uploads/parousiaseis-entypa/entypa/COMPANY_STATUTE_eng.pdf (accessed 1 May 2015).

Motor Oil Hellas, AArticles of Association, www.moh.gr/media/PDF_inside_texts/Etairiky_diakivernisy/Company%20Memorandum%20(Gr).pdf (accessed 1 May 2015).

National Bank of Greece, Articles of Association, www.nbg.gr/greek/the-group/corporate-governance/regulations-principles/Documents/GR_ARTICLES%20OF%20ASSOCIATION_22.07.2014.pdf (accessed 1 May 2015).

OECD, Doing Business, http://doingbusiness.org/methodology (accessed 21 November 2015).

OLP, Articles of Association, www.olp.gr/en/the-port-of-piraeus/organization-statute (accessed 1 May 2015).

OPAP, Articles of Association, www.opap.gr/documents/11503/3551006/%CE%9A%CE%91%CE%A4%CE%91%CE%A3%CE%A4%CE%91%CE%A4%CE%99%CE%9A%CE%9F%20%CE%A4%CE%97%CE%A3%20%CE%95%CE%A4%CE%91%CE%99%CE%A1%CE%95%CE%99%CE%91%CE%A3.pdf (accessed 1 May 2015).

OTE SA, Articles of Association, www.ote.gr/documents/10280/42094851/AOI_EGM_30_12_2013_eng_v2.pdf/445013f9-36fc-423f-9937-fb8245149246 (accessed 1 May 2015).

Piraeus Bank, Articles of Association, www.piraeusbankgroup.com/en/investors/corporate-governance/board (accessed 1 May 2015).

SOAS, University of London, www.soas.ac.uk/courseunits/C338.html (accessed 21 October 2015).

Terna Energy SA, Articles of Association, www.terna-energy.com/userfiles/5a12449c-be9f-43ce-9e75-ba74180074b6/TENERG_ARTICLES_OF_ASSOCIATION_13-05-2014_EN.pdf (accessed 1 May 2015).

World Bank, http://data.worldbank.org/indicator/NY.GDP.MKTP.KD?order=wbapi_data_value_2004+wbapi_data_value+wbapi_data_value-last&sort=asc&page=2 (accessed 21 November 2015).

World Bank, World Development Indicators, www.worldbank.org/data (accessed 21 November 2015).

World Justice Project, http://data.worldjusticeproject.org (accessed 1 November 2015).

Table of cases

ECHR

Marckx v Belgium (1979–80) 2 EHRR 330 22
Company S. and T. v. Sweden, no. 11189/84, Commission Decision of 11 December 1986, DR 50 22
Agrotexim and Others v. Greece (A/330) (1996) 21 EHRR 250 27, 31

English

Abouraya v Sigmund [2014] EWHC 277 (Ch) 89, 180, 182
Airey v Cordell [2007] BCC 785 103
Alexander Ward & Co Ltd v Samyang Navigation Co Ltd [1975] 1 WLR 673 30
Atwool v. Merryweather (1867) LR 5 Eq 464n 4
Bamford v Harvey [2012] EWHC 2858 (Ch) [2013] BCC 311 94, 246
Barrett v Duckett [1995] BCC 362 95, 106
Bhullar v Bhullar [2015] EWHC 1943 (Ch) 104, 250
Birch v Sullivan [1958] All ER 56, [1957] 1 WLR. 1247 111
Bird Precision Bellows Ltd, Re [1986] Ch. 658 135
Blue Arrow Plc, Re (1987) 3 BCC 618 134
Brannigan v Style [2016] EWHC 512 (Ch) 251
Bridge v Daley [2015] EWHC 2121 (Ch) 101, 204, 249
Carlen v Drury (1812) 1 Vesey & Beames 154 188
Clark v Cutland and Others [2003] EWCA Civ 810, [2004] 1 WLR 783 140
Colonial Bank v Whinney [1886] App Cas 426 25
Daniels v Daniels [1978] Ch 406 93
Ebrahimi v Westbourne Galleries Ltd [1973] AC 360 135
Edwards v Halliwell [1950] 2 All ER 1064 100, 142
Eley v Positive Government Security Life Association Co. Ltd (1876) 1 Ex D 88 131
Elgindata Ltd. Re (No. 2) [1992] 1 WLR 1207 139
Foss v Harbottle (1843) 67 ER 189, (1843) 2 Hare 461 4, 11, 18, 74, 80, 93, 94, 103, 104, 180, 186, 216

Franbar v Patel [2008] EWHC 1534 (Ch), [2008] BCC 885 101, 114, 193, 204, 240
Goodwin v Cook [2018] 6 WLUK 425 90, 104, 194, 253
Harben v. Phillips (1883) 23 Ch D 14 126
Hickman v Kent or Romney Marsh Sheep-Breeders Association [1915] 1 Ch 881 131
Hook v Sumner [2015] EWHC 3820 (Ch) 250
Hughes v Weiss [2012] EWCH 2363 (Ch) 95, 107, 245
Iesini v Westrip Holdings Ltd [2009] EWHC 2526 (Ch), [2010] BCC 420 96, 107, 193, 241
John Shaw & Sons (Salford) Ltd v Shaw [1935] 2 KB 113 30
Johnson v Gore, Wood & Co [2000] UKHL 65, [2002] 2 AC 27, 28
Kiani v Cooper [2010] EWHC 577 (Ch), [2010] BCC 463 59, 96, 240
Kleanthous v Paphitis [2011] EWHC 2287 (Ch), [2012] BCC 676 86, 95, 104, 244
Konamaneni v Rolls Royce Industrial Power (India) Ltd [2003] BCC 790, [2002] 1 WLR 1269 95, 107, 248
Mission Capital Plc v Sinclair [2008] BCC 866 (Ch) 874 76, 96, 239
Mumbray v Lapper [2005] EWHC 1152 (Ch) 95
Northwest Transportation v Beatty [1887] LR 12 App Cas 589 100
Nurcombe v Nurcombe (1984) 1 BCC 99, 269, [1985] 1 WLR 370 107
O'Neill v Phillips ***[1999] 1 WLR 1092*** 134, 135, 136
Pavlides v Jensen[1956] Ch 565 93
Parry v Bartlett [2011] EWHC 3146 (Ch), [2012] BCC 700 94, 101, 245
Prudential Assurance Co Ltd v Newman Industries Ltd (No2) [1982] Ch 204 28, 72, 100
Quin & Axtens Ltd v Salmon [1909] AC 442 131
R. v. Phillipou [1989] Crim LR 559 24
Regal (Hastings) Ltd v Gulliver [1967] 2 AC 134 100
Salomon v Salomon & Co Ltd [1896] AC 22 23, 89
Saul D Harrison & Sons Plc, Re [1995] BCLC 14 134, 136
SDI Retail Services Ltd v King [2017] EWHC 737 (Ch) 251
Seven Holdings, Re [2011] EWHC 1893 (Ch) 94, 104, 243
Shah v Shah [2011] EWHC 1902 (Ch) 135
Shandong Offshore Investment (HK) Co Ltd v Andresen [2018] EWHC 2874 (Ch) 112, 253
Sunrise Radio Ltd, Re [2009] EWHC 2893 (Ch), [2010] 1 BCLC 367 135
Singh v Singh [2014] EWCA Civ 103 101
Smith v. Croft (No. 2) [1988] Ch 114, [1987] 3 WLR 405, [1987] 3 All ER 909, [1987] BCLC 206 101
Smith v Croft (No 3) (1987) 3 BCC 218 101
Stainer v Lee [2010] EWHC 1539 (Ch) 86, 96, 204, 242

Stimpson v Southern Landlords Association [2009] EWHC 2072 (Ch), [2010] BCC 387 75, 107, 241
Taylor v National Union of Mineworkers (Derbyshire Area) [1985] BCLC 237 100
Universal Project Management Services Ltd v Fort Gilkicker Ltd and Others [2013] EWHC 348 (Ch), [2013] Ch. 551 88, 179, 247
Wallersteiner v Moir (No2) [1975] QB 373 80, 95, 206
Wilton UK Ltd v Shuttleworth and Others (No 2) [2018] EWHC 911 (Ch) 75, 102, 252
Wood v. Odessa Waterworks [1889] 42 Ch D 636 126
Zavahir v Shankleman [2016] EWHC 2772 (Ch) 194, 251

German

AG Nürtingen AG 1995 287, ZIP 1994 785 87
BVerfG 20.09.1999, ZIP 1999 1798, NJW 2000 349 (*Walter/Daimler-Benz*) 22
BVerfG 23.08.2000, NJW 2001 279, ZIP 2000 1670 (*Moto Meter*) 22, 24
BVerfG 12.12.2006 1, BvR 2576/04, NJW 2007 979 207
BVerfG, BVerfGE 13 331 23
BverfG, BverfGE 14 263, 276 (*Feldmühle*) 24
BverfG, BverfGE 100, 289, 301 (*DAT/Altana*) 24
BGH, BGHZ 20, 4, NJW 1956 785 23
BGH, BGHZ 83, 122, NJW 1982 1703 (*Holzmüller*) 158
BGH, BGHZ 90, 92 24
BGH 10.11.1986, ZIP 1987 29, WM 1987 13, 16 28
BGH 11.07.1988, ZIP 1988 1112 28
BGH, BGHZ 103, 184, 194 (*Linotype*) 136
BGH, BGHZ 94, 55 28
BGH, BGHZ 105, 121 28
BGH, BGHZ 129, 136, ZIP 1995, 819 (*Girmes*) 28, 137
BGH, BGHZ 142, 167, 170 (*Hilgers AG*) 136
BGH 29.1.2001, NJW 2001 1428, AG 2001 263 (*Aqua-Butzke*) 80
BGH, BGHZ 146, 179, NJW 2001 1425 (*MEZ*) 80
BGH, BGHZ 135, 244 (*ARAG/Garmenbeck*) 98, 104, 189, 190
BGH 27.9.2011, ZIP 2011, 2195 (*HVB/Unicredit*) 191
FG Hamburg Urt. v. 11.09.2009, Az. – 3 K 124/08, DStRE 2010 594 5
LG München I Beschluss v. 29. 3. 2007 – 5 HK O 12931/06, AG 2007 458 96
LG München I Beschluss v. 6.9.2007 – 5 HK O 12570/07, ZIP 2007 1809 191
OLG Hamburg, Beschluss v. 19.1.2007 – 11 Wx 33/06, AG 2007 331 5

OLG Köln Beschl. v. 22.02.2010, Az. – 18 W 1/10 114
OLG München Beschl. v. 11.5.2010 – 31 Wx 14/10, NZG 2010 7884, ZIP 201, 1032 85
OLG München, Beschl. v. 21.10.2010 – 7 W 2040/10, ZIP 2010 2202 201
OLG München, Urt. v. 28.11.2007 – 7 U 4498/07, ZIP 2008 73 191

Greek

Agrinio Single-Member Court 177/2009, EEmpD NI' 2009 560 155
Athens Multi-Member Court of First Instance 6881/2005, DEE 2006 625 108, 130
Athens Single-Member Court of First Instance 4421/1970, EEmpD 1971 42 119
Athens Single-member Court of First Instance 5079/2002, EEmpD 2002 572 130
Athens Single-Member Court of First Instance 12468/2012, EEmpD 2012 275 138, 139
Athens Single-Member Court of First Instance 9669/2014, DEE 2014 1055 27, 31, 40, 138, 139
Athens Court of Appeal 3469/1991, EEmpD 1993 424 27
Athens Court of Appeal 924/1998, Dikaiosyni 1999 407 24, 31
Athens Court of Appeal 252/2007, EpiskEmpd 2007 558; 27, 239
Athens Court of Appeal 3494/2007 DEE 2007 1193 82, 130
Athens Court of Appeal 5864/2011, DEE 2012 468 27, 31
Athens Court of Appeal 4960/2012, DEE 2013 248 138
Athens Court of Appeal 6900/2013, DEE 2014 136 138
Athens Court of Appeal 877/2014, DEE 2014 505 31, 138
Council of State 1861/1993, DForN 1994 41 128
Larissa Court of Appeal 24/2014, DEE 2014 965 247
Patrai Court of Appeal 266/2011, NOMOS Databank, Armenopoulos 2013 293 167, 198, 202, 243
Patrai Court of Appeal 226/1997, DEE 1997 591 77
Peiraeus Court of Appeal 277/2005 DEE 2005 685 18
Peiraeus Single-Member Court of First Instance 5826/2006, DEE 2007 452 44
Peiraeus Single-Member Court of First Instance 3884/2011, EEmpD 2012 684 31
Rodopi Multi-Member Court of First Instance 29/1995, EEmpD 1997 722 126
Supreme Court 1285/1980 EEmpD LB' 394 23, 27, 31
Supreme Court 1405/1998, DEE 1998 972 31
Supreme Court 795/2000, NoV 2001 1307 22, 23, 32
Supreme Court 1219/2001, DEE 2001 1128 131
Supreme Court 1888/2005, DEE 2006 392 27

Supreme Court 1121/2006, DEE 2007 583 136
Supreme Court 1844/2009, EllDni 2012 687 108, 241
Supreme Court 350/2011, ChrID 2011 691 130
Supreme Court 1256/2011, DEE 2012 29 199, 244, 247
Supreme Court 1280/2012, EEmpD 2013 616 201
Supreme Court 432/2016, DEE 2017 354 137
Supreme Court 189/2018, NOMOS database 253
Supreme Court Plenary Session 14/1999, DEE 1999 1017 22, 23, 32
Supreme Court Plenary Session 2/2013, DEE 2013 321 23
Supreme Court Plenary Session 5/2015, ChrID 2015 610 130, 248
Thessaloniki Court of Appeal 2500/1994, Armenopoulos 1995 1424 27, 31
Thessaloniki Court of Appeal 2399/2005, EpiskEmpD 2006 486 31
Thessaloniki Single-Member Court of First Instance 15126/2001, NOMOS database 196

Other jurisdictions

Cohen v. Beneficial Industrial Corp 337 US 541 (1949) 4
Waddington Ltd v Chan Chun Hoo Thomas [2009] 2 BCLC 82 27, 89
Wishart v Castlecroft Ltd & Ors [2009] CSIH 65 93, 94, 193
Gaillard v Natomas Company 173 Cal. App. 3d 410, 219 Cal. Rptr. 74 (1985) 170
Theodoros Pirillis and Another v. Eleftherios Kouis Civil Appeal No. 11387 (2004) 1A SCJ 136 18

Annex

Table A1 List of Published Cases on Derivative Claims and Corporate Actions under British and Greek Law

*Greek decisions (under Law 2190/1920 art 22b)**			*British decisions (under common law and CA 2006 Pt 11 ss 260–264)*		
Case/Year	***Instance***	***Decision***	***Case/Year***	***Instance***	***Decision***
252/2007 Athens Court of Appeal	Second Instance – Court of First Instance dismissed a direct action for damages	Appeal dismissed. The company itself is the proper plaintiff; the claimant in First Instance and appellant cannot claim restitution of reflective loss. Only means of redress is the corporate action under art 22b Law 2190/1920	***Mission Capital Plc v Sinclair*** [2008] EWHC 1339 (Ch) 17 March 2008	The parties agreed to combine the two stages. Application to costs indemnity for the derivative action.	Applications **dismissed**. Even though the claim satisfied the test laid by the mandatory requirements in CA 2006 s 263(2), **the discretionary factors weighed against it**: the claim was judged to be one to which little importance would be attached by the notional director; the availability of an alternative remedy (under CA 2006 s 994) was considered as a factor as well. Therefore, the issue as to indemnity did not arise.

(*Continued*)

Table A1 (Cont.)

*Greek decisions (under Law 2190/1920 art 22b)**			*British decisions (under common law and CA 2006 Pt 11 ss 260–264)*		
Case/Year	***Instance***	***Decision***	***Case/Year***	***Instance***	***Decision***
			Fanmailuk.com Ltd v Cooper [2008] EWHC 2198 (Ch) 11 June 2008	Application for permission to continue a derivative claim. First stage bypassed. No indemnity sought.	Adjourned. Preliminary issue to be decided first.
			Franbar v Patel [2008] EWHC 1534 (Ch) 2 July 2008	**Telescoping of the two-stage procedure**. Application for permission to continue a derivative claim, brought by a company holding 25% of the shares in the (nominally) defendant company (other applications not under CA 2006 Pt 11, discussed jointly). Claimant did not wish to be indemnified for costs at the time of the hearing.	**Permission refused**. In exercising its discretion and balancing the facts, the court decided that the claim was one to which little importance would be attached by the notional director; the availability of an alternative remedy (such as unfair prejudice remedy under CA 2006 s 994) was considered as a factor as well

1844/2009 Supreme Court 15 July 2009	Appeal against dec. No 44-2008 Athens Court of Appeal Petition under Law 2190/1920 art 22b. Dismissed on grounds of being premature at first instance, as it was filed before the six-months deadline. Petitioners were holders of 50% of the company's share capital	Appeal dismissed **The six-month deadline should have passed by the date of the court hearing** and therefore the petition is not to be dismissed as premature if it is filed before the aforementioned deadline.	***Iesini v Westrip Ltd* [2009] EWHC 2526 (Ch)** 16 October 2009	This was the second stage of proceedings; Norris J accepted that a prima facie case was established in the first stage.	Permission **refused**. The court held that, **the claim for breach of duty would not be pursued by any director** [263(2)(a)] **and, even if not so, little importance would be attached to continuing it** [263(3)(b)]. Furthermore, the combination of the costs liability of the company with the availability of an alternative and appropriate remedy would not allow the derivative claim to proceed (in relation to the rescission claim).
			***Stimpson v Southern Private Landlords' Association* [2009] EWHC 2072 (Ch)** 21 May 2009	Application for permission to continue a derivative claim in a company limited by guarantee. Ex parte stage bypassed (on	Permission refused. A hypothetical director would not pursue the claim (mandatory bar). The latter was weak and of

(*Continued*)

Table A1 (Cont.)

*Greek decisions (under Law 2190/1920 art 22b)**			*British decisions (under common law and CA 2006 Pt 11 ss 260–264)*		
Case/Year	***Instance***	***Decision***	***Case/Year***	***Instance***	***Decision***
				the initiative of the court).	little value, at least compared to the probable costs of litigation. Other factors such as the views of the members and the claimant's good faith considered.
379/2010 Ileia Single-Member Court of First Instance	First instance. Petition to appoint special representatives under Law 2190/1920 art 22b	Petition dismissed. **At the time the petition was filed the company lacked members of the board of directors**	***Kiani v Cooper*** **[2010] EWHC 577 (Ch)** 4 February 2010	Inter partes stage: Arnold J granted interim permission to commence the derivative claim. Applicant 50% shareholder in the company. Wallersteiner order sought.	**Permission granted. As to costs, they should be borne by the company, but, in case of a later adverse costs order, the applicant would not be entitled to indemnity**
			Stainer v Lee **[2010] EWHC 1539 (Ch)** 29 June 2010	Application for permission to continue a derivative claim; the decision is on the inter partes stage. The applicant is **holder of 0.08 of**	**Permission granted**. The court held that in the second stage (inter partes) whether a prima facie case exists may be revised. In this case, it was

				the company's issued share capital. Indemnity as to costs sought.	held, among others, that the existence of an alternative remedy was in itself not an adequate reason to dismiss the application. **Indemnity as to costs was granted but with a cap.**
			Cinematic Finance Ltd v Ryder **[2010] EWHC 3387** (Ch) 21 October, 2010	Second stage of admission proceedings (inter partes). Claimant was the majority shareholder in the company on whose behalf permission to continue the claim was sought	**Application dismissed. In exercising its discretion, the court asserted that the claimant fell short of the proper plaintiff principle; the judge Roth J) went on to hold that regarding companies in liquidation, the proper claimant will usually be the liquidator.**
266/2011 Patrai Court of Appeal 26 May 2011	Second Instance. Appeal against decision of the Court of First Instance to appoint a special	Appeal granted. Proceedings brought by the board effectively bar any minority petition; allegations that	***Re Seven Holdings (Langley Ward Ltd v Trevor)*** **[2011] EWHC 1893 (Ch)**	Applicant sought permission to continue a derivative claim in respect of the company in liquidation.	**Permission refused. The applicant did not satisfy the 'hypothetical director' criteria. Some**

(*Continued*)

Table A1 (Cont.)

*Greek decisions (under Law 2190/1920 art 22b)**			*British decisions (under common law and CA 2006 Pt 11 ss 260–264)*		
Case/Year	***Instance***	***Decision***	***Case/Year***	***Instance***	***Decision***
	representative under Law 2190/1920 art 22b (in this case a local lawyer). Petitioner is holder of 30% of the company's shares	the claim brought by the board was mala fide based on the unsatisfactory manner the relevant suit was drafted and submitted should not be considered	30 June 2011	The 'prima facie' stage was bypassed. Applicant 50% shareholder in the company. Indemnity as to costs sought.	**of the claims did not fit the scope of Part 11.**
1256/2011 Supreme Court 15 July 2011	Appeal against Patrai Court of Appeal 151/2010. Petition to appoint special representatives by a minority holding more than 10% of the company's shares	The issue at hand was the interpretation of Law 2190/1920 art 22b. Appeal granted by the Supreme Court. Under no interpretative construction of the said article can any qualification on the demand rule be inferred. Costs to be borne by the shareholders	***Kleanthous v Paphitis* [2011] EWHC 2287 (Ch)** 7 September, 2011	Inter partes stage. Application for permission to continue a derivative claim brought by a minority shareholder of 15%. Indemnity as to costs sought.	**Application dismissed**. The application failed to pass the test set in s 263(2)(a) regarding one of the defendants (Mr Childs); it also failed to satisfy a number of the factors enumerated in s 263(3), particularly the importance to be imputed by a director acting in accordance with s 172, the decision of the company

					not to sue and the availability of a more appropriate remedy.
141/2011 Volos Single-Member Court of First Instance	First Instance. Petition to appoint special representatives to continue an adjourned corporate action (dating all the way back to 2006)	Petition dismissed. Unless any of the defendants retain their positions in the board (position held in the proceedings in 2006), **there is no legal basis** for the claim to be initiated by a company's action.	***Parry v Bartlett* [2011] EWHC 3146 (Ch)** 29 November 2011	Application to continue a derivative claim by a shareholder/director owning 50 % of the shares in a private limited company	Permission granted. The claims had particular strength. Misconduct could not be ratified. Claimant was acting in good faith and in pursuit of the company's interests.
726/2011 Court of Appeal of Piraeus - 357/2011 Court of Appeal of Piraeus	Second Instance. Appeal against decision of the Court of First Instance dismissing a petition under Law 2190/1920 art 22b	Appeal granted. The appellant (50% shareholder) retained the right to file a petition for a corporate action; despite the fact that the company was insolvent and liquidation was pending.	***Phillips v Fryer* [2013] EWHC 1611 (Ch)** (12 June 2012)	Applicant 50% shareholder in a private limited company and director. Applicant had already brought proceedings under CA 2006 s 994	Permission granted. The derivative claim was in the company's interests and expedient in view of the circumstances.
			Hughes v Weiss and Ors [2012] EWHC 2363 (Ch) 15 August 2012	Inter partes stage. Application for permission to continue a derivative claim.	**Permission granted**. In establishing a prima facie case, the claimant had only to

(Continued)

Table A1 (Cont.)

*Greek decisions (under Law 2190/1920 art 22b)**			*British decisions (under common law and CA 2006 Pt 11 ss 260–264)*		
Case/Year	***Instance***	***Decision***	***Case/Year***	***Instance***	***Decision***
				Claimant is holder of 50% of the company's shares (also director of the company and barrister)	show that she had a case to make without going into detail as to its merits, as this would be the task for the court in the main proceedings. The deadlock the dormant company was in rendered considerations as to ratification and decision by the company not to pursue the claim immaterial.
			***Bamford v Harvey* [2012] EWHC 2858 (Ch)** 18 October 2012	This was the second stage of proceedings; Vos J accepted that a prima facie case was established in the first stage. Applicant is 50% shareholder and director of the company.	Permission refused. The appropriate means to bring the claim was the ordinary claim under Pt 7 of the CPR in the name of the company; in fact, what was largely at stake was the imposition of costs. Roth J) **expressly denied that by his judgment 'wrongdoer control' was 'elevated' to an absolute bar for derivative claims.**

			Universal Project Management Services v Fort Gilkicker [2013] EWHC348 (Ch) 13 February 2013	The claimant, a participant in a joint venture (and 50% shareholder of the respective LLP the latter was carried through), applied for permission to continue proceedings on behalf of a fully owned subsidiary of the latter (double derivative action)	**Permission granted.** The 'codification' of derivative claims by CA 2006 did not wash away multiple derivative actions. The claim could continue under common law.
44/2014 Larissa Court of Appeal	Second instance. Appeal against the decision of the court of first instance.	The court, granting the appeal, followed the rationale of Greek Supreme Court 1256/2011 that the demand rule may not be bypassed under no circumstances	***Singh v Singh & Ors*** [2014] EWCA Civ 103; 27 January 2014	Second instance; (renewed oral application for permission to) appeal against decision by Hodge J to refuse permission to continue a derivative claim. Indemnity as to costs sought. Appellant is holder of 50% of the company's shares.	Permission to appeal refused. The claim failed to satisfy the mandatory requirement set in s 263(2)(a). As to the discretionary grounds, claim under s 994 was more appropriate and the hypothetical director would not attach much importance to the claim.
			Abouraya v Sigmund [2014] EWHC 277 (Ch) 13 February 2014	Application for permission to continue an action as a derivative claim.	Permission refused. Even though the Court endorsed the judgment in *Gilkicker*

(*Continued*)

Table A1 (Cont.)

*Greek decisions (under Law 2190/1920 art 22b)**			*British decisions (under common law and CA 2006 Pt 11 ss 260–264)*		
Case/Year	***Instance***	***Decision***	***Case/Year***	***Instance***	***Decision***
				The claimant, member of a holding company incorporated in Hong Kong (holder of 50% of its shares) brought proceedings on behalf of the latter's British subsidiary (double derivative action).	as to the admissibility of multiple derivative actions in the post-CA 2006 era (and assumed jurisdiction; *Konamaneni v Rolls-Royce Industrial Power (India) Ltd* [2002] 1 WLR 1269 applied), the claimant failed to show a prima facie case that the action fell within the exceptions of the rule in Foss v Harbottle.
			McAskill v Fulton 31 October 2014	Application for permission to continue a derivative action. Applicant is holder of 50% of the company's shares. Inter partes stage. Indemnity as to costs sought.	Permission granted (up to conclusion of disclosure). Indemnity granted in part.
5/2015 Supreme Court 10 September 2015	Court of Appeal awarded the company, under the procedure of Law 2190/	The issue at hand being **whether a waiver of shareholder rights via**	***Cullen Investments Ltd v Brown* [2015] EWHC 473 (Ch)**	The claimant brought proceedings for permission to continue a derivative action;	Permission granted. The defendant did not establish that the applicant shareholder

	1920 art 22b, damages against the directors exceeding 1 million Euros, extinguishing the decision of the Court of First Instance (awarding a larger amount); proceedings initiated following a minority petition pursuant to Law 2190/1920 art 22b para 1. Petitioners are holders of 50% of the company's shares.	**shareholders' agreement blocked the applicants bringing the relevant petition,** the Supreme Court directed the case to the Full-Member Chamber, which found that the shareholders validly agreed not to exercise their right to file a petition pursuant to Law 2190/1920 art 22b para 1 and dismissed the claim.	27 February 2015	inter partes stage. No indemnity sought as to litigation costs.	did not satisfy the 'hypothetical shareholder' criteria set in ss 263(2)(a) and 263(3)(b). Other discretionary factors such as good faith and the availability of an alternative remedy taken into account.
			***Bridge v Daley* [2015] EWHC 2121 (Ch) 17 June 2015**	Application by a minority shareholder (holding 1.83 % of the shares) in a plc for permission to continue a derivative claim. Merger of the two stages. Indemnity as to costs sought.	Permission refused. No reasonable director would bring the claim. The views of disinterested members also weighed against litigation.

(*Continued*)

Table A1 (Cont.)

*Greek decisions (under Law 2190/1920 art 22b)**			*British decisions (under common law and CA 2006 Pt 11 ss 260–264)*		
Case/Year	***Instance***	***Decision***	***Case/Year***	***Instance***	***Decision***
			Bhullar v Bhullar [2015] EWHC 1943 (Ch); 07 July 2015	Application to continue a derivative claim under common law; double derivative action. Applicant is a 22% shareholder in a family-owned company. Indemnity as to costs of the proceedings sought.	Permission granted in part; no indemnity as to costs. Application of the 'hypothetical director' test; *Iesini* considered. The possibility of an alternative remedy (s 994) did not bar the derivative claim from proceeding.
			Peter Hook v Bernard Sumner and Or [2015] EWHC 3820 (Ch); 27 November 2015	The claimant brought proceedings for permission to continue a derivative claim. Indemnity as to costs sought.	Permission granted. The hypothetical reasonable director would pursue the claim for the purposes of s 263(2)(a), The claimant was acting in good faith. alternative remedy and ratification/ratifiability considered. No order for indemnity.

			Brannigan v Style [2016] EWHC 512 (Ch); *2 February 2016*	The claimant (minority shareholder) brought proceedings for permission to continue a derivative claim; inter partes stage. Indemnity as to costs sought.	**Permission refused.** The first respondent's conduct had been validly ratified by resolution. Given the cost-(in)effectiveness of the claim and the small chances of success, the court concluded that the applicant did not satisfy the 'hypothetical director' criteria.
			Zavahir v Shankleman [2016] EWHC 2772 (Ch); *10 November 2016*	The claimant brought proceedings for permission to continue a derivative action; inter partes stage. Indemnity as to costs sought.	**Permission refused.** Following a **risk/benefit analysis,** the court concluded that the applicant did not satisfy the 'hypothetical director' criteria.
			SDI Retail Services Ltd v King [2017] EWHC 737 (Ch) *22 March 2017*	Application for permission to continue a derivative claim. Claimant is a 49% shareholder. First stage bypassed.	Permission granted. The defendants did not establish that the applicant shareholder did not satisfy the 'hypothetical

(Continued)

Table A1 (Cont.)

*Greek decisions (under Law 2190/1920 art 22b)**			*British decisions (under common law and CA 2006 Pt 11 ss 260–264)*		
Case/Year	***Instance***	***Decision***	***Case/Year***	***Instance***	***Decision***
					shareholder' criteria set in s 263(2)(a), (3)(b).
			Wilton UK Ltd v Shuttleworth and others (No 2) [2018] EWHC 911 (Ch) *4 September 2017*	Application for permission to continue a derivative claim. First stage bypassed. No indemnity sought.	Permission granted, subject to further argument. The court held that the claimant taking steps (Service of claim to defendants etc.) without permission was acting without authority. However, in certain circumstances, such as the ones before it, the court may retrospectively grant permission, even when the ex parte stage has not taken place; **and validate with retrospective effect steps taken in the proceedings without permission.**

189/2018 Supreme Court 12 January 2018	The Court of First instance, acting as appellate court, reversed the replacement of the appointed (by petition of a 12.5% minority shareholder) special representative, on the grounds that the constant adjournment (since 2013) of the court hearing on the company's action does not constitute negligent performance of the representative's duties and the representative acting beyond powers does not constitute good cause for his replacement.	The issue at hand being the replacement of an appointed special representative, the Supreme Court advanced an interpretation of art 786 according to which a special representative may be replaced for good reason and that reason may be, inter alia, the representative acting beyond her/his powers and the hostile relationship between the representative and the shareholders.	*Goodwin v Cook [2018] 6 WLUK 425; 21 June 2018*	This was the second stage of proceedings; Rose J accepted that a prima facie case was established in the first stage. Applicant is holder of 50% of the company's shares.	Permission refused. No reasonable director would attach much importance to the claim. The court also concluded – and the applicant conceded generally – that this is an action that could be brought as an unfair prejudice claim.
			Shandong Offshore Investment (HK) Co Ltd v Andresen [2018] EWHC	Application for permission to continue a derivative claim. Claimant is holder of	Permission granted. The court considered, inter alia, the company's inability to

(*Continued*)

Table A1 (Cont.)

*Greek decisions (under Law 2190/1920 art 22b)**			*British decisions (under common law and CA 2006 Pt 11 ss 260–264)*		
Case/Year	***Instance***	***Decision***	***Case/Year***	***Instance***	***Decision***
			2874 (Ch) *15 October 2018*	50% of the company's shares.	have brought the claim in its own right.
			Montgold Capital LLP v Ilska [2018] EWHC 2982 (Ch) *16 October 2018*	Inter partes stage. Application for permission to continue a derivative claim. Claimant is holder of 50% of the company's shares. Indemnity as to costs sought.	Permission granted; defendants included non-directors in the private limited company. The claimant did not press for an indemnity for costs but obtained an order that the company's current cash assets of £190,000 would be preserved and that any sums to be drawn by the eighth and ninth defendants to be reviewed by the claimant before payment.

Note

* There is no reported decision yet (March 2019) on a claim filed pursuant to Law 4548/2018 arts 103–106.

Source: For the United Kingdom, Westlaw online Database; for Greece, NOMOS legal database

Index

abuse (of majority powers/rights): definitions 136–7; remedies for 136–42
accessibility of rights, Greece 148–52
accumulation of information 114–16, 208–11
admission stage: claimant's discretion following 116–19; proposals 184–205
agency costs 46–64
agency problems 33–46; corporate controllers–stakeholders 42–6; management-shareholders 33–8; minority shareholders–majority shareholders 38–42; monitoring 36–7; shareholder value 43–4; stakeholder interests 42–6; threat of enforcement 37–8
agency theory 33
Agrotexim and Others v Greece 31–2
Aktiengesetz: demand rules 113; scope of misfeasance 91–2; section 147 77, 85, 91–2, 96; section 148 79, 108, 113, 116, 170, 196; section 149 91–2, 96, 118; section 309 91
America (United States of) 11–12, 48–9, 110, 197, 198–9
anaklastikí zimía 26
ARAG/Garmenbeck 98, 104, 190
archí tis aflotélias tou n.p. 23–4

Bamford v Harvey 94
banking: accountability issues 40; freezing orders 138–40; risk appetite 63–4
Barrett v Duckett 95, 106
Baums, T. 86
behavioural psychology 58 behavioural economics 41, 173
'Berle and Means corporations' 34–5
block-holders 175; Greece 40, 156–7; path dependency 57–8
boards: dual structures 30; monitors 36–7
bonding costs 47
Borland's Trustee v Steel Brothers & Co Ltd. 126
boundaries, proprietary interests 26–9
Bridge v Daley 95
Britain *see* England
bubble-stock saga, 1999 39
Business Judgement Rule 38, 189, 196

Capital Markets Model Case Act (KapMuG) 132
Carlen v Drury 188
causality: 'law follows' thesis 55–6; 'law matters' position 50–5; path dependency 56–8
ceteris paribus 201–2
Civil Procedure Code: abuse remedies 133–42; article 786 113; information access 210; Practice Direction 19 C 2(2) 80; substitution rules 202–3
claimant's discretion 116–19
Clark v Cutland and Others 140
class actions 131–3
Coffee, J. 55–6, 185
collective litigation 131–3
common law: General Meeting impropriety 144; derivative action's scope 93–4
Companies Act 2006, UK: aims of 59; claimant's discretion 117–18; contractual freedom 126; demand rule 111–12; discharge/waiver rule 98–102; minority protection 83–5, 134; multiple derivative actions 88–9, 180–1; Part 11 76–8, 118; scope of misfeasance (derivative action) 90–7; section 239 100; section 260 92; section 261 117–18; section 263 75–7; section 371 118; section 994 134–5; section 996

134–5; shareholder value 43; special auditors 115
companies interest criterion 102–5, 192–7
company's action *see* corporate (or company's) action
comparative statistical analysis 50–1
comparison *see* functional comparisons
competences, General Meetings 30, 157–8
concentrated ownership 40, 51–2, 54
conflicts of interest: corporate governance 33–46; minority protections 82–3; special representatives regime 87–8
contemporaneous ownership 84–5, 177–9
contentious jurisdiction 184
contingency fees arrangements 207
continuous ownership 177–9
contractual freedom 125–31
convergence 15, 56, 57; contractual freedom 127–31; EU law in Greece 156–60, 217–18; corporate capital, maintenance of 28
corporate control, exit optionality 145–6
corporate controllers–stakeholders agency problem 42–6
corporate governance 33–46
corporate (or company's) action: definition 6, 7, 77; German transition 166–71
cost/benefit analysis 194–5, 205–8; *see also* economic efficiency
cost indemnification 207
costs allocation 78–81, 194–7, 205–8

D&O insurance *see* directors' and officers' liability insurance
Davis, K.B. 48
decision-makers: disinterest 199–200; rules and standards 35–6; *see also* directors...
Delaware law (DGCL) 197
demand rule 108–14, 197–201; *see also* futility of demand; redundancy of demand; universal demand
dependency, of share property 25
derivative actions: economic implications 46–64; in Europe 13–18; genuine 76–7; importance of 29–32; international debate 11–13; nature of 74–8; as a public good 42–6; rationale for 32
deterrence - threat of enforcement 37–8, 196
diffuse ownership 34, 40, 51, 174
direct derivative actions, Germany 91
directors: accountability 38–42; disinterest 199–200; supervision 36–7
directors' liability, enforcement 36–7, 38–42
directors' and officers' (D&O) liability insurance 38
discharge 98–102
disclosure: mandatory 114–16; proposals 208–11
disinterested directors 199–200
Doppelschaden 28
double derivate actions *see* multiple derivative actions
double recovery 28
dual board structures 30
duties of directors 35
duty of care 35, 180, 188-9

economic efficiency 46–64, 194–7, 205–8
einleitliche Leitung (common direction) 183
enforcement: accumulation of information 114–16, 208–11; admission stage proposals 184–205; claimant's discretion 116–19; companies interest criterion 102–5; corporate claims 69–123; costs allocation 78–81; demand rules 108–14, 197–201; deterrence 37–8; directors' liability 36–7; good faith 105–8; legal standing 81–90; ratification 97–102, 187–8; restrictions 81–114, 116–19; scope of misfeasance 90–7, 185–91; subsidiarity principle 108, 197–201; temporal restrictions 84–5
England 16–18; accumulation of information 115; aims of reforms 59; collective litigation 132; companies interest 103–4, 192–6; contractual freedom 126; costs allocation 80; discharge/waiver rule 98–102; equitable consideration 134–5; good faith 106–7; legal standing 83–5; minority protections 134; multiple derivative actions 88–9, 180–1; no reflective loss principle 27–9; ratification 97–102; remedies against abuse 136; scope of misfeasance 90–7, 187–8; shareholder value approach 43; substitution rules 202–3; *see also* Companies Act 2006, UK
enlightened shareholder value approach 43
equitable consideration 134–5
equity capital 23, 49–64
European Union (EU): derivative actions 13–18; influence on Greece 156–60
exit, as a method of control 145–6
externalities 47

fiduciary duties 35
Foss v Harbottle 11, 74, 93
frameworks, Greece 124–62
Franbar v Patel 101
fraud on the minority 93–4, 186
free-riding 78–9
freezing orders 138–40
frivolous litigation: proposed constraints for 184–205; *see also* restrictions
functional comparisons 69–123; accumulation of information 114–16; claimant's discretion 116–19; companies interest 102–5; costs allocation 78–81; demand rules 108–14; good faith 105–8; 'law matters' position 53–4; legal standing 81–90; ratification 97–102; scope of misfeasance 90–7
functional equivalence 9, 70–4
futility of demand 198–9
future prospects *see* proposals

Gall v Exxon Corp 12
gap-filling, Greece 152–5
General Meetings (GM): competences 30, 157–8; conflicts of interest 82–3; improper resolution remedies 142–4; ratification 97–102; right to place items, Greece 153–4, 156–60; subsidiarity 111–13
genuine derivative actions, definition of 76–7
Germany 16–18; abuse remedies 136–7; accountability issues 39; accumulation of information 114; admission stage 184–5; claimant's discretion 116, 118; collective litigation 132; companies interest 102–5; company's action v derivative actions 166–71; contractual freedom 126–7; costs allocation 79–80; double recovery 28; General Meeting impropriety 143; *Gesetz zur Unternehmensintegrität und Modernisierung des Anfechtungsrechts* 62; good faith 107–8; groups of companies 91–2; multiple derivative actions 91–2, 181, 183; qualified minorities 81, 83–6; ratification 97, 98; scope of misfeasance 90–2, 96, 185–8; shareholders' forum 83–4; shareholder value 44; special representatives regime 87–8; subsidiarity 108
Gesetzliche Prozessstandschafter 45–6; *see also* procedural stewards
Gesetz zur Kontrolle-und Transparenz im Unternehmensbereich (KonTraG) 167–8
Gesetz zur Unternehmensintegrität und Modernisierung des Anfechtungsrechts (UMAG) 62; claimant's discretion 118; insights from 166–71; scope of misfeasance 96–7; section 148 78, 79; section 149 78; *see also Aktiengesetz*
globalisation 61
GM *see* General Meetings
good faith 38, 105–8
governance, corporate 33–46
Greece 16–18; abuse remedies 133–42; accessibility of rights 148–52; accountability issues 38–42; accumulation of information 114–15; aims of reforms 59–60; claimant's discretion 116–17; collective litigation 131–3; companies interest 105; concentration of ownership 40; contractual freedom 125–31; costs allocation 79–81; demand rules 108–11; double recovery 28; European Union influence 156–60; framework, current 124–62; gap-filling 152–5; General Meeting impropriety 142–4; good faith 107–8; improvements, recent 146–60; no reflective loss principle 27, 28, 31–2; privatisations 41; proposals 165–213; qualified minorities 81–8; ratification 97, 98; rewordings 152–5; risk appetite 63–4; scope of misfeasance 90, 92, 97; shareholder value 43–4; subsidiarity 108–10; temporal restrictions 85; unfair prejudice 134–5; voice premia 151–2
gross violations 90–7, 104, 114, 185–9, 216
groups of companies: Germany 91–2; proposals 179–83

hard law 49–64; 'law follows' thesis 55–6; 'law matters' position 50–5; path dependency 56–8; role of 58–64
Holzmüller 158
Hughes v Weiss 107

Iesini v Westrip Holdings Ltd 103, 106
implementation, Law 4548/2018 147–8
indemnity of costs 207
independent directors 30
indirect ownership 23–5
individual rights vs. qualified minorities 171–7

information, accumulation of 114–16, 208–11
In re Walt Disney Derivative Legislation 12
inter-corporate control, Germany 91–2
interim administration 77, 113
investment, value of protection 49–50
Italian Legislative Decree 58 (of 1998) 62–3
iurisdictio voluntaria see non-contentious jurisdiction

Jensen, M.C. 47
Johnson v Gore, Wood & Co 27–9
jurisdictional focus 10–18

KapMuG *see* Capital Markets Model Case Act
Kershaw, D. 111–12
Klagezulassungsverfahren 184–5
Kleanthous v Paphitis 103
Konzernrecht 91–2, 181, 183

Law 2190/1920 59; article 2 128; article 22a 97; caveats 153–5; contractual freedom 127–8; date of replacement 147; General Meeting impropriety 142; ratification 97; scope of misfeasance 92
Law 3604/2007: aims of reforms 59–60; shareholders' rights 153
Law 4548/2018 73–4, 147–8; accessibility of rights 148–52; aims of reforms 59–60; article 102 116–17; article 105 113–14; article 108 97; article 144 150–1; articles 102-105 90, 92; articles 104-106 77, 79, 108–9; claimant's discretion 116–17; company's action 170; contractual freedom 128; demand rules 113–14; gap-filling 153–5; General Meeting impropriety 142–4; implementation 147–8; minority protections 82–3, 135–6, 149–50; ratification 97; Articles 102–105 scope of misfeasance 90, 92; subsidiarity per Articles 104 and 105 108–9; temporal restrictions per Article 104 198
'law follows' thesis 55–6
'law matters' position 50–5; criticisms 52–3; functional comparisons 53–4
'legal origins' thesis 52
legal standing 81–90; assessment 89–90; contemporaneous and continuous ownership 177–9; general principles 81–8; individual rights vs. qualified minorities 171–7; information access 209–10; multiple derivative actions 88–9, 179–83; proposals 171–83
legal transplant: examples 7, 12, 110, 121, 150, 151, 155; in general 10
legislation *see* hard law
leximetrics 50–5
liability cap 185–9
liability insurance, directors' and officers' 38
litigation: costs 78–81, 205–8; restrictions on 81–114
loser pays principle 79
loyalty: duty of 35; German thresholds 96

maintenance of corporate capital 28
management-shareholder agency problems 33–8
managers: accountability 38–42; rules and codes of conduct 35–6; supervision 36–7
market capitalisation: legislative effects 62; and protections 50–64
Meckling, W.H. 47
Merkel, A. 39
Minderheit 81
minority protection 81–8, 133–42, 149–50
minority shareholder–majority shareholder agency problems 38–42
misfeasance: deterrence 37–8; scope of 90–7, 185–91
Mission Capital Plc v Sinclair 76
Modern Corporation and Private Property, The 34
monitoring bodies 36–7
moral hazard, special representatives regime 87–8
multiple derivative actions 88–9, 179–83

nature of derivative actions 74–8
negligence 185–9
non-contentious jurisdiction (*iurisdictio voluntaria*) 184–5
no reflective loss principle 26–9, 31–2
Northwest Transportation v Beatty 100
notice of facts 197–8
numerical comparative methods 50–5

oppression, remedies for 133–42
organisational structures 29–30
ownership: concentration of 40, 51–2, 54; of the firm 23–5; Greek firms 40; proprietary interests 22–33; separation

from control 34–6; thresholds 81–90, 150–2, 168, 171–7, 209–10 see also diffuse ownership

Parry v Bartlett 101
path dependency 56–8
pending claims, substitution rules 201–5
'piercing the corporate veil' 23
Posner, R. 46
power of representation by statute 29–32
Practice Direction 19 C 2(2), Civil Procedure Rules 80
praesumptio similitudinis 189, 211
prelimary stage, proposals 184–205
pressure groups 60–1
prevention, and threat of enforcement 37–8
prima facie cases 26, 75–7; companies' interest 192–7; demand rules 197–201; importance evaluation 193–4; individual rights vs. qualified minorities 171–7; ownership, temporal restrictions 177–9; proposals 184–205; substitution rules 201–5
privatisations, Greece 41
procedural stewards 45–6, 184
proper plaintiff rule 74
property infringement 24
property rights 22–6
proposals 165–213; admission stage 184–205; companies interest 192–7; costs 194–7, 205–8; demand rules 197–201; duty of care 188; Germany, insights from 166–71; individual rights vs. qualified minorities 171–7; information access 208–11; ownership, temporal restrictions 177–9; rights to sue 171–7; scope of misfeasance 185–91; subsidiarity 197–201; substitution rules 201–5
proprietary interests 22–33; no reflective loss principle 26–9; organisational structures 29–30; rights 22–6; importance of derivative actions 29–32protection, as a facilitator of investment 49–50
Proton Bank 40, 138–40
proxy voting 156
public enforcers 36
public good, of derivative actions 42–6

qualified minorities 81–8, 150–2, 168, 171–7; doctrinal contestations 174–7; information access 209–10; problems entailed 171–4; vs. individual rights 171–7
quorum thresholds 62, 81–90, 150–2, 168, 171–7, 209–10

ratification 97–102, 187–8
rational apathy 78–9
recidivism 37
'record date' mechanism 157
recovery net of litigation costs 195–6
redundancy of demand 198–9
reflective loss 26
Reflexschäden 26
residual loss 47
restrictions 81–114, 116–19; claimant's discretion 116–19; companies interest criterion 102–5, 192–7; demand rules 108–14, 197–201; good faith 105–8; legal standing 81–90; ratification 97–102; scope of misfeasance 90–7, 185–91, 188–91; subsidiarity principle 108, 197–201; temporal 84–5
rewordings, Greece 152–5
rights: accessibility, Greece 148–52; proprietary 22–6
risk appetite, banking 63–4
rules, functional equivalence 69–123
rules of conduct 35

Salomon v Salomon 89
satzungstrenge 126–7
scope of misfeasance 90–7, 185–91
separate juristic personality principle 23–4
settlement 116–18
shareholder-appointed special auditors 114–16
Shareholder Rights Directive (SRD) 147, 153–4, 156–60
shareholders assembly *see* General Meetings
shareholders' forum 83–4
shareholder value, agency problems 43–4
shares: concentration of ownership 40, 51–2, 54; contemporaneous and continuous ownership 177–9; dependency of returns 25; ownership *see* ownership; rights of ownership 22–6, 138; value fluctuation following legislation 62
Siems, M. 54
SLCs *see* special litigation committees
small SA (kleine AG) 128–9
Smith v Croft (No 2) 84–5, 101–2
Smith v Croft (No 3) 72

Sonderprüfer 114–16
special auditors 114–16, 186–7, 196, 209
special independent committees 110
special litigation committees (SLCs) 110
special representatives regime 87–8, 168–9, 190, 192
SRD *see* Shareholder Rights Directive
stakeholders, interests of 42–6, 190–1
standards of conduct 35
state supervision 36
streitgenössischer Nebeninterventiente 116
subsidiarity principle 108, 197–201
substitution rule 201–5
supervisory boards 30
Supreme Court, Greece, abuse remedies 137–40

takeovers 145, 149
temporal restrictions 84–5; after admission stage 116; proposals 177–9, 198
terminological considerations 74–8
Trennungsprinzip 23
turnover ratios, legislative effects 62

UK *see* United Kingdom
UMAG *see Gesetz zur Unternehmensintegrität und Modernisierung des Anfechtungsrechts*
unfair prejudice 133–42
United Kingdom (UK) 16–18; abuse remedies 136; accumulation of information 115; aims of reforms 59; collective litigation 132; companies interest 103–4, 192–6; contractual freedom 126; costs allocation 80; discharge/waiver rule 98–102; equitable consideration 134–5; good faith 106–7; legal standing 83–5; minority protections 134; multiple derivative actions 88–9, 180–1; no reflective loss principle 27–9; ratification 97–102; scope of misfeasance 90–7, 187–8; shareholder value approach 43; substitution rules 202–3; *see also* Companies Act 2006, UK
United States (US) *see* America (United States of)
universal demand 200–1
Universal Project Management Services Ltd v Fort Gilikicker Ltd and Others 88–9
unwritten competences 158

Van Aaken, E. 47
vexatious litigation: companies' interest 192–6; proposed constraints for 184–205; *see also* restrictions
voice premia 151–2

waiver of claims 98–102
Wallersteiner order 80, 95
Wilton UK Ltd v Shuttleworth and Others (No 2) 75
Wishart v Castlecroft Ltd & Ors 75, 93
wrongdoer control 93–5, 180

Zavahir v Shankleman 194–5